CALIFORNIA

Titles in this series include:

- **New England**, with Boston and Cape Cod
- **California**, with Las Vegas and the Grand Canyon
- **New Zealand**, including outdoor activities and national parks
- **Scotland**, including the Highlands and Islands, Royal Deeside and the Whisky Routes
- **Brittany and Normandy**, with scenic routes from the Channel ports
- **Florida**, with a full guide to theme parks
- **Dordogne and Western France**, including Bordeaux, and the Atlantic coast
- **Ireland**, with Eire and Northern Ireland
- **Languedoc and Southwest France**, including Cathar country, the Cevenne, and the Tarn and Gard regions
- **Bavaria and the Austrian Tyrol**, with guides to Salzburg and Munich

For further information about these and other Thomas Cook publications, write to Thomas Cook Publishing, PO Box 227, Thorpe Wood, Peterborough PE3 6PU, United Kingdom

Signpost Guides

CALIFORNIA

The best of California,
including Los Angeles and
San Francisco, Palm Springs
and Hollywood, Disneyland
and Universal Studios, the
Grand Canyon, Death Valley
and the Napa Valley.

Maxine Cass and Fred Gebhart

Thomas
Cook
Publishing

Published by Thomas Cook Publishing
The Thomas Cook Group Ltd
PO Box 227
Thorpe Wood
Peterborough PE3 6PU
United Kingdom

Telephone: 01733 503571
E-mail: books@thomascook.com
Advertising sales: 01733 503568

Text:© The Thomas Cook Group Ltd
Maps supplied and designed by Lovell Johns Ltd, OX8 8LH
Map data © MapQuest.com Inc., Mountville, PA 17554
City maps © The Thomas Cook Group Ltd.

ISBN 1 900341 61 1

Publisher: Stephen York
Commissioning Editor: Deborah Parker
Map Editor: Bernard Horton

Series Editor: Christopher Catling
Copy editor: Karen Pieringer
Written and researched by: Maxine Cass and Fred Gebhart

About the authors

Fred Gebhart has lived in California for 41 years, interrupted by extended sojourns in Europe and West Africa that have eventually sent him back to his adopted state. He has logged thousands of miles in California, as a child as well as an adult, travelling by foot, horseback, balloon, bicycle, sailboat, RV and car. A freelance photojournalist for 16 years, Fred covers California and the Western United States for publications in Asia and Europe while focusing on Australasia for US readers. With his wife, Maxine Cass, Fred has written a number of Thomas Cook titles, including *On the Road around California, On the Road around Florida* (with Eric and Ruth Bailey) and *On the Road around the Pacific Northwest*. Fred's passion is scuba diving, a love that is more happily consummated in tropical climes than in the chilly waters off California.

Maxine Cass is a rare specimen, a California native. In the forty-some years since she was born on the Stanford University campus in Palo Alto, Maxine has studied Medieval European History at the University of California, Santa Barbara, lived in Greece and Senegal, and become a widely published photojournalist and author. Maxine is the author of the *AAA Photo Journey to San Francisco*, and she contributes to various travel and business publications in Europe, the US, Canada and Asia, as well as collaborating with other authors as contributor to the *On the Road guides*. Between research trips around the world, Maxine gardens at their home in San Francisco, and shares the indulgence of a very fat cat with her husband and series co-author, Fred Gebhart.

Acknowledgements

The authors would like to thank the following people and organisations for the invaluable help they gave in researching this guide: Laurie Armstrong, San Francisco Convention & Visitors Bureau; Molly Cahill; Chris Chrystal, Nevada Commission on Tourism; Ellen Clark & Geoffrey Williams; Kris Fister, Sequoia & Kings Canyon National Parks; Lou Gebhart; Elizabeth Harryman & Paul Lasley; Brian M Logan, BLM Arcata; Paul & Virginia McCarthy; Mendo & Panther; Mary Ellen Quesada; Sharon Rooney; San Diego Wild Animal Park; San Diego Zoological Society; Fred Sater, California Department of Tourism; Stanford Inn by the Sea; Joe Timko, San Diego Convention & Visitors Bureau; Town & Country Hotel; Marilyn Wagner; Keith Walklet, Yosemite Concession Services; Welk Resort Center; Whale Watch Inn.

Contents

About Signpost Guides

Above
The stark beauty of the desert

Symbol Key

ℹ Tourist Information Centre

⮂ Advice on arriving or departing

Ⓟ Parking locations

◉ Advice on getting around

⮎ Directions

🏛 Sights and attractions

Ⓒ Accommodation

🍴 Eating

🛍 Shopping

⚽ Sport

✦ Entertainment

Thomas Cook's Signpost Guides are designed to provide you with a comprehensive but flexible reference source to guide you as you tour a country or region by car. This guide divides California into touring areas – one per chapter. Major cultural centres or cities form chapters in their own right. Each chapter contains enough attractions to provide at least a day's worth of activities – often more.

Star ratings
To make it easier for you to plan your time and decide what to see, every sight and attraction is given a star rating. A three-star rating indicates a major attraction, worth at least half a day of your time. A two-star attraction is worth an hour or so of your time, and a one-star attraction indicates a site that is good, but often of specialist interest. To help you further, individual attractions within towns or theme parks are also graded, so that travellers with limited time can quickly find the most rewarding sights.

Chapter contents
Every chapter has an introduction summing up the main attractions of the area, and a ratings box, which will highlight the area's strengths and weaknesses – some areas may be more attractive to families travelling with children, others to wine-lovers visiting vineyards, and others to people interested in finding castles, churches, nature reserves or good beaches.

Each chapter is then divided into an alphabetical gazetteer, and a suggested tour. You can select whether you just want to visit a particular sight or attraction, choosing from those described in the

Practical information

The practical information in the page margins, or sidebar, will help you locate the services you need as an independent traveller – including the tourist information centre, car parks and public transport facilities. You will also find the opening times of sights, museums, churches and other attractions, as well as useful tips on shopping, market days, cultural events, entertainment, festivals and sports facilities.

gazetteer, or whether you want to tour the area comprehensively. If the latter, you can construct your own itinerary, or follow the author's suggested tour, which comes at the end of every area chapter.

The gazetteer

The gazetteer section describes all the major attractions in the area – the villages, towns, historic sites, nature reserves, parks or museums that you are most likely to want to see. Maps of the area highlight all the places mentioned in the text. Using this comprehensive overview of the area, you may choose just to visit one or two sights

One way to use the guide is simply to find individual sights that interest you, using the index, overview map or star ratings, and read what our authors have to say about them. This will help you decide whether to visit the sight. If you do, you will find plenty of practical information, such as the street address, the telephone number for enquiries and opening times.

Alternatively, you can choose a hotel, perhaps with the help of the accommodation recommendations contained in this guide. You can then turn to the overall map on page 10 to help you work out which chapters in the book describe those cities and regions that lie closest to your chosen touring base.

Driving tours

The suggested tour is just that – a suggestion. The routes are designed to link the attractions described in the gazetteer section, and to cover out-standingly scenic coastal, mountain and rural landscapes. The total distance is given for each tour, as is the time it will take you to drive the complete route, but bear in mind that this indication is just for the driving time: you will need to add on extra time for visiting attractions along the way.

Many of the routes are circular, so that you can join them at any point. Where the nature of the terrain dictates that the route has to be linear, the route can either be followed out and back, or you can use it as a link route, to get from one area in the book to another.

Accommodation and food

In every chapter you will find lodging and eating recommendations for individual towns, or for the area as a whole. These are designed to cover a range of price brackets and concentrate on more characterful small or individualistic hotels and restaurants. In addition, you will find information in the *Travel Facts* chapter on chain hotels, with an address to which you can write for a guide, map or directory. The price indications used in the guide have the following meanings:

$ budget level
$$ typical/average prices
$$$ de luxe.

Page 274

BRYCE CANYON

ZION CANYON

GRAND CANYON

Arizona

Fallon

Hawthorne

Tonopah

Basalt

Bridgeport

Lakeview

Reno

Carson City

South Lake Tahoe

Twain Harte

Alturas

Susanville

Page 114

Page 122

Truckee

SACRAMENTO

Stockton

Medford

Klamath Falls

Ashland

Yreka

Mt Shasta

Burney

Chester

Quincy

Oroville

Marysville

Chico

Page 246

Redding

Red Bluff

Page 226

Yuba City

Page 154 & 166

Napa

Artioch

Oakland

Grants Pass

Brookings

Crescent City

Garberville

Willows

Page 186

Willits

Ukiah

Page 176

Page 134

Page 146

Page 196

Eureka

Fortuna

Fort Bragg

Mendocino

Page 264

Las Vegas

Boulder City

Kingman

Parker

Needles

Bythe

Yuma

Brawley

Mexicali

Beatty

Shoshone

Baker

El Centro

Twentynine Palms

Indio

Escondido

El Cajon

Tijuana

Page 90

Page 94

Page 78

Page 256

Death Valley

Page 102

Lone Pine

Big Pine

Bishop

Ridgecrest

Barlow

Victorville

San Bernardino

Palm Springs

Anaheim

Encinitas

SAN DIEGO

Page 54

Page 42

LOS ANGELES

Pasadena

Bodfish

Mojave

Page 70

Santa Clarita

Malibu

Santa Monica

San Juan Capistrano

Long Beach

Giant Forest

Visalia

Oakhurst

Fresno

Bakersfield

Santa Maria

Santa Barbara

Ventura

Oxnard

Santa Catalina Island

San Clemente Island

Page 238

Mariposa

Merced

Madera

Lemoore

Coalinga

Paso Robles

Santa Maria

Lompoc

Page 62

Channel Islands

Yosemite Village

Fremont

San Jose

Palo Alto

Page 206

Hollister

Salinas

Soledad

King City

San Simeon

Morro Bay

San Luis Obispo

Arroyo Grande

Big Sur

Monterey

Page 214

FRANCISCO

Introduction

San Carlos Borromeo Mission

California is an asylum where the inmates have permanent control and the rest of the world is clamouring to get in. It's a hypermarket of people, places and experiences, from the vast horizons of the northeast to the teeming streets of Los Angeles and San Diego, from manicured vineyard rows to trackless forests that have never been properly mapped.

It's a land rife with myths, half-truths and outright lies stirred together to create a morality tale that is part admonition and part salacious entertainment. Even the handful of Californians who were born here can't always discern one tale from another. Most don't care. When Californians heard that 'perception is reality', they took it to heart as their own reality. California is a land of change, always moving toward an ever-better future. From that shared belief has sprung the California Dream, an ever-evolving mix of fact, fantasy and hope that suffuses the Golden State in a golden glow of arrested adolescence.

Named for a mythical land and nourished by generations of dreamers and schemers, California has come to epitomise a place where anything can happen – and usually does. Fortunes have been won, lost and won again by every means imaginable. More than a few sprang full-grown from the minds of men whose ambition overreached their good sense. Avarice, lust and fraud are as much part of the California Dream as peace, love and happiness. What all six share is an unshakeable faith in the positive power of change, a maniacal belief that tomorrow *will* be a better day.

Until the arrival of steam ships and transcontinental railways, simply travelling to California required an unhealthy dose of optimism. The journey from the Atlantic coast of North America offered the prospect of gruelling physical hardship by land or gnawing boredom by sea, both leavened by the very real prospects of death by disaster, disease or foul play along the way. Once arrived, rugged terrain and treacherous coastal shoals made travel up and down the state equally problematic. Despite the obvious difficulties, California has been portrayed as the Golden State – a paradise on earth – since it was first viewed by Europeans more than four centuries ago. It didn't seem to matter that just getting to California required either an extraordinary leap of faith or an equally extraordinary act of desperation. Once arrived, fame and fortune somehow seemed assured.

Generations of stubborn determination have turned that impenetrable faith in the future into a self-fulfilling prophecy that feeds upon itself and infects legions of newcomers from around the globe. The soaring spires of the Yosemite Valley and the cathedral silence of a grove of redwood trees wreathed in mist and spotlit by beams of sunlight are as much a part of modern California as the imagination, engineering and sheer sweat that created Disneyland, Industrial Light & Magic and generations of silicon chips.

California is a study in contradictions. It's the most populous state in America, yet has vast tracts of untouched wilderness. It produced the cult of youth, beauty and health that is sweeping the globe, yet has one of America's fastest growing populations of retired persons. It's a land built by immigrants whose political leaders fan the flames of anti-immigrant sentiment at every election. It's among the richest economies on earth, yet it refuses to feed, house and educate a growing minority of its population.

None of this is news to Californians. They revel in quirks and contradictions. Most of them are here by choice, not by birth. That they remain only reinforces the optimism that drew them, or their parents, here in the first place. One of the seldom-acknowledged joys of California is that everything that is said about the place is both true and untrue at the same time.

Below
Advertising mural on Melrose Avenue, in the shopping heart of upbeat Los Angeles

Travel facts

Accommodation

Thousands of chain hotels and motels provide the most reliable accommodation. Expect to pay $100–$250 per night in major cities, $50–$75 in smaller towns, single or double occupancy.

Camping pitches and RV sites must be booked in advance for popular national, state and local parks. RV parks are common in rural areas but rare in cities *(see Recreational vehicles, page 21)*. Bed and breakfast is often among the most expensive options. Fax or use the toll–free telephone numbers for booking; you can also book via e-mail or a website. Local tourist offices usually have lists of area accommodation but seldom make bookings.

Airports

Most international visitors fly into Los Angeles International Airport (LAX) or San Francisco International Airport (SFO). Luggage trolleys may be free for international arrivals; expect to pay $1.50–$2 at domestic terminals. For flight information and bookings, contact individual airlines. Major airports have foreign exchange and banking services as well as car-hire facilities. Secondary airports have cash machines (ATMs) and car-hire desks.

Children

Most attractions offer children's rates. Many hotels and motels can arrange for baby-sitters, a pricey service. Children up to 18 stay free in their parents' room with many motel chains.

Picnics offer mealtime flexibility. So does a small cooler filled with cold drinks and snacks. Most towns have roadside restaurants with long hours, cheap children's menus and familiar names.

Currency

US dollars come in denominations of $1, $2 (rare), $5, $10, $20, $50 and $100. All are the same colour, green and white, and the same size, the only differences being the US president on the front and the designs on the back. There are 100 cents to the dollar. Coins are: 1 cent (penny), 5 cents (nickel), 10 cents (dime), 25 cents (quarter), 50 cents (half-dollar – rare), and a rare quarter-sized Susan B. Anthony dollar. Oversized silver dollar coins are common in Nevada.

The safest forms of money are travellers' cheques and credit or debit

Thomas Cook Currency
Services
555 East Ocean Blvd #110
Long Beach
Tel: (562) 491 0846

Thomas Cook Currency
Services
Newport Fashion Island
1113 Newport Center Dr.
Newport Beach
Tel: (714) 644 9049

Thomas Cook Currency
Services
86 Stanford Shopping
Center, Palo Alto
Tel: (650) 321 3309

Thomas Cook Currency
Services
University Towne Center
4417 La Jolla Dr.
Suite N17, San Diego
Tel: (619) 457 2366

Thomas Cook Currency
Services
75 Geary St, Downtown
San Francisco
Tel: (415) 362 3453

Thomas Cook Currency
Services
Bank of America
One Powell St
San Francisco
Tel: (415) 849 8520

Thomas Cook Currency
Services
Bank of Los Angeles
8901 Santa Monica Blvd
West Hollywood
Tel: (310) 659 6093

Thomas Cook Currency
Services
1350 N. Main St
Walnut Creek
Tel: (510) 930 0486

cards. Carry at least one, preferably two, major credit cards such as **Access (MasterCard)**, **American Express** or **Visa**. Car-hire companies, hotels and motels require a credit card or a substantial cash deposit, even if the bill has been prepaid or will be settled in cash.

Thomas Cook Travellers Cheques free you from the hazards of carrying large amounts of cash. Thomas Cook Foreign Exchange Bureaux are listed in the sidebars. They all provide full foreign exchange facilities and will change currency and traveller's cheques (free of commission in the case of Thomas Cook Travellers Cheques. They can also provide emergency assistance in the event of loss or theft of Thomas Cook Travellers Cheques.

Banks can exchange foreign currency or traveller's cheques, but expect delays at small town branches. US dollar traveller's cheques from well-known issuers such as Thomas Cook are acceptable everywhere. To report Thomas Cook Travellers Cheque losses and thefts, *tel: (800) 223-7373* (toll-free, 24-hour service).

Customs allowances

Visitors to the US may bring 1 litre of spirits or wine, 120 cigarettes and 100 non-Cuban cigars and up to $100 worth of gifts duty-free. The age limit for alcohol is 21 and 18 for tobacco.

Check with customs officials at home for returning duty-free allowances, but don't buy duty-free. Alcohol, tobacco, perfume and similar items are cheaper at supermarkets and department stores than at airport and downtown duty-free shops.

Disabled travellers

Federal and state laws require that public businesses and services be readily accessible by persons with disabilities. Hotels, restaurants, offices, shops, cinemas, museums, post offices and other buildings must have access ramps and toilets designed for wheelchairs. Most cities also have kerb ramps at street corners. Major parks have at least a few sealed pathways for disabled visitors. For specific information, contact **SATH** (Society for the Advancement of Travel for the Handicapped), *347 5th Ave, Suite 610, New York NY 10016; tel: (212) 447-7284*. **RADAR**, *12 City Forum, 250 City Rd, London EC1V 8AF; tel: (0171) 250 3222*, publish a useful annual guide, *Holidays and Travel Abroad*, with details of facilities for the disabled in different countries.

Drinking laws

The drinking age is 21 and it is strictly enforced. Beer, wine and spirits can be purchased in food, drug and convenience stores as well as in liquor stores. Licensed establishments, bars, lounges, saloons and pubs may open between 0600 and 0200 in California and any hours in

Lunching al fresco in the North Beach restaurant district of San Francisco

Nevada. Laws against drinking and driving are severe and are also strictly enforced *(see Drinking, drugs and driving, page 25)*.

Earthquakes

Most of the 5000-plus earthquakes that shake California yearly are too small to be noticed. If the tremors are mild ie, dishes aren't rattling, treat it like an amusement park ride and thrill friends at home with tales of terror.

If it becomes difficult to stand or items fall from shelves, take cover beneath the nearest solid table. If there's no table, brace yourself in an interior doorway. Stay away from windows, bookcases or anything else that could collapse. *Don't* run outside, where glass, masonry and power lines could be falling.

If driving, pull off the road and stop on solid ground – you can't drive safely when the road is moving. If you are about to cross a bridge or flyover, stop, or get to the other side as quickly as possible. Then get ready for the next shake. There are always aftershocks, sometimes as strong as the mother quake.

Eating out

Expect to eat too much. An 'American breakfast' combines bacon, sausages or ham, hash browns, eggs, pancakes or French toast and toast. English muffins (crumpets), waffles, bagels, fresh fruit, yoghurt, porridge and cereal are other possibilities. A 'Continental breakfast' is juice, coffee or tea and bread or a pastry.

Lunch and dinner menus feature appetisers, salads, soups, pastas, entrées and desserts. Salads come at the beginning of the meal. Sunday brunch, self-service buffets piled high with hot and cold dishes, can be good value for hearty eaters (usually served 1100–1400).

Many fast-food outlets have drive-up windows. Look for A&W, Arby's Roast Beef, Burger King, Carl's Jr, Jack-in-the-Box, KFC (Kentucky Fried Chicken), McDonald's, Pizza Hut and Taco Bell.

Chain restaurants are ubiquitous. Denny's (open 24 hours) are common along freeways. Other familiar choices are Chevy's (Mexican), Fresh Choice (salads, soups and pastas), Olive Garden (Italian), Red Lobster (seafood) and Sizzler (American).

Entry formalities

Non-US citizens generally need a passport, visa and proof of return travel to enter the country. Check details with the nearest US

Electricity

America uses 110 volt 60 hertz current with two- or three-prong plugs. Power and plug converters are seldom available.

Beware of buying electrical equipment – it probably won't operate on your voltage at home. Exceptions are battery-operated items such as radios, cameras and portable computers.

Be equally wary of pre-recorded video tapes. America uses the NTSC format, most other countries use PAL or SECAM. When buying pre-recorded videos, check the box for compatibility. If no system is listed, it's probably NTSC.

Showtime at the Rio Hotel in Las Vegas.

Museums

Most museums are closed one day per week, usually Mon or Tue. Rural museums may open only on weekends or during the busy summer season. Most charge an entry fee.

consulate or embassy at least three months before departure. Weapons, narcotics and certain pharmaceutical products may not be imported. Carry documentation such as a doctor's prescription to prove that medications are legitimate.

Health

In the event of a life-threatening emergency, telephone 911 for an ambulance. If a life is at stake, treatment will be swift and professional, with payment problems left for later. For more mundane problems, urban areas and most rural communities have 24-hour walk-in clinics.

Because US medical providers do not accept non-US health plan coverage, health insurance is mandatory to ensure provision of non-emergency health services. Most travel agents who sell international travel offer travel insurance policies covering US medical costs.

Bring prescription medication for the entire trip, plus a few extra days and a copy of the prescription for emergencies. As names of drugs vary from country to country, the prescription should show the generic (chemical) name and formulation, not just a brand name.

California is basically a healthy place. No inoculations are required and common sense is enough to avoid most health problems. Eat normally (or at least sensibly) and don't drink water that hasn't come from the tap or a bottle. Most ground water is contaminated with *giardia* and other intestinal parasites.

Sun-glasses, broadbrimmed hats, and sunscreen help prevent sunburn, sunstroke and heat prostration. Be sure to drink plenty of non-alcoholic liquids, especially in hot weather.

Information

California Division of Tourism, *801 K St, Ste 1600, Sacramento CA 95814; tel: (916) 322-2881* or *(800) TO-CALIF; fax: (916) 322-3402; web: http://www.gocalif.ca.gov*. **Nevada Commission on Tourism**, *PO Box 30032, Reno NV 89520; tel: (702) 687-4332* or *(800) 638-2328; fax: (702) 687-6779; web: http://www.travelnevada.com*.

For national park, monument and seashore information, contact **National Parks of the West**, *Western Region Information Center, Fort Mason, Bldg 201, San Francisco CA 94125; tel: (415) 556-0560; web: http://www.nps.gov*

For California State Parks and Beaches, contact **State of California Department of Parks and Recreation**, *PO Box 942896, Sacramento CA 94926; tel: (916) 653-6995* or *(800) 444-7275; web: http://www.cal-parks.ca.gov*. For state park camping reservations, contact **ParkNet**, *PO Box 1510, Rancho Cordova, CA 95741; tel: (800) 444-7275*.

For Nevada State Parks, contact **Nevada Division of State Parks**, *Capitol Complex, Room 207, Carson City, NV 89710; tel: (702) 687-4384*.

Opening hours

Standard office hours are 0900–1700, Mon–Fri. Some tourist offices are open weekends. Most banks are open Mon–Thur 1000–1600, Fri 1000–1800, Sat 0900–1300. ATMs are open 24 hours.

Shopping malls usually open at 0900 or 1000 and close between 2000 and 2200, with shorter hours on Sun. Many restaurants, theatres and museums are closed Mon or Tue, but cinemas and most tourist attractions are open seven days a week.

Opening times and services in missions and places of worship vary widely. Call before visiting if possible.

Climate

Expect sunshine in Southern California, fog along the coast, and heat inland, but uneven terrain creates a patchwork of weather patterns which cannot be explained. Summer fog can hang heavy or burn away to reveal deep blue skies and a blistering sun. Winter temperatures generally drop with altitude and the further north you go, with snow above 1800m. In summer, look for increasing heat inland and to the south.

Packing

Take half as many clothes and twice as much money as you expect to need. Anything you can imagine is sold in California, plus some items you never thought of. Apart from a few restaurants which require business attire, dress is casual and informal, particularly in Southern California. It is a good idea to dress in layers as temperatures can change dramatically during the day, especially in the mountains and near the ocean.

Postal services

Every town has at least one post office. Most are open Mon–Fri 0900–1700 and Sat morning, closed Sun. For stamps, consult the telephone book white pages under US Postal Service. Some hotels and supermarkets also sell them. Letters or parcels sent abroad should go airmail to avoid delays. Domestic letters should arrive in three to seven days.

Public holidays

The following public holidays are observed in California and Nevada: New Year (1 Jan); Martin Luther King Jr Day (third Mon in Jan); Lincoln's Birthday (12 Feb); Presidents' Day (third Mon in Feb); Easter (Sun in Mar/Apr); Memorial Day (last Mon in May); Independence Day (4 July); Labor Day (first Mon in Sept); Columbus Day (second Mon in Oct); California Admission Day (9 Sept); Nevada Day, (31 Oct); Veterans Day (11 Nov); Thanksgiving Day (last Thur in Nov); and Christmas (25 Dec).

Unofficial holidays such as the lunar Chinese New Year and Cinco de Mayo (5 May, Mexican Independence from Spain) are celebrated with as much gusto as official days off.

Post offices and government offices close on public holidays, as do some businesses. Department stores hold huge holiday sales. Tourist attractions frequently have longer holiday hours. Accommodation is heavily booked in advance except for Easter, Thanksgiving and Christmas, which are usually celebrated at home.

Reading

- The AAA sells Automobile Club of Southern California regional guides: *Desert Area; Central Coast* (Ventura, Santa Barbara and San Luis Obispo Counties); and *San Diego County*.
- *The Adventurer's Guide to the Sierra Nevada Mountains*, by Claire & Marty Hiester, 1995, Design Works, Incline Village, NV.
- *Adventuring in the California Desert*, by Lynne Foster, 1998, Sierra Club Books, San Francisco.

Tipping

Tipping is standard except in the very rare restaurant where a service charge is added. Servers expect 15–20 per cent of the food and drink charge; bartenders at least 50¢ per drink. The traditional reward for poor service is two pennies.

Hotel porters get $1 per bag and the bellperson who shows you to your room several dollars more. Expect to pay $1–$5 for valet parking each time your car is delivered. Don't tip ushers in cinemas, theatres and similar establishments.

Casino employees depend on tips for survival. If you win, be generous with the dealer, croupier or slot machine change person. They can't help you beat the odds, but the dealer's attitude makes the difference between a good time and simply losing money.

For casino shows without reserved seating, $5–$20 to *the maître d'* usually gets better seats. If you want to change, ask discreetly, bill in hand, before sitting down. Showroom servers get $5–$10 per couple for a cocktail show, $10–$20 for a dinner show.

- *California Historical Landmarks*, Office of Historic Preservation, California Department of Parks and Recreation, 1990.
- *The Complete Nevada Traveler*, by David W Toll, 1998, Gold Hill Publishing Co, Virginia City, NV.
- *The Grapes of Wrath*, by John Steinbeck, multiple editions.
- *Humbugs and Heroes*, by Richard Dillon, 1983, Yosemite-DiMaggio, Oakland, CA.
- *Napa*, by James Conaway, 1990, Avon Books, New York.
- *The Painted Ladies Guide to Victorian California*, by Elizabeth Pomada and Michael Larsen, 1991, Dutton Studio Books, New York.
- *Roughing It*, by Mark Twain, multiple editions.
- *Two Years Before the Mast*, Richard Henry Dana, multiple editions.
- *The Ultimate Hollywood Tour Book*, by William A Gordon, 1998, North Ridge Books, El Toro, CA.
- *Weekend Adventures in Northern California*, by Carole Terwilliger
- Meyers, 1997, Carousel Press, Berkeley, CA.

Recreational vehicles

Recreational vehicles, or RVs (camper vans and caravans) are an increasingly popular way to travel. The higher cost of hiring and operating an RV is offset by savings on accommodation and meals and the convenience of not packing and unpacking at every stop. RVs are cramped, and savings evaporate if you give in to the temptation of high-priced hotels and fancy restaurant meals.

Get operating manuals and a full demonstration for *all* systems before leaving the hire lot. Buy a pair of sturdy rubber washing gloves to handle daily sewer chores. Pack old clothes to wear while crawling beneath the vehicle to hook up and disconnect at each stop.

For RV information, contact **Recreation Vehicle Industry Association**, *PO Box 2999, Reston, VA 22090; tel: (703) 620-6003.*

Safety and security

Dial 911 on any telephone for free emergency assistance from police, fire and medical authorities. Use normal common-sense precautions.

Safe travelling

Never discuss travel plans or valuables in public.

Use the same caution in rural areas as in cities, driving, parking and walking only in well-lit areas.

Don't wear expensive jewellery when walking about. A wallet in a back pocket or an open handbag are invitations to theft. Take precautions with anything that seems worth stealing – carry bags and camera cases across your chest and keep them between your feet or on your lap in restaurants.

Left
Giant redwoods in Sequoia National Park

Unwatched luggage can vanish in an instant. Most airports and bus or train stations have lockers; guard the key and memorise the locker number. Hotel bell staff may keep guest luggage for a few days, but always get receipts.

If attacked, hand over your bag or money. Resistance is likely to provoke physical harm. Report incidents to local police immediately, if only to get a report for your insurance company.

Safe driving

Car-hire counter personnel should recommend a safe, direct route on a clear map. Lock all valuables and luggage in the boot or glove box.
Keep car doors and windows locked. Don't drive into unlit areas or neighbourhoods that seem unsafe. If told by a passing motorist or pedestrian that something is wrong with your car, *do not stop*. If you must stop, wait for a well-lit or populated area, even if your car is hit by another vehicle.

If your car breaks down, turn on the flashing emergency lights, raise the bonnet and wait inside the vehicle. Lights on emergency vehicles are red or red and blue; never stop for flashing white lights or headlamps.

Have your keys out to unlock car doors before entering a car-park. Check the surrounding area and inside the vehicle before entering.

Don't pick up hitch-hikers or leave the car with the engine running.

Safe sleeping

Lock room doors, windows and sliding glass doors from the inside. Ground-floor rooms are convenient but easier to break into. When leaving the room at night, leave a light on to deter prowlers.

When someone knocks at the door, use the peephole to see who it is. If someone claims to be on the hotel staff, check with the front desk. Money, cheques, credit cards, passports and keys should be with you or in the hotel safe-deposit box.

Safe documents

Photocopy the important pages of your passport and visas. Carry the copies and extra passport photos separately from the documents themselves. If you are robbed, you will have identification and a head start on replacing crucial documents. To replace a passport, apply to your nearest consulate, probably in Los Angeles.

Shopping

Souvenirs include local wines; almonds, walnuts, dates and other dried fruits; sourdough French bread; and prepared mustards, oils and

Stores

Major department store chains:
Bloomingdales, JC Penney, Macy's, Mervyn's, Neiman Marcus, Nordstrom, Saks Fifth Avenue and Sears. Discount chains:
Kmart, Ross, Target and Wal-Mart. For the best prices, check the Sunday newspapers.

Time

California and Nevada are on Pacific Standard Time (PST), GMT -8. Both states jump ahead to Pacific Daylight Time (PDT), GMT -7, from the first Sun in Apr until the last Sun in Oct.

Insurance

Travel insurance should cover your belongings and your holiday investment. Buy cover for delayed or cancelled flights as well as weather problems and evacuation in case of medical emergencies.

National and State Parks

State Parks charge daily entry fees, National Parks charge by the week. Camping fees are extra.

If visiting several National Parks, save with a **Golden Eagle Pass**, $50 per year. For multiple State Park visits, consider an **Annual Day Use Pass**, $75. (See page 18 for details of addresses and telephone numbers.)

Festivals

California celebrates everything from independence (from England, July 4; from Spain, May 5) to garlic (Gilroy Garlic Festival, August) and homosexuality (Gay Pride Week, San Francisco and other cities, June). The state Division of Tourism lists major festivals state-wide, or check with local convention and visitor bureaux. Street fairs and Farmers' Markets thrive on sunny weekends.

condiments. Clothing is a bargain, especially at discount stores and factory outlets. The state sales tax, applicable to purchases except food and pharmaceuticals, is 7.5 to 8.5 per cent.

Sport

San Francisco, Los Angeles and San Diego have professional teams for baseball, football, basketball and other sports. Tickets may be available on short notice; ask at your hotel. Tickets for training games (late summer for football, spring for baseball) are considerably cheaper than regular season tickets. Better still are small-town minor league baseball games. The minor leagues (called Triple A or farm teams) lets you see tomorrow's stars at reasonable prices in small stadiums and a relaxed atmosphere.

Telephones

Public telephones (pay phones) are marked by a white telephone on a blue background. Dialling instructions are posted on the telephone or in the telephone directory. Most pay phones do not accept incoming or return calls. Local calls (800, 877 and 888 area codes) generally cost 35¢; toll-free and 911 (emergency) calls are free. To talk to an operator, dial 0. To locate local numbers, dial 411. For long-distance information, dial 1–(area code)–555-1212. There is a charge for all information calls.

Many hotels and motels add steep surcharges to the cost of phone calls from rooms; use a pay phone in the lobby. Few phone cards or calling cards issued outside the US are accepted by US phone companies, but prepaid calling cards are widely available at supermarkets, post offices, convenience stores and tourist offices.

For international enquires or assistance, dial 00. For international calls, dial 011 (access code) + country code + city code (omit the first zero if there is one) + local number. To call inner London, for example, dial 011-44-171-local number.

Many new area codes across California and Nevada will be phased in during the next two years. Area codes 209, 213, 310, 408, 415, 510, 619, 650, 702, 714, 805, 818, 909 and 916 will be split and new area codes will be added to provide a greater volume of phone numbers. We have used the latest available phone numbers in compiling this guide, but many of the details were not available at the time of going to press. If your call does not connect, check the area code in the telephone directory White Pages, or by dialling an information telephone operator.

The entrance to Zion National Park

Driver's guide

Fuel

Petrol (and diesel) is sold at gas stations in US gallons (about four litres per gallon). Most vehicles take unleaded petrol, which comes in regular, premium and super grades. Buy regular unless the car-hire company specifies otherwise. Most stations are self-service, although some offer a higher priced full-service alternative. Pump prices include all taxes. Gas stations generally accept credit cards and $20 travellers' cheques but will not take $50 or $100 bills due to counterfeiting concerns.

Information

For information on conditions, including road closures, call **Caltrans**; *tel: (800) 427-7623* for recorded information keyed to highway numbers. For **Northern Nevada (Reno area)**; *tel: (702) 793-1313*; **Southern Nevada (Las Vegas)**; *tel: (702) 486-3116*.

Local radio stations also broadcast weather and driving information. In urban areas, most stations have regular traffic reports.

Accidents

If you are involved in a collision, stop. Call the California Highway Patrol (CHP) or local police if there are injuries or obvious damage to any vehicle. Show police your driving licence, vehicle registration, proof of insurance and contact information, and exchange the same information with the other driver. Get the names and addresses of any witnesses. Accidents must also be reported to your car-hire company.

Collisions in California resulting in death, injury or property damage over $500 must be reported to the California Department of Motor Vehicles (DMV) within ten days. DMV offices are listed in the telephone book White Pages. In Nevada, report collision's resulting in death, injury or over $350 in property damage to police or the Nevada Highway Patrol. Other collisions must be reported to the Nevada Department of Motor Vehicles within ten days.

Automobile clubs

The **American Automobile Association** (AAA) is represented by two California affiliates, the **California State Automobile Association** (Northern California) and the **Automobile Association of Southern California** (Southern California). It prints the most useful road maps avaliable. These are free to members at AAA offices.

The RAC and other automobile clubs have reciprocal agreements with AAA. If a service is free at home, it's free at AAA when you show your membership card.

The best-known commercial maps are **Rand McNally** (large-scale maps) and **Thomas Brothers** (highly detailed road maps).

Breakdowns

Pull as far off the road as possible, turn on the flashing hazard lights and raise the bonnet. Change tyres only when out of traffic. Emergency call boxes are placed every half-mile on some highways to telephone for help. Otherwise, dial 911 from any telephone for police or medical assistance, but not for breakdown lorry.

Membership of the AAA or other auto club usually includes a free towing service to the nearest garage for repairs. Most car-hire companies either pay for repairs directly or reimburse the cost shown on repair receipts. If a hire car is going to be out of service for more than a few hours, ask the hire company for a replacement vehicle.

Documents

Your national driving licence is valid in California, but you must have it in your possession while driving. The minimum driving age is 16, but most car-hire companies require that drivers be at least 25. Be sure to have the vehicle registration and proof of liability insurance with you at all times.

Parking

Parking garages and car-parks are indicated by a white P on a blue background. Prices are posted at the entrance. Some city-centre garages charge $20 and more per hour.

Kerbside parking time is usually limited, either by posted signs or by coin-operated parking meters.

Kerbs may be colour-coded: *red* means no stopping or parking at any time; *white* is for passenger loading/unloading only; *green* is limited parking (usually 10 minutes); *yellow* is a commercial loading zone; *blue* is handicapped parking. Parking is not allowed within 15ft of a fire hydrant, within 3ft of a disabled kerb ramp, in bus stops, zebra crossings, pavements or on freeways. Fines vary from a few dollars to several hundred, depending on the infraction and jurisdiction. Fines levied against hired cars are charged against the hirer's credit card.

Car hire

Car categories vary, but most hire companies offer subcompact, compact, economy, mid-sized, full-sized, luxury and sport utility (SUV) vehicles. The larger the car, the faster it accelerates and consumes petrol. Book well in advance to ensure getting the type and size of vehicle you need. Standard features usually include automatic transmission, air-conditioning and unlimited mileage.

It's usually cheaper to pick up a vehicle at an airport than in the city centre. A surcharge, or drop fee, may be levied for dropping the vehicle off somewhere other than the place of hire. If you are considering an RV, ask about one-way rates if you aren't planning to arrive and leave from the same place.

All drivers must be listed on the hire contract. If an unlisted driver has an accident, you will probably be required to pay for repairs yourself.

Most car-hire companies require a credit card deposit, even if the hire has been prepaid. Before leaving, be sure you have all the necessary registration and insurance documents and that you know how to operate the vehicle.

Drinking, drugs and driving

DUI, driving under the influence of alcohol or any other drug, is illegal. The blood alcohol limit is 0.01 per cent and is strictly enforced. Drivers suspected of drunk driving have the choice of a breath, blood or urine test; refusing the test is an admission of guilt. Police establish random checkpoints and frequent roads near winery tasting rooms and popular roadside restaurants.

Driving conditions

California has almost every difficult driving condition imaginable outside the tropics. For desert travel, be sure that the air-conditioner and heater are both in good order. Carry extra water, food, warm clothing and a torch in case of trouble. If the car breaks down on a freeway, one person should walk to the next call box and phone for help, then return to the car to wait. On secondary roads, raise the bonnet. Either way, *always stay with your vehicle*. It's the only shade in sight and the breakdown lorry will be looking for a stranded car, not someone on foot.

Sandstorms can reduce visibility to zero. If visibility drops, pull off the road on to a spot higher than the surrounding terrain and wait it out.

RV drivers are often tempted to camp in dry riverbeds. Don't. Desert rains can create flash floods, even if the storm is out of sight, turning them into churning torrents in seconds. Check with park wardens (rangers) for safe camping spots.

In winter, blowing snow can reduce visibility to zero on mountain

California's native poppy, used to indicate one of the states' many waymarked scenic routes

roads and halt traffic for hours. Many passes over the Sierra Nevada mountains are closed late Nov–June. Highways that remain open frequently require the use of chains or other traction devices. If you are planning mountain driving in winter, ask the car-hire company to include chains or buy your own (under $50). When chains are required, petrol station attendants and roadside workers will install them for about $20. Carry warm clothing and food in case of traffic delays and always keep the petrol tank at least half-full. Useful items include an ice scraper and a small shovel.

Fog and blowing dust are frequent hazards, causing massive chain-reaction collisions in the Central Valley each year. When visibility drops, *slow down* and turn your headlamps on low beam. High beams blind oncoming drivers and reflect back to reduce your own vision.

Insurance

California requires third-party liability insurance cover of at least $15,000 for death or injury to one person, $30,000 for death or injury to more than one person and $5000 for property damage.

US and Canadian drivers may be covered by their own insurance, but other customers are strongly advised to take out their own coverage or purchase the collision damage waiver (CDW), sometimes called loss damage waiver (LDW) offered by hire companies. Without the waiver, you are personally liable for the full value of the vehicle. CDW is often required as part of fly-drive packages.

Police

Police signal drivers with flashing red and blue lights, sirens and loudhailers. Pull off the roadway as quickly as possible, turn off the engine and roll down the driver's side window. Stay inside the vehicle unless asked to step out. Have your driving licence and vehicle registration ready for inspection.

Officers occasionally let drivers off with a verbal warning. If issued a citation, arguing will only make a bad situation worse.

Road signs

European-style road signs are widely used, but not universally. *Red* signs indicate stop, do not enter or wrong way. *Yellow* signs are warnings or direction indicators. *Orange* means road repairs (road works) or detours (diversions). *White* shows speed limits and distances, almost always in miles. *Brown* indicates parks, camping and other recreation opportunities. *Blue* gives non-driving information such as services in a nearby town.

RVs

RVs are treated as lorries by traffic laws. The RV highway speed limit is 55mph (65mph for cars). Be cautious while driving. RVs are blown about by the wind more than cars and are more subject to rollover. As RVs are also taller and wider than cars, they can create hazards at gas stations, toll booths and car-parks or with low-hanging trees and signs.

Lights

It's wise to leave headlights on at all times for safety, but not required. Headlights must be used from dusk to dawn or whenever conditions require. In California, it is illegal to drive with only parking lights illuminated.

Left
Native American art in the Grand Canyon National Park

Speed limits

The highway speed limit is 65mph for cars (55mph for trucks and RVs) unless posted otherwise. Some rural freeways are posted for 70mph. In town, the speed limit is 25mph unless otherwise posted.

If driving conditions are poor, drivers are required to keep to a safe speed, no matter how slow. Police use radar, lasers and aeroplanes to track, stop and book speeders, but traffic normally flows at least 10mph above the posted limit.

Below
Route to the stars: street signs in downtown San Francisco

Seat belts

The driver and all passengers must wear seat belts. Children under the age of 4 or weighing less than 40lbs must ride in approved child safety seats. Safety seats can be hired with a car, or purchased for under $100 at a discount store. In an RV, passengers riding behind the driver's seat need not wear belts, but should be safely seated.

Security

Try not to accept a vehicle with a hire company logo visible – it's an advertisement for theft. You probably can't hide the hire company advert on an RV, but these vehicles are usually targets already.

Lock your vehicle when you are in it as well as when you leave it. Check for intruders before getting in, especially at night and in RVs any time. Never leave the engine running when the driver isn't behind the wheel and always park in well-lit areas.

Tolls

Major bridges in the San Francisco area charge tolls, as do scattered private freeways in Southern California, but most roads are free.

TYPICAL ROAD SIGNS IN CALIFORNIA

INSTRUCTIONS

Stop

Give way

Wrong way - often together with 'No entry' sign

No right turn

No U-turn

One-way traffic

Two-way left turn lanes

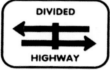

Divided highway (dual carriageway) at junction ahead

Speed limit signs: maximum and maximum/ minimum limits

WARNINGS

Crossroads

Junction

Curve (bend)

Winding road

Stop ahead

Two-way traffic

Divided highway (dual carriageway)

Road narrows on right

Roadworks ahead

Railway crossing

No-overtaking zone

Getting to California

The place to unwind after a long flight

Unless you already live within driving distance of California, flying is the most practicable way to get there. Transcontinental train and motor coach travel is slow, cramped and unpredictable, although AMTRAK operates popular coastal services from San Diego to Vancouver, British Columbia. Air travel is even more cramped, but travel time is counted in hours rather than days and timetables are almost always accurate.

Don't undertake a full day's touring after a long flight. Los Angeles and San Francisco may be only 10–12 air hours from much of Europe and 12–14 hours from Asia, but jet lag intensifies the effects of long-distance air travel. Expect to arrive fatigued, disorientated, short-tempered and otherwise *not* ready to drive.

Night-time flights are attractive because they seem to offer an extra day of sightseeing upon arrival. Resist the temptation. Most travellers do better by timing their flights to arrive in the late afternoon or early evening, then getting a good night's sleep before tackling the sights. Since many airport-area hotels and motels offer free shuttle service to and from the airport, you can take a shuttle to the hotel, recover from the flight and pick up your rental car the next morning at no additional cost.

Many fly-drive programmes offer what looks like an easy first-day drive, ie Los Angeles International Airport to the Disneyland area in Anaheim. It's a 45-minute jaunt that can stretch to hours in heavy rush-hour traffic. Better to rest the first night and hit the road refreshed in the morning – especially if you are not accustomed to urban traffic or driving on the right side of the road.

The reverse is equally true. Don't plan a tight schedule that gets you into Los Angeles or San Francisco and to the airport the requisite two hours before an international departure. Unexpected traffic can leave you stranded on a freeway as your plane takes off overhead. Airlines won't hold an entire flight for a carload of passengers flying on non-refundable bargain fares. Allow a safety margin by spending your last night in California near the departure airport, or at least in the same city.

Try to arrive with a few dollars in US currency and coins. Luggage trolleys are usually free in the international arrivals area but sometimes must be paid for. Some trolley stands accept credit cards, usually Visa or Access/MasterCard, but some require cash – and currency exchange facilities are located outside the arrivals area.

ATMs, automated teller machines, offer the best currency exchange rates and never close. Star and Cirrus are the most common international ATM networks.

International airports have currency exchange facilities in the international terminal that are open most hours. Domestic terminals and smaller airports have no exchange facilities at all. US dollar travellers' cheques from Thomas Cook and other major issuers are accepted almost everywhere, but travellers' cheques in other currencies must generally be cashed at a bank. Eurocheques and personal cheques drawn on banks outside the United States are usually not accepted.

California airports don't have duty-free shopping for incoming travellers, but it's no great loss. Prices for alcohol and other duty-free items are almost always lower in California supermarkets and discount stores than in duty-free shops. The same goes for other goods. Airport prices are generally higher than in similar shops near by and the selection is smaller. Airport fast-food outlets are comparable to chain outlets anywhere, but airport restaurants are generally higher in price than in quality.

A few car-hire companies have desks located near airport luggage claim areas, but nearly all require that you take a coach to an off-airport facility to pick up your car. Follow terminal signs for Rental Cars to the proper coach or van loading area.

Once at the car-hire location, have your booking number, passport, credit card and driving licence ready. Everyone who might drive the vehicle must show his or her driving licence and be listed on the rental contract. Drivers must generally be at least 25 years old, although some companies allow younger drivers for an additional fee.

Setting the scene

Lake Helen, in the Lassen
Volcanic National Park

The lure of California is as much mythical as real, but even the reality of the place borders on the unbelievable. The state, a bent rectangle 900 miles long by 200 miles wide, holds every climatic zone on earth except tropical rain forest and arctic wastes. The highest point in North America, Mount Whitney (14,494ft) and the lowest, Death Valley (282ft below sea level) are just 60 miles apart in southeastern California, but the winding 120-mile road trip between the two can take most of the day.

The state is a patchwork of awkward but awesome terrain, formed by tens of millions of years of earthquakes that have rent the landscape into a mosaic of mountains and fault lines. The biggest patch of flat land, the **Central Valley**, is 400 miles long by 50 miles wide. Nearly everything else is vertical.

California's entire coastline of 1264 corrugated miles is hemmed in by the **Coast Range**. Southern slopes are cloaked in explosively flammable brush, northern mountains by dense forests. **San Francisco Bay** is the only break in this natural wall.

The eastern side of the state is guarded by the **Sierra Nevada Mountains**, which rise gently from the Central Valley through the rolling hills of **Gold Country** to drop precipitously down eastern slopes into the Nevada deserts. A series of east–west ranges connects the Coast Range with the Sierras, making north–south travel a slow and tortuous task before the advent of modern roads. Fifty feet and more of snow blankets the Sierras every winter, closing most mountain passes from November until June. Each spring, the run-off roars through canyons up to 5000ft deep.

The climate is officially Mediterranean, even though the winter rain/summer drought pattern more resembles North Africa than Greece or Italy. Annual rainfall varies from less than an inch in the southeast deserts to more than 100ins in the northwest. Coastal redwood forests drip with accumulated mist while the deserts wither under scorching sun and some of the highest temperatures on earth.

In the beginning

The veil of myth and hyperbole that colours California was first woven in Spain. A 1510 Spanish romantic novel created Queen Califa, ruler of an island somewhere to the west of Europe, a land filled with black Amazons who rode griffins into battle and fought with weapons of pure gold. A few years later, Spanish conquistadores ventured north after subduing Native empires in Central and South America, hoping for more conquests, more gold and more glory.

Above
Joshua Tree National Park is named after these striking trees, so called because they resemble Joshua raising his arms to heaven

What they found instead was the peninsula of lower, or Baja California. The locals were hostile, the landscape barren and gold nowhere to be found. The would-be conquerors named the unpromising peninsula 'California', hoping that fiction would serve better than truth.

The first European to see Alta, or upper California, died there. **Juan Rodríquez Cabrillo** landed at San Diego in 1542, then broke his leg on San Miguel Island, now part of **Channel Islands National Park**, and died there, probably of gangrene. His crew sailed north as far as Oregon, then retreated back to Mexico. Spain called Cabrillo's voyage a failed and futile expedition.

Francis Drake, English privateer and later admiral, was the first European to make his fortune in California. Like many who followed, his scheme was not entirely legal but eminently successful.

Drake hunted Manila galleons, the lumbering Spanish treasure ships that sailed east from Manila each year laden with the plunder of Asia and the Philippines. The galleons sailed east to California, then turned south to Mexico and safety. Those that survived the trip were unloaded in Acapulco and other Mexican ports, their treasures transhipped to the east coast of Mexico, then sent through the Caribbean and on to Spain. Drake found the lightly armed galleons such easy prey that his ship, the *Golden Hinde*, was soon splitting from the weight of Spanish booty.

In 1579, he beached the *Hinde* for repairs, probably landing at Drakes Bay, now part of **Point Reyes National Seashore**, just north of San Francisco. Drake and his crew left a few undeniably English silver pennies behind for modern archaeologists. An engraved copper plaque claiming the land for Queen Elizabeth may or may not be authentic. Drake then sailed home to a knighthood while Spain ignored California for another 200 years.

Spain's neglect was a final reprieve for California's Native American population. Rugged terrain limited travel, but the climate was mild and food plentiful. Acorns were the staple, usually made into porridge or bread. Deer and small game were abundant. Rivers and bays were so rich in shellfish that coastal clans left heaps of discarded shells 30ft high. When the Spanish arrived in 1769, the Native American world quickly collapsed beneath the combined weight of disease, slavery and Christianity.

Gaspar de Portola and a Franciscan friar, **Junípero Serra**, led an expedition from Baja California north to San Diego. Serra stayed in San Diego to tend the sick and establish the first of 21 missions that stretched north to Sonoma. Portola explored north along what would become **El Camino Real**, 'the King's Highway', better known today as Hwy 101. The Spanish Empire had come to California.

An advance party climbed a ridge between today's cities of Pacifica and Millbrae and found their way blocked by an immense bay. Portola gave up and turned south again. Juan Crespi, a monk, recorded in his diary the sighting of a bay big enough to hold all the fleets of Europe. It was the first recorded description of **San Francisco Bay**.

Portola later sailed north with Serra from San Diego to Monterey, supposedly a fine harbour. Portola built a *presidio*, or fort; Serra built another mission. More missions were founded, including San Francisco in 1776, the year the United States declared independence from England.

Spain's empire declined during the early 19th century, but the California missions prospered. Vineyards, orchards, herds and maize fields flourished. Buildings began to assume a familiar form: whitewashed stone or brick churches topped by red clay tiles and bordered by arched colonnades. Fountains cooled lush central gardens.

San Carlos Borromeo del Carmel mission church

Above
Trail riders in Grand Canyon
National Park

Californios

Ecclesiastical prosperity was short lived. Mexico gained independence from Spain in 1821. Thirteen years later, Mexico secularised and sold the vast Mission estates to cattle ranchers (*Californios*). The Church's loss was California's gain.

The *rancho*, or ranch, became the basic social, cultural and economic unit. This gave California a rose-tinted heritage of dashing *caballeros*, gentlemen landowners, and swirling *señoritas*, glamorous young women. They created one of the largest and most prosperous pastoral societies the world has ever seen.

Californios sold 75,000 cattle hides yearly at $2 each to Yankee traders. With no enforceable taxes, plentiful food supplies and no need for armies, everything went to luxury imports. The *caballeros* raised cattle and bought them back as Boston-made boots. *Señoritas* slipped into fine Cantonese silk gowns to dance on floors of packed dirt. English and American merchants, most of them former sailors who had jumped ship, managed the trade.

The foreigners also managed the fur and whaling trade. New Englanders hunted whales migrating between Alaska and Baja California, nearly destroying every species of whale in the Pacific Ocean, while Russians hunted sea otters to the brink of extinction from their base at **Fort Ross**, north of San Francisco.

Furs lured English and American adventurers overland and the Hudson's Bay Company began California operations in 1829. In 1832, mountain man **Christopher 'Kit' Carson** helped map a trail from Santa Fe, New Mexico, to a lawless, dusty village called **Los Angeles**.

The first American overland immigrants arrived in 1841, the first wagon train in 1844. Then came the **Donner Party**, which had the misfortune to follow a guidebook written by an explorer who had never actually been to California. The party were snowbound in the Sierras near **Donner Summit**, on what is now the I-80, from November 1846 to February 1847. Forty of the 87 would-be pioneers survived by eating their livestock and their comrades.

Donner survivors arrived to find a new flag. Earlier settlers had been unhappy with a succession of weak Mexican governors, and when American Captain John Fremont 'happened' to appear in 1846 with a troop of 68 heavily armed soldiers, California's foreign population revolted. The rebels raised a flag over Sonoma carrying a star and a bear (which contemporaries said looked more like a pig) and declared the California Republic. Their new republic lasted one month.

The US declared war on Mexico in May; by July, naval units had occupied every California port and taken control of what little provincial government existed. The transition to American rule proceeded smoothly. *Californios* still ruled society and local government, foreign merchants ran the economy and there was land to spare for immigrants.

Los Angeles graffiti reflects the gun-law atmosphere of California in the Gold-Rush era

The Gold Rush

The discovery of gold in January 1848 changed California forever. The population mushroomed from 10,000 to 100,000 in two years. San Francisco metamorphosed from a windy, flea-bitten village into a city of 25,000. Gold, the first significant supply the world had seen since Spain had looted the Aztec, Inca and Maya empires in the 16th century, gave California the economic muscle to escape exploitation by New York and London financiers. The land nurtured its own collection of robber barons and a reputation as a place of eternal opportunity.

Americans of the era seized upon California gold as evidence of Divine favour and their right to rule the continent. After all, Spain and Mexico, the world's most experienced mining countries, had owned California for 300 years without finding significant deposits of the precious metal. American James Marshall spotted nuggets in a water wheel raceway just days before America paid Mexico $18.25 million for the entire southwestern quadrant of the continent. Miners pulled more than 30 times that much gold from California alone in less than a decade.

Most of the **49ers** sought their fortunes in what is now called Gold Country, the Sierra Nevada foothills along Hwy 49. When military officials called a constitutional convention in 1849, delegates split along regional lines. The south opposed joining the United States, rightly fearing that land, not mines, would be taxed. The north wanted statehood in order to assure a stable gold market. The northern faction won and California became a state in 1850.

The Gold Rush brought fortune to lucky miners and merchants who supplied the mines. The influx of miners from around the globe created shortages in everything from tea to tin. The American majority discriminated openly and violently against Chinese, Roman Catholics, Mexicans, Indians and anyone else who had the misfortune to be both non-American and successful.

Gold also destroyed the *Californios*. Inflation ravaged their finances as drought devastated their herds. Newly arrived Americans demanded title to the millions of hectares owned by a few hundred *Californio* families. Dubious land commissions awarded most acreage to American claimants whose best arguments were their nationality and ability to speak English.

The California Dream never faltered. As the goldfields played out, a tide of silver from Nevada brought new riches. The Comstock Lode beneath **Virginia City** produced $400 million for San Francisco mining companies before deposits were mined out in the 1880s.

Railroads were even better moneyspinners. **Mark Hopkins**, **Collis Huntington**, **Leland Stanford** and **Charles Crocker**, Sacramento merchants who backed the 1863 transcontinental railroad, became The Big Four. The quartet built fortunes on marginal land schemes and outright fraud, but California boomed. San Francisco ruled a commercial empire that stretched from China to Utah and Alaska to Mexico.

Even the weather contributed. As gold and silver lost their lustre, farmers realised that California was the one part of North America where rain fell only in winter. Agriculture flourished, from the vegetable farms that fed the cities to the vineyards that kept them drunk. With later irrigation schemes, the pattern of summer drought and winter water made the state an agricultural powerhouse in everything from apples and cotton to potatoes and marijuana.

In the 1880s, the railroad, by then called 'The Octopus' for its many-tendrilled influence in state and local politics, decided that California needed more people. Transcontinental fares fell to $1 per person just as farmers, real estate developers and the city of Los Angeles began extolling the virtues of sunny Southern California. Nature provided the sunshine, but California business designed the message, complete with alluring 'California Girl' posters.

The advent of the automobile and the fortuitous discovery of oil made the move west even easier. The burgeoning population demanded water, particularly in the desert that was most of Southern California. In 1913, Los Angeles built an aqueduct to pull water from the Owens Valley, east of the Sierra Nevada Mountains, to the parched city. The scheme was ridden with unscrupulous behaviour, corruption and scandal, as depicted in the film *Chinatown* which was produced half a century later, but Los Angeles had the water it needed to continue growing.

Agricultural interests saw the same future in irrigation; aqueducts carried water from the Colorado River to Southern California and the Central Valley. The Great Depression of the 1930s brought waves of migrant farmers into California from dusty, drought-plagued Oklahoma and Arkansas. Many joined indigenous Mexican farmworkers who migrated to harvest seasonal crops from Southern California to the Canadian border.

When World War II erupted, California became a wartime induction and shipping centre. Thousands of men passed through San Francisco, Los Angeles and San Diego on the way to battlefields in the Pacific, while naval operations brought an influx of military personnel and support services that remained through the 1990s.

After the war

With the war over, soldiers and sailors returned in droves to settle California's alluring coastal cities. The GI Bill provided free university education for veterans, many of whom attended the University of California in Berkeley, where much of America's atomic bomb research had been conducted. The new life and easy climate helped breed a new movement of artistic protest. Beatniks, dressed in black, given to recitals of free verse and the exercise of free love, flocked to the coffee houses in San Francisco's **North Beach**.

The protest movement that the Beats began spread to other segments of the population. By the early 1960s, agricultural workers, most of them originally from Mexico, began to organise against backbreaking working conditions in fields and agricultural factories, while university students in Berkeley began demanding more freedom to speak their minds.

By the mid-1960s, the first post-war generation was coming of age. Higher education received state funding and was no longer the reserve of the élite. Free thinking, free speech, free sex, free drugs, free everything came together in the hippie movement, while tie-dyed clothing, flowers, beads, incense, bare feet and jeans became the trademarks of a generation. Marijuana was the popular choice of drug, eclipsing the traditional favourites – alcohol and tobacco. Music recording studios in London suddenly had to contend with serious competition from Los Angeles and San Francisco.

Escalation of America's war in Vietnam in the late 1960s again brought thousands of soldiers pouring through California. Antiwar protesters from campuses state-wide took to the streets to demonstrate against the war even as the state's aerospace, communications and electronics industries grew wealthy from military spending.

The end of the Vietnam conflict in 1973 brought yet another wave

Golden Gate Bridge – San Francisco's world-famous engineering masterpiece

of immigration, this time from Indochina. Political turmoil in Central and South America sent new waves of Hispanic immigrants heading toward California.

Political turmoil at home created its own refugees. In 1978, California voters approved a ballot initiative, Proposition 13, which sharply cut taxes on homes and other real estate. Government revenues plummeted. Some mental sanatoriums were emptied, homeless shelters were reduced in size or closed and funding for education, libraries, museums and other public services was slashed. Government spending was brought into line, but the number of homeless people living on California streets skyrocketed.

The decline of the Cold War in the late 1980s and early 1990s brought stagnation and economic contraction to once-booming aerospace companies, but technology firms emerged to take their place. A bucolic agricultural area near San Jose, south of San Francisco, gradually lost its old name, 'Valley of Heart's Delight'. Its new name, **Silicon Valley**, appears on few highway maps, but the computer revolution that began in a Palo Alto garage continues to ricochet around the globe with the speed of email.

The same combination of university research, entrepreneurial drive, venture capital, and willingness to succeed that brought Silicon Valley to life has ignited other business booms. Biotechnology was born when an ambitious businessman and a biology researcher met over a jug of beer. Genentech, the company that emerged from a handshake and doodles on a serviette, brought genetic engineering out of the laboratory and into medical practices, kitchens, industrial plants and barnyards. Computer-based multimedia publishers have found a home in San Francisco's South of Market, or **SOMA** district, even as the more traditional entertainment moguls of Hollywood bring once-edgy computer technology to cinema and television screens worldwide.

California corporate upstarts like Netscape and Yahoo! have emerged to challenge the likes of IBM and Microsoft. Los Angeles-based automobile designers have helped Volkswagen, Nissan and Toyota knock some of the wind out of the sails of America's own car manufacturers in Detroit.

In the real world, there's no way to know just how long the string of successes and superlatives can continue. In the half-real, half-mythical allure of California, almost no one bothers to wonder, at least not in public.

California's population has nearly doubled every generation since the Gold Rush. The reasons to come change from one generation to the next – gold, silver, farms, oil, jobs – but the hopeful waves of immigrants keep coming, certain that the California Dream will come true for them, too.

Highlights

One of the best experiences of travel is tailoring an itinerary to match the your own interests and tastes. Here are some suggestions for itineraries that will show you different aspects of California, depending on how much time you have at your disposal.

The Top Ten Sights

Not the top ten places visitors *actually* go, but the ten not to miss.

Anza-Borrego Desert State Park *(page 90)*
California's most accessible desert.
Big Sur Coast *(page 214)*
Spectacular drive along golden, surf-baptised cliffs.
Grand Canyon National Park *(page 277)*
Forget the IMAX® and feast your imagination on the real place.
Hearst Castle *(page 219)*
Megalomania unhampered by good taste.
Las Vegas *(page 265)*
The ultimate theme park where the casino *always* wins.
Napa/Sonoma Wine Country *(page 154)*
Scenic home to some of the world's best wines.
The Redwoods *(page 196)*
The biggest living things on earth (Sequoia National Park) and the tallest (Redwoods National and State Park).
San Diego Wild Animal Park *(page 59)*
The best place in California to see exotic animals.
San Francisco *(page 134)*
Everybody's favourite city.
Yosemite National Park *(page 234)*
Mountain scenery so stunning it overawes you.

The Best of California

These two circular tours start and end in Los Angeles, but you can reverse them or pick them up in San Francisco or elsewhere. Suggested overnight stops are in **bold type**.

Two weeks
Marathon driving in 14 days!
Day 1: Arrive in **Los Angeles.**
Day 2: LA to Barstow, Baker, Shoshone and **Death Valley.**
Day 3: Death Valley to Lone Pine, Whitney Portal and **Bishop.**
Day 4: Bishop to Lee Vining, Mono Lake and **Yosemite National Park** (Hwy 120 to Yosemite closed in winter).
Day 5: **Yosemite**
Day 6: Yosemite to Gold Country (Mariposa, Sonora, Columbia) and **South Lake Tahoe.**
Day 7: Loop to Genoa, Carson City, Virginia City, Reno and **South Lake Tahoe.**
Day 8: Sqaw Valley, Tahoe City, Sacramento and **San Francisco.**
Day 9: **San Francisco.**
Day 10: Loop to Muir Woods, Point Reyes, Jenner, Guerneville, Healdsburg and **San Francisco.**
Day 11: San Francisco to Monterey, Carmel,Hearst Castle (advance tour booking needed) and **San Luis Obispo.**
Day 12: San Luis Obispo to Santa Maria, Solvang and **Santa Barbara.**
Day 13: Santa Barbara to Ojai, Malibu and **Los Angeles.**
Day 14: Home.

Three Weeks
See most of California, Grand Canyon National Park and Las Vegas in 21 fast-paced days.

Day 1: Arrive in **Los Angeles**.
Day 2: **Los Angeles**.
Day 3: LA to **Palm Springs**.
Day 4: Palm Springs to Blythe and **Prescott, Arizona**.
Day 5: Prescott to Sedona, Flagstaff and **Grand Canyon National Park**.
Day 6: Grand Canyon to Cameron, Marble Canyon, Kanab and **Bryce Canyon National Park, Utah**.
Day 7: Bryce to **Zion National Park** (the road into Zion Canyon, Zion Canyon Scenic Drive, will be closed to privite vehicles from Memorial Day weekend, 2000, through early Nov. Longer closures are planned for 2001; total closure to private traffic from 2002. Anyone with confirmed bookings at the lodge, however, will be allowed to drive to the hotel).
Day 8: Zion to St George and **Las Vegas, Nevada**.
Day 9: Las Vegas to Pahrump and **Death Valley National Park**.
Day 10: Death Valley to Lone Pine and **Bishop**.
Day 11: Bishop to Lee Vining, Mono Lake and **Yosemite National Park** (Hwy 120 to Yosemite closed in winter).
Day 12: **Yosemite**.
Day 13: Yosemite to Gold Country (Mariposa, Sonora, Columbia) and **South Lake Tahoe**.
Day 14: Loop to Genoa, Carson City, Virginia City, Reno and **South Lake Tahoe**.
Day 15: Squaw Valley, Tahoe City, Sacramento and **San Francisco**.
Day 16: **San Francisco**.
Day 17: Loop to Muir Woods, Point Reyes, Jenner, Guerneville, Healdsburg and **San Francisco**.
Day 18: San Francisco to Monterey, Carmel, Hearst Castle (advance tour booking needed) and **San Luis Obispo**.
Day 19: San Luis Obispo to Santa Maria, Solvang and **Santa Barbara**.
Day 20: Santa Barbara to Ojai, Malibu and **Los Angeles**.
Day 21: Home.

Wine Country

California has produced wine since Spanish Mission days, and with Napa Valley marketing and world-judged quality in over nine wine regions, California is second to none in tasting room accessibility. Microclimates produce distinctive bouquets in a recently introduced vintage appellation system.

San Francisco is the gateway to the **Napa Valley** and the multiple valley **Sonoma Wine Region**, and, to **Mendocino**'s wineries, a further two hours' drive north. South of **San Francisco**, **Monterey** and **Santa Cruz** wineries can be found amid redwoods and coastal mountains. The **Sierra Foothills**, **Amador** and **El Dorado**, off Hwy 49 in Gold Country, produce rich, dry wines from volcanic soil and winter snow.

An east-west mountain range funnels fog and ocean breezes far inland to create a long, cool-climate growing season for Southern California's best vintages from **Santa Barbara** wineries, north of Santa Barbara via Hwy 154 and 246 in the Santa Ynez Valley, and the **Santa Maria Valley**, north on Hwy 101. **Edna Valley** white wines, south of **San Luis Obispo**, and **Paso Robles'** heady reds and rich dessert wines, north of San Luis Obispo, create the flavour of summer heat. **Temecula**, 60 miles north of San Diego, provide easy access to wine-tasting rooms amid rugged mountains enshrouded with morning fog, but gets congested at weekends.

Los Angeles

Ratings

Museums	●●●●●
Shopping	●●●●●
Art	●●●●●
Food and drink	●●●●○
Nightlife	●●●●○
Architecture	●●●○○
Children	●●●○○
Historic sights	●●●○○

As your plane approaches Los Angeles International Airport, the flat sprawl which houses 9.4 million souls within Los Angeles County ends only at the great Pacific Ocean.

The denizens of the amorphous neighbourhoods, urban villages, slums, beach towns and creative colonies coexisting as Angelinos are an upbeat, eternally optimistic mix. One-third are Hispanic, many from Mexico; 8 per cent are African-American; and 9 per cent have an Asian or Pacific Island heritage.

Los Angeles has a relentless beat, a constant music of car horns, computer keys tapping away in cafés, thrumming generators, beeping signs, the whoosh of espresso coffee machines, mechanised leafblowers, and the hiss of water wastefully washing sidewalks in this desert. Angelinos call their home El-Lay, short, snappy, abbreviated, sassy, an entertaining name, like themselves. Often faintly visible through 'haze', Los Angeles's mountains rise startlingly to the north and east. *(For Long Beach, Santa Monica and the beach cities between, see Route 4, pages 69–76.)*

Getting there and getting around

Los Angeles International Airport (LAX); *tel: (310) 646-5252*, is 17 miles southwest of downtown. Taxi to downtown costs $26. All outbound transport except taxis are on the Lower Level/Arrival islands outside arrival baggage carousels. LAX to downtown door-to-door van service is $12 (single). A free shuttle runs to the Metro Green Line Light Rail Station; take the line to Wilmington, then transfer to the adjacent Imperial Terminal to take the Blue Line to 7th and Flower Sts in Downtown Los Angeles, $1.60 with transfer. There are free shuttles to car-hire locations and airport hotels.

Amtrak *(tel: (800) 872-7245)* trains pull into Union Station, where **Metrolink** *(tel: (800) 371-5465)* has its Mon–Fri commuter train hub for routes north to Oxnard, south to San Diego, and southeast to Irvine in Orange County, as well as to the San Fernando Valley and San Bernardino.

The Getty Center
Autry Museum of Western Heritage
Hollywood
Griffith Park
Pasadena
Rodeo Drive
Melrose Avenue
Beverly Hills
Museum of Tolerance
J. P. GETTY MUSEUM
Grand Central Market
Music Centre
Santa Monica
California Science Centre
LOS ANGELES

Parking

Parking meters are widely available, take change, and can be a good bargain if parking for less than one or two hours. Hourly restrictions are posted on detailed signs on the kerb. Downtown and in posh areas, car-parks may charge several dollars per hour. 2 Rodeo Drive in Beverly Hills offer two hours free parking, no validation required. For dining in any popular area, especially at night, valet parking is *de rigueur*, and costs from $5–$15.

Driving

Traffic flows slowly during rush hour on most LA area freeways, so it may be more efficient to take major surface streets (arterials) in the direction desired.

While much of the LA region is served by the **MTA** bus system; *tel: (213) 626-4455*, including the three-line Metro Rail light rail and subway, not all routes are convenient for visitors; most journeys take several hours. The $0.25 MTA **DASH** bus routes make frequent stops around Downtown LA, Hollywood, the beach areas and the northern valleys.

Listen to local radio stations for traffic reports, especially in the morning and evening rush hours. You will also get regular weather checks, including air pollution reports.

Sights

Angels Flight Railway $ 351 S. Hill St; tel: (213) 626-1901. Operates 0630–2200.

Bradbury Building 304 S. Broadway; tel: (213) 626-1893. Open to 1st landing 0900–1700.

Armand Hammer Museum of Art $ 10899 Wilshire Blvd; tel: (310) 443-7000. Open Tue–Sun at 1100; Tue–Wed, Fri–Sat to 1900, Thur to 2100, Sun to 1700; free Thur 1800–2100.

Autry Museum of Western Heritage $$ (Griffith Park) 4700 Western Heritage Way; tel: (323) 667-2000; web: www.autry-museum.org. Open Tue–Sun 1000–1700.

Downtown**

Whimsical design and classic elegance got lost for decades before Downtown Los Angeles underwent extensive redevelopment and a clean-up. Once shunned as dingy and crime-ridden, today's civic centre has soaring skyscrapers, a fanciful funicular, a pillar-like City Hall, a restored railway station, and a wealth of architecture. The **Los Angeles Conservancy** (tel: (213) 623-2489) offer tours of the notable monoliths, bank buildings and fine art deco, marble and terra-cotta architecture.

The orange **Angels Flight Railway**** is a charming funicular ride up steep Bunker Hill to California Plaza skyscrapers, many used as action film locations. Stroll through the ornate Spanish Renaissance-style lobby of the three-tower 1923 **Regal Biltmore Hotel*** (506 S. Grand Ave; tel: (213) 624-1011), across from Pershing Square's geometric sculptures and fountain. Stop at the **Bradbury Building****, five skylit levels of graceful, intricate ironwork and an exposed lift accented by marble, tilework and rich polished wood. This fanciful $500,000, 1893 masterpiece is a frequent film location; Harrison Ford and androids battled here in *Blade Runner* (1982).

Shimmering white **City Hall*** (200 N. Spring St), closed until 2003 for seismic repair, served as Superman's Daily Planet Building. The 1939 Spanish Mission exterior of **Union Station*** (800 N. Alameda St; tel: (213) 683-6875), encloses the cavernous marble mosaic-lined hallway of a railway station.

Armand Hammer Museum of Art*

Dwarfed by the Occidental Petroleum Building, the museum houses the late entrepreneur-philanthropist's third art collection: Old Masters, Impressionist and Post-Impressionist paintings, Dürer watercolours and satirist Daumier's lithographs. The museum opens into the heart of Westwood, the **University of California, Los Angeles (UCLA)** shopping and entertainment area.

Autry Museum of Western Heritage***

This Griffith Park museum offers a vibrant, honestly captioned collection of Western US art, artefacts and cowboy film memorabilia. Film star Gene Autry, 'The Singing Cowboy', amassed an extensive collection of cinema props, saddles, posters, cowboy costumes, boots, spurs and related 1950s-era outfits and toys for children. From the first Spanish conquerors to American wagon train expansion West, the museum doesn't shrink from the violence implied by the roomful of Colt firearms, the narrative diorama of the 'Shootout at the O.K. Corral', or descriptions of the decimation of Native Americans and buffalo. Even so, this is a deservedly popular museum, a great hit with visitors and not just those obsessed with cowboy films.

Museum of Television & Radio
$$ 495 N. Beverly Dr.; tel: (310) 786-1000; web: www.mtr.org. Open 1200, Wed–Sun to 1700, Thur to 2100.

California Science Center $ *(Exposition Park) 700 State Dr.; tel: (213) 744-7400; web: www.casciencectr.org. Open daily 1000–1700. Free, parking.*

Below
The California Science Center

Beverly Hills❖❖

Beverly Hills is a town and a state of mind, doing business within the aptly-named Golden Triangle, an area bordered by N. Crescent Dr. and Wilshire and Santa Monica Blvds. **Rodeo Drive's❖** three blocks of ultra-posh boutiques, where there are more tourists than shoppers, drip with sophistication. **2 Rodeo's❖❖** winding street of designer stores and quaint streetlamps offers a microcosm of *la crème de la crème*.

The film *Pretty Woman (1990)* put the **Regent Beverly Wilshire Hotel❖** *(9500 Wilshire Blvd; tel: (310) 275-5200)* on the must-see map. The **Museum of Television & Radio❖** is the best spot outside of the Museum's New York City venue to view television clips and listen to historic radio programmes and advertisements.

California Science Center❖

The **California Science Center** and adjacent IMAX® theatre are in Exposition Park, south of Downtown Los Angeles, within walking distance of the **LA Memorial Coliseum**, central site for the 1932 and 1984 Olympiad, the **California Afro-American Museum** and the **Natural History Museum of Los Angeles County**. Magenta light bathes a multi-storey entry pavilion hung with 1578 gold-leaf and palladium globes. You can balance on a bicycle suspended on a highwire, while another interactive machine uses astronaut training technology to simulate weightlessness. Check out the inner workings

🏛 **George C. Page Museum/La Brea Tar Pits $$** *5801 Wilshire Blvd; tel: (213) 934-7243; web: www.tarpits.org. Open Tue–Fri 0930–1700, Sat–Sun 1000–1700.*

The Getty Center $ *1200 Getty Center Dr., exit from I-405; tel: (310) 440-7300; web: www.getty.edu. Open Tue–Wed 1100–1900, Thur–Fri 1100–2100, Sat-Sun 1000–1800. Free admission and drop-off but parking reservations required.*

🛍 **Fashion District** *(Downtown) 7th St to I-10 (Santa Monica Fwy), Broadway to San Pedro; tel: (213) 488-1153; web: www.dpoa.com*

🛒 **Grand Central Market** *(Downtown) 317 S. Broadway; tel: (213) 624-2378. Open Mon–Sat 0900–1800, Sun 1000–1730; 90 mins free parking with a $15 purchase.*

and appropriate sound effects of the Digestion Diner mannequin and the Body Works, featuring a 50ft-long anatomically correct female body model, while 'she' discusses teenage physical strains with an inane cartoon character projected behind her.

Fashion District❖❖

Vendors of everything to do with clothing and accessories sell wholesale to the trade and retail to the public. Not all shops in this 56-block district are welcoming, but most offer a peek into an industry which generates $16.5 billion. Five thousand merchants operating from posh upper-floor shop-fronts or street-level outlets, employ 45,000 local residents, many immigrants, to design, pattern, sew, display and sell garments, buttons, zippers, coats, dresses, scarves, bolts of cloth and almost anything that can be used to adorn the body or decorate a house. For indoor browsing, try the **CaliforniaMart❖** *(110 E. 9th St; tel: (213) 630-3600)*. Mannequins lurch surreally into the walkway of **Santee Alley❖❖** *(between Santee St and Maple Ave, Olympic Blvd–11th St)*. The best day to find bargains is Sat, but some wholesalers also sell samples on the last Fri of the month.

George C Page Museum of La Brea Discoveries/La Brea Tar Pits❖❖

This Hancock Park museum belies the feeling of late 20th-century construction that characterises LA. Ice Age fossils around 40,000 years old have been found in bubbling tar pits once mined for natural asphalt. After the Age of Dinosaurs, giant ground sloths, sabre-toothed cats, wolves, and at least one human, La Brea Woman, roamed the once lush, rich land. More than 1.5 million bones and several million more plant and invertebrate fossils have been recovered just outside the museum building; excavations are ongoing in summer. A bas–relief around the building exterior depicts the world of gigantic birds, sloths, cats and mammoths. Inside, exhibits surround a garden planted with ferns and simple Ice Age-era flora. The current work of the palaeontology laboratory scientists is on view year-round.

The Getty Center❖❖❖

Shimmering white amongst the brown mountains above Los Angeles, this $1 billion art museum, with its signature wavy-line exterior, is free and has a pleasant tram ride up, a refreshing pool in the courtyard, a stream through a central garden landscaped to change seasonally, inexpensive shaded dining and an eclectic collection mixing masterpieces with over-indulgence. From photographs to illuminated medieval manuscripts, Van Gogh irises to flowery late 17th-century French paintings and decorative arts, the Getty Center takes in the past 12 centuries of Western, mostly European art. A one-hour, quick-tour brochure outlines a 'best of' overview. Sit down with Digital Experience computers to surf the Web for art tours, LA ethnic culture, archaeology digs or cyberpoetry.

Griffith Park *(Griffith Park Ranger Visitor Center), 4730 Crystal Springs Dr; tel: (323) 665-5188).*

Griffith Observatory $ *(Griffith Park) 2800 E. Observatory Rd; tel: (323) 664-1191.* **Planetarium** *and* **Laserium,** *free admission to* **Hall of Science.** *Open daily 1230–2200 in summer and weekends, Tue–Fri 1400–2200 in winter.* **Telescope** *viewing, open winter Tue–Sun 1900–2145, summer dark–2145.*

Travel Town Transportation Museum *5200 W. Zoo Dr.; tel: (323) 662-5874. Open Mon–Fri 1000–1600, Sat–Sun 1000–1700.*

Grand Central Market❖❖

Since 1917, Angelinos have shopped here for Mexican, Thai, Japanese, Chinese, Vietnamese, Armenian and Italian ingredients for their kitchens at home, finding exotic spices, candy and pastries, grains, rice and pastas, meat, fish, tortillas and other produce among 50 shops, restaurants and juice bars which wrap or dish up the freshest staples of ethnic life. Look for the bronze pig heads at the Broadway entrance; the Hill St entrance is across from Angels Flight.

Griffith Park❖❖

More than 4000 acres of green space in the Santa Monica Mountains above Hollywood are devoted to recreation and serious culture: cowboy-style at the **Autry Museum of Western Heritage❖❖❖** *(see page 44)*; or pop/folk music-style at the outdoor **Greek Theater❖❖** *(Griffith Park, 2700 N. Vermont Ave; tel: (323) 665-1927; $$$)*. There's free science and splendid sunset-watching above the Los Angeles sprawl at the copper-domed **Griffith Observatory❖❖**. The equestrian trail paradise is augmented by the 77-acre **Los Angeles Zoo❖** *(5333 Zoo Dr.; tel: (323) 644-4200; $$)*, and fascinating railway carriages, equipment and firefighting gear at the free **Travel Town Transportation Museum❖❖**. Golf courses and a merry-go-round top off the mix in this urban park.

Hollywood style – all tinsel and fluff

Hollywood❖❖

This district, its name emblazoned across the dry hills, always evokes the magic of film. Stars of film, television, radio, music and the stage have been celebrated with more than 2000 pink **Hollywood Boulevard Walk of Fame❖** stars, embedded in the pavement from La Brea Ave to Vine St. Bright murals, neon lights and colourful, risqué shop windows brighten the neighbourhood and add a touch of whimsy to the sidewalk clutter. Hand and footprints lure visitors to try out the stars' autographed imprints before the exotic pagoda façade of **Mann's Chinese Theater❖❖** *(6925 Hollywood Blvd). (See Route to the Stars, page 63, for more on Hollywood.)*

Los Angeles County Museum of Art (LACMA)❖❖❖

The Western US's largest art museum always has an outstanding special exhibition, like those on Picasso, Japanese

Los Angeles County Museum of Art (LACMA) $$ *5905 Wilshire Blvd; tel: (323) 857-6000; web: www.lacma.org*

Carole and Barry Kaye Museum of Miniatures $$ *5900 Wilshire Blvd; tel: (323) 937-6464. Open Tue–Sat 1000–1700, Sun 1100–1700.*

LACMA West $$ *(6867 Wilshire Blvd. Both open Mon, Tue–Thur 1200–2000, Fri 1200–2100, Sat–Sun 1100–2000. Free 2nd Tue of month except special events.*

Samurai, or colourful Panamanian *molas* (skilfully crafted cloth appliqués). LACMA shares a huge block with the **George C Page Museum** and **La Brea Tar Pits** *(see page 46)*, and is across wide Wilshire Blvd from the **Carole and Barry Kaye Museum of Miniatures**. Amongst LACMA's powerhouse collections are Textiles and Costumes, a world-renowned Indian and Southeast Asian Art Collection, and the Japanese Pavilion, two levels of galleries which include magnificent Japanese scrolls in a building designed in the shape of a pagoda. Large outdoor sculptures by Auguste Rodin, Alexander Calder and Henry Moore whet the appetite for what's inside.

LACMA West✦✦, a transformed department store building, is a fine example of the 1930s Steamline Moderne deco architecture for which the Wilshire Blvd **Miracle Mile** is known. LACMA West co-operatively displays the **Southwest Museum**'s Native American cultural artefacts.

Melrose Avenue✦

A decade of ultra-cool restaurants and Generation X boutique shopping has worn slightly thin around the edges of this punk-hair, black-garbed area between La Brea and Fairfax Aves, made slightly

Graffiti artists compete to produce the best art in ultra-cool Melrose Avenue

ⓘ Museum of Contemporary Art (MOCA) $$ *250 S. Grand Ave; tel: (213) 626-6222; web: www.moca-la.org. Open Tue–Sun 1100, to 1700 Tue–Wed, Fri–Sun, to 2000 Thur. Free 1700–2000 Thur.*

Museum of Tolerance $$ *9786 W. Pico Blvd; tel: (800) 900-9036 or (310) 553-8403. Open Mon–Thur 1000–1600, Fri 1000–1300, Sun 1030–1700.*

Music Center *(Downtown) 135 N. Grand Ave/717 W. Temple St; tel: (213) 972-7200. Free guided tours; tel: (213) 972-7483.*

El Pueblo de Los Angeles Historic Monument *Open daily 1000–1900. Sepulveda House Visitors Center open Mon–Sat 1000–1500. Los Angelinas del Pueblo, 130 Paseo de la Plaza, tel: (213) 628-1274, offers free walking tours of the park Tue–Sat 1000–1300.*

notorious by the television show *Melrose Place*. Evening dining means posh prices and handsome valets to park your auto – unless you opt for the ubiquitous American fast-food chains. Business façades sport half-sphere mirrors, shocking pink and aqua colours and flowerpot shards. Wander south on Martell Ave and turn right into the delivery alley to see some of LA's most masterful graffiti mural art, with truly striking icons of the city brightening the walls.

Museum of Contemporary Art (MOCA)✦

MOCA's downtown venue *(250 S. Grand Ave)*, presents an overview of the last 60 years of modern art. Large sculpture, abstract paintings, prints, multimedia and video presentations are in lower level galleries. The cheerful brick-red building entrance is flanked by an arch. The museum's other venue, the **Geffen Contemporary at MOCA✦** *(152 N. Central Ave)* in a warehouse-like converted garage, is accessible from **Little Tokyo**, the heart of Los Angeles' Japanese-American community.

Museum of Tolerance✦✦✦

The museum is a gripping introduction to – or reminder of – the effects of racism and intolerance. The World War II Holocaust is the final presentation after graphic interactive exhibits of Bosnian ethnic cleansing and the closer-to-home 'Final Solution' to the Jews' extermination.

Music Center✦✦

The performing arts is in the heart of downtown. The **Dorothy Chandler Pavilion✦** hosts the Los Angeles Opera, while cutting-edge theatre is presented in the **Mark Taper Forum✦✦** and Broadway plays and mainstream theatre are performed at the **Ahmanson Theater✦**. A Jacques Lipchitz 'Peace' fountain in the courtyard constantly varies its water flow, creating the illusion of an erratic brook in the city centre. By 2000, the Los Angeles Philharmonic should be ensconced in the modernistic, white **Disney Concert Hall**.

Olvera Street✦✦

The pedestrian street at the heart of downtown is the centre-piece of the **El Pueblo de Los Angeles Historic Monument**, where the first Spanish settlers arrived in 1781. Among among the park's 27 buildings is LA's oldest, the 1818 **Avila Adobe✦✦✦**, perfectly restored and furnished as an 1850s *rancho*. A Mexican-style **open-air shopping arcade✦** has well-crafted leather goods and Mexican tourist trinkets. Restaurants serve modest, authentic Mexican food.

Pasadena✦✦

Pasadena, northeast of Downtown LA, is beamed into millions of homes on New Year's Day with the televised **Rose Parade** *(tel: (626)*

Gamble House $ *4 Westmoreland Pl, Pasadena; tel: (626) 793-3334. Open Thur–Sun 1200–1500.*

Norton Simon Museum $ *411 W. Colorado Blvd, Pasadena; tel: (323) 681-2484; web: www.citycent.com/CCC/ nsmuseum.html. Open Thur–Sun 1200–1800.*

Huntington Library, Art Collections and Botanical Gardens $$ *1151 Oxford Rd, San Marino; tel: (626) 405-2141; web: www.huntington.org. Open Tue–Fri 1200–1630, Sat–Sun 1030–1630.*

Petersen Automotive Museum $$ *6060 Wilshire Blvd; tel: (323) 930-2277. Open Tue–Sun 1000–1800.*

449-7673; web: www:tournamentofroses.com) which precedes the Rose Bowl football match.

Wealthy Midwestern settlers spent the early 20th century building mansions in the balmy, orange-blossom-scented climate. The perfectly-proportioned **Gamble House✧✧✧**, designed with dark woods and stained glass, is Craftsman architecture at its finest. The 1927 **Pasadena City Hall✧** *(100 N. Garfield)* would look at home in Spain. Find designer wear and casual dining at Old Pasadena's **One Colorado✧** *(Colorado Blvd and Fair Oaks Ave)* complex.

The **Norton Simon Museum✧✧✧**, with its wealth of collections ranging from Picasso masterpieces to Hindu and Buddhist statues from India, Tibet and Nepal, is the marriage of a millionaire's exquisite taste with gallery display. In San Marino, close by, the **Huntington Library, Art Collections and Botanical Gardens✧✧** has fine art, medieval manuscripts, lovely gardens and a tea room.

Petersen Automotive Museum✧✧

One of the most complete car museums chronicles LA's love affair and dependence upon the automobile. Cars of the stars, hot rods, sport cars, roadside cafés, service stations – it's all here.

Accommodation and food

Rooms can be found everywhere in this world metropolis, including hundreds of chain properties. The LACVB *(see page 43)* lists member hotels in the *Destination Los Angeles* guide, but does not make bookings. To conserve time and energy, base yourself close to attractions you intend to see. Downtown, the Westside (Bel Air, Beverly Hills, West Hollywood), and Santa Monica are pricey; Hollywood area hotels and motels, and those in less touristic neighbourhoods, are more moderate. Always ask for secure parking.

If there's a cuisine you haven't tried, LA has a restaurant that prepares it. Local newspapers and the free monthly *Where Los Angeles* magazine list restaurants and reviews trendy newcomers.

Mel's Drive-in $ *8585 Sunset Blvd; tel: (310) 854-7200.* Serves quintessential American diner food along Hollywood's Sunset Strip 24 hours a day.

Chan Dara $$ *11940 W. Pico Blvd, West LA and other locations; tel: (310) 479-4461.* Draws diners for scrumptious Thai food – especially pad Thai noodles.

La Barca Jalisco $ *3501 Firestone Blvd, South Gate; tel: (323) 564-5140.* Dishes up traditional Mexican meals including seafood, *menudo* (tripe soup) and its famed *birra* (goat).

Entertainment

The Entertainment Capitol of the World is rich with amusements, from high culture to schlock to pornography. Look in the free weekly newspapers – *LA Weekly, New Times Los Angeles, Entertainment Today* – and the mainstream *Los Angeles Times, Calendar* (Sun) and *Weekend* (Thur) sections for listings. Pick a neighbourhood, refer to the listings and gamble that it will be good; many of the world's best and most industrious actors, artists, musicians, comedians and creative people live in the Los Angeles area to be where the action is.

Sunset Strip◊◊, Sunset Blvd in trendy West Hollywood, still offers **Whisky A Go Go** *(8901 Sunset Blvd; tel: (310) 652-4202)*, with other

Right
Posh-conservative styles in Beverly Hills department stores

The Angels Flight Railway rides up LA's steep Bunker Hill

star-making (Bruce Springsteen, Bob Marley) music venues such as **Roxy** *(9009 Sunset Blvd; tel: (310) 276-2222)* or American roots music at the **House of Blues**✦✦ *(8430 Sunset Blvd; tel: (323) 848-5100).* Gay clubs are a few blocks south in West Hollywood along Santa Monica Blvd. Most comedians learn to swim upstream to live audiences in LA clubs such as **The Improv**✦✦ *(8162 Melrose Ave; tel: (323) 651-2583)* and **The Comedy Store**✦✦ *(8433 W. Sunset Blvd; tel: (323) 656-6225).* Like the district, Hollywood clubs can be a little raw, attracting an audience of after-work slummers and devotées who seldom see daylight.

One of LA's best bargains is free tickets to live tapings of major television network talk shows and dramas. Though buskers at **Mann's Chinese Theatre** *(see page 65)* work hard to lure that day's audiences to CBS studio tapings, it's best to book ahead with **Audiences Unlimited** *(tel: (818) 506-0067,* **CBS Television City** *(tel: (213) 852-2624)* or **NBC Television** *(tel: (818) 840-3537).* Occasionally, location film shoots will permit visitors to watch, or filming may take place on city streets. **Paramount Studios $$** *(tel: (213) 956-5575),* **Warner Bros Studios $$** *(tel: (818) 954-1744)* and **Universal Studios Hollywood $$$** *(tel: (818) 508-9600),* offer a variety of behind-the-scenes tours.

Shopping

If it's made anywhere in the world, you can find in Greater LA. The LACVB offers a pocket-sized *Shopping in Los Angeles* guide for suggestions of where and what to purchase.

Dressing down and casual is almost a science. **Rodeo Drive** or the **Beverly Center** in Beverly Hills are starting places for posh-conservative with touches of Academy Award gown thrown in. For the raw materials, visit the LA **Fashion District.** Hundred-store malls are scattered throughout the area, usually anchored by two up-market department stores.

For art and books on cowboys and the West, the **Autry Museum of Western Heritage** *(see page 44)* is unparalleled. **Melrose Avenue** is where the trendoids shop to be 'bad'. Hollywood Blvd at Wilcox Ave is the centre for costumes, exotic shoes, and costume and film poster shops. Peruse 'in' furniture along La Brea Ave south of Sunset Blvd and search out antiques in **Old Pasadena**. **Third Street Promenade** in **Santa Monica** has up-market shops and a Farmer's Market patronised by film stars incognito within whiffing distance of the Pacific Ocean.

Suggested tours

Downtown, the **Los Angeles Conservancy Tours $** *(523 W. 6th St, Suite 1216, tel: (213) 623-2489)*, cover Art Deco, Biltmore Hotel, Broadway Movie Theatres, City Hall, Little Tokyo (Japantown), Pershing Square, Union Station and local architecture on guided walking tours.

Drive-by tours of the stars' homes are on offer via limousine or open-top double-decker bus. The quirkiest is **Grave Line Tours**✦✦✦ **$$$** *(tel: (213) 469-4149)* a narrated Cadillac hearse tour of death and sin sites of the famous.

Right
Shops in Olvera Street, Old LA

Southern California Theme Parks

Ratings

Theme parks	●●●●●
Children	●●●●●
Architecture	●●●○
Shopping	●●○○○
Food and drink	●●○○○
Parks and gardens	●●○○○
Wildlife	●●○○○
Art	●○○○○

If optimism and fantasy are Southern California's forte, the upbeat attitude is nowhere more evident than at amusement parks, lands of wonder for children of all ages. The secret is not to choose a park because it's famous, but because its attractions fit your interests.

Theme parks are geared for children. Disneyland, Knott's Berry Farm and Universal Studios Hollywood have oversized cartoon, television and film personalities strolling around the park to greet children, pose for pictures and give 'character' autographs. Baby buggies are ubiquitous, drinking fountains and other facilities are built to accommodate younger visitors, and some rides have safety in mind with posted size restrictions. Jurassic Park exists, but only as a water-soaked, high-spirited roller-coaster ride at Universal Studios Hollywood. San Diego Wild Animal Park is more an entertaining wildlife refuge than a traditional theme park à la Disneyland, the Granddaddy of them all.

DISNEYLAND✦✦

ⓘ Disneyland $$$ is a 30-minute drive southwest of Downtown Los Angeles, *1313 Harbor Blvd, Anaheim*; tel: (714) 781-4565; web: *www.disneyland.com*. During construction of Disney's new California Adventure, phone in advance for freeway exit directions and follow signs.

In 1955, Walt Disney took his flair for cinematic animation and dogged entrepreneurship beyond the Mickey Mouse film empire. Anaheim's orange groves were turned into Uncle Walt's rosy-coloured concept of nostalgia, patriotism, innovation, fairy-tale and adventure, all tied into his new television programme featuring many of the same characters, locales and themes.

Children, well-protected from real animal behaviour, cowboy and pioneers' guns, and inclement weather, could live out fantasies with simulated animals, robotic pirates and roller-coaster rides through Disney's Matterhorn. Snow White, The Mad Hatter and other fairy-tale characters portrayed in Disney animated films walked around in costumes to pose for photographs with children. Half a century later, the formula still works for the Walt Disney Company and its imitators around the world.

Springs
ANTELOPE
Rosamond
EDWARDS A.F.B.
Rogers Lake
Lenwood ○
Termo
New
Hodge
Daggett
(138)
Rosamond Lake
Hi Vista
Helendale
(15)
PIS
(49)
Antelope Acres
[N2]
Quartz Hill
Lancaster
Saddleback Butte S.P.
(395)
Oro Grande
(247)
Pt.
ke Hughes
Elizabeth Lake
Green Valley
Leona Valley
(14)
Palmdale
Wilsona Gardens
El Mirage
(31)
Victorville
SAN BERNARDIN
Vincent
Pearland Littlerock
Llano
Adelanto
Apple Valley
Lucerne Valley
(18)
(138)
Pearblossom
Pinon Hills
Hesperia
(18)
351
Placerita Canyon S.P.
(138)
Phelan
(2)
Silverwood Lake S.R.A.
SAN BERNARDIN
Six Flags Magic Mountain / Hurricane Harbour
Wrightwood
(138)
Lake Arrowhead
Big Bear City
EY
San Fernando
(2)
ANGELES NAT. FOR.
Crestline
Big Bear Lak
AND OAKS
Burbank
PASADENA
O
Rialto
SAN BERNARDINO
(38)
Pioneer
GLENDA
Universal Studio Hollywood and Citywalk
Redlands
verly Hills
POMONA
RIVERSIDE
Yucaipa
Beaumont
alibu
LOS ANGELES
(10)
Banning
Monica
FULLERTON
MORENO VALLEY
Cabazon
Palm Spring
GLEWOOD
Compton
Knotts Berry Farm
Corona
(60)
ORRANCE
ANAHEIM
ORANGE
(215)
San Jacinto
Rancho
LONG BEACH
Disneyland
Perris
(15)
SANTA ANA
IRVINE
Sun City
Hemet
Pa
HUNTINGTON BEACH
ORANGE
Mission Viejo
Lake Elsinore
Winchester Mountain Center
Newport Beach
(1)
Lake Elsinore S.R.A.
(74)
RAMONA I.R.
Anza
San Pedro
Laguna Beach
(74)
Murrieta
(79)
Sage
Cahuilla
San Juan Capistrano
CLEVELAND N.F.
Temecula
(371)
CAHU I.R.
Dana Point
San Onofre S.B.
Fallbrook
PECHANGA I.R.
(79)
Aguanga
San Clemente
Bonsall
Pala
PALA I.R.
Palomar Mtn. S.P.
(79)
Wa Spr
Channel
CAMP PENDLETON MARINE CORPS BASE
(5)
(15)
Pauma Valley
(76)
Avalon ○
(76)
RINCON I.R.
Santa Catalina Island
Vista
Valley Center
S.
Sa
Gulf of Santa Catalina
OCEANSIDE
(18)
(78)
ESCONDIDO
LEGOLAND California
San Diego Wild Animal Park
El Dios
(78)
Outer Santa Barbara Passage
Encinitas
Marcos
Poway
Ramona
Solana Beach
BARONA I.R.
Del Mar
(67)
CAPITAN GRANDE I.
U.S. NAVAL RES.
Santee
Lakeside
D
La Mesa
El Cajon
Alpi
Sea World Adventure Park San Diego
Spring Valley
SAN DIEGO
Lemon Grove
Jamul
CLEV
Dulzura
Coronado
(75)
(94)
0   10   20 Miles
Imperial Beach
CHULA VISTA
0   10   20 Kilometres
Border Field S.P.

Theme-park fun

Coping with queues

Summer is a hot, crowded time to visit a Southern California theme park, with long queues for rides, attractions, theme park restaurants, refreshment stands and souvenir shops. Pack for an outing in the country or an imaginary safari, with comfortable shoes, sun-hats, sun block and a large closed bag for your camera and souvenirs. Most parks discourage or forbid outside food or drink; non-alcoholic drinks are widely available in concession to the desert-like climate and cement construction.

Disney is building a second $1.4 billion park, Disney's California Adventure, next to the original Disneyland. A new hotel and Disneyland Center entertainment area, due for completion between 2001 and 2003, will augment new attractions. In the interim, construction squeezes traffic and may interfere with Monorail operations.

Just beyond Disneyland's Main Entrance, **Main Street, U.S.A.**✦ is an imitation 19th-century street lined by vaguely Victorian-style shop-fronts disguising trademark merchandise emporiums within. Balloon sellers, characters and streetcars wander around. Main Street is a good place to find ice-cream or snacks. The steam engine-powered **Disneyland Railroad**✦ circles 1½ miles around the park's distinct areas, or 'lands', accomplishing the park preview circuit in 20 minutes. Disney's first Mickey Mouse cartoon, the 1928 *Steamboat Willie*, plays at the **Main Street Cinema**✦.

Adventureland's✦ star is the **Indiana Jones Adventure**✦✦, a spin-off from the Steven Spielberg films. A rough group ride through a simulated archaeological temple dig protected by the malevolent whim of the forbidden Eye of Mara, translates into Disney's version of barely salvageable disaster when a boulder heads straight for your transport car. The **Jungle Cruise**✦ still sports mechanical hippos and elephants, an almost nostalgic visit to 1955 technology.

In **Critter Country**✦, Disney's Audio-Animatronic characters line the log ride route of **Splash Mountain** roller-coaster✦.

Fantasyland✦, anchored by the Disney signature **Sleeping Beauty's Castle**✦✦, is where fairy-tales live. **Peter Pan's Flight**✦, **Mad (Hatter's) Tea Party**✦ and **Pinocchio's Daring Journey**✦ are typical. Dancing dolls cavort for boats moving through the familiar theme music of **It's a Small World**✦. The **Matterhorn Bobsleds**✦✦ are a tame coaster through the imitation peak, but each afternoon, Goofy and Mickey Mouse climb the mountain where Minnie Mouse waits with picnic provisions.

Frontierland✦ evokes the 19th century of Mark Twain with the paddlewheel **Mark Twain Riverboat**✦✦, rafts to **Tom Sawyer Island**✦ where children can run off excess energy, the replica **Sailing Ship Columbia**✦, the Golden Horseshoe Stage country and Western music show, **Big Thunder Mountain Railroad** roller-coaster✦ and the evening outdoor song, dance and special effects **Fantasmic!** show✦✦ with Mickey Mouse acting as host to other Disney characters.

Mickey's Toontown✦ has attractions for the youngest. Weasels chase the macho hero bunny in **Roger Rabbit's Car Toon Ride**✦. New

🌙 Disneyland's own hotels are close to the park, reflected in higher lodging prices. It may be better value to pay more for accommodation to avoid traffic congestion close to park entrances.

🅿 Parks charge $5–$7 for parking, usually in covered car-parks. Note your vehicle's location in the car-park; it's easy to get disorientated after a long park visit. Most parks have kennel arrangements to keep pets cool and safe while their families enjoy the park.

Orleans Square*❖ is a 'land' with the ghostly, old-fashioned humorous horrors of the **Haunted Mansion**❖❖ and the politically corrected classic **Pirates of the Caribbean***❖ town invasion.

Tomorrowland❖❖ was rebuilt in 1998 to be more futuristic, including a Leonardo da Vinci astrolabe design transformed into a sculpture with moving spheres at the entrance, the **Astro Orbitor***❖. 'Honey, I Shrunk the Audience'❖❖ gives participants a chance to wear 3-D glasses. **Space Mountain**❖❖ and the **Star Tours**❖❖ ride from the *Star Wars* films Moon of Endor remain.

Evening parades and fireworks are worth waiting for, but find a vantage point early.

Accommodation and food for Disneyland

Disney presents a complete vacation package with hotel and special park passes (*tel: (714) 520-7070*). A variety of lodging offers choices, but the trade-off for not staying at one of the official two Disneyland Resort Hotels; the **Disneyland Hotel $$$** and the **Disneyland Pacific Hotel $$$** (*tel: (714) 956-6425*) may be a long wait in traffic to access the park area. Hotel chains abound, so compare the Disney package with other possibilities and ask for all available discounts upon arrival.

The 'no outside food or drink' policy virtually mandates dining on overpriced, generally dull park fare. All lands except Toontown have at least one vegetarian outlet. The official hotels offer children **Character Dining $$$**: **Breakfast with Minnie & Friends**, **Practically Perfect Tea** and **Goofy's Kitchen**.

KNOTT'S BERRY FARM❖❖

🍴 **Knott's Berry Farm $$** *8039 Beach Blvd, between La Palma, Western, Crescent and Stanton Aves, Buena Park; tel: (714) 220-5220; web: www.knotts.com*

America's first theme park started as a 1930s move by a berry farm family to survive the Great Depression. Chicken dinners with all the trimmings and pies are still served – more than a million annually, in a park well stocked with adrenalin-charged roller-coasters, Americana and some history education. Knott's current operators have not forgotten their roots – local residents enjoy admission discounts and everyone can find something tasty to eat in a cheerful, home-town atmosphere.

Knott's Berry Farm has six areas. **Ghost Town**❖❖ puts visitors in the Wild West, or at least a west with cowboys, gold panning, stagecoaches and *bandito* hold-ups of the **Ghost Town & Calico Railroad**❖❖. A 50-ft plunge down a waterfall climaxes **Timber Mountain Log Ride***❖. **GhostRider**❖❖, the longest and tallest wooden roller-coaster in southern California, drops 108ft over 4530ft of track.

Wild Water Wilderness❖❖ area's **Bigfoot Rapids**❖❖ is a damp

Making the most

The cost of park admission, food, drink and souvenirs may range from $40–$60 per person a day. It pays to research discounts on multiple-day or multiple-park passes, family discounts, senior/pensioner discounts or auto touring club rates in advance. If time or energy is limited, enquire if the park of your choice has guided VIP tours, a higher-priced admission which allows access to major attractions without queuing up. Behind-the-scenes views of attractions, entertainment studios, live filming and other pampering may be included.

whitewater river ride adjacent to a **Nature Center***** which delves into Bigfoot/Sasquatch lore. First Nations people from north of Vancouver Island, British Columbia, present a narrative of magic and origins based on authentic tradition at **Mystery Lodge******. Another area, **Indian Trails*****, marked with a 27-ft totem pole of incense cedar, has Native American dwellings and crafts, with face painting and arts and crafts for children.

Visit **Fiesta Village*** to ride the twisting Mayan/Aztec-theme **Jaguar** roller-coaster*** and **Montezooma's Revenge*****, accelerating to 55mph in less than 4 seconds. The South of the Border theme includes sombrero (hat) dances.

The Boardwalk* pays tribute to California's surfers with dolphins and sea lions performing at **Pacific Pavilion***, and to dino-mania with the genuine fossils displayed upon exiting the **Kingdom of the Dinosaurs*** ride into the **Discovery Center. Boomerang*** launches riders back and forth along a half-sphere path, and the **Windjammer*** coaster is actually a set of duelling tracks. The biggest adrenalin charge is **Supreme Scream*****, where strapped-in riders rise 300ft skyward, then plunge to earth in three seconds at 60mph.

The little ones have Peanuts cartoon characters in **Camp Snoopy***. Animals and tamer rides are reassuring, even the mini-Supreme Scream, **Woodstock's Airmail***, a 19-ft rise with an air-cushioned return to earth.

Accommodation and food for Knott's Berry Farm

Lodging abounds because of Disneyland's proximity and Anaheim's numerous conventions. The **Anaheim/Orange County Visitor and Convention Bureau** *800 W. Katella Ave, Anaheim; tel: (714) 999 8999 or (888) 598-3200; web: www.anaheim.co.org,* has an accommodation list.

Mrs. Knott's Chicken Dinner Restaurant**** \$** is a park institution, the place to try fried chicken, broiled chicken, barbecued beef ribs or chicken-fried steak. Add veggies, rhubarb, mashed potatoes, salad or soup, endless rolls and the obligatory boysenberry pie for one theme park meal that won't leave you hungry. A steakhouse, barbecue spot, Mexican restaurant and the **Hollywood Beanery \$** diner, serving pizzas and snacks, complete the sit-down dining.

LEGOLAND CALIFORNIA***

A new entry in the theme park competition is the Danish plastic brick LEGO company's third property (after Billund, Denmark and Windsor, UK), specifically for children aged 2 to 12. Thirty million LEGO bricks

LEGOLAND California $$$
near I-5 and Cannon Rd interchange, Carlsbad; tel: (877) 534-6526; web: www.lego.com/legoland/california.

decorate the Carlsbad site, a beach town famed for exclusive spas and colourful flower fields.

Among the main attractions are **Miniland❖❖**, with miniaturised versions of Washington, D.C., New Orleans, New York, New England and the California coast; **Imagination Zone❖**, a LEGO block hands-on and computer software play area; **Castle Hill❖**, a medieval-themed roller-coaster, with simulated jousting and gem-panning; a **Garden❖**; **Lake❖**; **Ridge labyrinth❖**; a **Village Green❖❖** boat ride by fairy-tale tableaux and LEGO African animals; and child-size cars, boats and helicopters in **Fun Town❖**.

San Diego Wild Animal Park❖❖❖

San Diego Wild Animal Park $$
15500 San Pasqual Valley Rd, Escondido; tel: (760) 747-8702; web: www.sandiegozoo.org/wap
Open-top, safari-style
Photo Caravan tours
tel: (760) 738-5022, get within a few feet of animals, a superb photographic experience for an additional charge.

When to come

Check on opening hours. Some parks, such as Six Flags Magic Mountain, close for most of the winter season; occasionally parks are hired for private groups. Weekdays are less crowded than weekends. Arrive when the park opens to avoid long queues and ask for a park map for each member of your party. Head instantly for the most popular attractions.

In the midst of rugged, rocky mountains 30 miles north of San Diego, lush savannah vegetation creates a scenario of blooming plants where African and Asian wildlife and birds live, relatively uncaged. Careful landscaping and the lack of obvious bars make this wildlife preserve a fascinating experience on foot.

The 55-minute **Wgasa Bush Line Monorail❖❖** is an excellent introduction before setting out for a gentle hike around the park. Shows include elephants, birds and **Rare and Wild America❖** species. Extensive botanical gardens with fuschia, epiphyllum, succulents, bonsai, native plants and conifers are connected by hiking paths centred around the **Kupanda Falls Botanical Pavilion❖❖** at the north end.

A large pond area shelters pink Chilean flamingos, African and other exotic birds. Gibbons, lowland gorillas, meerkats and red-ruffed lemurs have their own enclosures. The 1¾-mile **Kilimanjaro Safari Walk❖❖❖** features elephants, rhinos and other African species.

At the entrance to the stunningly accurate **Heart of Africa savannah❖**, pick up the area brochure, a field researcher's 1967 renderings of animals he encountered, a challenging guide to identification of species appearing along the route down to the main area. This is not a walk for the squeamish – very fresh animal kills are consumed in front of gawking park visitors. The twisting path ends near the **Okavango Outpost❖❖**, where cheetahs loll as giraffes and other exotic species wander near by.

Grazing giraffe at the San Diego Wild Animal Park

SeaWorld Adventure Park San Diego✦✦

SeaWorld Adventure Park San Diego $$$ *Mission Bay, San Diego; tel: (619) 226-3901; web: www.seaworld.com* SeaWorld organise a hands-on, in the water, **Dolphin Interaction Program** for an additional fee; *tel: (800) 380-3202.*

Denizens of the oceans are in residence here, anchored by the orca (killer whale) **Shamu Adventure✦✦** show, with special effects to enhance performances by Shamu, Baby Shamu and Namu. On **Wild Arctic✦✦✦**, a simulated helicopter takes off in San Diego and lands in a North Pole scenario with polar bears, beluga whales and walruses going about their business. Florida's gentle herbivores are being rehabilitated in **Manatee Rescue✦✦**, a 215,000-gallon freshwater tank with viewing of the sea cows from above and below. A plastic viewing tube protects visitors from the inhabitants of **Shark Encounter✦✦**. Bottlenose dolphins, pilot whales, sea lions, river otters and large birds perform routines, and aquariums introduce less tractable species.

Six Flags Magic Mountain✦/Hurricane Harbour✦

Six Flags Magic Mountain $$$, Six Flags Hurricane Harbor $ *both via I-5, Magic Mountain Parkway, Valencia; tel: (818) 367-5965; web: www.sixflags.com.* Ask for combo tickets if visiting both parks.

These adjacent parks offer roller-coasters and a water park in the Santa Clarita Valley, a half hour's drive north of downtown Los Angeles, but are open daily only in summer.

Magic Mountain's✦✦ themes include Warner Bros Superheroes and Looney Tunes cartoon characters. Stand up for three minutes on the **Riddler's Revenge✦✦✦**, six loop-de-loops with a maximum G-force of 4.2. Want weightlessness and similar Gs? try **Superman: The Escape's✦✦** 7-second acceleration to 100mph. Bottomless gondola cars whisk riders around the outside of **Batman: The Ride's✦** circular roller-coaster track. The **Colossus✦** is a double-track coaster, the **Log Jammer✦** drops straight down – twice, but the **Viper✦✦✦** loops three times vertically, flips riders over seven times, corkscrews, and provides drops to equal any roller coaster in the world. For a breather in summer, try the **Hurricane Harbor's✦** raft rides, water slides, tubing and pools.

Universal Studios Hollywood and Citywalk✦✦

Universal Studios Hollywood $$$ *100 Universal City Plaza, Universal City; tel: (818) 622-3801; web: www.universalstudios.com* Universal Studios Hollywood and Seaworld San Diego offer a combo park discount admission.

One of the world's oldest film studios is surrounded by a cinema-themed amusement park, and unique in the Western US, offers a **Backlot Tram Tour✦✦✦** past actual set locations and sound stages. A bridge drop-out, an appearance by King Kong and a simulated earthquake spice it up. The atmosphere is a touch more adult at USH, typified by the perfect singing and showmanship of the **Blues Brothers Show✦✦✦** concert from which the stars depart in a siren-wailing cop car.

Dinosaurs run amok in **Jurassic Park – The Ride✦✦**; prepare to get soaked when a humongous *Tyrannosaurus rex* dunks the ride's car. **Back to the Future – the Ride✦✦**, is a clever motion simulator combining the effects of ice cliffs and lava flows with another T-rex. **E.T. Adventure✦✦** puts you on a bicycle to save the beloved Extra

Terrestrial's home planet. **Backdraft**✧ re-creates the heat and fright of a raging fire. **Terminator 2 3-D**✧✧✧ premieres in 1999, a stunning integration of stunt actors, film and special effects to save the human race from cyborg imperialism.

Outside the park entrance gate is the free (with parking) **Universal CityWalk**✧✧, a pedestrian walking, shopping, dining and entertainment complex and a multiplex cinema area. **Marvel Mania Hollywood $$** adjoins both the park and CityWalk, providing comic-book superhero décor and morph effects as a dining backdrop. The **Hard Rock Café Hollywood $$** green and white guitar looms near the domed white restaurant building close to the car-park entrance. **B.B. King's Blues Club $$** serves Southern cooking and blues music, while magicians and bartenders mix it up at **Wizardz Magic Club and Dinner Theatre $$**, a cheerful place to dine while enjoying feats of magic and comedy routines. The car-park fee may be refundable with purchase of a cinema ticket.

Right
Pacific ray touch tank

Route to the Stars

Ratings

Star spotting	●●●●●
Scenery	●●●●
Beaches	●●●○○
Children	●●●○○
History	●●●○○
Museums	●●●○○
Architecture	●●●○○
Shopping	●●○○○

Star-struck! Hollywood conjures up images of sleek blonde starlets in form-fitting satin gowns wearing enormous sunglasses, impossibly handsome actors in evening wear, tyrannical directors, champagne, red convertibles and black limousines, Oscars, bigger-than-life heroes and an industry that conveys eternal life upon the chosen. Hollywood, the place, can be shockingly unkempt.

The film (and television) industry has never been physically limited to Hollywood, it has worked, lived and played all over Southern California. The chances of seeing a 'movie' star are best at a location shoot in the Greater Los Angeles area, and probably worst during the popular guided tours of the Homes of the Stars. Like everyone else, stars like to eat, drink and dance at trendy restaurants and clubs, shop for bargains, stroll in supermarkets and walk in parks. Most tolerate autograph seekers only when they are 'on', made up and dressed to meet their fans and satisfy the needs of a publicity circus to promote their careers. Don't overlook luck and chance – a star may run through the airport to catch a flight or go flower-shopping at a local farmer's market – providing you with your personal sighting and a unique story to take home.

BEVERLY HILLS✧✧

Beverly Hills has mansions, shopping and an aura of luxury few communities can match (*see Los Angeles, page 45*). The **Museum of Television and Radio**✧ (*495 N. Beverly Dr.; tel: (310) 786-1000*), covers the broadcast industry, but star buffs will enjoy the **Polo Lounge** at the **Beverly Hills Hotel**✧ (*9641 Sunset Blvd; tel: (310) 276-2251*) for the feeling of *luxe* and the power of moneymen doing deals for films. The **Regent Beverly Wilshire Hotel**✧ (*9500 Wilshire Blvd; tel: (310) 275-5200*) was the setting for Richard Gere's wooing of Julia Roberts in *Pretty Woman*.

Rodeo Drive Shops have back doors for stars' privacy, but hotel spas and hair salons cater to everyone, guests, patrons and celebrities alike. Shoppers can enjoy vintage clothing used by stars for the Academy Awards ceremony from **Lily's** (*9044 Burton Way; tel: (310) 724-5757*).

Westwood Village Memorial Park and Mortuary✧✧ (*1218 Glendon*

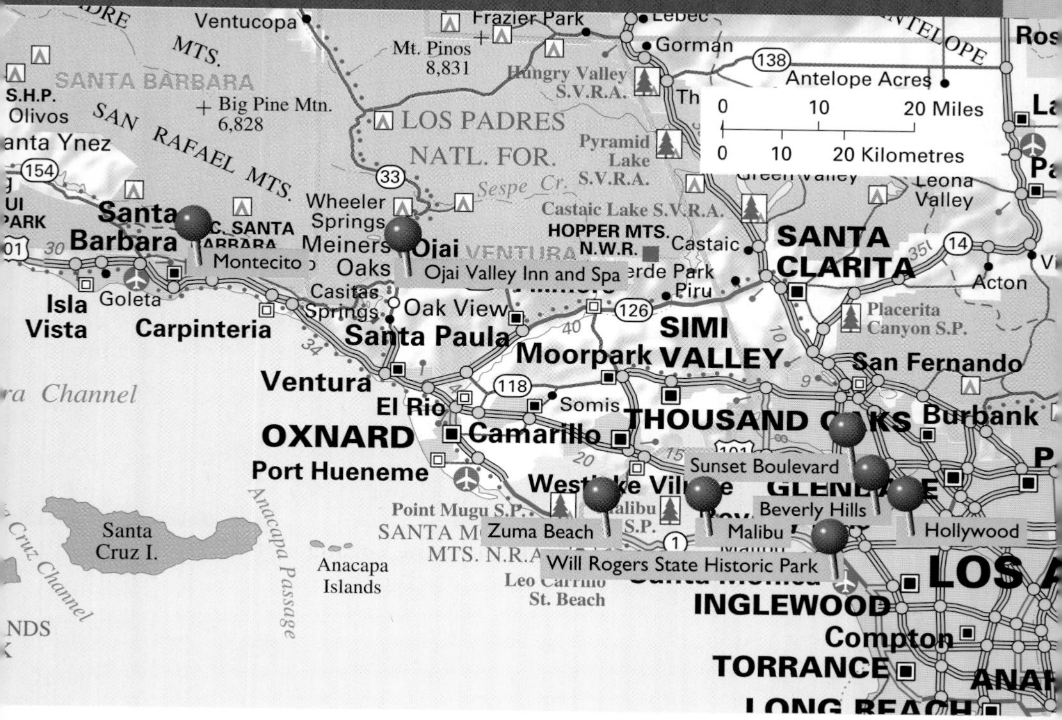

*Ave at Wilshire Blvd, behind a car-park, Westwood; (tel: (310) 474-1579)
is a peaceful cemetery where Marilyn Monroe is interred in the
Corridors of Memories, always graced by lovely roses.*

FOREST LAWN❖❖

**Forest Lawn
Memorial Park
Hollywood Hills** 6300
*Forest Lawn Dr.; tel: (800)
204-3131. Open 0900–1700.*

Forest Lawn Memorial Park Hollywood Hills is another spot to see
the stars, or rather their memorial tablets and a few opulent crypts.
Bette Davis's (*Courts of Remembrance*) white marble maiden belies the
crusty epitaph, 'She Did It The Hard Way.'

HOLLYWOOD❖❖

Tinseltown's glitter still shines a little, but most of Hollywood's
magnetism as a place where stars hung out on corners like Hollywood
(Blvd) and Vine (St) is gone. Politicos, businesspeople and developers
have begun pouring money into Hollywood as a spot where history
and image can be exploited for tourist dollars spent on more than thin
T-shirts, Maps of the Stars' Homes and a bus-bound whirl outside the
gates of purported stars' mansions. Several historic art deco theatres

Dolores del Rio, one of the many Hollywood stars that never die

ⓘ Los Angeles Convention & Visitors Bureau: Hollywood Visitor Information Center *The Janes House, 6541 Hollywood Blvd; tel: (800) 228-2452 or (323) 461-4213; web:www.lacvb. com/mod20/mod20fst. Open Mon–Sat 0900–1700.*

ⓘ Frederick's of Hollywood Lingerie Museum *6608 Hollywood Blvd; tel: (323) 466-8506; web: www.fredericks.com/museum Open Mon-Sat 1000–1800, Sun 1200–1700.*

have been restored and reopened as film palaces; Hollywood history-related museums supplement the oddity carnivals presented by Guinness, Ripley's and the inevitable wax museum.

The **Capitol Records Building**✧ (*1750 Vine St);* is a 1954 landmark, 11 storeys piled like long-playing records on a turntable. It has gold records on display in the lobby, but offers no tours.

The **Egyptian Theatre**✧✧ (*6712 Hollywood Blvd; tel: (323) 777-3456)* was Hollywood's original 1922 art deco movie palace, taking fanciful advantage of interest in the Near East in the year Howard Carter discovered King Tutankhamen's tomb. American Cinematheque's two film theatres show avant-garde, career tribute, foreign and independent films. The old interior is only partially restored. Filmgoers can admire the elaborate Egyptian décor until portable acoustic walls move into place as films begin. A *History of Hollywood* documentary film may be seen during the day.

El Capitan Theater✧ (*6838 Hollywood Blvd; tel: (323) 467-7674),* restored to its original 1926 art deco splendour, is where Orson Welles's 1941 *Citizen Kane* premiered.

Frederick's of Hollywood Lingerie Museum✧✧ is a free, cheerful voyage into the world of unmentionables worn by film stars, from Elizabeth Taylor and Mae West to Madonna's *bustier* and Cher's strapless bra.

Hollywood Boulevard Walk of Fame✧✧ (*Hollywood Blvd, from La Brea Ave–Vine St; Vine St from Yucca St–Sunset Blvd),* a 1960s marketing gimmick to stud the pavements with stars, has turned into an enduring icon. More than 2000 pink terrazzo stars honour stars of film, stage, television, radio, music and a few odd choices such as the Apollo XI astronauts.

Caution: tourists searching for stars can wander off kerbs!

ⓘ Hollywood Chamber of Commerce tel: (323) 469-8311; fax: (323) 469-2805; web: http://chamber.hollywood.com

Hollywood Entertainment District tel: (323) 463-6767; web: www.hollywoodbid.org, has a free historic district Visitors Guide and Map with a 16-stop walking tour.

ⓜ Hollywood Bowl Museum 2301 N. Highland Ave; tel: (323) 850-2058; fax: (323) 851-5617. Open Tue–Sat 1000–1630.

Hollywood Entertainment Museum $$ 7021 Hollywood Blvd, Hollywood Galaxy complex lower level; tel: (323) 465-7900; fax (323) 469-9576. Open Tue–Sun 1000–1800, daily July–Aug.

Hollywood History Museum $$ 1660 N. Highland Ave; tel: (323) 464-7776; fax: (323) 464-3777. Open Thur–Sat 1000–2400, Sun–Wed 1000–1900.

Hollywood Wax Museum $$ 6767 Hollywood Blvd; tel: (323) 462-8860. Open daily 1000–2400, Fri–Sat to 0100. Combo ticket with Guinness.

Ripley's Believe It or Not! Hollywood $$ 6780 Hollywood Blvd; tel: (323) 466-6335. Open 1000–2200.

Popular stars include:

Charlie Chaplin,	6751 Hollywood Blvd;
John Lennon,	1750 Vine St;
Marilyn Monroe,	6644 Hollywood Blvd;
Mickey Mouse,	6925 Hollywood Blvd; and
Elvis Presley,	6777 Hollywood Blvd.

Hollywood Bowl Museum＊ showcases the music and performing arts in the **Hollywood Bowl**＊, Tinseltown's quarter-sphere outdoor concert hall, with recordings of Hollywood Bowl performances.

Hollywood Entertainment Museum＊＊ is a good place to see the technology that goes into sound effects, special effects make-up, Hollywood costume design effect on fashion, behind-the-scenes sets, the bar from television's *Cheers* and *Star Trek* props.

Hollywood History Museum＊＊ uses the old art deco Max Factor building to display costumes, props, posters and film-making equipment illustrating Hollywood eras from silent film to technological wizardry. **Chasen's Hollywood Café**, capitalising on a now-closed West Hollywood landmark eatery, offers dining.

Hollywood Memorial Park Cemetery＊ (*6000 Santa Monica Blvd; tel: (323) 469-1181*), adjacent to Paramount Studios, is the resting place for director Cecil B De Mille, heart-throb Rudolph Valentino, and others who never went far away after making it big.

The first venue for the Academy Awards in 1929, **Hollywood Roosevelt Hotel**＊ (*7000 Hollywood Blvd; tel: (323) 466-7000*) is so rich with Hollywoodiana, it's haunted, allegedly, by Montgomery Clift playing a bugle in Room 928 where he practised when filming *From Here to Eternity*. The mezzanine has a fine collection of historic Hollywood photographs.

The **Hollywood Sign**＊ (*Mount Lee, Griffith Park*), seen from many Hollywood streets, is closed to visits from the public. Real estate developers created a 'Hollywoodland' sign in 1923 with 4000 light bulbs to promote a new housing estate; the decrepit sign was restored to its current 50-foot height in 1978, having lost the 'land' early on.

Hollywood Studio Museum (*2100 N. Highland Ave; tel: (323) 874-2276*), an historic studio building devoted to the silent film era, is under restoration.

Hollywood Wax Museum＊ shows how stars like Stallone, crooners like Elvis and legends like Marilyn would look like if eternally preserved in paraffin.

Hollywood and Highland Entertainment Complex, under construction (*Hollywood Blvd next to Mann's Chinese Theatre*), will host the Academy Awards ceremony in March 2001 at the **Theater for the Academy of Motion Pictures Arts and Sciences.**

Mann's Chinese Theater＊＊＊ (*6925 Hollywood Blvd; tel: (323) 464-8111*), Hollywood's best-known building, premiered Cecil B De Mille's *King of Kings* when it opened in 1927. The fanciful red and green pagoda tower presides over a courtyard of hands, feet and other body parts (Betty Grable's leg, Donald Duck's webbed feet) imprinted in cement. Original owner Sid Grauman is the target of many inscriptions, some suggestive, a few lewd, most laudatory. The cinema shows first-run films.

Pantages Theatre⁺ *(6233 Hollywood Blvd near Vine St; tel: (323) 468-1700)*, an ornate 1930 art deco film palace, now presents Broadway musicals.

A dinosaur and clock mark **Ripley's Believe It or Not! Hollywood**⁺ collection of curiosities, including a portrait of John Wayne rendered in laundry lint.

Suggested tours

Getting close to the stars and the action is the name of the game. Check the detailed Entertainment Industry Development Council Film Office daily *Shoot Sheet* for Television, Film, Commercial Advertisement, and Video filming. Walk-in at *7083 Hollywood Blvd, Ste 500; tel: (323) 957-1000, open Mon–Fri 0830–1800*, $10 for that day's schedule, or, for free, search on-line for several weeks' schedule; *web:www.eidc.com/community shoot*.

Major television productions crave live audiences. **Audiences Unlimited**, *(tel: (818) 506-0067* or *(818) 753-3470)*, acts as a clearing-house for free admission to studio tapings.

The alternative, with no guarantee of a star sighting, is a film studio tour. **Paramount Studios $$** *5555 Melrose Ave, Hollywood; (tel: (323) 956-1777* or *(323) 956-5575)*, offer 2-hour walking tours for those over 9 years of age *(Mon–Fri 0900–1400)*. **Universal Studios Hollywood Backlot Tour $$$** *(Universal City; tel: (818) 508-9600)*, is included in theme park admission. Near by, the two-hour **Warner Bros Studio VIP Tour $$$** *(4000 Warner Blvd, Burbank; tel: (818) 972-8687* or *(818) 954-1744)*, is by cart *(Mon–Fri 0900–1500 Oct–May, to 1600 June–Sept)*.

The best guided tour, **Grave Line Tours $$$** *(tel: (213) 469-4149)*, avoids a bus in favour of a hearse.

MALIBU✷✷

Eighteen miles of surfing and sunning beaches, stars' homes and pricey restaurants along Hwy 1, the Pacific Coast Hwy, are flooded out every few years. Despite the geological instability of homes built on stilts, Malibu (Movie) Colony stars have flocked here since 1926, when PCH's opening led a developer to create an exclusive strand as a hideaway for famous motion picture types. Those $2600 beach cottages are now multi-million dollar cottages.

Adamson House✷✷ (*23200 PCH, Malibu Lagoon State Beach; tel: (310) 457-8142*) incorporates locally made, late 1920s decorative tiles.

The **Malibu Lagoon Museum** covers Native American, Malibu Colony and tile history with guided house tours *Wed–Sat 1100–1400*. Just south near the pier is the obvious draw of **Malibu Surfrider Beach.**

Leo Carrillo State Beach✷ (*Mulholland Hwy at Hwy 1; tel: (818) 880-0350*), named after a comic sidekick actor who was the great-grandson of California's last Mexican governor, is favoured by surfers and windsurfers.

Point Dume State Reserve✷✷✷ (*access via Westward Beach Rd*), with **Paradise Cove** near by, is rugged golden and black rock cliffs close to nearly invisible stars' homes. A trail climbs 250ft above the beaches for a 30-mile view of Santa Monica Bay to Palos Verdes. Just west is the long strand of **Zuma Beach. Broad Beach**, 5 miles north, is celebrity row, well-guarded, but accessible on a public footpath at 31346 Broad Beach.

MONTECITO✷

Montecito is where stars, directors and technicians get away from the industry, or retire to semitropical foliage, nurseries, oak groves, flowering vines and horse trails. Watch for stars as spectators at first-run screenings at **Paseo Nuevo** or the 1931 **Arlington Theatre✷✷** (*1317 State St; tel: (805) 963-4408*), a film palace decorated as a Mexican village with a ceiling filled with painted stars.

OJAI✷✷

ℹ️ **Ojai Valley Chamber of Commerce** *150 W. Ojai Ave; tel: (805) 646-8126; fax: (805) 646-9762; web: www.the-ojai.org. Open Mon-Fri 0930-1630, Sat-Sun 1000-1600.*

Director Frank Capra saw sunset pink on the Los Padres Mountains around Ojai, and captured it as Shangri-la in the 1937 film, *Lost Horizon*. Stars, writers, artists and metaphysical devotees have liked this mountain town, 15 miles and a world away from the Pacific Ocean, as a getaway or part-time home since the 1920s. **Spa Ojai** at the **Ojai Valley Inn and Spa** (*Country Club Rd; tel: (805) 646-5511 or (800) 422-6542*), a recent addition to a smart golf resort famed since that era, mimics the white Spanish architecture so copied by the stars of silent and early talking motion pictures.

Sunset Boulevard**

Also known as **Sunset Strip**, this line of clubs and hot spots stretches from 7800–9200 Sunset Blvd in West Hollywood. Actor Johnny Depp co-owns the dark, atmospheric **Viper Room** (*8852 Sunset Blvd; tel: (310) 358-1880*), and **The Roxy** (*9009 Sunset Blvd; tel: (310) 276-2222*) is another over-the-top music joint. Check the scene for the latest in chic slumming or clubbing. **Melrose Ave** (*see Los Angeles, page 49*) is half a mile south. In between is the gay/lesbian mecca along Santa Monica Blvd. Posh **Chateau Marmont** (*8221 Sunset Blvd; tel: (323) 656-1010*) has hosted legions of stars, from Monroe and Garbo to Mick Jagger.

Will Rogers State Historic Park**

Will Rogers State Historic Park (*1501 Will Rogers State Park Rd, Pacific Palisades; tel: (310) 454-8212*) shows the good taste, 1924–35 home, stables and polo field of the beloved humorist, broadcaster and actor Will Rogers. The heavily used park has easy-to-rugged hiking trails, many with fine views to downtown Los Angeles and Santa Monica Bay. Will Rogers is also remembered at **Will Rogers State Beach** (*Pacific Palisades/Santa Monica boundary*) and as Beverly Hills' first mayor at **Will Rogers Memorial Park** (*across Sunset Blvd from the Beverly Hills Hotel*).

Suggested tour

Total distance: 125 miles

Time: 4 hours non-stop, but a stop in Ojai is less frantic.

Links: Los Angeles (*see page 42*). At Pacific Palisades, turn south on Hwy 1 to Santa Monica (*see Southern California Beaches, page 70*). Go north at Santa Barbara for **Big Sur/Central Coast** (*see page 214*).

Route: Take Hollywood Blvd west at Vine St to La Brea Ave, turn left two blocks, then right on Sunset Blvd to Pacific Palisades. Go right on Hwy 1, Pacific Coast Hwy, past Malibu beaches and celebrity houses and inland to Oxnard. Go west on Hwy 101 at Montalvo/Ventura. Take the Hwy 33 exit to Ojai. Return 3 miles west on Hwy 33, then take Hwy 150 past Lake Casitas. Continue northwest on Hwy 192, the scenic back road via Montecito to Santa Barbara.

Also worth exploring

Mulholland Drive/Mulholland Hwy** (with one detour at Encino to Hwy 101 going west; exit Hwy 101 at Topanga Canyon Blvd to rejoin the **Mulholland Scenic Drive**), winds west for 55 miles over the spine of the Santa Monica Mountains from Hwy 101 at Cahuenga Pass (Mulholland Dr. exit) to **Leo Carrillo State Beach** in Malibu (*see page 67*). Clear blue skies, rugged rocky mountains, creeks, ranches, canyons and unique mansions reflect the area chosen by many stars for their homes. State and regional parks, along with exclusive housing estates and an occasional golf course make for an incongruous mix of scenery and recreation enjoyed on foot, horse or bicycle.

Several major routes from the coast bisect the long, west–east stretch of Los Angeles' approximation of a national park, the **Santa Monica Mountains National Recreation Area** (*tel: (818) 597-9192*; **Visitors Center**, *401 W. Hillcrest Dr., Thousand Oaks, CA 91360; tel: (805) 370-2301; web: www.nps.gov/samo; open daily 0900–1700*). **Topanga Canyon Blvd, Malibu Canyon Rd/Las Virgenes Rd** and **Kanan-Dume Rd** all offer vistas at they approach their summits before plunging northward into the San Fernando and Conejo Valleys to Hwy 101.

Paramount Ranch**, set up in 1927 as a Western film set, is still used for productions, including *Dr Quinn, Medicine Woman*. False building façades are boarded up between productions, with each of several blocks having a complete saloon, marshall's office, general store and livery stables, for flexibility.

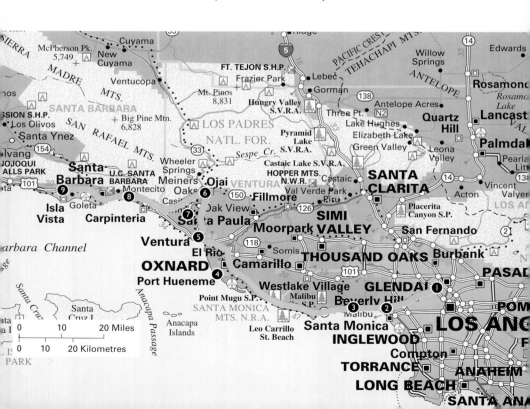

Southern California Beaches

In Hollywood mythology, life is a beach, and nowhere on earth has as much beach as Southern California. From the heart-throb days of the Annette Funichello and Frankie Avalon *Gidget* beach films to the feel-good bounce of the Beach Boys, Southern California has been associated with broad sandy crescents, curling waves and a carefree life where problems are as ephemeral as tomorrow's sand castle.

But into each beach a little reality must fall. Southern California is *not* all beaches. Cliffs intrude, providing spectacular viewpoints to watch the coast, migrating whales and surfers. Piers and harbours break up the coastline, sheltering massive ocean freighters as well as solitary sailboats. Offshore oil wells and natural oil seeps dribble bits of petroleum that wash up as tar, sticking to feet and bodies.

None of which matters. For residents as well as visitors, life in Southern California really *is* a beach. It doesn't matter that beaches can be crowded, the water cold, the parking impossible or the sunburn painful. The sand is waiting, the surf is up and true love could be just over the next crest.

CARLSBAD❖❖

ⓘ Carlsbad Convention & Visitors Bureau
400 Carlsbad Village Dr., Carlsbad, CA 92008; tel: (760) 434-6093 or (800) 227-5722; fax: (760) 434-6056; web: www.carlsbadca.org Open Mon–Fri 0900–1700, Sat 1000–1600, Sun 1000–1500.

⬤ Barnstorming Adventures $$$
6473 Montia Ct, Carlsbad, CA 92009; tel: (760) 438-7680 or (800) 759-5667; fax: (760) 931-2664.

Carlsbad is known mostly for the commercial flower fields at **Carlsbad Ranch**❖❖❖ *(east of 1-5, Palomar Airport Rd and Paseo del Norte; tel: (760) 431-0352. Open daily 0900–dusk late Feb – late May)* that burst into colour between February and May, and Southern California's newest theme park, **LEGOLAND California** (*see page 58*). The CVB publish self-guided maps to historical landmark buildings and extensive collections of public art.

The best overview of the area is from above, especially when the flower fields are in bloom. **Barnstorming Adventures**❖❖❖ offer low-level flightseeing from open cockpit biplanes.

Surfers congregate off **South Carlsbad State Beach**❖❖ (*tel: (760) 438-3143*). Further south is **Batiquitos Lagoon**❖❖❖ (*Batiquitos Dr., tel: (760) 943-7583*), an extensive wetlands restoration project. A ¼-mile interpretive trail departs from the visitor centre.

Canyon S.P.

Silverwood Lake S.R.A.

Wrightwood

San Fernando

2

138

Lake Arrowhead

EY

10

9

AND OAKS

Burbank

Rialto

SAN B

ANGELES NATL. FOR.

Redla

01

PASADENA

GLENDALE

ONTARIO

everly Hills

Santa Monica

POMONA

Malibu

RIVERSIDE

Monica

Venice Beach

OS ANGELES

10

GLEWO

Marina del Rey

FULLERTON

15

60

Compton

RIVERSIDE

ORRANCE

91

Corona

MORE VALLE

LONG BE

ANAHEIM

ORANGE

215

Long Beach

Perris

30

HUNTINGTON

SANTA ANA

IRVINE

ORANGE

Sun City

15

Lake Elsinore

Huntington Beach

Mission

Lake Elsinore S.R.A.

79

Wi

Newpor

Newport Beach

Viejo

74

Murrieta

Lagun

Laguna Beach

1

Pedro

San Juan Capistrano

CLEVELAND N.F.

Tem

Dana Point

San Onofre S.B.

27

Fallbrook

Pala

PAL I.R. R

San Clemente

Bonsall

15

San Pedro

Avalon

Santa Catalina Island

CAMP PENDLETON MARINE CORPS BASE

5

76

Vista

E

Santa Catalina Island

Channel

Oceanside

18

78

Santa Catalina Island

OCEANS

Carlsbad

Carlsbad

San Marcos

Del

P

Outer Santa Barbara Passage

Enci

Encinitas

Solana Beach

Del Mar

Gulf of Santa Catalina

La Jolla

Sant

U.S. NAVAL RES.

San Clemente Island

SAN DIEGO

La Mes

S

Coronado

75

Imperial Beach

Border Field S.P.

TIJUANA

0   10   20 Miles

0   10   20 Kilometres

Food in Carlsbad

Tip Top Meats $ *6118 Paseo Del Norte; tel: (760) 438-2620, open daily 0600–2000,* is a popular local breakfast and lunch stop with good picnic supplies.

ENCINITAS✢

Encinitas Visitor Center *138 Encinitas Blvd, Encinitas, CA 92024; tel: (760) 753-6041 or (800) 953-6041; fax: (760) 753-6270; web: www.encinitasca.org Open Mon–Fri 0900–1700, Sat–Sun 1000–1400.*

The town of Encinitas is a flower-growing centre, filled with commercial nurseries and spectacular private gardens. The best commercial display is **The Paul Ecke Poinsettia Ranch✢✢✢** (*441 Saxony Rd; tel: (760) 753-1134*), the largest poinsettia producer in the world. **Quail Botanical Gardens✢✢✢** (*230 Quail Gardens Dr; open daily*) are 30 beautifully landscaped acres planted with exotics from around the world.

Encinitas' serenity convinced the **Self-Realisation Fellowship** (*K St and First Ave*) to set up headquarters, with quiet cliffside **Meditation Gardens✢✢** (*216 K St*) just around the corner. The popular surfing beach below is called 'Swami's'.

HUNTINGTON BEACH✢✢

Huntington Beach Conference and Visitors Bureau *417 Main St, Huntington Beach, CA 92648; tel: (714) 969-3492 or (800) 729-6232; fax: (714) 969-5592; web: www.hbvisit.com Open Mon–Fri 0900–1700.*

Nicknamed 'Surf City' by 1950s surfers, Huntington Beach is also one of the largest cities in Orange County. The beach stretches 8½ miles, backed by a paved cycling, skating and walking path. Hwy 1, usually called **PCH, Pacific Coast Highway**, is lined with parking meters.

A favourite local surfing spot is just south of the concrete pier. The **Huntington Beach International Surfing Museum✢✢✢** (*411 Olive Ave; open daily*), is filled with photos and old-time surfing gear. Main St is lined with outdoor cafés and coffee houses.

Bolsa Chica Ecological Reserve, north of Huntingdon Beach, is a restored salt marsh and home to endangered bird species.

LA JOLLA✢✢✢

La Jolla Town Council *7734 Herschel Ave, La Jolla, CA 92037; tel: (619) 454-1444; fax: (619) 454-1848. Open Mon–Fri 0930–1600.*

La Jolla Cave and Shell Shop $ *1325 Coast Blvd; tel: (619) 454-6080). Open daily.*

This up-market San Diego neighbourhood is a mosaic of protected coves and cliffs battered by the surf. Most of the coastline is protected in public parks and beaches, as popular with seals as it is with human visitors. Art galleries cluster along **Prospect St**; new exhibitions usually open on Fri evenings.

La Jolla Cove✢✢, just off Prospect St, is popular with snorkelers; **Scripps Park✢✢**, beside the cove, attracts sun-worshippers and flocks of artists trying to capture views north and south along the cliffs. Just north are seven wave-carved caves; **Sunny Jim Cave✢** is accessible through **La Jolla Cave and Shell Shop**.

The **Salk Institute for Biological Studies✢**, a spectacular pair of

Salk Institute
10010 N. Torrey Pines Rd; tel: (619) 453-4100 ext. 1200; web: www.salk.edu. Open Mon–Fri 0830–1700. Guided architectural tours 1100 and 1200 by reservation.

San Diego Museum of Contemporary Art $
700 Prospect St; tel: (619) 454-3541; fax: (619) 454-6985; web: www.mcasd.org Open Tue–Sat 1000–1700, Wed to 2000, Sun 1200–1700.

La Jolla beach, sculpted by the waves

buildings overlooking the Pacific Ocean, specialises in research in biomedicine.

San Diego Museum of Contemporary Art* was built as the palatial Scripps family home in 1916. The museum specialises in emerging California artists, with an outdoor sculpture garden overlooking the sea.

Stephen Birch Aquarium-Museum* (*Scripps Institution of Oceanography; tel: (619) 534-3474; open daily*) features ocean life from the entire Pacific Ocean. **Torrey Pines State Reserve*** (*N. Torrey Pines Rd, tel: (619) 755-2063; open daily*) protects the only surviving mainland forest of Torrey pines (*Pinus torreyana*) on an isolated bluff fringed by multicoloured sandstone cliffs. The **University of California, San Diego*** (*9500 Gilman Dr.; tel: (619) 534-2117*) has the **Stuart Collection of Sculpture** scattered about the campus. Don't miss *Vices and Virtues*, flashing neon around the top of the Charles Lee Powell Structural Systems Laboratory; *Sun God*, a colourful bird near the car-park opposite Peterson Hall; and *Snake Path*, a 560-ft-long path tiled to resemble a snake, best seen from the **Central Library** upper floors.

LAGUNA BEACH***

Laguna Beach Visitor Information Center *252 Broadway, Laguna Beach, CA 92652; tel: (949) 497-9229 or (800) 877-1115; fax: (949) 376-0558; web: www.lagunabeachinfo.org*

Festival of the Arts $$ *Box 1659, Laguna Beach, CA 92652; tel: (949) 494-1145 or (800) 487-3378.*

Laguna Beach spawned one of California's first artistic organisations, the Laguna Beach Art Association. Most of the artists are long gone, but their heritage remains with some 90 galleries and studios and three annual art festivals. The June–July **Festival of the Arts**** draws 200,000 visitors, most to see the 'Pageant of the Masters', live tableaux reproducing famous classical paintings.

The coastline is scalloped with beaches separated by rugged cliffs. **Crescent Bay Point Park**** (*off Crescent Dr.*) offers striking views across the bay and cliffs to the town centre. **Heisler Park** (*north of the Art Museum*) is the beginning of a pleasant path to **Main Beach*** (*foot of Broadway*), the town's largest and most popular beach. The **Laguna Beach Art Museum*** (*307 Cliff Dr.; tel: (949) 494-8971*) specialises in American art, particularly modern art in California.

LONG BEACH✤

ℹ Long Beach Area Convention & Visitors Bureau
One World Trade Center, Ste 300, Long Beach, CA 98031; tel: (562) 436-3645 or (800) 452-7829; fax: (562) 462-5653; web: www.golongbeach.org. Open Mon–Fri 0830–1700.

🏛 Aquarium of the Pacific $$$
100 Aquarium Way; tel: (562) 590-3100 or (888) 826-7257; fax: (562) 590-3109. Open daily 1000–1800.

Once a tawdry military town, Long Beach, America's largest container port (with adjoining San Pedro, part of Los Angeles) has 6 miles of uncluttered sandy beach stretching south from Rainbow Harbor. The easiest way to explore the waterfront attractions is by **AquaBus**✤✤ water taxi.

The incredibly clear tanks of the **Aquarium of the Pacific**✤✤✤ re-create local temperate waters, the subarctic Bering Sea and coral lagoons from Micronesia. Don't miss the outdoor touch tanks.

Belmont Shores✤ (*along Second St, south of downtown*) is a restored 1920s district filled with trendy boutiques, galleries, bookstores and restaurants. **Pine Street**✤, Long Beach's restored city centre, is lined with early architecture, restaurants and boutiques and is great for people-watching.

The former luxury liner the *Queen Mary*✤✤ (*open daily*) is moored across Queensway Bay from the Aquarium of the Pacific. It has been fitted out as a hotel, with many of the elegant first-class areas refurbished for tours. A Russian **Scorpion submarine**✤✤ is also open for tours.

Shoreline Village (*fronting on Rainbow Harbor; tel: (562) 435-2668*) has waterfront shopping and entertainment.

MARINA DEL REY✤✤

ℹ Marina Del Rey Visitor Information Center *4701 Admiralty Way; tel: (310) 305-9547; fax: (310) 822-0119; web: www.co.la.ca.us/beaches. Open daily 0900–1700.*

This immense marina north of LAX is lined with expensive restaurants known mostly for their harbour views. **Fisherman's Village** (*13755 Fiji Way; tel: (310) 823-5411*), a New England-style shopping and entertainment area, has boutiques, eating places, sport equipment rentals and harbour cruises.

Volleyball on Laguna Beach

NEWPORT BEACH**

Newport Harbor Area Chamber of Commerce
1470 Jamboree Rd, Newport Beach, CA 92660;
tel: (949) 729-4400;
fax: (949) 729-4417; web: www.newportbeach.com.
Open Mon–Fri 0800–1700.

Six miles of beaches line the seaward side of **Balboa Peninsula****. The Victorian lace of **Balboa Pavilion*** (*400 Main St*) was once the terminus for a tourist trolley line from Los Angeles. It now marks an official **Fun Zone** with Ferris wheel, carousel, shops and restaurants. Several harbour cruises leaving from nearby piers.

Marinas along Newport Bay boast one of the largest concentrations of pleasure boats in America, while the upper end of the bay is an ecological preserve.

OCEANSIDE**

Oceanside Visitor Information Center 928 N. Coast Hwy, Oceanside, CA 92054;
tel: (760) 722-1534;
fax: (760) 722-8336; web: www.oceansidechamber.com

Oceanside hosts several national surfing competitions each year. The **California Surfing Museum*** (*233 N. Coast Hwy; tel/fax: (760) 721-6876; open Wed–Mon 1000–1600*) displays of vintage surf boards, just up from the **Oceanside Pier***, which stretches more than 900ft into the Pacific. The **Buena Vista Audubon Nature Center*** (*2202 S. Hill St; tel: (760) 439-2473; open Tue–Sat 1000–1600, Sun 1300–1600*) explores the mouth of the San Luis Rey River. **Mission San Luis Rey****** (*see page 261*) is 4 miles inland.

SANTA MONICA***

Santa Monica Visitor Center
1400 Ocean Ave, Santa Monica, CA 90401;
tel: (310) 393-7593;
fax: (310) 319-6273;
web: www.santamonica.com.
Open daily 1000–1600.

Santa Monica Museum of Flying $
2772 Donald Douglas Loop N.; tel: (310) 392-8822;
fax: (310) 450-6956;
web: www.mof.org/mof.
Open Tue–Sun 1000–1700.

A walking pier, carousel, up-market pedestrian mall, palm-lined beachfront park and youthful style make Santa Monica an oceanside version of what Hollywood would like to be. **Montana Avenue*** (*7th–17th Sts*) is a trendy shopping area sporting everything from baby clothing to racy lingerie and trendy restaurants to wear it in.

Palisades Park**** (*clifftop along Ocean Ave*) provides convenient benches to watch the sunset. An excellent collection of vintage aircraft can be found at the **Santa Monica Museum of Flying*** on the former site of the pioneering Douglas Aircraft Company.

Santa Monica Pier* (*end of Colorado Ave*) features an historic carousel, arcades, restaurants, an amusement park and the **UCLA Ocean Discovery Center****, which covers the marine life of Santa Monica Bay.

Third Street Promenade**** (*Third St, Wilshire Blvd–Broadway*) is an outdoor pedestrian mall with fountains, dinosaur topiary and cafés.

SANTA CATALINA ISLAND****

Twenty-one miles off the coast from Long Beach, Catalina Island is a vision of Southern California before LA. Nearly 90 per cent of the island is undeveloped, a mix of sandy beaches and crumbling cliffs.

The art deco **Casino**✣✣ overlooking the harbour in Avalon, Catalina's one real town, was a summer escape for Hollywood stars during the 1930s and 1940s; the interior murals of undersea scenes and Southern California history are stunning.

VENICE✣✣

Toning up at the Muscle Beach Gym in Venice

Just south of Santa Monica, Venice was laid out as a romantic replica of the Italian city. It became rundown, but bounced back as a trendy beach town. The beach scene revolves around **Venice Boardwalk**✣✣✣, a winding pedestrian, bicycle, skate, dog-and-everything-else path. The Boardwalk is a free-form circus packed with an ever-changing crowd of exhibitionists, onlookers, jugglers, fire-eaters, musicians, magicians and wanderers, busiest around the T-shirt booths at weekends and in summer. **Muscle Beach**✣✣ (*south of Windward Ave at 19th Ave*) is a legendary outdoor body-building studio.

Suggested tour

Total distance: 250 miles.

Time: One long day, or 3–4 days with stops in Carlsbad/Oceanside, Laguna Beach and Santa Monica Bay.

Links: San Diego to the south, Los Angeles to the north, and Route to the Stars.

ⓘ Los Angeles Convention and Visitors Bureau *685 S. Figueroa St, Los Angeles, CA 90017; tel: (213) 689-8822.*

Route: From **La Jolla ❶**, follow La Jolla Blvd north to Hwy S21 north of the **Salk Institute ❷** and through **Torrey Pines State Reserve ❸** to **Carlsbad ❹**, **Oceanside ❺** and I-5. Continue north through **Camp Pendleton ❻** to **San Clemente ❼**.

Take the Hwy 1/El Camino Real/Pacific Coast Highway exit from I-5. Drive north through **Orange County ❽** to **Laguna Beach ❾**, **Newport Beach ❿**, **Huntington Beach ⓫** and into **Los Angeles County ⓬**. Follow Hwy 1 inland through **Long Beach ⓭** and several smaller areas to the 'South Bay', the southern end of **Santa Monica Bay ⓮**. Hwy 1 turns inland through **Los Angeles International Airport (LAX) ⓯** to skirt **Marina del Rey ⓰** and **Venice ⓱**, returning to **Santa Monica ⓲**.

Acton Valyermo Piñon Hills

Placerita Canyon S.P. LOS ANGELES Phelan Hesperia

Wrightwood

San Fernando 138 Silverwood Lake S.R.A.

Crestline Lake Arrowhead

ANGELES NAT. FOR.

Burbank

AND OAKS

PASADENA

GLENDALE ONTARIO Rialto SAN BE

verly Hills Redla

POMONA 10

alibu LOS ANGELES RIVERSIDE

onica FULLERTON

GLEWOO Compton 12 Corona MORE

RRANCE 91 VALLE

LONG BEACH ANAHEIM ORANGE 215

Perris

SANTA ANA IRVINE Sun City 74

HUNTINGTON BEACH ORANGE Lake Elsinore Win

Newport Beach Mission Lake 79

Laguna Beach Viejo Elsinore S.R.A.

San Juan Capistrano 74 Murrieta Teme

Dana CLEVELAND N.F.

Point San Onofre Fallbrook Pala

San S.B. PALA

San Pedro Clemente Bonsall I.R. RI

Channel Vista 15

Avalon OCEANSIDE 76 78

Santa Carlsbad San

Catalina Marcos Del D

Island Encinitas

Outer Santa Barbara Passa Solana Beach Po

Del Mar 3

Gulf of 2

Santa Catalina Sant

U.S. 1

AVAL La Mesa

RES.

0   10   20 Miles

0   10   20 Kilometres

SAN DIEGO

Coronado 75

Imperial Beach

Border Field S.P.

Ratings

Museums	●●●●●
Architecture	●●●●○
History	●●●●○
Art	●●●○○
Children	●●●○○
Food and drink	●●●○○
Shopping	●●●○○
Beaches	●●○○○

San Diego

San Diego is as tropical as California gets. Bright sun and ocean breezes combine with the influence of Mexico, 20 miles south, to concoct a casual, easy-going atmosphere in California's second largest city. Visually, San Diego is uncongested; homes and businesses do not pile above or against one another.

East over the mountains is desert; north along the coast are round, eroded cliffs and golden sand beaches. Coronado Island offers resort dining and shopping a few minutes from Downtown San Diego. Mission Bay has beaches, SeaWorld San Diego and marinas filled with pleasure boats. Downtown bustles with business, gracefully proportioned high-rises lining the waterfront. Ten inches of annual rainfall encourage *al fresco* dining most of the year.

While San Diego thrives on tourism and manufacturing, a military presence still defines the city. California's first city was founded in 1769 by soldiers seeking to settle this little-explored area to thwart economic incursions by Russian fur traders – while Spanish Franciscan friars simultaneously Christianised the local native peoples. Mexico ruled from 1821 until 1847, when the United States took over.

Getting there and getting around

San Diego is 120 miles south of Los Angeles; allow three hours to drive from downtown to downtown, more during rush hour. For information on traffic hotspots tune into a local radio station.

San Diego International Airport, Lindbergh Field (*tel: (619) 231-7361*), is 3 miles north of downtown. Taxi to Downtown $7. San Diego Transit (MTS) bus No 992 runs every 15 minutes, 0513–0121, $2. Hotels and other shuttles also operate from between Terminals 1 and 2. Pick up car-hire shuttle vans from ground transportation islands outside arriving baggage areas.

Parking
Downtown parking meters are inexpensive. Horton Plaza offers three hours' free parking with any mall purchase, a cheaper alternative to valet parking at trendy 5th St restaurants. Seaport Village has two-hour validation.

San Diego Convention & Visitors Bureau
401 B St, Suite 1400, San Diego, CA 92101-4237; tel: (619) 236-1212; fax: (619) 696-9371; web: www.sandiego.org

International Visitors Information Center
11 Horton Plaza (1st Ave at F St). Open Mon–Sat 0830–1700, June–Aug 1100–1700 Sun.

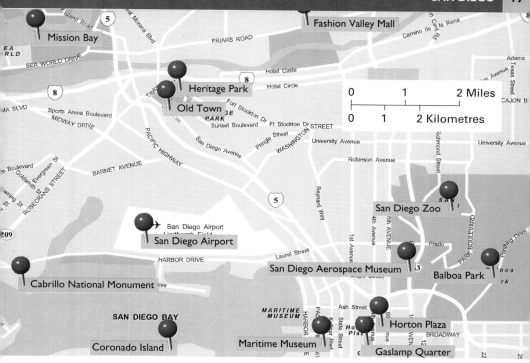

Mission Bay

Fashion Valley Mall

Heritage Park

Old Town PARK

San Diego Zoo

San Diego Airport
San Diego Airport

San Diego Aerospace Museum

Balboa Park

Cabrillo National Monument

SAN DIEGO BAY

MARITIME MUSEUM

Ash Street

Horton Plaza
BROADWAY

Coronado Island

Maritime Museum

Gaslamp Quarter

0   1   2 Miles

0   1   2 Kilometres

San Diego Visitor Information
Center *2668 E. Mission Bay Dr., San Diego, CA 92109;*
tel: (619) 276-8200;
fax: (619) 276-6041;
web: www.infosandiego.com
Open 0900–dusk.

Driving

Freeways can clog abysmally at rush hour. I-5 parallels the coast from Capistrano Beach south to San Diego. Hwy S21 is the much slower scenic route on the coast from Carlsbad to Mission Bay/Mission Beach. I-8 goes east from Old Town, past Mission Valley lodging, to East San Diego County. Around downtown, many streets are one-way; follow directional signs to attractions.

San Diego's transportation is inexpensive and a good alternative to city driving. The **San Diego Metropolitan Transit System (MTS)** (*102 Broadway at 1st Ave; tel: (619) 685-4900 or (619) 233-3004*), co-ordinates the **North County Coaster** train, buses and the **San Diego Trolley** (*100 Harbor Dr.; tel/fax: (619) 232-4002*).

Naval San Diego

By 1908, US expansionism dictated a Southern California base for naval operations. San Diego remains headquarters for the Pacific Fleet. North Island (Coronado) houses the US Naval Air Station. Aerospace companies thrived from the 1920s until aerospace and naval downsizing shocked the region in the 1970s.

The response? San Diego restored its historic downtown, built a convention centre, accommodated cruise ships, revamped the waterfront, and capitalised on the presence of the hi-tech industry stimulated by the La Jolla-based Scripps Institution of Oceanography, Salk Institute for Biological Studies and a large University of California, San Diego campus

ⓘ Balboa Park
Visitors Center in the House of Hospitality, 1549 El Prado; tel: (619) 239-0512; web: www.balboapark.com/index.html. Open daily 0900–1600.

ⓘ Botanical Building
near the Lily Pond. Open Fri-Wed 1000–1600.

Marston House $
3525 7th Ave, northwest corner of Balboa Park; tel: (619) 298-3142. Open Fri–Sun 1200–1630

Mingei International Museum $ *1439 El Prado; tel: (619) 239-0003; web: www.mingei.org. Open Tue-Sun 1000–1600.*

Museum of Man $ *1350 El Prado; tel: (619) 239-0001; web: www.museumofman.org. Open 1000–1630.*

Reuben H Fleet Science Center; *tel: (619) 238-1233; web: www.rhfleet.org. Open 0930 daily, to 1800 Mon–Tue, to 2100 Wed–Sat, to 2000 Sun.*

San Diego Automotive Museum $$
2080 Pan American Plaza; tel: (619) 231-2886. Open 1000–1630, summer to 1730.

San Diego Model Railroad Museum $
1649 El Prado, Lower Level; tel: (619) 696-0199; web: www.globalinfo.com/noncomm/SDMRM/sdmrm. Open Tue-Fri 1100–1600, Sat–Sun to 1700.

Sights

Balboa Park✦✦✦

Balboa Park, the 1400 acres of greenery north of Downtown San Diego, is *the* city park. The collection of plants, trees, California-Spanish baroque architecture, museums and the world-renowned **San Diego Zoo** have rendered its original 1868 chaparral and cacti desertscape unrecognisable outside the sculptured **Desert Garden✦** *(Park Blvd, east side)*. Many of the Spanish baroque buildings were installed for the 1915 Panama-California Exposition.

A free **Balboa Park Tram** from the Inspiration Point car-park makes a circuit of 11 stops. The 7-day, 12-museum **Passport to Balboa Park** provides bargain admission; many museums are free on one Tue each month. The park is full of interesting museums, botanical displays, artists' studios and performing arts venues.

Alcazar Garden✦✦, behind the Mingei International Museum, is a formal garden enclosed by arcades with a postcard view of California Tower's tile dome.

The plain name of the **Botanical Building✦✦** disguises the beautiful orchids and heliconia which bloom amid exotic palms.

The elegant façade of **Casa del Prado Theater✦** *(tel: (619) 239-1311)* would not be out of place in Spain. Enjoy youth productions of ballet, theatre and dance.

Marston House✦ is a Craftsman-style mansion with lovely landscaped English-style gardens.

Mingei International Museum✦ *(House of Charm building)* displays worldwide folk arts.

The **Museum of Man✦✦** is an eclectic, fun collection of ethnic artefacts from all over – don't miss the mummies.

The **Museum of Photographic Arts✦✦** offers changing exhibitions by the world's finest (closed for renovation until spring, 2000). It is renowned for the largest photography-oriented bookstore in the US. During renovation, exhibits and the bookstore continue at the **Museum of Contemporary Art** *(Broa and Kettner Blvd, Downtown, across from the Santa Fe Depot)*.

The **Old Globe Theatre✦✦✦** *(Simon Edison Center for the Performing Arts; tel: (619) 239-2255)*, a reproduction of the London original, presents Shakespeare plays and more on several stages.

Reuben H Fleet Science Center✦ offers hands-on exhibits and an OMNIMAX® Space Theater.

• **San Diego Aerospace Museum✦✦✦** *(see page 84)*.

• **San Diego Automotive Museum✦✦** rotates exhibits of Southern California's *raison d'être* from a fine collection of historic vehicles.

• **San Diego Model Railroad Museum✦✦** is heaven for train buffs, where six scale-model, mini-gauge trains circle, enhanced by realistic sound effects.

• **San Diego Museum of Art✦** combines contemporary California art

San Diego Museum of Art $$
Plaza de Panama; tel: (619) 232-7931; web: www.sddt.com/sdma. Open Tue–Sun 1000–1430.

Spanish Village Arts & Crafts Center *tel: (619) 233-9050. Open 1100–1600.*

Spreckels Organ Pavilion *tel: (619) 702-8138. Organ concerts 1400 Sun, 2000 Mon June–Aug.*

Timken Museum of Art, *1500 El Prado, Plaza de Panama, tel: (619) 239-5548; web: http://gort.ucsd.edu.sj.timken/ Open Oct–Aug Tue–Sat 1000–1630 , Sun 1330–1630 .*

with Chinese, Japanese and 15th- to 18th-century European works, supplemented by the outdoor **Sculpture Garden Café.**

Spanish Village Arts and Crafts Center✶✶, with its wide, colourful courtyard, offers studios where artists work, display and sell sculpture, jewellery, paintings and other arts.

Spreckels Organ Pavilion✶ has 4445 organ pipes which thrill music lovers with free outdoor Sun afternoon concerts (and Mon eve, June–Aug).

The European art collections at the **Timken Museum of Art**✶ include magnificent Russian icons.

Right
Sculptor's studio in San Diego's Spanish Village

Cabrillo National Monument $
Hwy 209 to 1800 Cabrillo Memorial Dr.;
tel: (619) 557-5450;
fax: (619) 557-5469;
web: www.nps.gov/cabr

Monument, visitor centre and Old Point Loma Lighthouse
Open daily 0900–1715, to 1815 4 July–Labor Day.

Coronado Beach Historical Museum $
1126 Loma Ave, Coronado; tel: (619) 435-7242. Open Wed–Sat 1000–1600, Sun 1200–1600.

Cabrillo National Monument at Point Loma**

In 1542, three Spanish ships under Portuguese commander Juan Rodriguez Cabrillo found a 'closed and very good port' and Kumeyaay Indians. The explorers landed, claimed 'San Miguel' for the Catholic Majesties, then sailed north to the Channel Islands. The **Cabrillo National Monument**, atop cliffs at the end of Point Loma peninsula sheltering San Diego Bay, is a majestic, oversized white statue of the explorer flanked by cross, crown and the Spanish coat of arms. Cabrillo's head faces east, above the sweep of the bay channel, Coronado Island and Downtown San Diego to the mountains flanking the border with Mexico. Below the statue, an observation area offers stunning vistas of sailboat regattas and the to and fro of US Naval traffic, comprising vessels of the Pacific Fleet.

Old Point Loma Lighthouse*, a 5-minute walk from the monument, sits 422ft above the Pacific. Operational from 1855 to 1891, the light tower sits in the middle of the house, furnished as it was for the last keeper's posting. A 2-mile return **Bayside Trail*** passes through a mix of prickly pear and succulents with black sage and chaparral as it descends 300ft. A well-marked path close to the monument entrance gives on to accessible **tide-pools***, and the **Whale Overlook** is a prime spot for grey whale spotting from December to March. Below Point Loma, the eroded **Sunset Cliffs** are a popular rendezvous for photographers and view lovers at sundown.

Coronado Island*

In the 1880s, the arrival of railways in San Diego cried out for a resort – and the **Hotel del Coronado*** (*1500 Orange Ave; tel: (619) 522-8000*), just a short ferry ride across the beautiful San Diego Bay, met the need. The white Victorian building with its bright red roof and towers still stands as a luxury landmark.

The **San Diego-Coronado Bay Bridge*** arcs gracefully over the bay, a lovely drive except at rush hour. The **San Diego-Coronado Ferry*** (*tel: (619) 234-4111*) transports passengers and bicycles between the Broadway Pier and Ferry Landing Marketplace. Marriott's Coronado Island Resort offers a pricey but fast 6-minute **water taxi*** service to the San Diego Convention Center area (*tel: (619) 435-3000*). Romantics can board a **Venetian gondola*** (*Gondola di Venezia; tel: (619) 221-2999*) at Loews Coronado Bay Resort.

Ocean Blvd northwest of the Hotel del Coronado is a superb spot for sunsets. North-side shops and restaurants centre around **Ferry Landing Marketplace*** (*1201 1st St and B Ave; tel: (619) 435-8895*) which, with its four parks 1½ miles west, has fine views of the afternoon sun glowing on downtown high-rises, while **Orange Ave**, near the **Hotel del Coronado**, is a trendy area to shop, dine, sip espresso, browse art galleries and people-watch. The **Coronado Beach Historical Museum*** displays a small collection of photographs and artefacts in an 1898 Victorian house.

Horton Plaza
*Broadway-G St,
1st–4th Aves;
tel: (619) 238-1596; web:
www.hortonplaza.com
Shops open 1000,
1100 Sun.*

Gaslamp Quarter✦✦

Opulent late-Victorian architecture and streetlamps grace downtown San Diego's 16-block Gaslamp Quarter *(Broadway and Harbor Dr., 4th and 6th Aves), the* shopping, dining and entertainment area. Alone among California's major cities, this civic and business centre has remained visually intact since its beginnings as 'New Town' in 1887, when San Francisco merchant Alonzo E Horton bought up the waterfront and moved the action from Old Town. The 1850s **William Heath Davis House**✦ *(tel: (619) 233-4692)* was an early merchant-developer's residence.

Through the next century, the boom town catered to lawman Wyatt Earp's three gambling halls, bordello patrons, sailors and homeless men, evolving into an infamous skid row as population and business shifted north and east. Some homeless missions remain, but the Gaslamp Quarter's 1970s restoration continues, cemented by great music clubs, fine dining and a cheerful ambience of rediscovery. **Horton Plaza**, a multi-level shopping mall with excellent fast food, theatres and a cinema, anchors the district on the north side.

Heritage Park✦

On the edge of Old Town San Diego, **Heritage Park** *(access Heritage Park Row from Juan and Harney Sts)* preserves six Victorian mansions and a Jewish synagogue arranged along a pedestrian walk. All of the buildings are still in use: look for wedding parties on weekends. The turret marks the **Heritage Park Bed & Breakfast Inn** in the 1889 Queen Anne **Christian House**, and there are Victorian-style souvenirs in the 1893 Classic Revival **Burton House**. The 1893 **Temple Beth Israel**'s clean Classic Revival lines appealed to Christian congregations, who used the building before they had permanent sites for their churches.

Horton Plaza✦

Geometric wedges, odd angles, tilework, the eagle-topped Jessops 'San Diego Time' Clock and 41 cheerful colours make this chic downtown shopping mall a destination for San Diegans. **Horton Plaza**, at the north edge of the Gaslamp Quarter, has 140 shops, including F.A.O. Schwarz for toys and Nordstrom and Macy's department stores. The **San Diego Lyceum Theatre**✦ *(tel: (619) 235-8025)* has comic and classic performances in repertory.

Mission Bay✦

Mission Bay sprang from the imagination when mud dredged from San Diego Harbor created a huge waterside parkland, with beaches on the bay and Pacific Ocean. The best-known attraction is **SeaWorld Adventure Park San Diego** *(see page 60)*. The sheltered bay offers hotels, restaurants, children's playgrounds, jet skiing, fishing, sailing, boardsailing, jogging, tennis and golf – even camping.

Mission San Diego de Alcalá

10919 San Diego Mission Rd; tel: (619) 281-8449. Museum open daily 0900–1700.

Old Town San Diego State Historic Park

2645 San Diego Ave; tel: (619) 220-5422. Open daily 1000–1700. For a self-guided walking tour, purchase an Old Town San Diego State Historic Park Tour Guide & Brief History, $2 at Seeley Stables, or take a ranger-led tour.

Junipero Serra Museum and Tower Gallery $

2727 Presidio Dr., Presidio Park; tel: (619) 297-3258. Open Fri–Sun 1000–1630.

Mormon Battalion Memorial

2510 Juan St; tel: (619) 298-3317. Open 0900–2100.

San Diego Aerospace Museum $$

2001 Pan American Plaza, Balboa Park; tel: (619) 234-8291; web: www.aerospacemuseum.org. Open 1000–1630, free 4th Tue of the month.

San Diego Maritime Museum $$

1306 N. Harbor Dr.; tel: (619) 234-9153; web: www.sdmaritime.com. Open 0900-2000, to 2100 in summer.

Old Town Trolley Tours $$

tel: (619) 298-8687; fax: (619) 298-3404; web: www.historictours.com/sandiego/trolley. Operate daily 2-hour, 9-stop tours 0900–1600.

Mission San Diego de Alcalá✦, California's first mission *(see page 260)*, seems strangely isolated 7 miles from the coast or downtown, but its white façade and lush front gardens are exactly the austere and imposing image the Spanish Church and Empire wished to project. A small museum displays vestments and manuscripts written by California Missions' founder Fra Junípero Serra.

Old Town San Diego✦✦

Old Town San Diego State Historic Park, northwest of downtown, anchors a larger area of motels, restaurants and shops which serve the tourist trade visiting the city's 19th-century settlement. Three original family adobes, **La Casa de Estudillo, Machado y Stewart** and **Machado y Silvas** are excellently restored house museums. On weekends, volunteers dressed in mid-19th-century military uniforms are inspected in front of the **Robinson-Rose House** park visitors centre, then drill on the green and parade around the park. A blacksmith demonstrates his skills near **Seeley Stables Museum**; carriages and stage-coaches are on display inside, supplemented by a film on transport in California. The **First San Diego Courthouse**, the first **San Diego Union** (newspaper) building, a school and a dental museum offer insights into daily life while the **Wells Fargo Museum** in the reconstructed **Colorado House** explains the economics of stage-coaches and the Gold Rush in California.

Candy and reproduction period knick-knacks are for sale in several historic buildings. San Diegans visit Old Town to enjoy margaritas and warm tortillas at several good restaurants, including **La Casa de Bandini**✦ *(tel: (619) 297-8211)* or one of five restaurants along the courtyard of **Bazaar del Mundo**'s hibiscus-entwined shopping arcade, complete with dancers and mariachi bands *(tel: (619) 296-3161)*.

The **Old Town Trolley Tour** begins on Twiggs St. The **Mormon Battalion Memorial**, celebrating the 1847 arrival of Latter Day Saints troops to support American troops in the fight against Mexico, is between Old Town and Heritage Park. North of Old Town, **Presidio Park** was the site of the original 1769 fort and mission. The artefacts and scale models in the **Junípero Serra Museum and Tower Gallery** explain San Diego's pre-American history.

San Diego Aerospace Museum✦✦✦

Aviation fans flock to the **San Diego Aerospace Museum**. The combined influence of naval aviation and the aerospace industry in San Diego make the 66 aircraft on display in the doughnut-shaped Ford Building one of the best history lessons of airborne flight.

San Diego Maritime Museum✦✦✦

San Diego's embarcadero **Maritime Museum** is dominated by the majesty of the square rigging of the *Star of India*✦✦✦. One of three ships open for touring, this, the oldest merchant vessel still afloat, has

San Diego Zoo $$$
2900 Zoo Dr., Balboa Park; tel: (619) 234-3153; web: www.sandiegozoo.com. Open 0900–1600.

been restored to the condition of her launch from the Isle of Man in 1863. The 1898 *Berkeley*✦✦✦ ferry boat is the sister ship of the *Eureka*, displayed along the Hyde Park Pier of the National Maritime Museum in San Francisco. Both ferries plied San Francisco Bay. The steamer *Medea,* a Scots-built luxury yacht, is tied up alongside.

San Diego Zoo✦

The **San Diego Zoo** was among the first to pioneer habitats for 3900 animals and hundreds of birds, freeing them from traditional caged confinement. On several levels of jungle-type vegetation, the zoo wanders through Cat and Bear Canyons and Horn and Hoof Mesa. Guided (double-decker) bus tours see most of the zoo; **Kangaroo Bus Tours** provide eight drop-off points. Both depart from **Flamingo Lagoon**✦ in the main area. **Skyfari Aerial Tram** provides a gondola overview with a quick hop to the other side of the park. Queue up early for a glimpse of two pandas on research loan from China. The **Polar Bear Plunge**✦ is happily incongruous in the balmy climate, but **Gorilla Tropics**✦ and the South African klipspringer habitat feel like authentic exotic locales.

Below
Victorian houses in San Diego's Old Town Historic Park

Seaport Village *849 W. Harbor Dr.; tel: (619) 235-4014; web: www.spvillage.com. Shops open 1000–2100, to 2200 June–Aug.*

Seaport Village✦

Seaport Village has nautical theme shopping and dining near the San Diego Convention Center. A bayside boardwalk at the south end of the embarcadero offers year-round outdoor music, fashion shows and mimes. Take a spin on the 1890 Looff **Broadway Flying Horses Carousel** (*tel: (619) 234-6133*) or try the **Village Café** (*tel: (619) 544-9444*) for a wide assortment of breakfast and other fare for a cheerful wake-up. **Wyland Galleries** (*tel: (619) 544-9995*) have the famous artist's whale paintings and marine art. If you're looking for a gift for those back home, the **San Diego City Store** (*tel: (619) 234-2489*) has local-name souvenirs and T-shirts.

The tall-masted *Star of India* lies at anchor in San Diego's Maritime Museum

Entertainment

Local newspapers and the free *San Diego Weekly Reader* list clubs, nightlife and restaurants. Hopping jazz, blues and rock clubs are attached to Gaslamp Quarter restaurants along 5th Ave, south of Horton Plaza. The **San Diego Performing Arts League** (*tel: (619) 238-0700*) has bi-monthly listings in its free *What's Playing in San Diego Guide.*

San Diego Visitor Information Center, 2668 E. Mission Bay Dr., San Diego, CA 92109; tel: (619) 276-8200; fax: (619) 276-6041; web: www.infosandiego.com Open 0900–dusk.

One of the most venerable companies in the country, the **Old Globe Theatre** *(see page 81)* in Balboa Park, fills three theatres with 12 productions a year. **TIMES ARTS TIX** *(southwest corner of Horton Plaza)* offers on-the-spot, half-price tickets for theatre, dance or concert performances on the day. The proximity of UC San Diego draws big-name music groups to the area.

San Diegans love sports: the **Padres** play baseball Apr-Oct and the **Chargers** play NFL football Oct–Dec/Jan at QUALCOMM Park while a new stadium is built. Weather encourages outdoor sports with numerous golf courses and tennis courts.

Shopping

Perhaps because of the pleasant climate, it's easy to shop in the San Diego area. **Horton Plaza** *(see page 83)*, has restaurants, shops, stores and theatres, and validated parking makes a Gaslamp Quarter exploration a bargain. Shops in the whimsical-coloured shopping hub include **The Disney Store, Warner Bros Studio Store,** the **Discovery Channel Store,** the local educational television station **KPBS Store of Knowledge,** and **Sports Fantasy** for genuine US sports team clothing and accessories.

Fashion Valley Mall *(7007 Friars Rd; tel: (619) 688-9113)* in Mission Valley is filled with clothing, cosmetic and home furnishing shops, a food court and a multi-screen cinema. Shop for nautical souvenirs at **Seaport Village,** Mexican at Old Town's **Bazaar del Mundo,** or search for unexpected bargains at **Kobey's Swap Meet**⁺ *(3500 Sports Arena Blvd; tel: (619) 226-0650, Thur–Sun).*

Accommodation and food

San Diego's interest in attracting convention-goers keeps hotel/motel rooms available at reasonable cost almost anytime. Coronado, Mission Bay, coast and downtown hotels are pricey; look for easy freeway access from I-8 in Mission Valley's Hotel Circle, a 15-minute drive to downtown. Prices drop 15–40 per cent Nov–Mar; what's pricey then may be offered at discount later.

The *SDCVB Official Visitors Planning Guide* lists accommodation by area. **San Diego Visitor Information Center** *2668 E. Mission Bay Dr., San Diego, CA 92109; tel: (619) 276-8200; fax: (619) 276-6041; web: www.infosandiego.com,* and **San Diego Hotel Reservations** *tel: (800) 728-3227 or (619) 627-9300; web: www.savecash.com,* book accommodation area-wide.

Heritage Park Inn $$$ *2470 Heritage Park Row; tel: (619) 299-6832 or (800) 995-2470,* is Victorian cosseting two blocks from **Old Town State Historic Park** *(see page 84).*

Above
The San Diego skyline

Hotel del Coronado $$$ *1500 Orange Ave, Coronado; tel: (619) 522-8000 or (800) 468-3533,* is the *grande dame*, picture-postcard resort hotel, complete with ghosts.

Town & Country Resort Hotel $$$ *500 Hotel Circle North; tel: (800) 772-8527,* is a convenient, large convention hotel with posh rooms, cheerful staff, and easy freeway access to the area.

Welk Resort Center $$$ *8860 Lawrence Welk Dr., Escondido CA 92026; tel: (760) 749-3000,* offers golf and resort getaway in the rugged mountains 30 miles north of San Diego.

San Diego's proximity to Mexico makes it easy to find a variety of Mexican food, from bland to chilli-pepper spicy, especially in **Old Town**. San Diego is also getting a reputation for 'fusion cuisines', mixing California's fresh produce with delicate recipes, sauces and presentation from Asia.

The **Gaslamp Quarter** has a good choice of restaurants, from moderate to pricey, many with live music in the evening.

Croce's $$ *5th Ave and F St; tel: (619) 233-4355,* have three venues: **Top Hat Bar & Grille** has nightly rhythm and blues; **Croce's West** has Southwest cuisine; and **Croce's Restaurant & Jazz Bar** has all-American cuisine with live jazz.

Buffalo Joe's $$ *600 5th Ave; tel: (619) 236-1616,* is the place to try baby back ribs.

Sadaf Restaurant $$ *828 5th Ave; tel: (619) 338-0008,* draws a loyal crowd for its Persian dishes.

For seafood, walk to Seaport Village's several bayside restaurants or enjoy gleaming white boats nestled in marinas in Mission Bay.

Hornblower $$$ *1066 N. Harbor Dr.; tel: (619) 686-8715,* offers dinner-dance and Sun Champagne brunch cruises on San Diego Bay.

Suggested tours

San Diego's **59-Mile Scenic Drive**❖❖ signs have a flying white seagull on a blue and yellow field. The half-day circuit begins at the foot of Broadway near the Santa Fe Depot (Amtrak/Coaster), and includes La Jolla and Coronado.

The orange and green motorised trams of **Old Town Trolley Tours**❖❖ (*tel: (619) 298-8687*) can be boarded from Old Town or any of eight other stops for a two-hour narrated circuit, or reboarded after spending some time in each area. Have a passport and (for non-US citizens or resident aliens) a multiple-entry visa or visa waiver to hand on the **San Diego Trolley** if you want to make a day trip to the border and walk to **Tijuana** in Mexico.

San Diego Harbor Excursions❖ (*tel: (619) 234-4111*) cruise the bay sights daily and **Gondola di Venezia**❖❖ (*tel: (619) 221-2999*) departs from Coronado Island for a one-hour Venetian gondola cruise of San Diego Bay.

Below
San Diego's Horton Plaza

Anza-Borrego Desert State Park

Ratings

Nature	●●●●●
Geology	●●●●●
Outdoor activities	●●●●●
Scenery	●●●●○
Historical sights	●●●○○
History	●●●○○
Children	●○○○○

A short journey east of San Diego or south of Palm Springs is true desert, a desert park surrounding a few golf courses, resort hotels and basic services. Anza-Borrego Desert State Park is rugged, more rocky and mountainous than stereotypical sandy dunes, a place for solitude away from the cities of Southern California. The town of Julian, nestled in forests and apple orchards, is a world in-between, a popular and historic getaway for San Diegans. Stop there for an alpine respite before venturing on to Anza-Borrego and an overnight stay in Borrego Springs.

ANZA-BORREGO DESERT STATE PARK✧✧✧

ⓘ Anza-Borrego Desert State Park $ *200 Palm Canyon Dr., Borrego Springs, CA 94004; tel: (760) 767-4205 or (760) 767-5311.*

Visitors Center
1½ miles west of Christmas Circle, Borrego Springs. Open daily 0900–1700 Oct–May, weekends and holidays June–Sept. **Wildflower Hotline** *for Jan–March season; tel: (760) 767-4684. Ask at visitors centre for details of trails.*

Two-thirds of the 600,000 acres of this largest state park in the contiguous US is wilderness. Thanks to its proximity to the Colorado River, Anza-Borrego Desert State Park (ABDSP) is technically a Colorado Desert section of the Sonoran Desert, with arid, eye-stretching badlands, palm canyons, desert bighorn sheep camouflaged by raw mountain scarps, temperature- and saline-adaptable pupfish, seas of spring wildflowers and fossils of mammoth elephants and sabre-toothed cats.

In a few places, such as the 3-mile return **Borrego Palm Canyon Trail**, native California fan palm trees, North America's largest palms, offer shade against blistering temperatures from June to September, even as the *borrego* (desert bighorn sheep), move down to water at palm-lined waterholes. Elsewhere, the panoramas and vistas are worth a well-provisioned hike into a sere desert – follow established trails, or risk being caught in a rare, but potentially fatal flash-flood downpour. Brilliant expanses of **wildflowers✧✧✧**, between late-January and March, are legendary.

Accommodation in Anza-Borrego Desert State Park

Reserve park camp pitches for **Borrego Palm Canyon** and **Tamarisk Grove** (*tel: (800) 444-7275*). **Bow Willow Camp** has 16 pitches (no facilities); **Borrego Springs** has standard accommodation.

BORREGO SPRINGS❖

ℹ Borrego Springs Chamber of Commerce *622 Palm Canyon Dr., Borrego Springs, CA 92004; tel: (800) 559-5524; web: www.borregosprings.com. Open daily 1000–1600.*

🏍 The Coffee & Book Store *$ 590 Palm Canyon Dr.; tel: (760) 767-5080, open 0600–1800, serves light fare and java with a good book selection.*

Surrounded by Anza-Borrego Desert State Park, and a service point for park visitors, Borrego Springs holds its own as a desert resort centre and citrus fruit producer for worldwide export. April's Grapefruit Festival celebrates the local product, though oranges, lemons and limes also grow in north-side groves.

Accommodation and food in Borrego Springs

Cooler weather between October and May draws a million tourists a year – book in advance, even for tee times. Accommodation includes ABDSP camping, RV parks, bed and breakfast, motels and three resort hotels. Prices can drop 40 per cent in summer.

The Palms at Indian Head $$–$$$ *2220 Hoberg Rd; tel: (760) 767-7788 or (800) 519-2624; fax: (760) 767-9717, on the site where 1950s film stars went for a ranch getaway.*

Palm Canyon Resort Hotel $$–$$$ *221 Palm Canyon Dr; tel: (760) 767-5341 or (800) 242-0044; fax: (760) 767-4073,* has a Western theme and is close to the park.

La Casa del Zorro Desert Resort Hotel $$$ *3845 Yaqui Pass Rd; tel: (760) 767-5323 or (800) 824-1884; fax: (760) 767-5963,* offers rooms, individual *casitas,* and formal dining.

JULIAN✥✥

Julian Chamber of Commerce *2129 Main St; tel: (760) 765-1857; web: www.julianca.com. Open daily 1000–1600*

Cuyamaca Rancho State Park $ *12551 Hwy 79, Descanso, CA 90216; tel: (760) 765-0755; web: www.cuyamaca.statepark.org /park*

Julian's wooden shopfronts evoke the 1869 gold rush which created the town. **The Eagle and High Peak Mine**✥ has guided tours. The town also attracts visitors for its alpine climate and delicious apples served in pies or quaffed as juice. **Cuyamaca Rancho State Park**✥✥, 17 miles south on Hwy 79, is a good introduction to the region's pine, cedar and oak forests, **Stonewall Goldmine**✥ site and a museum of Kumeyaay Indian culture.

Accommodation and food in Julian

The Chamber of Commerce has an accommodation list. The **Julian Bed and Breakfast Guild,** *PO Box 1711, Julian, CA 92036; tel: (760) 765-1555; web: www.julianbnbguild.com,* represents 21 bed and breakfast lodgings.

Dudley's Bakery *at the Junction of Hwys 78 and 79, northwest of Julian; tel: (760) 765-0488,* is famous for its jalapeno pepper and potato bread.

Julian Drug Store *corner of Main and Washington Sts; tel: (760) 765-0332,* has an 1886 wooden soda fountain counter – complete with milk shakes and ice-cream desserts.

Suggested tour

Total distance: 90 miles.

Time: 3 hours driving.

Links: From the Erosion Road Auto Tour, Hwy S22, east of Borrego Springs, continue east. Turn left at Hwy 86, the Salton Sea, going 32 miles north to Hwy 111 at Indio at the eastern side of the Coachella Valley to join the Palm Springs Route (*see page 94*). To include San Diego Wild Animal Park (*see page 59*), continue west of Julian on Hwy 79 to the Hwy 78 junction, and go southwest for 25 miles on Hwy 78 through Ramona and San Pasqual.

Eagle and High Peak Mine $
end of C St;
tel: (760) 765-0036.
Open year-round, weather permitting, from 1000–1500, for one-hour guided mine tours and gold panning.

Palomar Observatory⁺⁺
northwest of Julian and Santa Ysabel Mission, via Hwy 76, right on Hwy S7, then right on Hwy S6;
tel: (760) 742-2119.
Open daily 0900–1600.

Route: North of downtown San Diego ❶, take I-8 east for 38 miles. Turn left (north) on Hwy 79 to **Cuyamaca Rancho State Park** ❷ and **Julian** ❸. For the most direct route from Julian **to Anza-Borrego Desert State Park** ❹/**Borrego Springs** ❺, take Hwy 78 18 miles east, veer left on to Hwy S3 (Yaqui Pass Rd) for 7 miles, then follow Borrego Springs Road to town.

An alternative route to ABDSP continues 18 miles northwest of Julian ❸ on Hwy 79 passing **Santa Ysabel Mission⁺** ❻ *tel: (760) 765-0810,* a reconstructed chapel and museum which served as a satellite of Mission San Diego (*see page 260*). Turn east on to Hwy S2/S22 24 miles to Borrego Springs ❺.

Also worth exploring

Palomar Observatory⁺⁺⁺ ❼ has a museum and video explaining astronomical phenomena sighted using the huge 200-inch Hale Telescope. The white-domed research facility does not offer night visits, but a special platform allows visitors to view the apparatus' works.

The mountains in the **Cleveland National Forest** ❽ are rocky, stark and impressive. Close by the observatory is **Palomar Mountain State Park⁺⁺** ❼ (*2 miles west of the Hwys S6/S7 junction; tel: (760) 742-3462*), with high meadows rivalling the Sierra Nevada Mountains for scenic beauty.

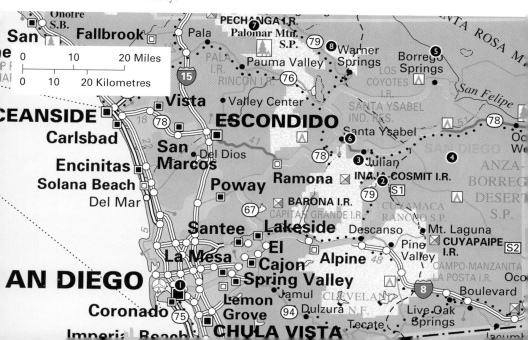

Palm Springs

Ratings

Golf	●●●●●
Shopping	●●●●●
Scenery	●●●●●
Nightlife	●●●●○
Museums	●●●○○
Historical sights	●●●○○
Food and drink	●●●○○

Surrounded by thousands of square miles of stark desert beauty, Palm Springs is an artificial oasis overrun with the rich, the famous and the star-struck, all joined in the common pursuit of golf, eternal youth and the perfect sun tan. It's California's desert destination for those who *don't* want to get away from it all.

Palm Springs was originally an isolated hot springs among the desert palms, known only to the Agua Caliente band of the Cahuilla Indians and a few health fanatics. In the 1930s, Hollywood discovered the joys of distant desert getaways, with real estate developers and golf course designers in close pursuit. Three generations later, the town created for luxury and leisure has become a string of eight resort cities strung along Hwy 111 through the Coachella Valley. The valley remains one of America's richest agricultural areas, though fields and orchards are now disappearing beneath a jigsaw puzzle of interlocking golf courses and malls.

Getting there and getting around

ℹ Palm Springs Tourism *333 N. Palm Canyon Dr., Ste 114, Palm Springs, CA 92262; tel: (760) 778-8415 or (800) 347-7746; fax: (760) 323-3021; web: www.palm-springs.org* **Visitor Center** *2781 N. Palm Canyon Dr. (at Hwy 111). Open daily 0900–1730.*

Palm Springs is 110 miles from Los Angeles (about 2½ hours) off I-10 on Hwy 111, which becomes North Palm Canyon Dr. From San Diego, follow I-15 north to Hwy 215, then to Hwy 60 and I-10. From Anaheim/Orange County, take Hwy 55 north to Hwy 91. Go east on Hwy to I-10.

Palm Springs Regional Airport *3400 E. Tahquitz Canyon Wy, Palm Springs; tel: (760) 323-8161.* A taxi to Palm Springs is about $10, to Rancho Mirage, $40. Most hotels offer a free or reduced-rate shuttle service.

Traffic can be slow on Palm Canyon Dr. near major shopping malls and in central Palm Springs. There is plenty of parking, almost always free, but watch for golf carts – drivers occasionally swerve without warning or signal as though they were still on the course. Palm Springs is busiest during the winter months, and traffic is heaviest in the evening when crowds come out to shop and drive.

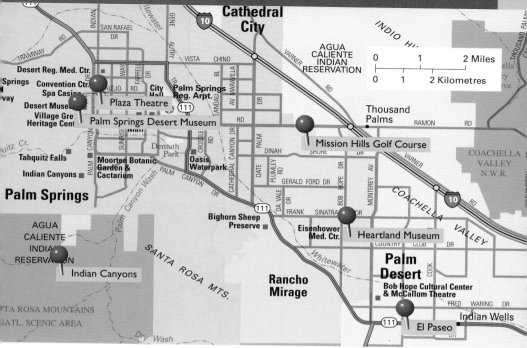

Cities

The eight cities that make up the Palm Springs resort area tend to blur into each other, especially along Palm Canyon Dr. (Hwy 111), an endless strip of low-rise development.

Cathedral City was named for the rocky spires that are all but hidden behind new sporting complexes and other higher-rise development. The city is family-orientated during the day, but has a bustling gay scene at night, second only to Palm Springs itself.

Desert Hot Springs is noted for the underground wells that supply most of the area's spas and swimming pools. Located north of Palm Springs, it's a convenient location for day-trippers to Joshua Tree National Park (*see page 107*) and other desert sights.

Indian Wells became famous as a golf venue thanks to US President Eisenhower's frequent golf holidays here in the 1950s. The town has the valley's largest concentration of grand resorts and private courses.

Indio is the low-key agricultural heart of the Coachella Valley, as well as the commercial, gambling and polo centre.

La Quinta is named for the area's first exclusive resort, which opened in 1927. Hollywood director Frank Capra wrote the script for his

ⓘ Palm Springs Desert Resorts Convention and Visitors Bureau
69-930 Hwy 111, Ste 201, Rancho Mirage, CA 92270; tel: (760) 770-9000; fax: (760) 770-9001; web: www.desert-resorts.com.
Visitor Center *Open daily 0830–1730*

Indian Canyons $
End of S. Palm Canyon Dr.; tel: (760) 325-1053 or (800) 790-3398; web: www.aguacaliente.org/icmai. Open Sept–Mar 0800–1700 Apr–Aug 0800–1800

Living Desert Wildlife Reserve and Botanical Park $$ 47-900 Portola Ave, Palm Desert; tel: (760) 346-5694; fax: (760) 568-9685; web: www.living desert.org Open daily 0900–1630 Sept–mid June, varies mid June–Aug.

Fabulous Palm Springs Follies $$$
Plaza Theater, 128 S. Palm Canyon Dr.; tel: (760) 778-7654; fax: (760)322-3196. Performances Nov–May.

Academy Award-winning *It Happened One Night* at the resort and kept coming back with stars such as Clark Gable and Greta Garbo in tow.

Palm Desert is mostly a place to shop, relax, play golf and watch wildlife at the **Living Desert Wildlife Reserve and Botanical Park** (*see page 97*). The best time to visit is Nov, when the growing golfing population stages America's first (and possibly only) golf cart parade.

Palm Springs is where it all began with a primitive mineral hot springs in the 1890s. Most of the city's hotels remain small, a hold-over from earlier days.

Rancho Mirage, the Valley's high-profile neighbourhood, attracts presidents, kings and stars to its golf courses. Golf links share centre stage and newspaper headlines with the Betty Ford Center, California's celebrity health clinic.

Desert Tours❖❖
The only way to appreciate the desert is to see it up close and off the main roads. **Jeep Eco-Tours $$$** (*tel: (760) 324-5337*) offers a variety of off-road jeep tours through local canyons, over the San Andreas Fault and into nearby mountains with experienced naturalist guides.

Fabulous Palm Springs Follies❖
The best introduction to Palm Springs' image of itself, this feathers-and-sequins tribute to 1930s and 1940s musicals gives veteran showgirls a chance to strut their stuff – all are over the age of 50. So is the historic **Plaza Theater**, where they perform each winter.

Indian Canyons❖❖❖
The Agua Caliente band of Cahuilla Indians was forced to give up half of the Coachella Valley in the 1890s, but they retained three picturesque canyons in the lower slopes of the San Jacinto Mountains south of Palm Springs. All three canyons contain extensive groves of California fan palms *(Washingtonia filifera)*, California's only native palm, nourished by year-round streams. Pleasant hiking and equestrian trails climb the canyons from the car-park at the head of Palm Canyon. Horses can be hired from Smoke Tree Stables (*tel: (760) 327-1372*) for individual or guided rides – Western style only.

A new **Tahquitz Canyon Visitor Center** is scheduled to open in 1999 with a canyon observation deck, cultural presentations and tribal museum.

Palm Canyon❖❖❖ shelters about 3000 palms. Most grow in groves that extend 2 miles up the canyon from below the car-park, with shady walking paths through the sandy flats. The trail becomes more difficult and rockier higher in the canyon. **Andreas Canyon**❖❖ is smaller and equally lush, but an initial section of trail clambers over boulders that have fallen from the canyon rim above.

The trail into **Murray Canyon**❖ passes through a mile of

low, unshaded brush before dropping into a shady grove of palms in the stream bed. It's a pleasant walk in winter, but beware the sun in summer.

Living Desert Wildlife Reserve and Botanical Park❖❖❖

The Living Desert is a 1200-acre botanical garden with rare plants and animals from arid climes around the world. The core of the reserve represents the main deserts of North America, including the Upper Colorado, Yuman and Baja California. Animals include bighorn sheep, Arabian oryx, gazelles, zebras and Bactrian wapiti, many of them endangered or already extinct in the wild.

Below
Shaggy giants in Palm Springs

Moorten Botanical Garden $ 1701 S. Palm Canyon Dr.; tel: (760) 327-6555. Open Mon–Sat 0900–1630. Sun 1000–1600.

Moorten Botanical Garden✤✤

This private garden and plant store displays more than 3000 varieties of desert plants from around the world, often in whimsical, seemingly haphazard displays. Though technically a nursery, few specimens are actually for sale.

Mount San Jacinto✤✤✤

Fifty miles of trails at the crest of Mount San Jacinto (pronounced 'ha-seen-toe') are Palm Spring's escape from itself. In summer, altitude tempers the blazing desert temperatures while conifer forests provide welcome shade. In winter, the Mount San Jacinto Wilderness becomes a busy Nordic skiing centre. The only access is via the Aerial Tramway.

Below
Springs Jeep Tour

Agua Caliente

US Government survey reports originally dismissed the Coachella Valley as 'an immense waste of uninhabited country', but it was neither waste nor uninhabited to the Agua Caliente band of Cahuilla Indians. The band hunted and harvested the valley floor in winter and retreated up the canyons to cooler country as summer temperatures climbed towards 120°F (49°C).

Early White settlers appropriated what land and water sources they pleased with little regard to traditional Agua Caliente uses. In the 1890s, railway developers took half the valley for real estate development, forcing the band to accept a chequerboard pattern of alternative square-mile blocks. The Agua Caliente lost control of their land, but financially, at least, they got the last laugh.

Rather than evicting settlers, the band began charging rent. The group owns 6700 acres, nearly 10¼ square miles, of Palm Springs itself, plus similar sections across the Valley. As the area's largest landowner, the Agua Caliente have long been amongst the most prosperous Native American groups in the country. With legal changes that effectively open Native lands to unrestricted gambling and casino operations, the Agua Caliente have been the biggest winners in Palm Spring's steady explosion of popularity.

Palm Springs Aerial Tramway $$ One Tramway Rd; tel: (760) 325-1391 or (888) 515-8726; fax: (760) 325-6682; web: www.ps tramway.com Open Mon–Fri 1000–2145. Sat–Sun 0800–2145

Palm Springs Aerial Tramway◆◆◆

The **Palm Springs Aerial Tramway** floats 2½ miles from the valley floor to Mount San Jacinto (8516ft) in 14 minutes. The views up (or down) are breathtaking, stretching from the San Jacinto Mountains east to the highlands of **Joshua Tree National Park◆◆◆** (*see page 107*). Be prepared for a 40°F (4°C)-plus temperature change between top and bottom, including deep snow in winter.

Palm Springs Air Museum $ 745 N. Gene Autry Trail; tel: (760) 778-6262; fax: (760) 320-2548; web: www.airmuseum.org Open daily 1000–1700.

Palm Springs Air Museum◆

World War II is the focus for the Air Museum. Ageing air buffs (and occasionally their grandchildren) slaver over 30 restored aircraft, including a Curtiss P-40 Warhawk, a P-51 Mustang and a Boeing B-17 Flying Fortress.

Palm Springs Desert Museum $ 101 Museum Dr.; tel: (760) 325-0189; web: www.psmuseum.org Open Tue–Sat 1000–1700 Sun 1200–1500.

Palm Springs Desert Museum◆◆

The museum is dedicated to desert art, natural science and performing art. The natural science wing is a solid introduction to desert geology, flora, fauna and ecology, while the art collection focuses on the 20th century and California artists.

Village Green Heritage Center $ 221 S. Palm Canyon Dr.; tel: (760) 323-8297; fax: (760) 320-2561. Open Wed and Fri 1200–1500 Thur 1000–1600 mid Oct–May.

Village Green Heritage Center◆

The **Village Green Heritage Center** contains Palm Springs' first two permanent buildings, a hotel and home, both now used as museums by the Palm Springs Historical Society.

Wind Farm Tours $$ I-10, Indian Rd exit; tel: (760) 251-1997. Tours daily by advance booking.

Wind Farms◆

It's impossible to miss the ranks of windmills off I-10 at the San Gorgonio Pass just before Palm Springs. Look for the spreading groves of more than 4000 wind turbines, their steel blades glinting in the desert sun. Steady breezes blow through the pass nearly every day of

Golf

The Coachella Valley boasts between 90 and 100 golf courses, some with up to 54 holes. Most of the world's best-known course designers have at least one Palm Springs course to their credit. But regardless of the designer, nearly every Palm Springs course incorporates the almost jarring juxtaposition of rolling emerald green fairways with dusky cacti and stark rock formations leading to mountain heights. The scenery can be as hazardous as any sand trap or hidden lake.

Most courses are open for public play, but tee times can be difficult to obtain on short notice, especially the much sought-after early morning slots in winter. Major resorts can arrange tee times to match guest hotel bookings, but public courses generally only accept tee reservations between one and seven days in advance. Several local companies guarantee tee times up to six months in advance, but demand full prepayment of course fees. The Palm Springs Desert Resorts CVB *Golf Guide* offers current details.

the year (carrying Los Angeles smog into the desert in the process), generating enough electricity to power a small city. The only way to see the turbines up close is with **Wind Farm Tours**, driving among the whirling generators in electric-powered carts. The visitor centre has an ever-changing collection of unusual electric vehicles.

Shopping

Shopping in Palm Springs has become entertainment, a way to see, to be seen and confirm one's place in the world of conspicuous consumption. Most shops and boutiques open by mid-morning, but serious shoppers restrain themselves until after lunch. That's when the crowds begin to trawl the pavements along **North Palm Canyon Drive**✦✦✦ in Palm Springs.

All of the famous brand names are represented, usually at full price, as well as the requisite number of T-shirt shops, souvenir stands and Southwestern art that ranges from the exquisite to exquisitely painful. Best bet is the Thursday evening Village Fest **street fair** which features a collection of stands hawking anything from tawdry souvenirs to artful jewellery.

Serious shoppers make a pilgrimage to **Palm Desert**, just down Hwy 111, and **El Paseo**, a 2-mile strip of trendy boutiques that can match anything on offer along LA's Rodeo Drive. The slightly younger set heads for the nearby **Gardens on El Paseo**, which bills itself as Palm Springs' first development for shoppers in their 20s, 30s and 40s, touting prices more in line with Los Angeles than Beverly Hills.

Accommodation and food

Palm Springs was built for the rich and famous. Luxury resorts abound, especially in Indian Wells, La Quinta and Rancho Mirage. Rates can be exorbitant in winter, but look for summer discounts of up to 70 per cent at major resorts and 20–30 per cent at smaller hotels. The Palm Springs Desert Resorts CVB offers a free booking service; *tel: (800) 417-3529*, for accommodation, golf and other activities.

La Quinta Resort & Club $$$ *49499 Eisenhower Dr., La Quinta; tel: (760) 564-4111 or (800) 598-3828; fax: (760) 564-1578; web: www.LaQuintaResort.com.* La Quinta is 'Old Palm Springs', the Coachella Valley's original 1920s resort. It's still one of Palm Spring's most attractive, a collection of flower-bedecked *casitas* at the foot of the Santa Rosa Mountains, surrounded by the inevitable golf courses.

Spa Hotel and Casino $$$ *100 N. Indian Canyon Dr, Palm Springs; tel: (760) 325-1461 or (800) 854-1279; fax: (760) 325-3344; web: www.aguacaliente.org/spa.* The spa is built around mineral hot

Opposite
La Quinta Hotel golf and tennis resort

The Coachella Valley made its first fortune on farming, watered by an immense Ice Age aquifer that lies beneath the sands. Early immigrants who saw the physical and climactic resemblance to North Africa and the Middle East planted groves of date trees. A number of growers remain, most notably **Shields Date Gardens**✧✧✧ *80225 Hwy 111; tel: (760) 347-0996 or (800) 414-2555; fax: (760) 342-3288.* Built in the 1920s and refurbished in the 1950s, Shields produce the best date milk shakes in the Valley, the perfect accompaniment to its tongue-in-cheek film, *The Romance and Sex Life of the Date* – and the dates are hard to resist.

springs long used by the Agua Caliente band for healing; the elegant buildings, hotel and casino are more recent (and more profitable) additions.

Two Bunch Palms $$$ *67-425 Two Bunch Palms Trail; Desert Hot Springs; tel:(760) 329-8791 or (800) 472-4334; fax: (760) 329-1317; web: www.twobunchpalms.com.* Two Bunch was the area's original resort escape, a favourite with gangster Al Capone as well as Hollywood celebs of the 1930s. It's still Palm Spring's most sybaritic, private and star-ridden resort – no sightseers allowed.

All of the major resorts have much-advertised restaurants, most offering Californian or Southwestern fusion cuisine at top prices. Other possibilities:

John Henry's Café $$ *1785 Tahquitz Canyon Way; tel: (760) 327-7667*, serves an eclectic American menu at reasonable prices.

Las Casuelas $$ *368 N. Palm Canyon Dr.; tel: (760) 325-3213*, is the original of a string of family-owned Mexican restaurants (and most popular with locals).

Louise's Pantry $ *124 S. Palm Canyon Dr.; tel: (760) 325-5124*, is one of the Valley's original 1950s diners, especially good for breakfast.

Desert Parks

Ratings

Scenery	●●●●●
Children	●●●●○
History	●●●●○
Geology	●●●●○
Food and drink	●●●○○
Outdoor activities	●●●○○
Museums	●●○○○
Architecture	●○○○○

California's desert parks include the lowest and the hottest corners of the western hemisphere. To the uninitiated, desert is dry and dangerous, at best an empty quarter to be skirted or transited as quickly as possible. On closer look, it's a delicate balance of extremes between too hot and too cold, too dry and too wet, stark, twisted and irresistibly alluring.

The harsh midday sun seems to bleach all colour and texture from desert landscapes, leaving neither shade nor relief from the ceaseless glare. But the softer light of morning and afternoon reveal a rugged grace, a palette of colours and shapes that change almost by the second. Far from the crowds, the pollution and the enveloping vegetation of the coast, the desert is California in its finest and most unabashed grandeur.

DEATH VALLEY JUNCTION*

Once a railway junction town, Death Valley Junction is little more than the **Amargosa Opera House***. Owner Marta Becket produces and performs mime-ballets in winter; call for schedule and bookings. The Opera House also has accommodation.

DEATH VALLEY NATIONAL PARK*

ⓘ Death Valley National Park $
Box 579, Death Valley, CA 92328;
tel: (760) 786-2331;
fax: (760) 786-2236;
web: www.nps.gov/deva/

Only 90 miles long and 10 miles across, Death Valley offers the nation's most dramatically desolate scenery. America's hottest temperature, 134°F (56°C), was recorded in Death Valley in 1913; average summer days hit 116°F (47°). The National Park protects vast stretches of mountain and desert surrounding the basin.

Death Valley was formed as the basin floor subsided, leaving precipitous mountains on all sides. The Sierra Nevada blocks nearly

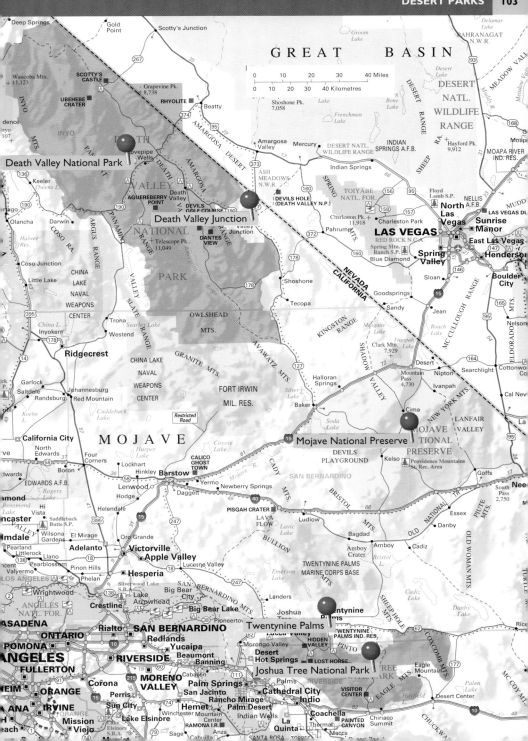

Death Valley National Park

Death Valley Junction

Mojave National Preserve

Twentynine Palms

Joshua Tree National Park

ⓘ **Death Valley
Chamber of
Commerce**
*Box 157, Shoshone, CA
92384; tel: (760) 852-4524;
fax: (760) 852-4414.
Open daily 0900–1600.*

all rainfall; Furnace Creek averages barely 1½ins of rain yearly. Climactic changes turned an enormous lake 600ft deep into desert pans cracked into hexagons and piled high with salt crystals. Softer sediments have eroded into vast badlands stained every colour of the rainbow.

Despite its name, Death Valley is anything but dead. Conifers grow on the cooler, wetter heights of the Panamint Mountains. The lower slopes are generally too dry and too salty for cacti, but creosote and other coarse bushes thrive. Even the valley bottom, 282ft *below* sea level, sports unique plants and animals in hot, salty marshes.

Errant immigrants gave Death Valley its name and reputation. Hoping to avoid snowy Sierra passes to the north, two bands of gold prospectors stumbled into the valley in 1849. Nearly all survived but were impressed enough by the harsh terrain to call it Death Valley.

There were several abortive mining booms in the 19th century, but only a late-century borax boom brought much permanent change. Millennia of evaporation concentrated boron salts into fluffy

Below
Badwater – nearly as low as you
can get in North America

Furnace Creek Visitor Center and Museum *tel: (760) 786-2331. Open daily 0800–1800.* Visitor centres at **Stovepipe Wells** and **Scotty's Castle** *Open 0800–1700.*

'cottonball' crystals. Workers collected the cottonballs which were processed into borax and used to make fine jewellery, glass and washing powder.

Twenty-mule teams hauled wagons from **Harmony Borax Works**✦ 165 miles to the railway at Mojave. In 1907, a railway (now abandoned) began hauling borax to **Death Valley Junction**✦. Hoping to stimulate tourism and boost revenues, railway owners built the **Furnace Creek Inn**✦✦✦ in 1927. As the inn prospered, less expensive cabins were added at **Furnace Creek Ranch**✦✦. Death Valley became a National Monument in 1933 and a National Park in 1994.

Paved roads are passable all year, but most of Death Valley's gravel roads are meant for four-wheel drive. Always check with park rangers before venturing off-road.

Artists Drive✦✦ (*south of Furnace Creek, off Badwater Rd, vehicles over 25ft prohibited*) is a 9-mile, one-way loop through brightly coloured badlands and alluvial fans. **Artists Palette**✦✦✦, half-way through the drive, displays a startling patchwork of intense red, yellow, orange, green, violet, brown and black tones. Colours are most vivid in late afternoon.

Badwater✦✦ (*south of Furnace Creek*), 279.8ft below sea level, was long accepted as the nadir of North America. More accurate surveys have found two lower spots, both 282ft below sea level, a few miles away and unmarked. The highly mineralised water isn't poisonous, just a very effective laxative.

Dantes View✦✦✦ (*off Hwy 190 east of Furnace Creek*) is one of the most stunning vistas in Death Valley. Located one mile directly above Badwater, the view stretches across the basin to **Telescope Peak** (11,049ft) and beyond to **Mount Whitney** (14,496ft), the tallest peak in the continental US. Colours and views are best in early morning.

Devil's Golf Course✦✦✦ (*south of Furnace Creek*) is more than 200 square miles of crystalline salt towers sculpted by wind and rain. The salt cracks and groans audibly with temperature changes.

Furnace Creek✦✦✦ is an oasis that has become Death Valley's centre for accommodation (Furnace Creek Inn and Ranch) and activities (park visitor centre). The natural spring that watered hay fields in the last century now keeps the world's lowest golf course green. The **Borax Museum**✦ (*Furnace Creek Resort; tel: (760) 786-2345, open daily 0830–1600*) was originally the office and bunkhouse for 20-mule team borax trains. Museum collections include borax mining equipment as well a 20-mule wagon.

Harmony Borax Works✦ (*north of Furnace Creek*) commemorates the 1880s borax boom. A short path passes the refinery ruins and outlying buildings; a 3-mile trail leads to the borax 'cottonballs' labourers collected.

Rhyolite*** (*northeast of Furnace Creek, near Beatty, Nevada*) is a stark, imposing collection of stone and concrete ruins from a 1904 boom town. The ruins are haunting at sunset.

Salt Creek* (*north of Furnace Creek*) shows the resilience of the inch-long pupfish (*genus Cyprinodon*) which has adapted to the heat, salinity and periodic drought of Death Valley. Related species are found in **Anza-Borrego Desert State Park** (*see page 90*) and other desert water courses.

Scotty's Castle*** (*north of Furnace Creek; tel: (760) 786-2392, open daily 0830–1700*) represents the extravagant marriage of money (Chicago insurance magnate Albert Johnson) and myth (local cowboy, occasional miner and full-time prevaricator Walter 'Scotty' Scott). 'Scotty' convinced Johnson to build the Spanish-Moorish mansion in 1924 as a restful retreat. Grounds surrounding the $2.4 million extravaganza were never completed, but the interior is elegantly finished with tiles, handcrafted furniture, leather and textiles. The interior is open by guided tour only – expect long queues in winter.

Stovepipe Wells** (*northwest of Furnace Creek*) was Death Valley's original settlement; stovepipes driven into the sand to create wells gave it its name. Visitor facilities at Stovepipe Wells Village are a few miles south of the original well, across an immense field of **sand dunes*****. The dunes are at their sensuous best in the long shadows near dawn and sunset.

Ubehebe Crater** (*west of Scotty's Castle*), 600ft deep and 2600ft wide, was created by an immense volcanic explosion in the last few thousand years. The sides of the cauldron are layered with tones of orange and grey.

Zabriskie Point*** (*south of Furnace Creek*) overlooks the Golden Canyon badlands from the east. The heavily eroded landscape glows pink in the first few minutes after dawn.

Accommodation and food in Death Valley

Furnace Creek Inn $$$ *Furnace Creek; tel: (760) 786-2345; fax: (760) 786-2361; web: www.furnacecreekresort.com*, was built in the 1920s as a vaguely Moorish resort, still among the poshest accommodation in an American desert park.

Furnace Creek Ranch $$–$$$ *Furnace Creek; tel: (760) 786-2345; fax: (760) 786-9945; web: www.furnacecreekresort.com*, is the Inn's motel-like alternative.

Panamint Springs $$ *Hwy 190; tel: (702) 482-7680*, has a motel, restaurant, campground and RV park.

Stovepipe Wells Village $$ *Stovepipe Wells; tel: (760) 786-2387; fax: (760) 786-2389*, offers accommodation, supplies and information for the northern end of Death Valley.

All four accommodation locations have restaurants and general stores. Picnic supplies are more reasonable outside the park.

JOSHUA TREE NATIONAL PARK✧✧✧

Joshua Tree National Park $
74485 National Park Dr., Twentynine Palms, CA 92277; tel: (760) 367-5500; fax: (760) 367-6392; web: www.nps.gov/jotr/

Named for wildly gesticulating trees that are actually lilies, Joshua Tree is an anomaly among national parks. There are no IMAX® theatres, no grand lodges, no biggest-smallest-best-tallest-only-on-earth attractions. In fact, there isn't much of *anything* here except nature – more than 800,000 acres, nearly all of it wilderness.

The park is an eerie, almost mystical landscape. Early and late in the day, long shadows and reddish sunlight seem to animate the bizarre landforms and even stranger plants. Jumbled piles of rounded golden boulders rise from the surface, immense mounds of monzogranite that have been cracked, broken, stacked and eroded into shapes reminiscent of twisted Henry Moore sculptures. Climbers from around the world revere the sheer faces of Wonderland Rocks.

Namesake Joshua trees (*Yucca brefifolia*) seem to march across the rolling hills, a vast army of stick figures with multiple arms raised to the heavens as though pointing the way to unseen oases fringed with palm trees and willows. Fuzzy cacti that glow like soft velvet in the sun are actually covered with microscopic spines that are nearly impossible to remove.

In spring, the arid hills and canyons disappear beneath carpets of wildflowers. Just weeks later, the same hillsides have become a blazing midday furnace, parched by the sun. In summer, stick to the Joshua tree forests where temperatures top out around 100°F (38°C), a good 25°F (-4°C) cooler than the lowlands. In winter, the lowland canyons are a comfortable 75°F (24°C) as the highlands shiver in snow.

The two temperature zones are actually two different deserts, the Mojave and the Colorado. There are few sharp distinctions between the two, no boundary signs to mark the amorphous transition. It's a matter of altitude and, even more, of rainfall, variations.

The lower, hotter and drier Colorado Desert is marked by spindly ocotillo bushes, thorny green sticks dripping scarlet blossoms in spring and practically leafless most of the year. With an average of 3ins of rain yearly, double the moisture of Death Valley, the Colorado Desert also supports a varied cacti community. The most common is the jumping cholla (pronounced *'choi-yuh'*), named for its proclivity to hook into unwary passers-by.

Life is easier in the higher and moister Mojave Desert. Lying above 3000ft, the Mojave gets nearly 6ins of rain annually, enough to support vast groves of Joshua trees. Though they grow up to 60ft tall,

Cottonwood Visitor Center
Cottonwood Springs entrance. Open daily 0800–1630.

Joshua trees aren't proper trees, but yuccas, a lily with woody stems. Clumps of spindly leaves at the end of the branches give the appearance of arms waving wildly against the sky. The trees were named by Mormon immigrants who likened the trees to the Biblical prophet Joshua, pointing the way across the desert with raised arms.

One main road bisects the park, from **Cottonwood** in the south, near I-10, to **Twentynine Palms** and Hwy 62 on the north. Another major road runs from the town of **Joshua Tree** south into the park to meet Pinto Basin Rd. Most of the dirt tracks are passable only by four-wheel-drive vehicles; check for current conditions at ranger stations before venturing off the pavement in passenger vehicles. Trailers and RVs are generally not recommended on dirt roads.

Cholla Cactus Garden✦✦✦ (*near Pinto Basin Rd*) provides an easy opportunity to see (but *not* to touch) the most common indicator plant of the Colorado Desert. A short, easy trail winds through an especially dense stand of cholla cacti (*Opuntia bigelovii*). Also called 'teddybear cholla' for their soft, fuzzy appearance, 'jumping cholla' is more painfully accurate. Chunks of cactus seem to leap out, propelled by microscopic spines which snag skin, clothing and almost anything else that brushes past. The large piles of dead cholla are nests built by packrats, which use the prickly pads to protect their dwellings, usually built at the base of a creosote bush.

Just south along Pinto Basin Rd is the **Ocotillo Patch**✦✦✦, the park's most accessible ocotillo thicket. This spiny shrub, noted for its brilliant crimson flowers, is the Colorado Desert's other indicator plant. It's also called Jacob's staff, candlewood, coachwhip and vine cactus, a testament to the thorns along the limber, nearly leafless branches.

Cottonwood Spring✦✦ (*south entrance, off I-10*) is a pleasant oasis one mile east of the visitor centre. The springs are natural, the palms a human addition much used by birds and other wildlife.

Desert Queen Mine✦ (*off a dirt road running north opposite Geology Tour Rd*) lies ¾-mile along an easy trail, a collection of rusting mine machinery. The mine shafts and tunnels are extremely dangerous. A more strenuous half-day walk leads to the **Lost Horse Mine**✦✦ and the remains of a ten-stamp mill.

Desert Queen Ranch✦✦✦ (*open by guided tour only, check with ranger stations for current tour schedule*) is a one-family ghost town that died in 1969. The ranch includes an adobe barn from the 1880s, a schoolhouse, junked cars, a windmill, antique mining equipment and ranch fittings crafted from Joshua tree wood.

Fortynine Palms Oasis✦✦✦ (*off Canyon Rd, 4 miles west of Twentynine Palms*) is the best area for spring wildflowers. Desert annuals carpet the ground, barrel cacti explode with blooms and the canyon pool is rimmed with native fan palms. The 3-mile return hike is moderately

Wind-eroded boulders in the Joshua Tree National Park

strenuous; the trail may be closed during late summer against fire danger.

Geology Tour Road✦✦✦ (*from Queen Valley, check road conditions at the visitor centre before setting out*) is an 18-mile gravel loop (*sometimes* passable by passenger cars) through some of the parks most spectacular geological features. Great alluvial fans spill toward the road and massive monzogranite heaps tower over the Joshua trees surrounding a desert *playa*, or dry lake bed. Visitor centres sell an excellent road guide.

Keys View✦✦✦ (*20 miles south of Joshua Tree town, via Quail Springs and Keys View Rds*) offers the most spectacular panoramas in the park, from atop the San Bernardino Mountains (5185ft) across the Coachella Valley to the San Jacinto Range and south to the Salton Sea.

Oasis of Mara✦✦✦ (*Oasis Visitor Center, Twentynine Palms*) was the original oasis of 29 palms first recorded in an 1855 survey. The name *mara* means 'little water' in the language of the Chemehuevi people who occupied the area before White prospectors and settlers arrived. The oasis once held an open pool of water, but years of overdrafting have lowered the water table. An easy ½-mile trail leads from the visitor centre to the oasis.

ⓘ **Oasis Visitor Center** *Twentynine Palms; tel: (760) 367-7511, Open daily 0800–1700.*

🏛 **General Patton Memorial Museum** *$ off I-10, 4½ miles east of Cottonwood Spring Rd; tel: (760) 227-3483. Open daily 0930–1630.*

Queen Valley✦✦✦ (*Pinto Valley Rd, centre of the park*) has the park's largest and healthiest stands of Joshua trees, thousands of them marching toward the horizon in every direction. **Jumbo Rocks Campground** offer fine vistas with Joshua trees set against soaring monzogranite towers and spires.

General Patton Memorial Museum✦ contains World War II memorabilia, with special displays of tanks and artillery used by Patton's training camps in Joshua Tree and ten other southwestern desert camps. Camp Young was just off I-10 on Cottonwood Spring Rd.

Accommodation and food in Joshua Tree National Park

There are a number of camp-grounds in the park, but no accommodation or restaurants. The Palm Springs area (*see page 94*) has the best variety near the park, although Twentynine Palms (*see page 112*) the closest centre.

Mojave National Preserve ❖❖❖

Joshua trees thrive even in the hot dry desert

ⓘ Mojave National Preserve *222 E. Main St, Ste 202, Barstow, CA 92311; tel: (760) 255-8801; web: www.nps.gov/moja/, open Mon–Fri 0800–1700.*

This 'Lonesome Triangle' of Mojave Desert between I-40, I-15 and the Nevada border is more mountain than sand. The vast expanse (1.4 million acres) is accented by cinder cones, sand dunes, caverns, precipitous mountains and lava mesas. Joshua tree forests thrive in the upper elevations; the lower slopes are threadbare beneath a sparse carpet of creosote brush.

Though desolate in human terms, this rugged triangle is home to 700 species of plants and 300 different kinds of animals. It's also an historic thoroughfare. Native Americans have been traversing the region for at least 10,000 years, trading Coastal California goods as far east as Central Mexico. Spanish explorers followed in the 1770s, then American explorers, ranchers, railway lines and highways.

But except for scattered ranches and mines, there has been little permanent settlement. The Eastern Mojave has been a land where anything goes and no one much minded so long as it was safely out of sight. Growing recreational use has changed the government's traditional hands-off policies. The area became a National Preserve in 1994 over fierce local opposition. Ranchers, miners, off-road vehicle users and landowners still object to stricter controls over what many see as *their* land, by right of use if not of ownership.

Signs of human use are never far away, from abandoned mine sites to shot-out Preserve signs, rusted railway tracks and decrepit buildings, but the desert has managed to preserve its expansive emptiness. Without four-wheel drive, stick to the main roads. Rutted side-tracks often disappear into fields of sand or boulders bounded by steep cliffs.

The tiny town of **Amboy**, south of **Mojave National Preserve**, was once an important stop for the transcontinental railway service and auto traffic on Route 66, America's first trans-continental highway. More modern routes have since bypassed Amboy.

Cima Dome❖ (*off Cima Rd, south of Valley Wells*) is best seen from a distance. The almost-perfectly formed white batholith (molten magma that solidified before reaching the surface) rises 1500ft above the surrounding plain, but the gentle rise is difficult to see up close. The 75-square-mile dome is cloaked in Joshua trees. The tiny town of

ℹ️ Needles Information Center *707 W. Broadway, Needles, CA 92363; tel: (760) 326-6322; fax: (760) 326-4119.*

Hole-in-the-Wall Ranger Station *Hole-in-the-Wall Campground; tel: (760) 928-2572. Open winter.*

California Welcome Center *2796 Tanger Way, Ste 100 (Tanger Outlet Center), Barstow, CA 92311; tel: (760) 253-4813; fax: (760) 253-4814. Open daily 0900–2000.*

🏛️ Mitchell Caverns Providence Mountains State Recreation Area *Box 1, Essex, CA 92332; tel: (760) 928-2586. Caverns open by guided tour, call for times.*

Cima originated as a railway siding.

Cinder Cones Natural National Landmark✦✦ (*off Kelbaker Rd, north of Kelso*) is a collection of young (1000–10 million-years-old) cinder cones.

Hole-in-the-Wall Campground✦✦ (*Essex Rd, off I-40*) is named for the wall of rhyolite lava, filled with holes like rocky Swiss cheese.

Kelso Dunes✦✦✦ (*near Kelso, centre of the Preserve*) are among the tallest sand dunes in California, 600–700ft at the crest fanning out across 45 square miles. The golden rose quartz sand has blown in from the Mojave Sink, to the northwest. Allow about two hours to walk to the dune crest and back, plus time to play. The dunes 'sing' as sand slides from the crest, reverberations that sound like a whispering Tibetian gong. Best times to visit are early or late in the day, preferably sunrise/sunset, when long shadows highlight the undulating dune ridges.

Mitchell Caverns✦✦ (*Essex Rd off I-40*) are the only caves in Southern California developed for tourism. Water-borne deposits have created a wonderland of limestone curtains, stalactites, stalagmites and other rocky formations, all accessible by stairs and walkways. The cave is open for guided tours only. The easy **Mary Beal Nature Trail✦✦** offers a scenic introduction to the surrounding **Providence Mountains State Recreation Area✦✦✦**

Shoshone is a small supply town for Death Valley at the junction of Hwy 178 (the route from Pahrump and Las Vegas, Nevada) and Hwy 127 from Baker.

Zzyzx✦✦ (*Zzyzx Rd, off I-10 west of Baker*) is the remains of a 60-room spa, hotel, church, castle and radio station built in the 1940s by self-proclaimed minister/healer Curtis Springer. Springer invented the name (pronounced 'zye-zix', to rhyme with 'size six') to be the last entry in the telephone book. The spa was closed in 1974 when Springer was convicted on tax, health and drug charges; the facility is now a California State University research station.

Researchers are usually more than happy to be interrupted. If the station is unstaffed (as it usually is), signboards describe local natural history and the endangered Mojave chub (a desert fish). The old bathhouse offers good views of dry Soda Lake and the picturesque mountains beyond.

Accommodation and food in Mojave National Preserve

There is camping, but no accommodation, within the Preserve. Fuel and very limited picnic supplies are available in Cima and Nipton. Pick up supplies before entering the Preserve.

Twentynine Palms

i **Twentynine Palms Chamber of Commerce** 6455 Mesquite Ave, Twentynine Palms, CA 92277; tel: (760) 367-3445; fax: (760) 367-3366. Open Mon–Fri 0900–1700.

H **Hi-Desert Nature Museum $** Community Center Complex, 57116 Twentynine Palms Hwy, Yucca Valley; tel: (760) 369-7212; fax: (760) 369-1605. Open Tue–Sun 1000–1700.

Edchada's $ Hwy 62; tel: (760) 367-2131, open for lunch and dinner, serves good Mexican dishes.

The Finicky Coyote $ Hwy 62; tel: (760) 367-2429, open breakfast–dinner, has solid home-made soups, sandwiches and desserts.

Named for the palm trees surrounding Mara Oasis (Joshua Tree National Park headquarters), Twentynine Palms has become a busy desert town as headquarters for the **Marine Corps Air Ground Combat Center** (the US Marine Corps' largest base) and **Joshua Tree National Park**. The Chamber of Commerce publishes a free map to public murals depicting area history. **Hi-Desert Nature Museum** covers Southern California flora, fauna and natural history.

Accommodation and food in Twentynine Palms

Circle C Lodge $$ 6340 El Ray Ave; tel: (760) 367-7615; fax: (760) 361-0247, includes Continental breakfast and a swimming pool.

The 29 Palms Inn $$–$$$ adjacent to the Visitor Center; tel: (760) 367-3050; fax: (760) 367-4425, open for lunch and dinner, is the closest accommodation to the park. The inn also has the best restaurant $$ in the area, with steaks, seafood and chicken.

Suggested tour

Total distance: 260 miles.

Time: One gruelling driving day, **Palm Springs** ❶ to **Furnace Creek** ❷; three–five days touring with overnight stops in **Twentynine Palms** ❸, **Baker** ❹ and **Death Valley** ❺.

Links: Palm Springs to the west, Las Vegas to the east, Anza-Borrego Desert State Park to the south.

Route: From **Indio** ❻, follow I-10 24 miles east to Cottonwood Springs Rd and **Joshua Tree National Park** ❼. Drive north through the Park to **Twentynine Palms** ❸, then east and north to **Amboy** ❽ and the **Mojave National Preserve** ❾. Follow Kelbaker Rd through the Preserve to **Kels** ❿.

Also worth exploring:

Shimmering **Salton Sea**✳, south of Palm Springs, was created when a Colorado River aqueduct ruptured in 1905. Measuring 35 miles by 15 miles, it's one of the world's largest inland bodies of salt water, the result of agricultural runoff. Bird-watching is extremely good along the shoreline, as is fishing, but the polluted, sometimes foul-smelling lake is generally unattractive for swimming.

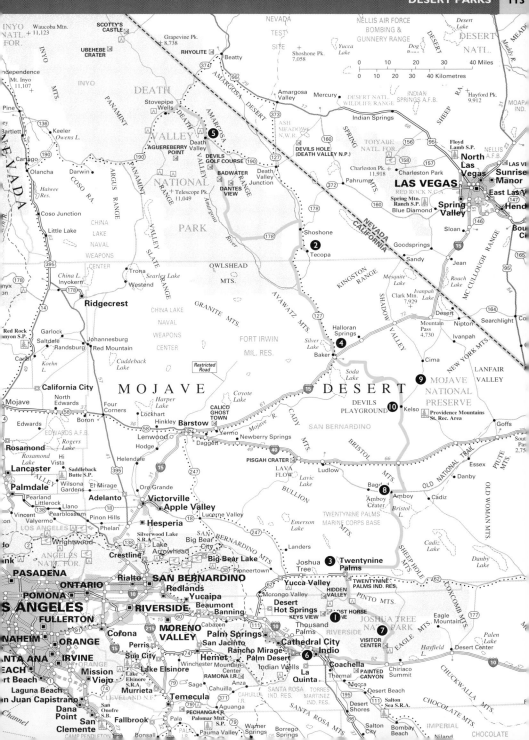

Spine of the Sierras

Ratings

Outdoor activities	●●●●○
Geology	●●●●○
Scenery	●●●●○
Wildlife	●●●○○
History	●●●○○
Children	●●●○○
Food and drink	●●○○○

The eastern slope of the Sierra Nevada is steeper and more dramatic than the gentle foothills leading up from the Central Valley, a mix of serrated peaks, blistering desert, alkaline lakes and rushing streams squeezed into a narrow corridor between snowcapped summits and The Great American Desert in Nevada. It's also an area almost devoid of people – no Interstate highways, no flashing neon resorts, no rush hour. Hwy 395 provides easy north–south travel, but winter snows close most westbound mountain passes during November to May.

BIG PINE✦

ⓘ Big Pine Chamber of Commerce
126 S. Main St, Big Pine, CA 93513; tel: (760) 938-2114.

Ⓗ Ancient Bristlecone Pine Forest *off Hwy 168 east of Big Pine; tel: (760) 873-2500. Open in summer.*

The town of Big Pine is little more than a collection of petrol stations and motels, but it is the gateway to two of the region's top attractions, the **Ancient Bristlecone Pine Forest**✦✦✦ (*off Hwy 168; tel: (760) 873-2500*) and **Palisade Glacier**✦ (*Glacier Lodge Rd, west*).

Bristlecone pines (*Pinus longaeva*) are the oldest living things on earth, usually clinging to inaccessible mountain slopes. The world's only drive-up stand of bristlecones is 10,000ft up the **White Mountains**, east of Big Pine. Bristlecones have been growing on these mountains for at least 4500 years, gnarled branches bleached blonde by centuries of blasting wind, snow and sand beneath a burning sun. The twisted trunks grow only an inch in diameter each century, dead as any chunk of driftwood except for an occasional ribbon of bark leading to a splash of needles and cones on some remote branch.

Schulman Grove✦✦, named for the researcher who first dated the trees in the 1950s, lies at the end of a twisting paved road. Look for

two self-guiding trails, the 1-mile **Discovery Trail** and the slightly longer **Methuselah Trail**, which passes the 4700-year-old Methuselah Tree and the **visitor center**. **Patriarch Grove**, 11 miles beyond on a gravel road, offers spectacular views of the Sierras, the Great Basin in Nevada, and the Patriarch Tree, the largest bristlecone. **Palisade** is the southernmost glacier in the US, looming above Big Pine Canyon west of town at the end of Glacier Lodge Rd, 11 miles west from Hwy 395.

BISHOP

Bishop Chamber of Commerce 690 N. Main St, Bishop, CA 93514; tel: (760) 873-8405; fax: (760) 873-6999; web: www.bishopvisitor.com

Bureau of Land Management (BLM) 785 N. Main St (Cottonwood Plaza); tel: (760) 872-4881. Open Mon–Fri 0800–1600.

Paiute-Shoshone Indian Culture Center $ 2300 W. Line St; tel: (760) 873-4478. Mar–Oct open daily 1000–1500, Nov–Feb Mon–Fri 1000–1600.

Red Rock Canyon Petroglyphs Off Hwy 6; tel: (760) 872-4881. Stop at the BLM office for free permit and maps.

Bishop is the largest town in the Owens Valley, one of the few to survive Los Angeles' insatiable thirst. In 1910, about 4500 people lived between Bishop and Owens Lake, just south of Lone Pine. The valley floor was once a maze of orchards, vineyards and fields of corn, wheat and potatoes, while a steamship plied the waters of **Owens Lake**.

But Los Angeles, one of California's fastest growing cities, needed more water. The **Owens Valley** had the bad luck to be the nearest source. LA's Department of Water and Power (DWP), chief engineer William Mulholland and his cronies bought up most of the Valley, either through sham corporations or questionable legal tactics. Local officials were bribed or intimidated with the sort of semi-legal real-estate schemes depicted in the 1974 Jack Nicholson film *Chinatown*.

When the Owens Valley Aqueduct opened in 1913, nearly all of the water that once ran through the Owens Valley was diverted to Los Angeles. Steely blue Owens Lake became a pinkish salt flat, and fields and orchards gave way to dunes as the population drifted away.

Bishop, at the head of the Valley, survived to become a burst of civilisation surrounded by mountain wilderness that lures anglers (fantastic fly-fishing), hikers, mountain climbers and other outdoor lovers. The **Owens Valley Paiute-Shoshone Indian Culture Center** (2300 W. Line St; tel: (760) 873-4478) displays basketry, weaving, food gathering and other traditional activities carried out by the area's original inhabitants. The most visible signs of Native American history are the **petroglyphs** scattered about the valley. The meaning of the figures pecked into rocks is long lost, but the best place to see them is the **Red Rock Canyon Petroglyphs** (off Hwy 6). Most of the images are found at places where water used to be, nearly all of them now dry, courtesy of Los Angeles.

Food in Bishop

Jack's Waffle Shop $ 437 N. Main St; tel: (760) 872-7971, is an institution. **Erick Schat's Bakery** $ 763 N. Main St; tel: (760) 873-7156, has good espresso, light meals and Dutch-style baked goods. **Whiskey Creek** $$ 254 N. Main St; tel: (760) 873-7174, offers American cuisine and Bishop's liveliest bar.

BRIDGEPORT*

Film buffs might recognize Bridgeport as the village that gave fugitive Robert Mitchum a new start in the 1947 film *Out of the Past*. Mitchum's Mono Motor Service petrol station has disappeared, but the tiny town is otherwise little changed. Those not addicted to the *film noir* genre might watch for the turnoff to **Bodie***** (*see page 120*), 6 miles south.

INDEPENDENCE*

Eastern California Museum
155 Grant St; tel: (760) 878-0364. Open Wed–Mon 1000–1600.

The small town was named for Fort Independence, established in 1862 to protect White settlers from Paiutes angry at the usurpation of their lands. It is better known for the **Manzanar Relocation Camp****, 6 miles south.

Manzanar (the name means 'apple orchard' in Spanish) was a thriving apple- and pear-growing town around the turn of the century that died when Los Angeles diverted its water south. It was reborn during World War II as a desolate internment camp for 10,000 mostly California-born Americans of Japanese ancestry. Considered a threat by military officials, Japanese-Americans were imprisoned until 1944 and their property confiscated.

Most of the internees had owned businesses and homes in coastal California; Manzanar gave them 20sq ft per family in flimsy, paper-covered wooden barracks behind barbed wire fences, buffeted by freezing winter winds and sweltering summer heat. It took the US government more than 40 years to settle compensation claims and apologise.

All that remains are a few foundations visible amidst the sagebrush, a pair of ornamental gates, a garage and a cemetery obelisk marking the National Historic Site.

The **Eastern California Museum*** details the impact of Manzanar on the many children who grew up behind the barbed wire. Other displays cover Owens Valley environments, Paiute and settler artefacts, farming implements and mining equipment.

Just north of town is **Mount Whitney State Fish Hatchery** (*Fish Hatchery Rd; tel: (760) 878-2272*), a stone monastery-style building with a Tudor tower and the ruins of Fort Independence, abandoned in 1877.

LONE PINE*

This is a convenient base for exploring the nearby mountains, including 14,494ft **Mount Whitney*** and desert areas. It's also the first touch of civilisation west from Death Valley. The best stop is the **Eastern Sierra Interagency Visitor Center***** (*Hwy 395/136 junction;*

ⓘ **Lone Pine Chamber of Commerce** *126 S. Main St, Lone Pine, CA 93545; tel: (760) 876-4444; fax: (760) 876-9205; web: www.lone-pine.com*

tel: (760) 876-6222) which has complete information on Owens Valley attractions as well as routes into Death Valley.

If the scenery seems familiar, it probably is. Cowboys, Indians (Native Americans), outlaws, Bengal lancers and space aliens have been parading before cinema cameras in the **Alabama Hills**✦✦ since the early 1920s. Six-mile **Movie Flat Rd**✦✦✦ (*Hwy 395 to Whitney Portal Rd*) remains a favourite with film-makers. The gravel road is easily passable by cars and RVs, but unsigned side roads can be rough.

Having driven Movie Flat Rd, visit the **Indian Trading Post**✦ (*137 S. Main St; tel: (760) 876-4641*). The souvenir stock is standard, but the front door frame was signed by Gary Cooper, Errol Flynn, John Wayne and other film stars.

MAMMOTH LAKES✦

ⓘ **Mammoth Lakes Visitors Bureau** *437 Old Mammoth Rd, Suite Y, Minaret Village, Mammoth Lakes, CA 93546; tel: (760) 934-2712, (888) 466-2666 or (800) 367-6572; web: www.visitmammoth.com*

Mammoth Lakes/US Forest Service Visitors Center *Hwy 203; tel: (760) 924-5500. Open daily 0800-1700.* The centre dispenses outdoor recreation and camping information and backcountry pemits.

Originally a short-lived gold-rush town, Mammoth is California's second most popular mountain resort after Lake Tahoe. A major ski centre in winter, more than 50 miles of skiing trails become mountain bike runs in summer. Either season, the gondola to the top of Mammoth Mountain provides stunning **views**✦✦ north to Mono Lake. **Mammoth Lakes Basin**✦, just south, is a glacial depression with six scenic lakes as alluring to winter alpine skiers as to summer hikers. **June Lake**✦✦, just north, is a quieter alternative with similar scenery.

Right
Tufa formations at Mono Lake echo the peaks of the Sierra Nevada Mountains

Devil's Postpile National Monument
14 miles on Hwy 203; tel: (760) 934-2289. Open June–Oct. In summer, day visitors (but not campers) must take public transport from Mammoth Mountain Inn.

Mammoth's most unusual sight is **Devil's Postpile National Monument✦✦**, a wall of basalt columns 60ft tall, rising above the middle fork of the San Joaquin River. The pile was formed about 100,000 years ago as a basalt flow from Mammoth Mountain cooled and cracked into hexagonal and octagonal posts. A glacier cut through the area about 10,000 years ago, exposing the formation.

The pile is less than a half-mile by trail from monument head-quarters; a second trail leads to the top of the pile, which resembles a tiled floor. The main trail continues 2 miles to **Rainbow Falls✦✦**, a 101ft waterfall renowned for rainbows refracted in the spray around midday. A shorter trail leads to the Falls from **Reds Meadow**, accessible by shuttle from Mammoth Mountain Inn.

Mammoth is famous for its **hot springs✦**, which may be the legacy of North America's most destructive volcanic eruption (about 760,000 years ago) or the forerunner of eruptions yet to come. A favourite soak is **Hot Creek Geothermal Area** (*Airport/Hot Creek Fish Hatchery Rd, off Hwy 395*), an icy mountain stream that mixes with near-boiling water from natural vents. Don't expect solitude and don't settle too close to heat sources – bathers have been scalded to death by unexpected blasts of superheated water.

Accommodation and food in Mammoth Lakes

Beware of winter weekends, when Los Angeles skiers pour into Mammoth, and summer weekends, nearly as popular with mountain bikers and climbers. Midweek is more reasonable. **Mammoth Mountain Inn $$$** *tel: (760) 934-2581*, is *the* place to sleep, at the base of the ski lifts, next to the bike park and overlooking the climbing rock. **Mammoth Lakes Visitors Bureau** provides lodging assistance.

The Stove $ *644 Old Mammoth Rd; tel: (760) 934-2821*, is a long-time favourite for gargantuan portions of American favourites. **Whiskey Creek $$** *Main St and Minaret Rd; tel: (760) 934-2555*, is one of Mammoth's liveliest restaurants and bars and has its own good micro-brews.

MONO LAKE✦✦✦

Mono Basin Scenic Area Visitor Center
Hwy 395, 1 mile north of Lee Vining; tel: (760) 647-3044. Open daily 0900–1700 Apr–Oct, Thur–Mon 0900–1600 the rest of the year.

This other-worldly lake, rimmed by salt flats, twisted mineral towers and new-born mountains, may be the oldest lake in North America. It is also the nesting ground for 85 per cent of all California gulls, which feed on the trillions of shrimp and flies that hatch in the salty, alkaline shallows. The towers are made of tufa, limestone deposited underwater when mineral-laden springs bubbled into the alkaline lake. A new aqueduct to Los Angeles that opened in 1941 dropped water levels by more than 40ft, exposing the bizarre towers and nearly

Mono Lake Committee Information Center/Chamber of Commerce Hwy 395 & 3rd St, Lee Vining; tel: (760) 647-6595. Open daily 0900-1700.

Laws Railroad Museum and Historical Site (operated by the Bishop Museum and Historical Society); tel: (760) 873-5950. From Bishop, take Hwy 396 to Hwy 6, drive 4 miles north and east to Silver Canyon Rd. Laws is a half-mile east. Open daily 1000–1600 except Christmas and Thanksgiving.

Bodie State Historic Park $ Hwy 270 (last 3 miles gravel); tel: (760) 647-6445. Park open all year, but the road may be closed in winter.

destroying the lake. Twenty years of environmental battles forced LA to cut its water usage and agree to restore Mono Lake to historic levels.

The best place to see the tufa towers is **Mono Lake Tufa State Reserve✦✦✦**, on the south shore. The volcanic cones to the south are the **Mono Craters✦**, explosion pits, cinder cones and lava flows from California's youngest mountains. A short trail leads up to the rim of **Panum Crater**, about 650 years old. **Lee Vining**, just north, sits next to Hwy 120 east of **Tioga Pass✦✦** (summer only) and **Yosemite National Park✦✦✦** (see page 234).

Suggested tour

From **Reno**, follow Hwy 395 south to **Carson City**, the twin towns of **Minden** and **Gardnerville** and back into California. The scenic highway continues south over **Devil's Gate Summit** (7519ft) and down to **Bridgeport**, starting point for a detour to **Bodie State Historical Park**. Hwy 395 climbs up over **Conway Summit** (8138ft) before dropping down to **Mono Lake** and **Lee Vining**, then climbing past **June Lake** to **Deadman Summit** (8041ft) and down past **Mammoth Lakes** into the **Owens Valley**, a desert corpse sucked dry to keep Los Angeles green. **Bishop** is the starting point for a side trip to **Laws**. Continue south on Hwy 395 through **Big Pine** and **Independence** to **Lone Pine** and **Mount Whitney**. Take Hwy 136 southeast to **Panamint Springs**, over **Towne Pass** (4956ft) and down into **Death Valley National Park**.

Also worth visiting

Laws✦✦
The **Laws Railroad Museum and Historical Site** was once a major stop on the narrow-gauge Carson and Colorado Railroad between Carson City, Nevada and Owens Lake. The 11-acre open-air museum preserves the old station, the *Slim Princess*, the last steam locomotive engine to work the line, and other rolling stock. Buildings include a frontier physician's office and dispensary, the station agent's home, Wells Fargo office, library and post office, all furnished with period antiques. The drover's cottage across the road was built for the 1966 Steve McQueen film *Nevada Smith*.

Bodie✦✦✦
'Goodbye, God, we are going to Bodie' is how one girl faced the prospect of moving to Bodie in the last century. In its gold-rush glory during the 1880s, Bodie boasted the widest streets, the meanest men and the most disgusting whisky in the West. A local preacher called the booming town of 10,000 'a sea of sin lashed by tempests of lust

and passion'. He probably understated the daily tally of murder and mayhem that wracked California's most remote and lawless outpost. When the gold disappeared, so did the town, along with the churches, saloons, shops, brothels, schools and newspapers. Most people left possessions behind as though they expected to return.

About 170 buildings remain, all in a state of 'arrested decay'. Dusty shop windows are still loaded with merchandise; bedrooms still have tattered lace curtains and sagging mattresses. Pick up a self-guiding brochure at the former **Miner's Union Hall**.

Below
Sierras ghost town

Lake Tahoe and Reno

Ratings

History	●●●●●
Scenery	●●●●○
Gambling	●●●●○
Sport	●●●●○
Lake cruises	●●●○○
Children	●●●○○
Architecture	●○○○○
Food and drink	●○○○○

Lake Tahoe is California Mountain Country at its best, a 12-mile sapphire oval, 6227ft above sea level, more than 1600ft deep and surrounded by snow-capped Sierra peaks laced with hiking, cycling and skiing trails. Although the California–Nevada border divides Lake Tahoe east–west, the real division is north–south. South Shore revolves around Stateline, a miniature Las Vegas just inside Nevada, and the urban clutter of South Lake Tahoe on the California side of the border. North Shore sports a sprinkling of casinos, but the focus is firmly fixed on outdoor activities, from hiking and water skiing in summer to snoeshowing and snowskiing in winter.

Hwys 28, 50 and 89 link to circle Tahoe, a scenic 72-mile drive that can take two hours mid-week or most of the day on weekends. The towns of Virginia City, Carson City and Reno, in the historic heart of Nevada, lie just east.

LAKE TAHOE CIRCUIT✦✦

ⓘ Lake Tahoe Visitors Authority *(South Shore) 1156 Ski Run Blvd; South Lake Tahoe, CA 96150; tel: (530) 541-5255 or (800) 288-2463 (accommodation booking); fax: (530) 544-2386. Open Mon–Fri 0800–1700.*

🏛 DL Bliss State Park $ *Hwy 89, South Shore; tel: (530) 525-7277. Open May–Sept.*

Most drivers circle Lake Tahoe in a clockwise direction to avoid left turns into car-parks. Allow at least a full day for the drive. Must-sees include **Emerald Bay✦✦✦** and **Inspiration Point✦✦✦**, on the southwest shore, and **Cave Rock Tunnel✦✦**, **Sand Harbor State Park✦✦✦** and **Zephyr Cove✦✦** on the Nevada side. *Around Lake Tahoe*, a two-hour audio cassette on sale at visitor centres and chambers of commerce, is a good introduction to Tahoe history and scenery.

Tahoe's greatest concentration of hiking trails is on the south–west shore around **Fallen Leaf Lake✦✦✦**. The **Tahoe Rim Trail✦✦✦** circles the lake in 150 ridge-top miles, although parts of the route make pleasant day hikes. The **US Forest Service Visitor Center** *¾-mile north of Camp Richardson; tel: (530) 573-2674)* offers good recommendations, maps and brochures for everything from easy strolls to high-altitude leg burners. South Shore is dominated by America's only bi-state ski resort, **Heavenly**; North Shore has California's greatest concentration

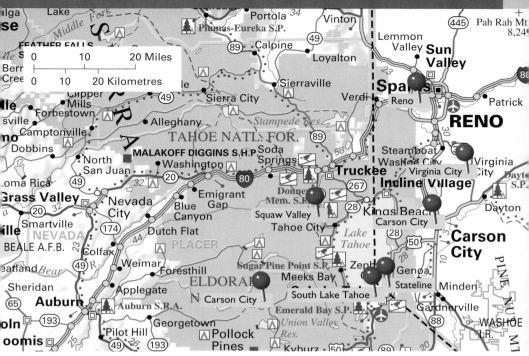

Emerald Bay State Park
Hwy 89, South Shore;
tel: (530) 525-7277 or
(530) 541-3030. Open daily.
Vikingsholm $ Open for
guided tours every half-hour
daily 1000–1600 mid
June–Labor Day, Sat–Sun
Memorial Day–mid June.

**Incline Village &
Crystal Bay
Visitors & Convention
Bureau**, 969 Tahoe Blvd,
Incline Village, NV 89451;
tel: (775) 832-1606 or
(800) 468-2463; fax: (775)
832-1605. Open Mon–Fri
0830–1730, Sat–Sun
1000–1600.

of ski resorts. Most ski mountains are open in summer for sightseeing, hiking and mountain biking.

D L Bliss State Park✷ (*South Shore*) has one of Tahoe's most scenic beaches, though the water is icy and the car-park fills up early. **Balancing Rock Nature Trail**✷✷ is a half-mile loop to a 130-tonne boulder that appears balanced precariously on a granite slab. The **Rubicon Trail**✷ is 4½ miles of spectacular lake views from **Rubicon Point** south to **Emerald Bay**.

Emerald Bay State Park✷✷ (*South Shore*) surrounds **Emerald Bay**✷✷✷, a shallow, glacier-carved inlet named for its colour. The Bay is best viewed from **Inspiration Point**✷✷✷ on Hwy 89. A steep trail (2 miles return) leads from a car-park at the north side of the bay down to **Vikingsholm**✷✷, a 1929 summer residence built to resemble a 9th-century Nordic castle. Just offshore is **Fanette Island**✷, with a ruined tea-house.

Incline Village (*North Shore*) is the largest town on Tahoe's Nevada shore, with the closest casinos to Tahoe City and other North Shore hideaways. **Lake Tahoe Nevada State Park**✷, a largely undeveloped forest and lakeshore, is dotted with house-sized boulders and

ⓘ **South Lake Tahoe Chamber of Commerce**
*3066 Lake Tahoe Blvd;
tel: (530) 541-5255;
fax: (530) 541-7121;
web: www.tahoeinfo.com
Open Mon–Sat 0900–1700.*

ⓘ **Ponderosa Ranch**
*$$ 100 Ponderosa
Ranch Rd; tel: (775) 831-
0691; web:
www.ponderosaranch.com
Open 0930-1700 mid-Apr-
Oct.*

occasional patches of sandy beach. **Sand Harbor***, the largest beach, has a small boat dock. Hwy 28 joins Hwy 50 just south of the park to continue around the lake or east toward Carson City.

Die-hard fans of the long-gone *Bonanza* television series may recognise the **Ponderosa Ranch**, 1 mile south off Hwy 28. The Western theme park is built around sets used for the original series and later cinematic spin-offs, including the ranch house (complete with removable walls and ceilings), barn and a fanciful re-creation of Virginia City – the real one is less than 30 miles away *(see page 132)*. Pony rides, a petting zoo and wooden sidewalks appeal to children.

Accommodation in Incline Village

Hyatt Regency Lake Tahoe Casino $$$ *Lakeshore & Country Club Dr.; Incline Village, NV 89415; tel: (775) 832-1234* or *(800) 233-1234*, is North Shore's most luxurious lakeside hotel and biggest casino.

South Lake Tahoe (*South Shore*) is a collection of hotels, motels, restaurants and businesses sprawling from **The Y**, the junction of

Right
Snowy peaks rise from
Emerald Bay

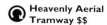

Heavenly Aerial Tramway $$
Ski Run Blvd;
tel: (775) 586-7000;
web: www.skiheavenly.com.
Open daily.

Hwys 50 and 89. South Lake Tahoe has the bulk of Tahoe's accommodation, restaurants and other tourist services, and casinos are a free shuttle ride away just across the border in Stateline, Nevada.

South Lake Tahoe also has a series of fine beaches, though the icy water keeps most people on the sand even in mid-summer. The best people-watching is at **Jamison Beach** (*Camp Richardson, 2½ miles north of The Y*), **Nevada Beach** (*Elk Point Rd, 1 mile east of Stateline*) and **El Dorado Beach**, in the centre of town.

Heavenly Aerial Tramway provides one of the best and easiest views across Lake Tahoe from the flanks of Monument Peak (10,167ft). In winter, the tram opens access to one of the largest ski resorts in North America; in summer, it is the starting point for the 2-mile **Tahoe Vista Trail** (open June–Sept), which lives up to its name. Views are nearly as good from the broad decks and view windows of the tram terminus lodge.

Accommodation and food in South Lake Tahoe

Lake Tahoe Visitors Authority *tel: (530) 544-5050* or *(800) 288-2463*, handles bookings for the South Shore.

Embassy Suites Resort $$$ *4130 Lake Tahoe Blvd; tel: (530) 544-5400* or *(800) 362-2779; fax: (530) 544-4900*, is next to Stateline; room rates include breakfast.

Tahoe Seasons Resort $$$ *3901 Saddle Rd; tel: (530) 541-6700* or *(800) 540-4874; fax: (530) 541-0653*, across the road from Heavenly, is a boon to skiers.

Evan's American Gourmet Café $$$ *536 Emerald Bay Rd; tel: (530) 542-1990, open daily,* offers an eclectic mix of Italian, Caribbean, Asian and Southwestern dishes and a wine list with around 300 labels. **Scusa! on Ski Run $$** *1142 Ski Run Blvd; tel: (530) 542-0100, open daily* is Tahoe's top Italian restaurant despite the casino-like lighting. **Sprouts Natural Foods Café $** *3123 Harrison St; tel: (530) 541-6969, open daily,* is an easy stop for picnic ingredients, but the queue snakes out the door at lunchtime.

SQUAW VALLEY

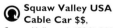

Squaw Valley USA Cable Car $$,
Squaw Valley; tel: (530) 583-6985 or (888) 766-9321; fax: (530) 581-7106
web: www.squaw.com.
Open daily 0900–2100.

Aerial trams make it easy to explore the near-vertical mountains that lured the 1960 Olympic Winter Games to Squaw Valley. The **Squaw Valley USA Cable Car** climbs more than 2000ft to **High Camp**, with ice-skating, swimming, bungee jumping, tennis, restaurants and killer views. Skiing, hiking and mountain biking are among Tahoe's best. Down below, golf courses and hotels have taken over what was one of Tahoe's most tranquil corners.

Accommodation and food in Squaw Valley

PlumpJack Squaw Valley Inn $$$ *1920 Squaw Valley Rd; tel: (530) 583-1576 or (800) 323-7666*, is a low key, big-city-sophisticated restaurant and ski resort.

The **Resort at Squaw Creek $$$** *400 Squaw Creek Rd; tel: (530) 583-6300 or (800) 327-3353; fax: (530) 581-5407; web: www.squawcreek.com*, is Tahoe's most luxurious resort, complete with adult toys like a private golf course and ski lift.

River Ranch Lodge $$ *Hwy 89 and Alpine Meadows Rd; tel: (530) 583-4264 or (800) 535-9900*, is an old-fashioned inn midway between Squaw Valley and Alpine Meadows ski areas.

River Ranch Lodge Restaurant $$ *open daily*, is a long-time local favourite overlooking the Truckee River.

STATELINE*

🏛 Sugar Pine Point State Park $
Hwy 89, *South Shore*; tel: (530) 525-7982. *Open daily year-round.*

Ehrman Mansion
Open by guided tour only July–Labor Day 1100–1600.

Gatekeeper's Log Cabin Museum $ *130 W. Lake Blvd, William B Layton Park*; tel: (530) 583-1762. *Open Jun–Aug daily 1100–1700, May and Sept Wed–Sun, other times by appointment.*

Stateline is the Nevada side of South Lake Tahoe, dominated by the jangling slot machines and flashing neon of **Caesars** (*tel: (775) 588-3515 or (800) 648-3353*), **Harrah's** (*tel: (775) 588-6611 or (800) 427-7247*), **Harvey's** (*tel: (775) 588-2411 or (800) 427-8397*), **Horizon** (*tel: (775) 588-6211 or (800) 648-3322*) and a handful of smaller casinos.

Casino accommodation packages can be good value mid-week and the buffets are always popular with teenagers and others with gargantuan appetites. Lounges and showrooms offer scaled-down versions of Las Vegas spectacles and the gambling is non-stop. Most restaurants and other services are in South Lake Tahoe.

Sugar Pine Point State Park** (*South Shore*) is Tahoe's largest state park and the only one with year-round camping. Sugar Pine Point also holds several of Tahoe's oldest buildings. **Phipps Cabin** was built in 1872 by early resident William Phipps. The 1903 **Ehrman Mansion****, made of local wood and stone quarried from nearby Meeks Bay, is furnished in mid-1930s styles; the expansive grounds were used as the opulent Lake Tahoe mansion setting in *Godfather II*.

Tahoe City* (*North Shore*) is the hub of North Shore. Hwy 89 meets Hwy 28 at the western edge of town and **Fanny Bridge***, named for the view pedestrians present as they peer down at the enormous trout in the Truckee River, which flows from lakeshore gates to Pyramid Lake, in the desert near Reno.

The gates were once opened and closed by a gatekeeper who lived at **Gatekeeper's Log Cabin Museum****, a reconstruction of the original 1910 lodgepole pine cabin. The museum covers pioneer and Native

Above
Pioneer transport

American settlement in the area, with an extensive basket collection.

One of the most popular summer pastimes is rafting the Truckee River from Tahoe City to River Ranch Lodge (*see page 126*). Whitewater enthusiasts need not apply – the placid 4-mile, 3-hour trip is more suited to inner tubes and air mattresses than crash helmets. Operators provide raft, life-jacket, paddle and a lift back to Tahoe City, but arrive before 1100 to avoid the worst of the crowds. Lunch or drinks at the River Ranch Lodge Restaurant is the traditional float finale. The **Truckee River Bike Trail**✢ offers similar scenery from land.

Watson Cabin Living Museum✢ **$** (*560 N. Lake Blvd; tel: (530) 583-8717*), built in 1908, is the oldest North Shore building still in its original location. The museum replays early 20th-century life on Lake Tahoe.

ⓘ **North Lake Tahoe Resort Association**

*245 N. Lake Blvd,
Tahoe City, CA 96145;
tel: (530) 581-8736 or
(800) 824-6348;
fax: (530) 581-4018;
web: www.tahoefun.org
Open Mon–Fri 0900–1700,
Sat–Sun 0900–1600.*

Kings Beach Visitor Center

Open Memorial Day–Labor Day 1000–1800.

Accommodation and food in Tahoe City

The **North Lake Tahoe Resort Association** (*tel: (530) 581-8736 or (800) 824-6348*) makes bookings for the North Shore. Last-minute accommodation *may* be available north of Tahoe City towards the towns of **Tahoe Vista** and **Kings Beach**, but advance bookings are advisable all year and necessary at weekends, holidays and June-Aug.

Christy Hill $$$ *115 Grove St; tel: (530) 583-8551, dinner only Tue–Sun,* is one of Tahoe's best restaurants with traditional California combinations.

Fire Sign Café $$ *1785 W. Lake Blvd; tel: (530) 583-0871, breakfast and lunch daily,* is a long-time local breakfast favourite.

Bridgetender Tavern and Grill $ *Fanny Bridge; tel: (530) 583-3342, lunch and dinner daily,* is Tahoe City's busiest tavern.

Right
Lake Tahoe

Lake cruises

Traffic and heavy lakeshore development can make the drive around Lake Tahoe disappointing. A more scenic way to tour Tahoe is from the lake itself. Several commercial boats ply the lake with breakfast cruises, several trips during the day, and sunset/dinner cruises. Some boats also ferry skiers in winter. Advance bookings are required all year.

MS Dixie II $$ *760 Hwy 50, Zephyr Cove; tel: (775) 588-3508 or (888) 673-4943.* A replica paddlewheeler sails to Emerald Bay all year.

Tahoe Gal $$ *Lighthouse Marina, 850 N. Lake Blvd, Tahoe City; tel: (530) 583-0141 or (800) 218-2464.* Breakfast, scenic and dinner/dance cruises Apr-Oct.

Tahoe Queen $$ *Ski Run Marina, South Lake Tahoe; tel: (530) 541-3364 or (800) 238-2463.* This sternwheeler once hauled cotton on the Mississippi River.

Woodwind Sailing Cruises $$ *Camp Richardson and Zephyr Cove; tel: (775) 588-3000 or (888) 867-6394; web: www.sailwoodwind.com.* Summer-only sailing cruises.

ⓘ US Forest Service Visitor Center
South Shore, ¾ mile north of Camp Richardson;
tel: (530) 573-2674.
Open daily 0800–1730 mid June–Labor Day, to 1630 Sept, Sat–Sun 0800–1630 Oct and Memorial Day–mid June.

US Forest Service Headquarters
South Shore, 870 Emerald Bay Rd, Ste 1;
tel: (530) 573-2600; web: www.fs.fed.us/r5/laketahoe.
Open Mon–Fri 0800–1630.

Road conditions
Tel: (800) 427-7523 (California only) or (775) 793-1313.

ⓘ Tallac Historic Site
Hwy 89, 3 miles north of The Y; tel: (530) 573-2600. Grounds open daily.
Museum $ *Open 1000–1600 Memorial Day–Sept.*

Tallac Historic Site✦✦ is Tahoe's original resort area. The site contains several late 19th- early 20th-century mansions, when Tahoe was the elegant escape of choice for upper crust Californians. The grounds are open all year; buildings are open in summer.

Baldwin-McGonagle House Museum✦ is furnished in the opulent rustic style favoured by early 20th-century summer residents. An excellent **photo exhibit**✦✦ explores the life and times of the Washoe Indians who also summered at the lake; other exhibits show early resort life.

Pope-Tevis Estate✦✦ is the most lavish of the mansions. **Valhalla**✦ features wide verandahs and walk-in fireplaces; the interior is open only during special events or cultural performances.

The **US Forest Service Visitor Center**✦✦ is the best source of information on outdoor activities around Lake Tahoe. Rangers lead nature walks and campfire programmes daily in summer; there are also a number of self-guiding hikes.

Taylor Creek Stream Profile Chamber✦✦✦ offers a glimpse beneath a genuine mountain stream. Bright red kokanee salmon make their way from Lake Tahoe past the chamber in Oct to spawning beds farther upstream.

Zephyr Cove✦ (*South Shore, 2 miles north of Stateline*) is the most heavily developed beach on the Nevada shore, with a sandy strand, water toys for hire and a public pier. Hwy 50 turns east toward Carson City north of **Cave Rock Tunnel**.

CARSON CITY*

ⓘ Carson City Convention & Visitors Bureau *1900 S. Carson St, Ste 200, Carson City, NV 89701; tel: (775) 687-7411 or (800) 638-2321; fax: (775) 687-7416.*

ⓘ Mormon Station State Historic Park *Foothill Rd, Genoa; tel: (775) 782-2590. Open May–Oct.*

Nevada State Capitol *101 N. Carson St; tel: (775) 687-6800. Open during business hours.*

Nevada State Museum *$ 600 N. Carson St; tel: (775) 687-4810. Open daily 0830–1630.*

Ask the Convention & Visitors Bureau for their free self-guided walking and driving maps to the **Kit Carson Trail** historic district, west of Carson St. The tours include a home used as a set in John Wayne's final film, *The Shootist* (1976).

Nevada settlement began in 1851 at **Mormon Station State Historic Park***. When silver was discovered beneath what became **Virginia City** *(see page 132)*, the Territorial Legislature moved the capitol to **Carson City**, nearer the mines.

The silver-domed **Nevada State Capitol*** is open to the public, including the old legislative chambers. **Nevada State Museum*** nearby occupies the US Mint where Virginia City silver was turned into legal tender. Exhibits include a mine reproduction, ghost town, minerals, a mint-mark coin collection, guns and a mammoth.

The **Nevada State Railroad Museum*** *(2180 S. Carson St; tel: (775) 687-6953. Open daily 0830-1630. Historic rides Mon–Fri 1000–1600 Memorial Day–Labor Day; call to confirm departures)* has more than 60 pieces of rolling stock from the Virginia and Truckee Railroad, which ran from Virginia City to Carson City. Historic steam trains and motor cars make short trips in summer.

Native American history is on display at **Stewart Indian School Museum** *(5366 Snyder Ave, tel: (775) 882-6929. Open daily 1000–1700)*, a former residential school for Native Americans .

RENO**

ⓘ Reno/Sparks Convention & Visitor Authority (RSCVA) *4590 S. Virginia St, Reno, NV 89504; tel: (775) 827-7600, (800) 367-7366 or (888) 447-7366; fax: (775) 827-7646; web: www.playreno.com.*

ⓘ National Automobile Museum *$$ 10 Lake St; tel: (775) 333-9300. Open Mon-Sat 0930-1730, Sun 1000-1600.*

Reno's slogan, 'The Biggest Little City in the World', blazes from a neon **arch*** (*N. Virginia St and Commercial Row*) in the downtown casino district. Reno is also a burgeoning commercial city with a relatively mild winter climate and desert summers made bearable by air-conditioning. Spreading suburbs blend imperceptibly into the town of **Sparks**, which has its own set of casinos along I-80, just east of Reno.

The **National Automobile Museum**** is one of America's finest auto collections. Galleries trace the automobile from the 'horseless carriage' of the 1890s through modern and experimental models.

Spectators are welcome to view some of the world's largest bowling tournaments at the domed **National Bowling Stadium**. A large-screen cinema lies beneath the dome.

The **Nevada Historical Society Museum*** is Nevada's oldest museum. Displays include Native American artefacts, pioneer relics, antique furniture, guns and minerals.

Pyramid Lake* 30 miles long by 9 miles wide (*36 miles north on Hwy 445*), is the remnant of a prehistoric lake that once covered central Nevada. The sparkling lake, named for a pyramid-shaped formation, is surrounded by sagebrush and brown sandstone

Opposite
Glittering lights welcome visitors to Reno

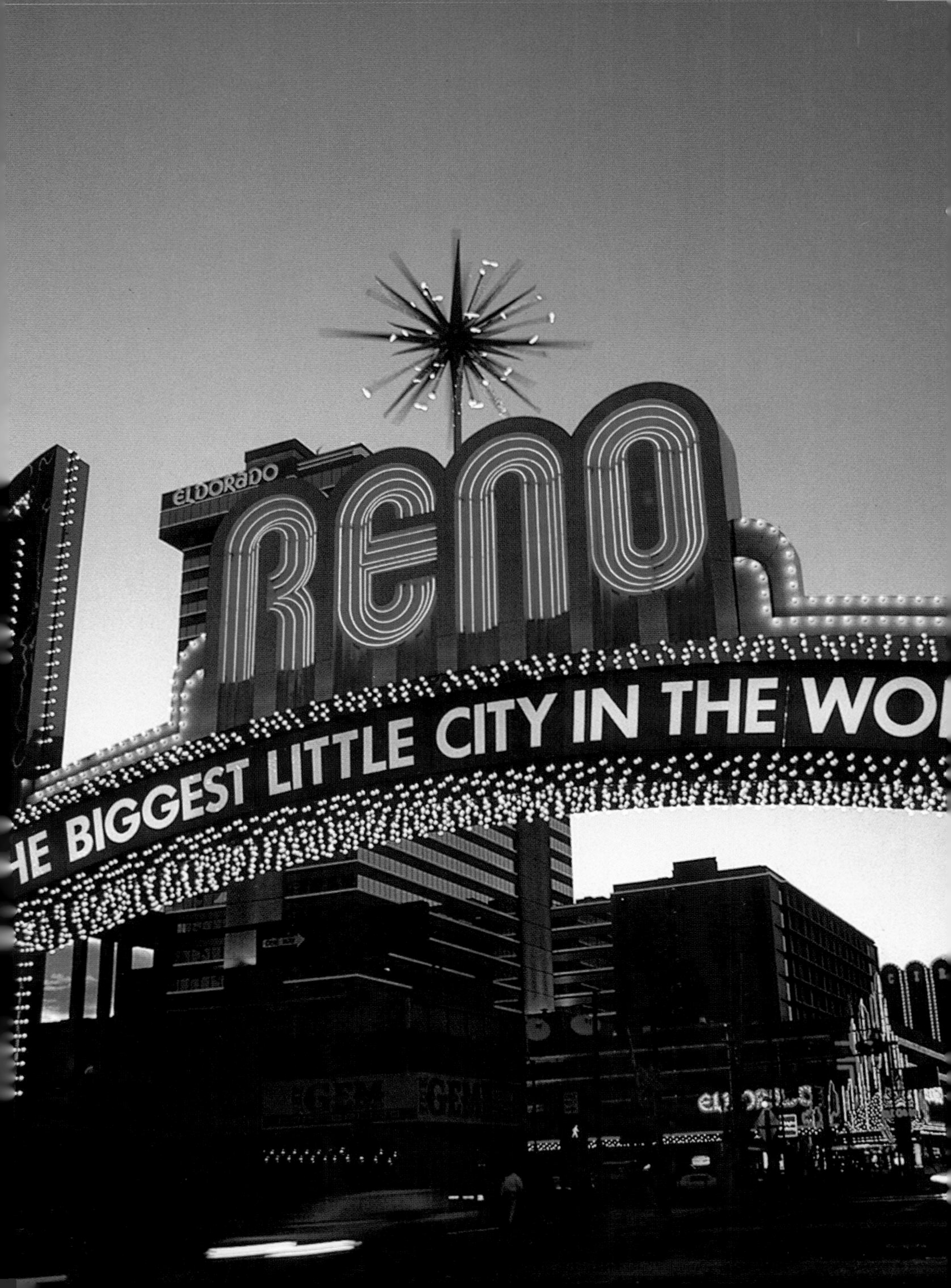
ELDORADO
RENO
BIGGEST LITTLE CITY IN THE

Nevada Historical Society Museum $,
1650 N. Virginia St; tel:
(775) 688-1190. Open
Mon-Sat 1000-1700

Great Basin Adventure
$ Open daily 1000–1700
Memorial Day
weekend–Labor Day.

Wilbur D May Center
Rancho San Rafael Park,
1502 Washington St; tel:
(775) 785-5961.

National Bowling Stadium 300 N.
Center St; tel: (775) 334-
2600. **Cinema $** tel: (775)
334-2634. Open daily.

mountains, but has some of Nevada's finest trout fishing.

Riverwalk* (along the Truckee River, Lake St–Idlewild Park) is all but deserted in winter, but becomes a shady escape for downtown office workers and casino habitués spring to autumn.

The **Wilbur D May Center**** includes the **Wilbur May Museum, Arboretum and Botanical Garden** and **Great Basin Adventure**. The museum is a hodgepodge of tourist trinkets and *objets d'art* collected by department store heir Wilbur D May. The botanical garden re-creates a dozen different eastern Sierra Nevada plant habitats; Great Basin Adventure is a children's park.

Accommodation and food in Reno

Downtown casinos offer good-value accommodation mid-week, but prices jump dramatically at the weekend. Special offers appear in the pink *Datebook* section of the *San Francisco Chronicle & Examiner* (Sun), or contact the RSCVA.

Casino buffets (breakfast, lunch or dinner) are barely more expensive than fast-food. The best restaurant in town is **La Strada $$$** *Eldorado Hotel & Casino; tel: (775) 786-5700, open daily for dinner.* Northern Italian dishes from the owners of the Ferrari-Carrano Winery in California's Dry Creek Valley *(see page 166).*

The local speciality is Basque, thanks to generations of Basque shepherds who have settled across Nevada. The best is **Louis' Basque Corner $$** *301 E. Fourth St; tel: (775) 323-7203. Open daily for lunch and dinner.*

VIRGINIA CITY✦✦✦

Virginia City Chamber of Commerce
131 S. C St, Virginia City, NV
89440; tel: (775) 847-0311.
Open daily 1000–1800.

Chollar Mine $
S. B St; tel: (775) 847-
0155. Open daily
1200–1700 May–Oct.

Comstock Firemen's Museum 125 S. C St;
tel: (775) 847-0717. Open
May–Oct daily 1000–1700,
Nov–Apr 1000–1600.

Home to 30,000 residents and 110 saloons during the 1860s–1880s Comstock Lode silver mining boom years, Virginia City nearly died when the mines played out around the turn of the century. Slopes above, beneath and around the town are riddled with hundreds of miles of unmapped mine shafts.

The almost-ghost town resurrected itself as a tourist destination after World War II, building on a reputation laid by former residents Mark Twain and Bret Harte. Twain's novel *Roughing It* recounts his days as a sometime miner, sometime journalist in Virginia City. The best place to see what Twain and company endured is the **Chollar Mine✦✦✦**, an 1861 Comstock Lode mine with original square-set timbers. Wear good walking shoes and expect mud in the tunnel.

Comstock Firemen's Museum* displays antique fire wagons and fire-fighting equipment in the original volunteer fire hall. **Julia Bulette's Red Light Museum**** is all that remains of what was once the biggest and busiest red-light district between Chicago and San Francisco.

Julia Bulette's Red Light Museum $
5 N. C St; tel: (775) 847-9394. Open Mon–Fri 1200–2000, Sat–Sun 1100–1900.

Ponderosa Saloon $
106 S. C St; tel: (775) 847-0757. Open daily.

Virginia and Truckee Railroad $ Washington and F Sts; tel: (775) 847-0380. Open daily 1030–1745 May-Sept, Sat–Sun in Oct.

Piper's Opera House $ B and Union Sts; tel: (775) 847-0433. Open daily 1100–1630 mid May–late Oct for guided tours.

Piper's Opera House✶✶ was the cultural centre of the entire West during the 1880s. Highlights include original 19th-century scenery and furnishings and a floor built on ore cart springs to dampen dynamite blasts in the tunnels deep below. Most of those old tunnels have flooded or collapsed, but the **Ponderosa Saloon✶** offers guided tours of a small section of mine directly below the building.

The **Storey County Courthouse✶** (B St near Union St) acknowledges the legal realities of the profitable years through the 1880s – the statue of Justice on the building façade is without her traditional blindfold.

Virginia and Truckee Railroad✶✶✶ trains travel part of the railway's original line to Carson City. The V&TR runs through countryside just as rugged, just as dry and just as starkly beautiful as it was when Mark Twain worked the same hills. The entire railway line to Carson City is being restored and could reopen for passenger traffic around 2000.

Driving guide

Circle **Lake Tahoe ❶** on Hwys 28, 50 and 89 and continue east to **Carson City ❷** on Hwy 50, with awesome desert views snaking down the eastern side of the Sierra Nevada. Take Hwy 395 north to **Reno ❸**, or, for a more scenic route, follow Hwy 50 east to Hwy 341/342 and **Virginia City ❹** before looping north to **Reno ❸**.

SAN FRANCISCO

Ratings

Food and drink	●●●●
Nightlife	●●●●
Shopping	●●●●
Art	●●●
Architecture	●●●
Children	●●●
Museums	●●●
Parks	●●●

San Francisco

F or those who live here, San Francisco is *never* 'Frisco'; it's *The City*, a refuge of civilisation in an otherwise Wild West. It was, after all, The City the world encountered on the way to Gold Rush riches and The City where the successful few returned to splurge on wine, women and real estate along the Barbary Coast. After The City was destroyed by earthquake in 1906, it rebuilt itself to host the 1915 Panama-Pacific Exhibition, then rebuilt reality.

The Beatniks of the 1950s shook American society, political demonstrations in the 1960s shook government and the 1967 Summer of Love shook the world. Los Angeles may be California's cultural capital, but San Francisco remains its fractious soul, an aggregation of minorities who dislike each other but still manage to live together. Precipitous hills, a sparkling bay, bridges, cable cars, 3000 restaurants and benign tolerance for almost anything short of mayhem are eternal touchstones.

Getting there and getting around

San Francisco International Airport (SFO); *tel: (650) 876-7809*, is 14 miles south on Hwy 101. Taxi to downtown $35. Airporter Bus to downtown hotels $10 single; door-to-door van service $12 single. Free shuttles to car-hire locations and airport hotels.

Parking

Public parking is scarce downtown. Fees range from $2–$20 per hour. Best bets are city-operated garages: **Stockton-Sutter Garage** *near Union Square*; **Fifth & Mission Garage** *between Union Square and Yerba Buena Gardens*; **Police Garage** *766 Vallejo St*; **Portsmouth Square Garage** *Clay and Kearny Sts*. Charges are exorbitant at **Fisherman's Wharf** and **Pier 39**.

Street parking is nearly impossible in Chinatown, North Beach, Fisherman's Wharf and Union Square, scarce elsewhere. Parking meters accept only quarters, good for 15–60 mins, depending on the neighbourhood. Try to park and explore on foot rather than driving, or use MUNI transport when possible.

ⓘ San Francisco Convention & Visitor Bureau (SFCVB)
Hallidie Plaza, Lower Level, Powell and Market Sts; tel: (415) 391-2000; fax: (415) 227-2668; web: www.sfvisitor.org. Open Mon–Fri 0900–1700, Sat–Sun 0900–1500. 24-hour recorded information: *(415) 391-2001. The San Francisco Book is the complete tourist reference.*

cipal

Hyde Street

Jefferson Street

atic

Bay Cruises **ANCHORAGE**

Herb Caen Way

CANNERY

Fisherman's Wharf

PIER 39 UNDERWATER WORLD AQUARIUM

PIER 35 CRUISE

Fishermans Wharf IAL

North Point Street

ONAL TIME EUM

GHIRARDELLI SQUARE

BAY STREET

Francisco Street

Chestnut Street

LOMBARD STREET HILL

Lombard Street

Greenwich Street

Filbert Street

North Beach

Washington Square

Beach Blanket Babylon Blvd

Columbus Avenue

HERB CAEN WAY (THE EMBARCADERO)

Lombard Street

CO TOWER

Telegraph Hill

Telegraph Hill

Filbert Street

UNION STREET

North Beach

Green Street

Vallejo Street

Broadway

Front Street

Davis Street

PIER 29 SUNDAY ANTIQUE MARKET

Russian Hill

Union Street

Green Street

Vallejo Street

VAN NESS AVENUE

Polk Street

Larkin Street

HYDE STREET

Pacific Avenue

Jackson Street

Broadway

Nob Hill

CABLE CAR BARN

Leavenworth Street

Jones Street

Taylor Street

MASON STREET

Powell Street

STOCKTON STREET

GRACE CATHEDRAL

Portsmouth Square

t Avenue

ey Street

ntery Street

Sansome St.

BATTERY STREET

Front Street

Davis Street

Jackson Street

Pacific Avenue

JACKSON SQUARE

WASHINGTON STREET

TRANS-AMERICA RAMID

Chinatown

FERRY BUILDING

Steuart St

Spear Street

WASHINGTON STREET

Clay Street

Sacramento Street

CALIFORNIA STREET

Pine Street

Bush Street

101

Sutter Street

Post Street

GEARY STREET

O'Farrell Street

MARY'S THEDRAL

Ellis Street

Eddy Street

Turk Street

Golden Gate Avenue

McAllister Street

Civic Centre

Center

City Hall

CITY HALL

STREET

CHINAT N

Union Square

Financial District

CROCKER GALLERIA

Yerba Buena Gardens Complex

Union Square

M

EAR MUNI METRO

EMBARCADERO CENTER

M

RT/

Muni etro

SOMA

BEALE

Fremont Street

First

M

Museum of Modern Art

POWELL STREET BART/Muni Metro

M

HALLIDIE PLAZA

YERBA BUENA GARDENS

M

SAN FRANCISCO SHOPPING CENTER

OLD MINT

MARKET STREET

MISSION STREET

Howard Street

Fifth Street

Fourth Street

MUSEUM OF MODERN ART

SECOND STREET

Third Street

STREET

TO OA

80

South

EMERGENCY HOSPITAL

M CIVIC CENTER BART/Muni Metro

ayes Street

Seventh Street

EIGHTH STREET

ell Street

SIX

Bryant Street

Brannan Street

RAILROAD STATION

M Muni Metro

0		1		2 Miles

0	1	2 Kilometres

Driving

One-way streets, steep hills and lack of parking turn driving into a challenge. Coloured signs point the way to key areas:

- A green outline of Italy for **North Beach**

- A red Chinese lantern for **Chinatown**

- An orange crab for **Fisherman's Wharf**

- A blue Victorian house for **Union Street**

- A white female statue for **Union Square**.

Below
Golden Gate bridge

Public transport

The Municipal Railway, or **MUNI** (*tel: (415) 673-6864*), reaches most major tourist attractions, but schedules vary from erratic to fictional. **Buses** follow numbered routes on city streets. **Streetcars** follow lettered routes under-ground in the city centre and on the surface in outlying districts. **Cable cars** serve Nob Hill, Fisherman's Wharf, Aquatic Park and California Street. **Muni Passport** offers one- to seven-day discounts. **BART**, the Bay Area Rapid Transit District (*tel: (510) 992-2278*), provides service from San Francisco beneath the bay to Oakland and other East Bay cities. Fares vary by distance.

Ferries

Blue & Gold Fleet (*tel: (415) 705-5555*), depart from Pier 39, Pier 43½ and the Ferry Building, *foot of Market St*, for the East Bay, Alcatraz, Angel Island and sightseeing cruises. **Golden Gate Ferry** (*tel: (415) 923-2000*), serves Sausalito and Tiburon (Marin County, north of San Francisco) from the Ferry Building.

Sights

Cable Car Barn & Museum $
Mason & Washington Sts; tel: (415) 474-1887. Open daily 1000–1700. Barn is free.

Alcatraz Island✦✦✦
The list of prisoners incarcerated in the infamous federal penitentiary reads like a *Who's Who* of Hollywood celebrity criminals. Al 'Scarface' Capone, Robert 'Bird Man of Alcatraz' Stroud and George 'Machine Gun' Kelly were among the 1554 convicts who spent an average of eight years within sight of San Francisco, yet completely out of touch.

The tiny island is 1½ miles off shore, accessible only by boat. Blue & Gold Fleet operate daily tours of what was once touted as America's only 'escape proof' prison.

Visitors may wander freely through the former cellblocks, including the 'dark holes', or solitary confinement cells used to punish prisoners. To appreciate fully the dank, depressing atmosphere of Alcatraz, take a **self-guided audio tour✦✦✦** narrated by former prison guards.

The pervasive security apparently worked. Only 36 prisoners tried to escape: ten were killed in the attempt; 21 captured; and five were never found.

Angel Island✦✦✦
Once the main port of entry from Asia, the largest island in San Francisco Bay is a rural state park with stunning views of San Francisco, Alcatraz and the Bay Area. Facilities include restored immigration buildings, picnic grounds, hiking and cycling trails and a tram ride around the island. Access is by private boat or Blue & Gold Fleet ferry service.

Bay Cruises✦✦
The budget version is a commuter ferry ride. Bigger spenders can choose from the official Blue & Gold Fleet tour that circles beneath the **Golden Gate Bridge** and the **San Francisco-Oakland Bay Bridge** with views of **Alcatraz**, **Angel Island**, **Treasure Island** and the **San Francisco waterfront**, as well as luxury yacht cruises and overnight escapes (*tel: (415) 705-5555*). The winds that make San Francisco a sailor's delight can bring shivers to the sunniest day; remember to bring a jumper or a coat.

Cable Cars✦✦✦
San Francisco's original mechanised public transport still climbs half-way to the stars up **Nob Hill** between the Bay and **Hallidie Plaza** (*Powell and Market Sts*) and along California St. The **Hyde St Line** runs to **Aquatic Park** (*Beach St between Hyde St and Van Ness Ave*) for easy access to **Fisherman's Wharf**, the historic ships at **Hyde St Pier** in **San Francisco Maritime National Historic Park** and **Ghirardelli Square**, a former bayside chocolate factory – the hot fudge sundaes at **Swenson's Ice Cream Parlor** (*tel: (415) 399-9415*) are divine.

Exploratorium $
*Palace of Fine Arts,
3601 Lyon St at Marina
Blvd; tel: (415) 561-0399 or
(415) 561-0362 (recorded
information).
Open Labor Day–Memorial
Day Tue–Sun 1000–1700,
Wed to 2130, closed Mon;
Memorial Day–Labor Day
daily 1000–1800,
Wed to 2130.*

Fisherman's Wharf
*Jefferson and Taylor Sts.
Open daily.*

Queue up (sometimes for hours) to board at the end of each cable car line or follow the locals who walk a couple of blocks up the street to climb aboard without waiting. To see how the system works, visit the **Cable Car Barn**✧ (*Mason and Washington Sts; tel: (415) 474-1887*). Don't miss the gallery overlooking the 14ft pulleys that haul miles of steel cable beneath city streets to power the cable cars at a constant 9mph. The **Cable Car Museum** in one corner of the Barn displays the history of the system.

Chinatown✧✧

What began as a shanty town of Chinese miners expelled from the gold fields around 1850 has become the largest Chinese community outside Asia (*Pine St to North Beach between Kearny and Powell Sts*). Dr Sun Yat Sen planned the revolution that became the Chinese Nationalist Republic from a tiny building on Spofford Alley. More recently, Chinatown's Waverly Place featured prominently in San Franciscan Amy Tan's best-selling novel *The Joy Luck Club*. Place-names used in the book are as real as the slap of mah jongg tiles that can still be heard through neighbourhood doorways.

Grant Ave, Chinatown's official high street, is a tourist trap. Stockton St, one block west, is piled high with fresh vegetables, live fish, smoked ducks and other necessities of life. *Dim sum* (filled dumplings), noodles and Chinese bakeries are a sure bet for a delicious slice of reality and local colour.

Exploratorium✧ and Palace of Fine Arts✧

This museum of science, art and perception is designed for children, but adults are at least as eager to get their hands on 500 do-it-yourself exhibits. The highlight is the **Tactile Dome**✧✧, manoeuvring by touch through a maze of shapes and textures in pitch blackness. The Exploratorium adjoins the beautiful Palace of Fine Arts, built to resemble a classical ruin for the 1915 **Panama-Pacific Exposition**.

Fisherman's Wharf✧

This one-time home to San Francisco's commercial fishing fleet now has more T-shirt and souvenir shops than fishing boats. The **USS Pampanito** submarine is open for tours on the east side of Pier 45. Explore on foot between **Pier 39**, **Fisherman's Wharf**, **Aquatic Park** and the **San Francisco Maritime National Historic Park**, **Ghirardelli Square**, **The Cannery** and **Fort Mason**.

Fort Point✧✧✧

The red brick fort beneath the Golden Gate Bridge was built to defend San Francisco during America's Civil War, 1861–5. Costumed guides re-create life inside the fort while waves sweeping through the **Golden Gate** blast spray 30ft into the air.

Golden Gate Bridge *Hwy 101 between San Francisco and Marin County. $3 auto toll southbound, pedestrians and cyclists free.*

Golden Gate National Recreation Area *Headquarters on MacArthur St, upper Fort Mason; tel: (415)556-0560. Open daily.*

Nature in the city's midst – basking sea-lions on San Francisco's Pier 39

Golden Gate Bridge✦✦✦

The bridge opened in 1938, linking the gap above the tides churning through the Golden Gate, the narrow passage into San Francisco Bay. 'Golden' refers to the Golden Horn in Istanbul, after which adventurer-explorer John Fremont named the entrance in 1846. The bridge is painted orange for better visibility in heavy fog. Park at the San Francisco end to walk or cycle across; drive to the vista point just beyond the north end of the bridge to look back toward San Francisco.

Golden Gate National Recreation Area (GGNRA)✦✦✦

A string of former military bases and coastal defences has become the world's largest urban park, stretching west from **Aquatic Park** and **Fort Mason** along the Bay to the **Presidio**, then south along the Pacific beyond San Francisco. Also included are **Alcatraz** and **Angel Islands**, the **Marin Headlands**, **Muir Woods National Monument**, **Mount Tamalpais** and much of **Tomales Bay** shoreline. Best views

Golden Gate Park
*Stanyan St between
Fulton St and Lincoln Ave.*

Asian Art Museum $$
*Golden Gate Park next to
M H de Young
Memorial Museum;
tel: (415) 379-8801;
web: www.asianart.org.
Open Wed–Sun
0930–1700. Free first Wed
0930–2045 of every month.
Single admission valid for
Asian and de Young
Museums.*

**M H de Young
Memorial Museum $$**
*Golden Gate Park, next to
Asian Art Museum;
tel: (415) 750-3600 or
(415) 863-3330
(recorded information);
web: www.thinker.org.
Open Wed–Sun
0930–1700. Free first Wed
1000–2045 of every month.
Single admission valid for
de Young and Asian Art
Museums.*

**California Academy of
Sciences $**
*Golden Gate Park;
tel: (415) 750-7145
(recorded information);
web: www.calacademy.org.
Open daily Memorial Day
weekend–Labor Day
0900–1800, 1000–1700
rest of year. Free the first
Wed of every month.*

can be had from **Crissy Field**, the Golden Gate Bridge to downtown San Francisco; **Baker Beach**, facing the Golden Gate Bridge from the ocean; **Lands End** with the city's most natural landscape and best sunsets; and **upper Fort Mason** for bay vistas.

Golden Gate Park✦✦✦

America's second great urban park (after Central Park in New York), Golden Gate Park is 1000 acres of drifting sand dunes transformed into shady forests, winding drives, lakes surrounded by open glades and museums. Don't miss jasmine tea and fortune cookies amid exquisite landscaping in the **Japanese Tea Garden✦✦**, an oasis of calm next to the **Asian Art Museum**, which houses the largest collection of Asian art and artefacts in any Western museum. The Asian adjoins the **M H de Young Memorial** and its collection of American art from the 17th to the 20th centuries. One ticket provides entry to both museums.

Just across the **Music Concourse** stands the **California Academy of Sciences✦**, the oldest scientific institution in the Western US. Among the attractions are **Steinhart Aquarium**, **Morrison Planetarium** and the **Natural History Museum**, all included in a single admission. Don't miss the delightfully retro crocodile pit and underwater views of cavorting seals and sea-lions in the Aquarium. The park is also home to **Strybing Arboretum and Botanical Gardens**, 7000 plant species arranged in 17 distinct garden habitats.

Right
San Francisco's Yerba Buena
Gardens

Strybing Arboretum & Botanical Gardens
9th Ave at Lincoln Way, Golden Gate Park; tel: (415) 661-1316. Open Mon–Fri 0800–1630, Sat–Sun 1000–1700. Free guided walks daily at 1330, also 1030 weekends. Free.

Coit Tower $ *1 Telegraph Hill Blvd; tel: (415) 362-0808. Open daily. Parking is extremely limited; walk up or take bus 39. The hilltop view is free.*

Palace of the Legion of Honor $$ *34th Ave & Clement St, Lincoln Park; tel: (415) 750-3600 or (415) 863-3330 (recorded information); web: www.thinker.org. Open Tue–Sun 0930–1700. Free the second Wed of every month.*

San Francisco Museum of Modern Art (SFMOMA) $$
151 Third St (Yerba Buena Gdns); tel: (415) 357-4000; web: www.sfmoma.org. Open Fri–Tue, 1100–1800, Thur to 2100. Free first Tue of each month, Thur 1800–2100 half-price.

San Francisco National Maritime Historic Park $
Beach St between Hyde St and Van Ness Ave; tel: (415) 556-3002. Open daily.

The Mission (District)✦✦

Named after **Mission Dolores** (*17th & Dolores Sts*), founded in 1776, The Mission is Central and South America come north. Look for brilliant murals blazing messages of equality, ethnic pride and hope and a wide range of Mexican and other Hispanic restaurants.

North Beach✦

Once a northern beach on San Francisco Bay, North Beach (*blocks surrounding Broadway and Columbus Ave*) was settled by Portuguese and Italians. The area has been an entertainment and nightlife district for more than a century. The topless and nude dancing clubs that have spread across American began at **The Condor** (*300 Columbus Ave*), now a sports bar, in the 1960s.

The Beatnik era survives at poet Lawrence Ferlinghetti's **City Lights Bookstore** (*261 Columbus Ave; tel: (415) 362-8193*) and **Vesuvio Café** (*255 Columbus Ave; tel: (415) 362-3370*). It's a short, if steep, walk from the coffee houses to the high point of North Beach, tiny **Telegraph Hill**, topped by 212-ft **Coit Tower**. The nozzle-shaped tower was built by Lillie Coit, an early City socialite with a notorious fondness for burley firemen. The interior features splendid Depression-era murals.

Palace of the Legion of Honor✦✦

This copy of Napoleon's Hôtel de Salm Paris displays ancient and European art from 2500 BC to the 20th century. Check for touring exhibitions and the Rodin sculpture collection.

Pier 39✦

The state's most popular tourist attraction is an abandoned pier converted to retail shops, entertainment and restaurants with fine views of Alcatraz and the bay (*The Embarcadero at Beach St; tel: (415) 981-7437, open daily*). The Pier's most famous residents are the barking **sea-lions**✦✦ that have taken over the north side marina. Most Blue & Gold Fleet ferries leave from Pier 41, just west.

San Francisco Museum of Modern Art (SFMOMA)✦

Northern California's largest collection of modern art is most noted for its distinctive architectural design by Mario Botta and the extremely popular Caffé Museo.

San Francisco National Maritime Historic Park✦✦

The nation's only floating National Park includes the **Maritime Museum**✦ housed in a gleaming white art deco streamline modern building in Aquatic Park and several historic ships docked at the **Hyde Street Pier**✦✦. The square rigger *Balclutha* and the *Eureka*, a former San Francisco Bay ferry featured in the *Nash Bridges* television series, are open for tours.

Half-price tickets for theatre, dance and music events on performance day, cash only (*Stockton St side of Union Square; tel: (415) 433-78277827; web: www.theatrebayarea.org*). Credit cards are accepted for full-price advance tickets to area performance events. *Open Tue–Thur 1100–1800, Fri–Sat to 1900.*

SOMA*

The South of Market (Street) Area (SOMA) was once an industrial haven filled with brick buildings and dark alleyways, but has metamorphosed into a trendy residential and entertainment neighbourhood. Clubs suit every taste from Springstein to Grunge, Goth and House mixes.

Union Square*

The heart of the shopping and theatre district (*Powell, Post, Stockton and Geary Sts*), nowadays the square is down at the heel.

Yerba Buena Gardens*

A former SOMA slum, Yerba Buena (*north of Moscone Convention Centre between 4th, Mission, 3rd and Howard Sts*) has become a lively nexus with SFMOMA, a Performing Arts Center, ice-skating rink, Moscone Convention Center, cinemas, shopping, entertainment venues, hotels, restaurants and a landscaped garden.

The **Cartoon Art Museum*** (*tel: (415) 227-8666*) is one of three museums in America devoted to cartoon art. Look for comic books, editorial cartoons, cartoon strips, animation cels, advertisements, greeting cards and the odd video. Other museums are planned for the area.

Entertainment

San Francisco has taken entertainment seriously since the days when admiring miners tossed bouquets of roses to touring opera stars and pouches of gold dust to bouncing dance hall girls. City stages offer the gamut from Punk to Pavarotti, plus theatre, dance and concerts. The *Datebook Section* in the *San Francisco Sunday Chronicle* is the most complete listing for traditional diversions; the *SF Bay Guardian* and *SF Weekly* concentrate on more avant-garde offerings.

Audium *1616 Bush St; tel: (415) 771-1616. Fri–Sat.* Sound sculptures from 136 speakers surround the audience, sitting in a darkened theatre.

American Conservatory Theater (ACT)** **$$$** *415 Geary St, Union Sq; tel: (415) 749-2228; web: www.actsfbay.org. Daily except Mon.* San Francisco's leading repertory theatre company.

Beach Blanket Babylon*** **$$** *Club Fugazi, 678 Beach Blanket Babylon Blvd (Green St, North Beach); tel: (415) 421-4222; web:www.beachblanketbabylon.com, open Wed–Sun, adults only except Sun afternoon.* Zany cabaret-style musical spoof of popular culture, updated regularly to reflect current events.

Above
Chinatown's heritage captured
in mural form

Clubs

Most clubs are in SOMA, catering to every taste from old-line jazz to the latest electronic creations. See the *SF Bay Guardian* or *SF Weekly*, free in racks around the city, for current listings.

Grace Cathedral Concerts⁺ \$\$ *1100 California St; tel: (415) 749-6350.* Concerts in California's finest Gothic cathedral.

Old First Concerts \$\$ *Old First Church, Van Ness Ave and Sacramento St; tel: (415) 474-1608. Year-round.* Solo, chamber, chorale, jazz and world concerts.

San Francisco Ballet \$\$\$ *455 Franklin St; tel: (415) 865-2000.* Annual dance season Jan–May; annual *Nutcracker* performances in Dec.

San Francisco Blues Festival⁺⁺ \$\$ *Great Meadow, Fort Mason; tel: (415) 979-5588. Third week in Sept.* The oldest blues festival in the nation, mid Oct.

San Francisco Opera \$\$\$ *War Memorial Opera House, Van Ness Ave and McAllister St; tel: (415) 864-3330. Sept-Jan.* A world-famous company in a newly restored opera palace.

San Francisco Symphony \$\$\$ *Davies Symphony Hall, Van Ness Ave and Grove St; tel: (415) 864-6000; web: www.sfsymphony.org.* Year-round symphony, summer Pops and holiday programmes.

Stern Grove Midsummer Music Festival⁺ *Sigmund Stern Grove, 19th Ave and Sloat Blvd. Summer Sun afternoons.* Free outdoor summer classical, opera, popular and jazz by top performers.

The Chinese in California

The Chinese have been part of California since 1848, when the first three immigrants from Guandong Province disembarked in San Francisco. Tens of thousands followed, lured by the promise of untold wealth in *Kum Saan*, or Gold Mountain, as it was known in China. Most early immigrants were men, expecting to work hard for a few years, save a small fortune then return to their ancestral village. Few ever left California and even fewer made their fortunes.

Chinese labourers were systematically exploited, first by agents at home who charged exorbitant fees, then by employers in California who paid them half the going rate for White workers. Those who tried their luck in the gold fields were driven out amid accusations of working too long, too hard and too successfully. Many found work in railway construction, where they were generally given the most dangerous assignments blasting tunnels and chiselling ledges into sheer cliff-faces. The Chinese were easy targets in the days when anyone who wasn't White, Anglo-Saxon and Protestant was suspect.

Anti-Asian sentiment was fanned by Chinese Exclusion laws designed

Street performers✦✦✦

The Cannery (*2801 Leavenworth St; tel: (415) 771-3112*), Pier 39 and other centres offer stages for buskers, but most jugglers, mimes and musicians set up shop on any convenient patch of pavement. Don't miss Fisherman's Wharf punks of various (sometimes indeterminate) sexes posing for photos with piercings, brands, tattoos and scars on display.

Theatre on the Square $$$ *450 Post St; tel: (415) 433-9500. Tue–Sun.* New York off-Broadway theatre in San Francisco.

Shopping

San Francisco is a shopper's dream regardless of budget. **Factory Outlets** are always busy. **Yerba Buena Square**, *899 Howard St; tel: (415) 543-1275*, has six floors of merchandise, and **Six Sixty Center**, *600 Third St; tel: (415) 227-0464*, has 20 shops.

The hip, or those who wish to be, gravitate to **Haight St**. The Haight's latest reincarnation is a trendier-than-thou mix of fashion, food and body piercing. **Union Square** is shopping central with the most expensive marquees, from Disney and Nike to Saks Fifth Avenue and Tiffany. **Union Street** caters to the stylishly trendy, pricey shops in fine Victorian buildings offering jewellery, marbled paper, clothing, antiques, furnishings and bric-à-brac from around the world.

Accommodation and food

San Francisco has been famous for high prices since Gold Rush days. It's one of America's most-visited cities, which keeps hotels and restaurants busy all year. *Always* book ahead. **Union Square** is the best location if you don't have a car, near the main shopping and theatre areas, most major tourist sights and public transport routes. Add $20–$25 per day for parking. Motels along **Lombard St** and **Van Ness Ave** generally offer free parking; ask for a room at the back to minimise street noise. **Fisherman's Wharf** is group-tour territory. **San Francisco Reservations**, *22 Second St; tel: (800) 677-1550*, makes free bookings for more than 225 local hotels.

The Archbishop's Mansion $$$$ *1000 Fulton St; tel: (415) 563-7872*, is the stately and elegant former home of the Archbishop of San Francisco. The other end of the spectrum is the ultra-trendy **Hotel Triton $$$** *342 Grant Ave; tel: (415) 394-0500*, filled with irregular shapes, wavy lines and corners that appear not to meet. The **Sheraton Palace Hotel $$$** *Market and New Montgomery Sts; tel: (415) 512-1111*, is one of the oldest, most historic hotels in San Francisco – and one of to keep them out. Local laws banned Chinese (and other Asians) from most occupations; sporadic anti-Chinese riots encouraged them to band together for self-protection. Los Angeles, Sacramento, San Francisco and isolated Delta towns such as Lock gained significant Chinatowns and other Asian neighbourhoods.

Discrimination began to ease after World War II, when the US and China found themselves allied. Immigration opened for refugees fleeing the Chinese Communist government after 1949. By the time quotas were raised again in the 1960s, San Francisco had the largest Chinese population outside Asia – and the Golden Dragon continued an annual New Year dance down Grant Ave that began in the 1860s.

the few major buildings to survive the 1906 earthquake. Don't miss the Garden Court, a brilliant palm-filled restaurant beneath a scintillating restored stained-glass dome covering what was originally the *porte-cochère* (carriage entrance).

San Francisco calls itself the food capital of America, a title justly contested by Los Angeles, New York and New Orleans. The *SF Bay Guardian* offers the best selection of current reviews. Local favourites change almost weekly, but **Boulevard $$$$** *1 Mission St; tel: (415) 543-6084*, is a long-term survivor for its French-inspired dishes. **Aqua $$$$** *252 California St; tel: (415) 956-9662*, may serve the best fish in town. **Boudin Sourdough Bakery & Café $** *156 Jefferson; tel: (415) 928-1849*, has the best Fisherman's Wharf sandwiches. **Golden Spike $$** *527 Columbus Ave; tel: (415) 421-4591*, has been serving up gargantuan portions of North Beach antipasto, pasta and main dishes for 60 years. **McCormick & Kuleto's Seafood Restaurant $$$** *900 North Point (Ghirardelli Square); tel: (415) 929-1730*, has food to equal the views across Aquatic Park and the Bay. The **Beach Chalet $$** *1000 Great Highway (Golden Gate Park); tel: (415) 386-8439*, is a brewery, restaurant and Golden Gate Park visitor centre. The beer and food are as good as the restored frescoes depicting Depression-era life in San Francisco.

Suggested tours

49-Mile Drive✥✥
Allow at least a half-day and avoid downtown during rush hours.The drive was created for the 1939 Golden Gate International Exposition. Blue and white seagull signs still mark an outstanding driving circuit. The route is marked on the SFCVB's free city map, but it's easier to follow the Bureau's own 49-Mile Drive brochure.

Walking tours
San Francisco is best seen on foot. Top guided walking tours: **City Guides** *tel: (415) 557-4266*, for culture, history and architecture; **Cruisin' The Castro✥** *tel: (415) 550-8110*, for The City's gay subculture from 1849 to the present; **Wok Wiz Chinatown Tours✥** *tel: (415) 981-8989*, for Chinatown alleys, tea and secrets with chef and author Shirley Fong-Torres; **Italians of North Beach✥✥** *tel: (415) 397-8530*, for Italian food, history and culture with chef and columnist GraceAnn Walden; **Victorian Home Walk** *tel: (415) 252-9485*, for an exploration of San Francisco's version of Victorian architecture, lifestyle and history.

Do-it-yourselfers can follow 150 sidewalk plaques on the 3.8-mile **Barbary Coast Trail✥✥**, matching San Francisco history with today's best sights. The CVB has a free self-guiding brochure.

San Francisco Bay Area

Ratings

Scenery	●●●●○
Food and drink	●●●●○
Art	●●●●○
Architecture	●●●○○
Children	●●●○○
History	●●●○○
Nature	●●●○○
Museums	●●○○○

San Francisco has given its name to the Bay Area, but it's hardly the dominant force in a region filled with vibrant cities, each with its own distinctive look and feel. The bay unites a montage of soaring bridges, windswept islands, distant skylines piercing the fog, sailboats and boardsailors weaving past lumbering cargo vessels, Nobel Prize-winners and world-renowned chefs. It's possible to breeze through the entire Bay Area in a day, but more productive to spread the sights over several days. Bridges and freeways can become stop-and-go car-parks during rush hours.

BERKELEY✧✧

ⓘ Berkeley Convention & Visitors Bureau
2015 Center St, Berkeley, CA 94704; tel: (800) 84-4823 or (510) 549-7040; fax: (510) 644-2052; web: www.berkeleycvb.com. Open Mon–Fri 0900–1700.

University of California Berkeley Campus Visitor Center *101 University Hall, 2200 University Ave; tel: (510) 642-5215. Open Mon–Fri 0830–1630.*

It's hard to separate Berkeley from the **University of California, Berkeley✧✧**. The campus, usually called Cal, lends a schizophrenic air to a town already known as 'Berserkely' for its benign loonies and strident politics. It also has America's greatest concentration of Nobel laureates.

Thirty thousand students make Cal the physical heart and soul of Berkeley. **Sather Tower**, aka **The Campanile✧✧**, towers 307ft above them all, slightly shorter than the original in St Mark's Square, Venice. From an observation platform below the 61-bell carillon, views span the bay. On the ground, **Sproul Plaza** (*north of Telegraph Ave and Bancroft Way*) is a non-stop circus, dominated by the student union in **Sproul Hall**.

Campus collections worth seeing are: the **Phoebe A Hearst Museum of Anthropology** (*open Wed–Sun*), with artefacts used by 'Ishi', last survivor of California's Stone Age Yaki aboriginals; modern and contemporary art at the **UC Berkeley Art Museum** (*2626 Bancroft*

Way, open Wed–Sun); the **Pacific Film Archive** (*below the UC Berkeley Art Museum; tel: (510) 642-1412*), which screens popular, foreign, independent and avant-garde films; the **Lawrence Hall of Science**, a popular participatory museum with a fine Bay view from the Berkeley Hills; and the enormous fossil collection at the **Museum of Paleontology**.

The **UC Botanical Garden** (*200 Centennial Dr., open daily*) has over 12,000 species from around the world, neatly labelled and divided into regional habitat zones. The rhododendron collection is stunning during the spring bloom. Cacti, a Chinese medicinal herb garden and California native plants are major collections, and views of San Francisco Bay are eye-catching.

Off-campus Berkeley swirls around **Telegraph Ave**, an ever-changing collection of coffee houses, booksellers, street musicians, panhandlers, students and homeless people. The **Judah L Magnes Museum**, the first Jewish museum in the Western US, collects fine art, ceremonial objects and rare books. Berkeley's best bookseller is **Cody's**.

Food in Berkeley

Berkeley takes everything seriously, including food. California cuisine got its start here, the idea that fresh ingredients, cultivated on small plots by happy farmers, are absolutely vital to health, taste, prosperity and peace on earth. To see the raw ingredients, tiny 'baby' vegetables and exotically coloured produce, visit the **Monterey Market** (*1550 Hopkins St; tel: (510) 526-6042: open Mon–Sat 0930–1800*).

High temple to the Cult of Cuisine is **Chez Panisse $$$** (*1517 Shattuck Ave; tel: (510) 548-5525*), whose reputation exceeds its execution. Downstairs tables book weeks in advance, but upstairs **Café Fanny** offers better value.

The area around Chez Panisse, Shattuck Ave near Cedar and Vine Sts, is called **Gourmet Ghetto** for the enormous concentration of fine restaurants.

People-watchers head for **Bette's Oceanview Diner $$** (*1807 4th St; tel: (510) 644-3230*), a casual breakfast and lunch-only diner with some of the area's tastiest American traditions: pancakes, French toast, blintzes, sandwiches, soup, meatloaf and to-die-for milk shakes. It sits in the bustling **Fourth Street Shopping District**✷, a former warehouse area that has become a lively artistic, shopping, dining and entertainment district.

Modelled on Venice, the Campanile at the Berkeley campus of the University of California

OAKLAND*

ℹ **Oakland Visitor Marketing**
*(mail: 250 Frank Ogawa Plaza, Ste 3330, Oakland, CA 94612-2032);
tel: (510) 238-2935;
fax: (510) 238-6422;
web: www.oaklandnet.com*

🏛 **Oakland Public Library Oakland History Room** *125 14th St; tel: (510) 238-3222. Open Mon, Tue and Sat 1000–1730, Wed–Thur 1200–2000, Fri 1200–1730, Sun 1300–1700.*

Ebony Museum of Arts *Jack London Sq, 2nd level; tel: (510) 763-0745. Open Tue–Sat 1100–1800, Sun 1200–1800.*

Pardee Home Museum *$ 672 11th St; tel: (510) 444-2187. Tours Fri-Sat 1200.*

Oakland Museum of California *$$ 1000 Oak St; tel: (510) 238-2200. Open Wed, Thur, Sat 1000–1700, Fri 1000–2100, Sun 1200–1700.*

Sailboat House *$$ tel: (510) 238-2196. Open Tue–Sun except rainy days*

⛰ **Children's Fairyland** *$ Grand & Bellevue Aves; tel: (510) 238-6876. Open daily 1000–1730 in summer, Fri–Sun 1000–1600 in winter.*

Oakland doesn't get much respect. Derided as high crime and low brow by San Franciscans and Berkeleyites, it is best known as the place about which native daughter writer Gertrude Stein complained 'There's no *there* there'.

It's no longer true. Oakland is a sunny, diverse city with a long cultural, musical and artistic heritage. Jack London, Oakland's first literary light, has his named plastered along the waterfront where he once stole oysters and lobsters for a living.

Jack London Square** (*west of downtown*) is a modern complex of shops, restaurants and museums. The **Jack London Museum*** (*30 Jack London Sq; tel: (510) 451-8218*), is devoted to the adventure writer and his contemporaries, though the **Oakland Public Library Oakland History Room** and **Jack London State Historic Park** (*see page 174*) have better collections. The Square's only genuine Londoniana is **Heinold's First and Last Chance Saloon** (*56 Jack London Square; tel: (510) 839-6761*), where London drank. The **USS *Potomac**** (*tel: (510) 839-8256*), the one-time American presidential yacht, is open for tours near by.

The **Ebony Museum of Arts*** features African American art and counterculture collectables. The Square's other highlights are a **ferry terminal** with hourly connections to San Francisco and **Yoshi's**, a Japanese restaurant and the East Bay's top jazz club.

The best place to see early Oakland is **Preservation Park*** (*Martin Luther King Jr Way and 12th St*), a re-created neighbourhood with restored buildings from 19th-century Victorian to early 20th-century Craftsman. Most are private offices, but **Pardee Home Museum** is open for guided tours. **Old Oakland*** (*Broadway, Clay, 8th and 10th Sts*) is the former commercial district, largely restored. **Chinatown**** (*Broadway, Fallon, 6th and 8th Sts*), more Pan-Asian than Chinese, has shops, restaurants and bakeries that are as busy – and far less touristy – than San Francisco.

Many of Oakland's grand buildings from the early 20th century survive in downtown, including **City Hall*** (*14th St*) and the **Tribune Tower**** (*Franklin St*), former home of the *Oakland Tribune* newspaper. A restored 1920s movie palace, the **Paramount Theater**** (*2025 Broadway; tel: (510) 465-6400),* shows Hollywood classics as well as stage productions. Surrounding buildings are equally flamboyant.

The stunning **Oakland Museum of California** is California's *de facto* state museum. Oakland's other must-see is **Lake Merritt****, the nation's oldest wildlife refuge. **Camron-Stanford House**** is the last of the elegant Victorian mansions that once lined the lake. Canoes, rowboats, paddleboats and sailboats can be hired from the **Sailboat House**. **Children's Fairyland*** was reputedly the model for Fantasyland in Walt Disney's original Disneyland.

Accommodation and food in Oakland

Farmers Market
Broadway and 9th St.
Open Fri 0800–1300.

The white gleam against the hills is the **Claremont Resort, Spa & Tennis Club $$$** (*Ashby and Domingo Aves; tel: (510) 843-3000*). For art-deco splendour, check into the **Clarion Suites Lake Merritt Hotel $$** (*1800 Madison St; tel: (510) 832-2300*).

Oakland is filled with colourful eateries, from a rainbow of Asian flavours in Chinatown to Oakland's own Gourmet Ghetto, **Rockridge** (*College Ave between 63rd and Alcatraz Sts*).

Bay Wolf $$$ (*3853 Piedmont Ave; tel: (510) 655-6004*) avoids Berkeley-like flights of fancy for restrained Mediterranean-California dishes.

Citron $$ (*5484 College Ave; tel: (510) 653-5484*) shows distinct French and Italian touches.

Soizic Bistro-Café $$$ (*300 Broadway at 3rd St; tel: (510) 251-8100*) emphasises the French amid flowers and *trompe-l'oeil* wall paintings.

Sausalito✦✦✦

ⓘ Sausalito Chamber of Commerce
Village Fair Center, 777, Bridgeway, Sausalito, CA 94966; tel: (415) 332-0505. Visitors Center open Tue-Sun 1130-1600.

ⓐ Blue & Gold Fleet (ferry) *Pier 41, San Francisco; tel: (415) 773-1188.*

Golden Gate Transit (ferry) *Ferry Bldg, San Francisco; tel: (415) 923-2000.*

ⓜ Bay Area Discovery Museum $$ *557 McReynolds Rd; tel: (415) 487-4398; web: www.badm.org. Open Tue-Thur 0900-1600, Fri-Sun 1000-1700.*

Bay Model *2100 Bridgeway; tel: (415) 332-3870. Open Tue-Sat 0900-1600.*

A small 19th-century summer resort and fishing town expanded as a ship-building centre during World War II, then sank into happy obscurity as a haven for 1950s artists, poets and Beats. A free-thinking reputation was assured when Sally Stanford, one of San Francisco's infamous bordello madams, retired to Sausalito, opened a restaurant and was elected mayor.

Sausalito marinas and houseboats orient the town to the bayfront. Multi-storey shopping complexes wind and twist like rabbit warrens. Much of the town centre is a National Historic Landmark District, including the **Plaza de Viña del Mar✦**, with its Spanish-style fountain and elephants from the 1915 Panama-Pacific Exposition.

At the north end of Sausalito is the **Bay Model✦✦**, a scale model of San Francisco Bay used to test the impact of development, dredging and clean-up efforts. The best ways to see the Bay up close are a three-hour guided sea kayak tour from **Sea Trek Ocean Kayaking Center✦✦✦** or a 30-minute **ferry ride✦✦** from San Francisco.

Getting out of the car in Sausalito

Sausalito's best bay vistas are from Bridgeway, walking south to Second St, Alexander Ave and Fort Baker Rd to the former military base. It's a 2-mile walk with unexpected views of the **Golden Gate Bridge✦✦✦** to reach the **Bay Area Discovery Museum✦✦✦**, with lively science, art and media exhibits geared to children aged one to ten.

Accommodation and food in Sausalito

Sea Trek Ocean Kayaking Center $$ *tel: (415) 488-1000. Open daily, advance booking required.*

Inn Above Tide $$$ *30 El Portal; tel: (800) 893-8433*, is the only hotel built *over* San Francisco Bay. **Casa Madrona Hotel $$$** *801 Bridgeway; tel: (415) 332-0502*, is a collection of cottages stretching up the hillside from Bridgeway to an 1885 Victorian mansion.

Avatar's Restaurant $$ *2656 Bridgeway; tel: (415) 332-8083*, offers Indian specialities.

Mikayla $$$ *Casa Madrona Hotel; tel: (415) 331-5888*, has the best views, best food and highest prices in town.

Scoma's $$$ *588 Bridgeway; tel: (415) 332-9551*, has the best Bay views.

TIBURON✦✦✦

Tiburon Peninsula Chamber of Commerce *96B Main St, Tiburon, CA 94920; tel: (415) 435-5633; fax: (415) 435-1132; web: www.citysearch.com/sfo/tiburon. Open Mon–Fri 0800–1600.*

Below
Going to Angel Island from Tiburon

Originally called Punta de Tiburon (Shark Point) by Mexican fishermen, today's town was born in 1884 as the terminus for the San Francisco and North Pacific Railroad ferry to San Francisco. Sweeping bay views – and daily ferry service – helped turn Tiburon and neighbouring **Belvedere** into exclusive dormitory communities for San Francisco.

Tiburon's tiny and almost always sunny **waterfront**✦✦✦ has become a trendy San Francisco getaway. Restaurants with outdoor decks surround the ferry landing. A long park offers space to run and enjoy views of San Francisco shimmering beyond Angel Island, a few hundred yards offshore. Central Tiburon was once a lagoon dotted with houseboats, or arks, that were eventually placed on pilings. **Ark**

ⓘ **Richardson Bay**
Audubon Center
and Sanctuary
(Tel: (415) 388-2524. Open
Wed–Sun 0900–1700.

Row** has become a popular dining and shopping area. Other sites include **Old St. Hilary's**, a restored Carpenter Gothic church overlooking the town; **Tiburon Uplands Nature Preserve;** and the **Richardson Bay Audubon Center and Sanctuary***. The Chamber of Commerce has free self-guided walking tour maps.

Food in Tiburon

Frequent ferry connections make Tiburon an easy restaurant excursion from San Francisco.

Sam's Anchor Cafe $$ *27 Main St; tel: (415) 435-4527*, is noisy, hospitable, busy and worth the wait for simply prepared seafood and burgers. Arrive about an hour early, leave your name with the *maître d'* and go explore.

Guaymas $$$ *5 Main St; tel: (415) 435-6300*, Mexican, and **Tutto Mare $$$** *9 Main St; tel: (415) 435-4747*, Northern Italian seafood, have similar views and require reservations.

Treasure Island*

ⓘ **San Francisco**
Convention &
Visitor Bureau
Lower Level, Hallidie Plaza,
San Francisco CA 94103;
tel: (415) 391-2000;
web: www.sfvisitor.org, Open
Mon–Fri 0900–1700,
Sat–Sun 0900–1500

The tabletop expanse of Treasure Island was created for the 1939 Golden Gate International Exposition, with access via the **San Francisco-Oakland Bay Bridge**. The large art moderne building facing San Francisco was originally the control tower and terminal building for Pan American Airways' flying boat service to Asia.

The island became a Naval base during World War II and reverted to the city of San Francisco 50 years later. Many of the former Navy buildings are now studios and sound stages for cinema and television productions. Part of the island has become a small marina and public park with seldom-visited views of the **San Francisco waterfront**. Best vistas are in the morning and at sunset.

Suggested tour

From San Francisco, follow I-80 east on the **San Francisco-Oakland Bay Bridge ❶** to **Treasure Island ❷**, then continue through the toll plaza area. Follow I-580 southbound to **Oakland ❸**. From Oakland, return northbound on I-580 to I-80 eastbound. Take the **University Ave ❹** exit into **Berkeley ❺** toward the **University of California, Berkeley ❻**.

Return to I-80 eastbound along San Francisco Bay to the **Richmond-San Rafael Bridge ❼** to **Marin County ❽**. The golden structure just south of the Marin County end of the bridge is **San Quentin Federal**

Prison ❾. Take Hwy 101 south to Paradise Dr. and the **Tiburon Peninsula** ❿. The road becomes narrow, windy and steep, but passengers can expect good bay views.

Continue around the peninsula to **Tiburon** ⓫ and **Belvedere** ⓬. Follow Tiburon Blvd along the shores of **Richardson Bay** ⓭ to Hwy 101 and turn south to **Sausalito** ⓮. Cross the **Golden Gate Bridge** ⓯ into San Francisco or, for pleasant afternoon views of the bridge, take the last exit before the bridge on to the **Marin Headlands** ⓰ and drive uphill to any of several car-parks.

Also worth exploring

Belvedere✷✷ ⓬ is Tiburon's smaller and wealthier neighbour. The name means 'beautiful view' in Italian, an assessment of the panorama west toward Sausalito and south across San Francisco Bay. The **China Cabin**✷✷ (*52 Beach Rd; tel: (415) 435-1853*) is an elegantly restored Victorian social saloon salvaged from the 1867 steamship SS *China*. The floor is made of oak and walnut; cut-glass floral window panes provide light and the cabin is trimmed in 22-carat gold.

Napa Valley Wine Country

Ratings

Food and drink	●●●●●
Wine	●●●●○
Scenery	●●●○○
Outdoor activities	●●●○○
Shopping	●●●○○
Walking	●●○○○
Wildlife	●●○○○
Children	●○○○○

This 30-mile strip of valley covered with lush vineyards could be a theme park version of Southern France. Some of America's finest wines and extraordinary promotional skills have made Napa the self-proclaimed Capital of California Wine – and turned Hwy 29 into one long traffic jam during the summer and at every weekend. The best time to visit is mid-week during the spring and autumn. If you must visit in summer, traffic is less congested on the Silverado Trail, which runs along the eastern side of the valley.

CALISTOGA❖❖

ⓘ Calistoga Chamber of Commerce
Railway depot, 1458 Lincoln Ave, # 9, Calistoga, CA 94515; tel: (707) 942-6333; web: www.calistogafun.com. Open Mon–Fri 0900–1799, Sat 1000–1500, Sun 1100–1600.

ⓗ Sharpsteen Museum
$ 1311 Washington St; tel: (707) 942-5911; web: www.nap anet.net/vi/sharpsteen/. Open daily 1200–1600 in winter, 1000–1600 in summer.

The town's mud baths and hot springs are better known than its wineries, thanks to Sam Brannan, the entrepreneur who quietly bought up San Francisco's entire supply of picks and shovels before shouting news of James Marshall's gold discovery on the streets of San Francisco in 1848. In 1860, Brannan founded a town he intended to promote as the 'Saratoga of California' after a famed resort town in New York state. What purportedly emerged was the 'Calistoga of Sarifornia'. Brannon's other historic contributions survive at the **Sharpsteen Museum❖**.

Hot springs, volcanic mud and a low-key atmosphere have come together in California's most relaxed spa town. Treatments run the gamut from simple soaks in hot mineral water to wallows in volcanic mud, herbal wraps and deep tissue massage. **Dr Wilkinson's Hot Springs** caters to the famous and the film stars. **Lavender Hill Spa** is known for its 'unthick' mud baths of volcanic ash mixed with kelp.

Lower Lake
Cobb
Guinda
Dunnigan
Robbins
Knights
Landing
Zamora
175
Middletown
Geyserville
NAPA
29
R.L. Stevenson
S.P.
20 Miles
0 10 20 Kilometres
0 10
Healdsburg
128
Calistoga
Pope
Valley
Lake
Berryessa
Woodland
West Sacramento
113
17
Windsor
SANTA
ROS
Angwin
the-Napa Valley S.P.
St. Helena
Winters
Davis
Forestville
Rio
St Helena
Rutherford
128
Dixon
Clarksburg
Graton
dental
116
Oakville
Loaf Ridge
S.P.
Yountville
ville
Vacaville
Courtland
Sebastopol
Glen Ellen
121
Fairfield
Clarksburg
Rohnert Par
30
Napa
TRAVIS A.F.B.
Walnut Grov
Sonoma
Napa
80
12
160
116
121
SOLANO
Rio Vista
Islet
Petaluma
20
Brannan I. S.R.A
160
37
29
11
680
Tern
eyes Station
Novato
Vallegio
Carquinez Straits
Antioch
VALLEJO
Benicia
Pittsburg
19
4
Fairfax
Martinez
San Rafael
14
CONCORD
Brentw
Mill Valley
Richmond
24
Walnut Creek
4
SAN
BERKELEY
OAKLAND
CONTRA
COSTA
FRANCISCO
580
Danville
San Ramon
SAN FRANCISCO
880
San Leandro
580
Daly City
Pacifica
San Bruno
HAYWARD
Pleasanton
Livermor
San Mateo
Redwood City
84
880
FREMONT
ALAMEDA
Half Moon Bay
SAN MATEO
Milpitas
Palo Alto
280
SUNNYVALE
84
Pescadero
Cupertino
Saratoga
Los Gatos
Campbell
85
SAN JO
SANTA
CLARA
101

ⓘ Dr Wilkinson's Hot Springs $$ *1507 Lincoln Ave; tel: (707) 942-4102. Open 0800–2200.*

Lavender Hill Spa $$ *1015 Foothill Blvd; tel: (707) 942-4495. Open 0900–2100.*

Nance's Hot Springs $ *1614 Lincoln Ave; tel: (707) 942-6211. Open Mon–Fri 0900–1600, to 1700 Sat–Sun.*

Old Faithful Geyser $ *1299 Tubbs Ln; tel: (707) 942-6463; web: www.oldfaithfulgeyser.com. Open 0900–1600 in winter, to 1700 in summer.*

Petrified Forest $ *4100 Petrified Forest Rd; tel: (707) 942-6667; web: www.petrifiedforest.org. Open Wed–Sun 1000–1630 in winter, daily 1000–1800 in summer.*

Schramsberg Vineyards *tel: (707) 942-4558; web: www.schramsberg.com. Open daily 0900–1700 by appointment.*

Calistoga Gliders $$ *tel: (707) 942-5000, advance booking required.*

Chateau Montelena *01429 Tubbs Ln; tel: (707) 942-5105; web: www.montelena.com. Open daily 1000–1600, tours by appointment. Free.*

Sterling Vineyards $ *1111 Dunaweal Ln; tel: (707) 942-3344; web: www.aboutwine.com. Open daily 1030–1630.*

Ordinary people flock to the down-to-earth spas along Lincoln Ave. **Nance's Hot Springs** is one of the more popular, with a full mineral bath, blanket wrap, steam bath and massage for less than the cost of a single treatment at one of the classier spas.

Napa's hot underground also surfaces at **Old Faithful Geyser**✦, which spits boiling water and steam every half hour or so. The geyser was born when an exploratory oil rig drilled into a geothermal source in the 1920s. After numerous failed attempts to cap the regular eruptions, landowners turned the inevitable into a tourist attraction. The source is part of the volcanic plumbing system that gave rise to eruptions at nearby **Mount St Helena**✦ (4344ft) and turned a lush grove of redwood trees into the **Petrified Forest**✦✦ about three million years ago.

The mountain is protected within **Robert Louis Stevenson State Park**✦✦ (*7 miles north on Hwy 29; tel: (707) 942-4575*). A 2½-mile trail leads to the top of the Napa Valley, with spectacular views stretching north to **Mount Shasta** on clear days. The park is named for the Scottish novelist Robert Louis Stevenson, who honeymooned in an abandoned miner's cabin on Mount St Helena in 1880. The cabin is long gone, but a trailside plaque marks the site. The highlight of his stay, Stevenson wrote in *Silverado Squatters*, was sampling 18 different champagnes from wine baron Jacob Schram's nearby **Schramsberg Vineyards**✦.

Calistoga's other high-altitude viewpoint is **Calistoga Glider Rides**✦✦, a 20- to 30-minute glider descent from about 5000ft. The ride can be as smooth as a toddler's roller-coaster or as acrobatic as a stunt plane, according to passengers' preference.

Don't miss winery visits around Calistoga. **Chateau Montelena**✦✦ has a formal Chinese garden with a traditional pagoda-pavilion overlooking a lake with a half-sunken junk. The French château-like architecture is also worth the drive, as is the Cabernet Sauvignon. **Sterling Vineyards**✦✦✦ sits atop a small hill, an extravagant white mission-style mansion accessible by aerial tram.

Accommodation and food in Calistoga

Rooms in all categories are snapped up quickly at peak periods, ie summer, weekends and holidays, so book in advance all year. **Bed and Breakfast Inns of Napa Valley** *tel: (707) 944-4444*, makes bookings throughout Wine Country.

Mount View Hotel & Spa $$$ *1457 Lincoln Ave; tel: (707) 942-6877*, is one of Calistoga's oldest spas. **Calistoga Wine Way Inn** $$ *1019 Foothill Blvd; tel: (707) 942-0680 or (800) 572-0679; web: www.napavalley.com/wineway*, offers a similar atmosphere without the spa. **Bosko's Ristorante** $$ *1364 Lincoln Ave; tel: (707) 942-9088, open daily 1100–2200*, is Calistoga's best Italian choice. **Fellion's Delicatessen** $, *1359 Lincoln Ave; tel: (707) 942-6722* is a favourite for picnic supplies.

CARQUINEZ STRAITS*

Benicia Chamber of Commerce & Visitors Center *601 First St, Benicia, CA 94510; tel: (707) 745-2120; web: www.ci.benicia.ca.us. Open Mon-Fri 0830–1700, Sat–Sun 1100–1500.*

Benicia Capitol State Historic Park *$ First and West G Sts; tel: (707) 745-3385. Open daily 1000–1700.*

Below
Stirling Vineyards, at Calistoga

This narrow channel is the sole outflow for Central Valley rivers draining the Sierra Nevada. The tiny port town of **Crockett** is cut into the hills along the south side of the Straits, dominated by the gigantic C&H Sugar refinery. **Carquinez Straits Scenic Drive**✧ leads 2 miles to the former ferry town of **Port Costa**, which lost its *raison d'être* when the **Carquinez Straits Bridge** was built at Crockett. The town is still a good spot to watch huge freighters sailing to the inland ports of **Sacramento** and **Stockton**.

On the north side of the Straits is **Benicia**✧, a one-time rival to San Francisco and the state capital for 13 months. **Benicia Capitol State Historic Park** preserves the 1852 Greek Revival capitol building, as well as the **Fischer-Hanlon House**✧, a renovated Gold Rush-era hotel. The capitol is furnished in the legislative style of the era, complete with polished spittoons. The Chamber of Commerce publishes a free self-guided walking tour map of this Victorian town which is still largely intact.

NAPA✤

ⓘ **Napa Valley
Conference &
Visitors Bureau**
*1310 Napa Town Center
(off First St), Napa, CA
94559; tel: (707) 226-7459;
web: www.napavalley.com.
Open daily 0900–1700.*

ⓜ **Napa County
Historical Society
Museum $** *1219 First St;
tel: (707) 224-1739.
Open Tue, Thur 1200–
1600.*

**Napa Valley Wine
Train $$**
*1275 McKinstry St;
tel: (707) 253-2111;
fax: (707) 253-9264;
web: www.winetrain.com.
Excursions daily.*

RMS Alambic Distillery
*1250 Cuttings Wharf Rd (off
Hwy 12/121, south west of
Napa); tel: (707) 253-9055.
Open daily 1030–1630
(free).*

Hakusan Sake Gardens
*One Executive Wy;
tel: (707) 258-6160; web:
www.hakusan.com/index.htm
l. Open Thur–Tue 1000–
1700 (free).*

Domaine Carneros $
*1240 Duhig Rd (off Hwy
12/121); tel: (707) 257-
0101; web:
www.domaine.com. Open
daily 1030–1800, tours at
1100, 1300, 1500, hourly
Mon-Fri 1100–1600 Sat–
Sun.*

Hess Collection $
*4411 Redwood Rd;
tel: (707) 255-1144; web:
www.hesscollection.com.
Open daily 1000–1600.*

Napa, the town, is the economic heart of Napa, the valley. Like many ageing hearts, its arteries have become clogged as its waistline sprawls. The town centre, west of the Napa River, however, remains a scenic reminder of a less hurried past, filled with Victorian homes, spreading trees and quiet sidewalks. Napa also has the majority of the Valley's hotels, restaurants and tourist facilities, if not the most famous names. The **Napa County Historical Society Museum**✤ explores local history from the days when Napa was a sunny riverside resort retreat for San Franciscans.

To see (but not to visit) the greatest number of wineries in the shortest possible time, ride the **Napa Valley Wine Train**✤, an elegantly restored passenger train that makes 36-mile lunch and dinner runs up and down the valley – but doesn't stop.

One of Napa's best non-winery stops is **RMS Alambic Distillery**✤✤. Owned by France's Rémy Martin, RMS is one of the state's top brandy producers. State law prohibits tasting of spirits, but sniffing is strongly encouraged. Napa's other non-winery must-see is **Hakusan Sake Gardens**✤, a modern sake brewery.

Not far away on the highway to Sonoma is **Domaine Carneros**✤, Taittinger's Napa Valley sparkling winery modelled on the French champagne maker's 18th-century Château de la Marquetterie.

Art lovers should make time to visit the **Hess Collection**✤✤, a restored turn-of-the-century winery and eclectic modern art collection neighbouring a calm Franciscan retreat centre.

Accommodation and food in Napa

The best way to absorb wine country is to spend a night or two in an inn or bed and breakfast (usually pricey). **Bed and Breakfast Inns of Napa Valley** *tel: (707) 944-4444*, and **Reservations Unlimited** *tel: (707) 252-1985* or *(800) 251-6272*, can book most Valley rooms.

Napa town isn't known for its food. **Alexis Baking Company $** *1517 Third St; tel: (707) 258-1827, open Mon–Wed 0630–1800, Thur–Fri 0630–2000, Sat 0730–1500, Sun 0800–1400*, has picnic supplies. **La Boucane $$$** *1778 Second St; tel: (707) 253-1177, open 1730-late*, serves Napa's best classic French cuisine. Downtown **Joe's Restaurant & Brewery $$** *902 Main St; tel: (707) 258-2337, open daily 0830–2200* is great for California-style bistro dishes, beers and ales. **High Tech Burrito $** *641 Trancas St: tel: (707) 224-8882, open daily 1100–2100* offers international verisons of *burritos*. **Sciambra French Bakery**, *$, 685 S. Freeway Dr (off Imola Ave); tel: (707) 252-3072, open daily 1000–1600*, is another well-regarded picnic provisioner.

RUTHERFORD/OAKVILLE⁘

Robert Mondavi Winery
7801 St Helena Hwy, Oakville; tel: (707) 226-1335 or (888) 766-6328. Open daily 1000–1600.

St Supery Winery
8440 St Helena Hwy, Rutherford; tel: (707) 963-4507; web: www.stsupery.com. Open daily 0930–1700, tours hourly 1000–1500.

Niebaum-Coppola Estate Winery & Vineyards
1991 St Helena Hwy, Rutherford; tel: (707) 963-9099. Open daily 1000–1700.

Mumm Napa Valley
8445 Silverado Trail, Rutherford; tel: (707) 942-3434. Open daily 1000–1700, tours hourly 1100–1500.

Rutherford Hill Winery
200 Rutherford Hill Rd, Rutherford; tel: (707) 963-9099. Open daily 1000–1700.

The tiny hamlets of Rutherford and Oakville, along Hwy 29, are ground zero in the continuing explosion of Napa wineries. **Robert Mondavi Winery**⁘ is the standard bearer for the Napa Valley, the first American wine-maker in modern times to commit to the French heresy that wine tastes better if made in small barrels rather than in 40,000-litre vats and that Cabernet Sauvignon demands different vinification than Cabernet Franc or Sauvignon Blanc. Mondavi's tours are among the most informative and the best suited to wine beginners. The down side is that the winery is so well known it attracts enormous

Robert Mondavi, standard bearer for Napa Valley wineries

crowds. Make tour bookings five days in advance in summer and at holiday weekends. There are a number of other good tours on offer.

St Supery Winery⁘ has the valley's best interactive exhibit, with a 3-D valley map, samples of the varied aromas found in fine wines and enormous windows overlooking winery operations.

Niebaum-Coppola Estate Winery & Vineyards⁑ is an historic château (formerly the Inglenook Estate Winery) with tasting room and cinema memorabilia museum owned by director Francis Ford Coppola.

Mumm Napa Valley⁑ offers sweeping views of the valley.

Rutherford Hill Winery⁑ has an excellent cave tour as well as shady picnic grounds.

Food in Rutherford/Oakville

The **Oakville Grocery Co**⁘ 7865 St Helena Hwy, Oakville; tel: (707) 944-8802, open daily 0900–1800, has been selling oil, vinegar and barbed wire since 1881, but the valley's oldest mercantile has grown into a gourmet haven. The store is packed with food, wine and – usually – with people. The lunchtime sandwich queue sometimes snakes out the door. The **Oakville Grocery Cafe $$** open daily 0500–1500, Thur-Mon 1700–2100, is a local favourite.

St Helena ❖❖

ℹ️ **St Helena Chamber of Commerce**
1010-A Main St (Hwy 29), St. Helena, CA 94574; tel: (707) 963-4456; web: www.sthelena.com. Open Mon–Fri 1000–1700, Sat 1000–1500.

🏛️ **Silverado Museum**
1490 Library Rd; tel: (707) 963-3757; web: www.napanet.net/vi/silverado/. Open Tue–Sun 1200–1600.

Below
The Auberge du Soleil Inn, in Rutherford

St Helena's town centre is the valley's finest collection of historic buildings. The literati should visit the **Silverado Museum**, with more than 8000 items related to Robert Louis Stevenson. The other half of the former library building is occupied by the **Napa Valley Wine Library**, a collection of photographs and newspaper cuttings related to local viticulture. **Ambrose Bierce House** (*1515 Main St; tel: (707) 963-3003*), where the misanthropic author lived for 15 years before disappearing into the Mexican Revolution, is a bed and breakfast with a small collection of Bierce memorabilia.

The town also has two of the valley's better outdoor attractions. **Bale Grist Mill State Historic Park❖** (*3 miles north on Hwy 29; tel: (707) 942-4575*) surrounds an 1847 grist mill that is still used for demonstrations. Hiking trails lead to the mill pond and **Bothe-Napa Valley State Park❖❖** (*4 miles north on Hwy 29; tel: (707) 942-4575*), once home to the Wappo Indians. The park has several fine hiking trails, a swimming-pool, camping and horseback riding (Western style only) summer to autumn.

California Wine

Rules about drinking white wine with fish and red wine with meats seemed sensible enough when both food and wine were predictable. But today's recipes incorporate a wider range of ingredients and flavours – and not just in California. It's more useful to find out what a wine actually tastes like than to look to the colour for guidance. Here are the major California grapes and wines, with an important caveat: every wine develops a different taste, depending on where and how the grapes were grown and how they were vinified, or made into wine. No two wines taste precisely the same and no two drinkers experience precisely the same taste from the same bottle. If it doesn't taste good to *you*, it doesn't taste good, no matter how long or loudly the 'experts' declaim. Most California wineries sell their own wine by the bottle or the case. Case purchases usually bring a 10–20 per cent discount off the list price, but it's often cheaper to buy wine at a local supermarket or discount store than at the winery or a wine shop. The disadvantage: smaller wineries have limited distribution, so their wines may be available only at the winery. If in doubt, ask at the winery.

Blanc de Blancs Literally 'white from whites', wine (often a delicate sparkling wine) made from white grapes, usually Chardonnay.

Blanc de Noirs 'White from blacks', sparkling white wine made from red grapes, usually Pinot Noir. The skins, which contain most of the colour, are separated from the juice immediately after pressing to preserve the light colour. Blanc de Noirs normally has a richer, fruitier taste than Blanc de Blancs. Both are quite dry in California.

Blush Pink wines, usually white Zinfandels, are somewhere between almost-white and almost-red. The longer the juice is left with the skins after crushing, the darker the colour and the more intense the flavour. Most blush wines are light, sweet and meant to be drunk as young as possible.

Cabernet Sauvignon California 'Cabs' are normally dry, medium to full-bodied, and can be tannic, a less direct way to say astringent. The dominant flavours are berries and cherries.

Chardonnay Heavy advertising has turned Chardonnay into the white wine of choice for many people. Pick your style: light, with simple flavours like apples, citrus and flowers; rich, with oak, butter and nuts; or steely, with very little taste at all.

Gewürztraminer California wine-makers usually opt for a slightly sweet German style, but Gewürz can also be made dry, in the Alsacian style, or as an almost too-rich dessert wine. All three styles taste of spice, flowers and fruit.

Merlot This red is softer than Cabernet, ie, it is less astringent and more 'fruity'. Wine-makers traditionally blend Merlot with Cabernet to create a softer, more drinkable wine that requires less ageing.

Petit Sirah A delicate red that is less common in California. Look for it as Syrah in French blends or Shiraz in Australia.

Pinot Noir Usually a silky-smooth light red that leaves a lingering freshness rather than the heaviness more typical of Cabernet and Merlot.

Riesling Germany's other white grape is the classic for sweet dessert wines, but can also be made as a delicate dry wine filled with flower and fruit flavours.

Sauvignon Blanc or **Fumé Blanc** By either name, wines made from this white grape are normally lighter and less pronounced in flavour than Chardonnay.

Sparkling wine California's way around Champagne's legal lock on the name Champagne. Look for 'methode champenoise' or 'fermented in this bottle' for top quality. 'Charmant' is plonk produced in bulk. Most of the major French champagne houses also produce sparkling wine in California.

Zinfandel This rich red is usually spicy, with a strong hint of berries.

Beringer Vineyards
$ 2000 Main St;
tel: (707) 963-7115; web:
www.beringer.com.
Open daily 0930–1700,
tours every half-hour.

**Kornell Champagne
Cellars** $ 1091 Larkmead
Ln; tel: (707) 942-0859.
Open daily 1000–1700.

Don't miss **Beringer Vineyards**✴ and the **Rhine House**✴✴✴, the valley's most-photographed building, modelled after an ancestral Gothic German homestead. The winery can be crowded, but it's worth slogging through the mob to see the rich, wood-panelled interior and regal tasting room. **Kornell Champagne Cellars**✴ is one of the valley's pioneer sparkling wine producers.

Accommodation and food in St Helena

Two of Napa's finest resorts are tucked into the hills above the Silverado Trail. **Auberge du Soleil**✴✴✴ $$$ 180 Rutherford Hill Rd, Rutherford; tel: (707) 963-1211 or (800) 348-5406; web: www.auberge dusoleil.com, is a Mediterranean-inspired retreat surrounded by olive groves and valley vistas.

Meadowood Resort✴✴✴ $$$ 900 Meadowood Ln, St Helena; tel: (707) 963-3646 or (800) 458-8080; web: www.placestostay.com, surrounds a private croquet lawn and golf course. Both have rabid followers and receive rave reviews for their pricey restaurants.

Tra Vigne✴✴✴ $$$ 1050 Charter Oak Ave; tel: (707) 963-4444, open 1130–2200, specialises in Italian-laced California cuisine.

The **Wine Spectator Greystone Restaurant**✴✴✴ $$$ 2555 Main St; tel: (707) 967-1010, open 1130-2200, part of the Culinary Institute of America's nearby campus at the former Christian Brothers Winery, has California versions of Mediterranean staples.

VALLEJO✴

**Vallejo Convention
& Visitors Bureau**
495 Mare Island Way,
Vallejo, CA 94590;
tel: (707) 642-3653;
fax: (707) 644-2206;
web: www.visitvallejo.com.
Open Mon–Fri 0830–1700,
Sat-Sun 0930–1430.

**Vallejo Naval &
Historical Museum**
$ 734 Marin St;
tel: (707) 643-0077.
Open Tue–Sat 1000–1630.

Vallejo was California's first state capital, named for General Mariano Vallejo, one of California's few Mexican leaders who became a successful American politician. Vallejo was also home to a major US Navy repair facility and mothball fleet, the **Mare Island Naval Shipyard**, which closed in 1997. The rusting hulks that once lined the mouth of the Napa River are gone and the former shipyard is being turned to civilian uses.

Local history is recounted in the **Vallejo Naval and Historical Museum** (734 Marin St; tel: (707) 643-0077), in the old city hall building. Many of Vallejo's graceful Victorian buildings were replaced or altered beyond recognition during the frantic growth and ship building of World War II. Enough historic structures survived to create a small **Architectural Heritage District**, between Georgia, Sutter, Carolina, Monterey and York Sts.

The most popular reason to visit Vallejo is **Six Flags Marine World** (tel: (707) 643-6772, closed winter), the most scenic way to visit is aboard a Blue & Gold Fleet ferry from San Francisco (see page 150 for details).

YOUNTVILLE✦

ⓘ Yountville Chamber of Commerce
6516 Yount St, Yountville, CA 94599;
tel: (707) 944-0904.

ⓜ Napa Valley Museum $
55 Presidents Circle;
tel: (707) 944-0500.
Open Wed–Mon
1000–1700.

Domaine Chandon
1 California Dr.;
tel: (707) 944-2280;
web: www.dchandon.com.
Open Jan–Mar Wed–Sun
1000-1800, daily Apr–Dec.

This is the culinary heart of the Napa Valley and the beginning of serious, shoulder-to-shoulder wineries. Art lovers head for the **Napa Valley Museum**✦, an art gallery, wine museum and cultural centre. **Vintage 1870** (*6525 Washington St; tel: (707) 944-2451*) is a one-time winery turned shopping mall.

Domaine Chandon✦✦✦ has the valley's most informative sparkling winery tour. Hot-air balloons frequently take off from the winery grounds or nearby.

Food in Yountville

Yountville is Napa's answer to Berkeley's Gourmet Ghetto, with prices to match. Make bookings as far in advance as possible.

The French Laundry✦✦✦ **$$$** *6640 Washington St; tel: (707) 944-2380, open 1130-2130,* is one of the valley's original name eateries, followed by **Mustards Grill**✦✦✦ **$$$** (*7399 St Helena Hwy; tel: (707) 944-2424, open 1130–2100, to 2200 Fri–Sat*, **Brix Restaurant & Wine Shop**✦✦✦ **$$$** *7377 St Helena Hwy; tel: (707) 944-2749, open daily 1130-1500, 1600-2130,* **Bistro Jeanty**✦✦✦ **$$** (*6510 Washington St; tel: (707) 944-0103, open 1130-2230* and a constantly changing constellation of would-be stars.

California Wine History

California has been producing wine since Mission friars first planted criolla grapes for sacramental use. In 1857, Hungarian immigrant Agoston Haraszthy planted European *Vinifera* grapes in Sonoma. His successful **Buena Vista Winery** soon attracted competitors **Gundlach-Bundschu** (1858), **Charles Krug** (1861), **Schramsberg** (1862) and a host of other familiar names. By the 1890s, California wines were winning gold medals in every major European competition.

The 1906 San Francisco earthquake and subsequent fire destroyed enormous stocks of wine ageing in San Francisco warehouses as well as wineries up and down Wine Country. By the time the industry was back on its feet, America was plunging into Prohibition. From 1919–33, it was illegal to make or consume wine (or any other alcoholic beverage) except for sacramental, medicinal or family purposes.

A few vineyards hung on, but most switched to fruit trees and other crops or went bankrupt. Robert Mondavi and the few other 1940s and 1950s wine-makers who dreamed of re-establishing the glory days were dismissed as dreamers. Today, they're worshipped as saints.

Their dogged vision, plus research from the University of California at Davis, near Sacramento, and technological improvements from bulk wine-makers such as Gallo, gave California vintners more control over the art of turning grape juice into wine than any wine-makers in the world. When **Stag's Leap** bested Mouton Rothschild in a Paris competition in 1976, the California wine rush was on.

Wine Country from the air

Balloons Above the Valley *tel: (707) 253-2222 or (800) 464-2724; web: www.balloonrides.com*

Napa Valley Balloons *tel: (707) 253-2224 or (800) 253-2224.*

Sonoma Thunder *tel: (707) 538-7359 or (800) 759-5638; web: www.balloontours.com*, are experienced operators.

Ballooning over the vineyards of the Napa Valley

One of the most common sounds on a Napa morning is the gentle roar of propane burners from hot-air balloons drifting above the vineyards. Balloon tours nearly always lift off near dawn, when breezes are light, just as the night mists burn away to reveal rank upon rank of trellised vines sweeping across valley contours. Plan on landing 90 minutes later to a champagne breakfast.

It's not cheap – about $175 per person – but it's worth the experience. Advance booking is required.

Driving guide

Take the **San Francisco–Oakland Bay Bridge** ❶ to I-80 eastbound. Cross the **Carquinez Straits Bridge** ❷. Detour through **Vallejo** ❸ or continue on I-80 to Hwy 37 to Hwy 29. Follow Hwy 29 north through **Napa** ❹, **Yountville** ❺, **Oakville** ❻, **Rutherford** ❼, **St Helena** ❽ and **Calistoga** ❾.

Follow Hwy 101 north from San Francisco across the **Golden Gate Bridge** ❿ through Marin County to **Rohnert Park** ⓫, **Santa Rosa** ⓬ and **Healdsburg** ⓭. Take Healdsburg Ave and Alexander Valley Rd north, then east to **Jimtown** ⓮ and Hwy 128. Turn south to **Kellog** and Franz Valley Rd to Porter Creek Rd and follow Calistoga Rd to Hwy 12 and **Kenwood** ⓯. Take Warm Springs Rd south to **Glen Ellen** ⓰. Continue south to **El Verano** ⓱ and turn east to **Sonoma** ⓲. Return to San Francisco via the Carneros Hwy and the Napa Valley or take Hwy 121 to Hwy 37 and back to Hwy 101.

28
Navarro
Ukiah
Lake
Leesville
Co
20
Williams
Meridian

Hendy Woods S.P.
Philo
29
Indian Valley Res.
Nice
Lucerne

Boonville
253
33
Clear L.
Lakeport
23
Clea
rimes

0   10   20 Miles

0   10   20 Kilometres

oint Arena
Hopland
175
Clear Lake S.P.
Kelseyville
Lake S.P.
Clearlake
53

128
Lower Lake
16
Dunnigan

ay
Gualala
29
Cobb
Guinda
YOLO

Annapolis
Lake Sonoma
SONOMA
Geyserville
Middletown
NAPA
505

Black Pt.
warts Point
Cloverdale
175
R.L. Stevenson S.P.
Pope Valley
Lake Berryessa
Esparto
Wood
West

Salt Point S.P.
Austin Creek S.R.A.
Healdsburg
128
14
Calistoga
9
Angwin
Winters

Cazadero
13
Bothe-Napa Valley S.P.
St. Helena
128

Northwest Cape
Guerneville
Monte Rio
Windsor
Forestville
SANTA ROSA
8
7
Sugarloaf Ridge S.P.
5
Yountville

Jenner
Graton
12
12
15
Glen Ellen
121

Sonoma Coast St. Beach
Occidental
Sebastopol
116
16
Napa
Va
Fair

Bodega Bay
11
Rohnert Park
17

Dillon Beach
Tomales
30
101
18
Sonoma
4
80

POINT REYES NATL. SEASHORE
1
Petaluma
116
121
29
SOLANO
R

Tomales Bay S.P.
Novato
20
37
680
Bra

Inverness
Point Reyes Station
Samuel P. Taylor S.P.
VALLEJO
3
2
Pittsbu

Pt. Reyes
MARIN
Fairfax
Benicia
Martinez
CO

GOLDEN GATE N.R.A.
San Rafael
14
19

Mill Valley
Richmond
24
Wal

Farallon Islands
SAN FRANCISCO
BERKELEY
OAKLAND
Da

FARALLON N.W.R.
10
1
580
San Lea

SAN FRANCISCO
880

Daly City
101

Pacifica
San Bruno
HAYWARD

San Mateo
Redwood City
84
880

Half Moon Bay
Palo Alto

SAN MATEO
1
280
SUN
84

Sonoma Wine Country

Ratings

Scenery	●●●●●
Wine	●●●●●
Food and wine	●●●●●
Architecture	●●●○○
History	●●●○○
Children	●●○○○
Wildlife	●●○○○
Museums	●●○○○

Sonoma is an agglomeration of several wine valleys, one of which is actually called Sonoma. The geographic variety makes Sonoma slower to drive through than neighbouring Napa, but far more rustic and interesting. California's wine industry was born in Sonoma, but the region has been far less aggressive in promoting itself than Napa. For visitors, that makes Sonoma a less expensive, less crowded and far more pleasurable experience – and Sonoma wines win at least as many medals as their Napa counterparts.

DRY CREEK VALLEY❖

Dry Creek, running north from Healdsburg to **Lake Sonoma**, was one of Sonoma's first official wine appellations. It's hard to find mediocre wine or boring scenery in the twisting valley. **Dry Creek Vineyards**❖❖ (*3770 Lambert Bridge Rd; tel: (707) 433-1000; open daily 1030–1630*), is one of Dry Creek Valley's first and most-awarded wineries. **Preston Vineyards**❖❖❖ (*9282 W Dry Creek Rd; tel: (707) 433-3372;. open daily 1100–1630*) offers enticing picnic tables in a flowering garden, *bocce* courts and home-made bread to go with its rich red wines. **Ferrari-Carano Vineyards & Winery**❖❖❖ (*8761 W. Dry Creek Rd; tel: (707) 433-6700; open daily 1000–1700*) is an architectural masterpiece with killer Chardonnay.

GEYSERVILLE❖❖

The most imposing structure on view is **Château Souverain**❖, an ordinary winery in an extraordinary, château-inspired building.

Hendy
Woods
S.P.
Philo
Boonville
oint Arena

Ukiah
253
Hopland
128

Clear L.
Lakeport
175
Kelseyville

Nice
Lucerne
Res.
37

29

29   53
Cobb   Lower Lake   16

Guinda

Cloverdale
Lake Son
Dry Valley Creek
SONOMA

Russian River

Geyserville ille
175   37
Middletown   NAPA
29
R.L. Stevenson
S.P.

Pope
Valley
Lake
Berr

Gualala
Annapolis

Black Pt.
warts Point
Salt Point S.P.

Austin
Creek
S.R.A.
Healdsburg
Windsor
Cazadero
Gu Guerneville
Monte Rio
Jenner
Occidental
Sonoma Coast St. Beach

Healdsburg
128
Calistoga
SANTA
ROSA
Forestville
Graton
116
Sebas
Rohnert Park
Valley of the Moon

Bothe-Napa Valley
St. Helena
Angwin
Sugarloaf Ridge
S.P.
Yountvi
Glen Ellen
Park
Sonoma

Northwest Cape
Santa Rosa
12

Sonoma
Na

Bodega Bay
Dillon Beach
Tomales
101
Sonoma
116   121

30

121

29

Tomales Bay S.P.
POINT REYES NATL. SEASHORE
Inverness
Point Reyes Station
Samuel P. Taylor S.P.
Pt. Reyes
GOLDEN GATE N.R.A.
MARIN

Petaluma

Novato
VALLEJO
Benicia
Martine
37
14

Fairfax
San Rafael
Mill Valley
Richmond

Farallon
Islands
FARALLON N.W.R.

SAN
FRANCISCO
SAN FRANCISCO
Daly City
Pacifica
Sa Bruno

BERKELEY O
880

101

HAY

0   10   20 Miles

0   10   20 Kilometres

ⓘ Geyserville Chamber of Commerce *21060 Geyserville Ave, Geyserville, CA 95441; tel: (707) 894-3695.*

🏛 Château Souverain *400 Souverain Rd; tel: (707) 433-3141. Open daily 1000–1700.*

Pedroncelli Winery *1220 Canyon Rd; tel: (707) 857-3531. Open daily 1000–1700.*

Trentadue Winery *19170 Geyserville Ave; tel: (707) 433-3104. Open daily 1100–1630.*

Château Souverain, in Geyserville

Fortunately, the Alexander Valley has better to offer, starting with **Pedroncelli Winery**, one of the area's last family-owned wineries to go corporate, and Italian-inspired **Trentadue Winery✴✴**.

Accommodation in Geyserville

Victoriana lovers may swoon at **Hope-Merrill House✴✴✴ \$\$** *21253 Geyserville Ave; tel: (707) 857-3356*, a three-storey bed-and-breakfast jewel with strictly symmetrical landscaping, extravagant silk-screened wallpaper, carved armchairs and velvet-covered divans.

Hope-Bosworth House✴✴ \$\$ *across the street at 21238 Geyserville Ave; tel: (707) 857-3356*, is a more cheerful, less formal and less expensive Queen Anne restoration.

GUERNEVILLE❖

ⓘ Russian River Region Visitor Information Center
14034 Armstrong Woods Rd, Guerneville, CA 95446; tel: (707) 869-9212; web: www.russianriver.com. Open Mon–Fri 0930–1700 and holiday weekends 1000–1500 in winter, daily 0930–1700 in summer. This Visitor Information Center carries an excellent Russian River Wine Road map listing all the wineries along the river. Unlike their more formal counterparts in the Napa and Sonoma valleys, Russian River and nearby wineries seldom charge for tasting or organise formal tours.

ⓘ Armstrong Redwoods State Reserve $ 2 miles north, Armstrong Woods Rd; tel: (707) 869-2015. Open 0800–one hour after sunset.

Korbel Champagne Cellars 13250 River Rd; tel: (707) 824-7000. Open Nov–Mar 0900–1630, Apr–Oct 0900–1700.

Topolos at Russian River Vineyards 5700 Gravenstein Hwy N., Forestville; tel: (707) 887-1575. Open 1030–1730.

Mark West Winery 7010 Trenton-Healdsburg Rd, Forestville; tel: (707) 544-4813. Open 1100–1600.

Pronounced *gurnvil*, the biggest settlement in the Russian River Valley began as a logging town in the 1880s, blossomed as a San Francisco summer resort and slipped into the hippie era. Wealthy city escapees have since filtered into the valley, creating an appealing mix of counter-culture, urban sophisticates, gay holiday-makers and local wine-makers, none of them in a rush to get anywhere.

Wine touring and lazing about the Russian River are the main activities. **Johnson's Beach**❖❖, a placid strand in the centre of town, offers sand, canoes, paddle-boats and rubber rafts in summer. The beach is also the main stage for the wildly popular **Russian River Jazz Festival**❖❖, held each Sept. The river is less benign in winter, when heavy rains produce periodic floods. Many river-front homes and businesses have been raised to the first floor to escape the high waters.

Guerneville's most often-ignored asset is **Armstrong Redwoods State Reserve**❖❖❖, 750 acres of virgin coast redwood groves, hiking trails and primitive camping. Don't stray off the trails as it's easy to get lost in the tangled thickets in the centre of the park. **Armstrong Woods Pack Station** (*tel: (707) 887-2939*) offer half-day tours and overnight forest expeditions on horseback (advance booking required).

The Russian River is lined with vineyards and wineries, most of them upstream (east) from Guerneville. One must-see, even if you are not doing the wineries, is **Korbel Champagne Cellars**❖❖❖, which makes beer, wine, brandy, and yes, champagne-style sparkling wines. The red brick buildings are swathed in ivy and surrounded by hundreds of varieties of roses with plenty of shaded picnic tables.

Topolos at Russian River Vineyards❖❖ produces mostly reds and is one of the River's friendliest wineries. The winery restaurant (*tel: (707) 887-1562*) is a pleasant forest retreat.

Mark West Winery❖❖ combines wine and **California Carnivores**❖❖❖, the area's only nursery specialising in carnivorous plants.

Accommodation and food in Guerneville

The river resort is well supplied with places to sleep and eat. The best of both is **Applewood** $$$ *13555 Hwy 116; tel: (707) 869-9093* or *(800) 555-8509; web: www.applewoodinn.com*, the Russian River's most luxurious inn and best gourmet restaurant (*open for dinner Tue-Sat*). **Fife's** $$ *16467 River Rd; tel: (707) 869-0656*, was Guerneville's original gay resort.

Brew Moon $$ *16248 Main St; tel: (707) 869-0201, open 0800–1500*, has good barbecued food, while **Burdon's Restaurant** $$ *15405 River Rd; tel: (707) 869-2615, open Wed–Sun 1700–2100*, is more up-market American-Continental.

HEALDSBURG✦✦

❶ Healdsburg Chamber of Commerce *217 Healdsburg Ave, Healdsburg, CA 95448; tel: (707) 433-6935. Open Mon–Fri 0900–1700, Sat–Sun 1000–1400.*

ⓘ Trentadue✦✦ *320 Center St; tel: (707) 433-1082. Open daily 1000–1700.*

Windsor *308B Center St; tel: (707) 433-2822. Open Mon–Fri 1000–1700, Sat–Sun 1000–1800.*

Healdsburg Museum *221 Matheson St; tel: (707) 431-3325. Open Tue–Sun 1100–1600.*

This is one of the few wine country towns that still seems to have more grape growers and farm workers than tourists. Founded in 1857 by a migrant farmer turned merchant, the tranquil town remains focused on its tree-lined **central plaza✦✦✦**. Healdsburg straddles an invisible border between the Russian River, Dry Creek and Alexander valleys, which makes it a popular starting point for wine tours.

If time is short, several wineries have tasting rooms on or near the plaza, including **Trentadue✦✦** and **Windsor.** More than 20 wineries are within easy cycling distance of the bed and breakfasts that have sprung up all over town, and dozens lie within a quick drive. And when wine touring gets too much, try **Veterans Memorial Beach✦** on the Russian River, a mile south of the plaza. Canoes and rubber rafts can be hired for a cooling float downstream; the hire company provides the return trip.

The **Healdsburg Museum✦**, in the 1910 Carnegie Library building, has a collection of Pomo Indian baskets and artefacts from California's Mexican period. Extensive displays explain local history, assisted by one of the area's largest photographic archives.

Accommodation and food in Healdsburg

Those who fail to appreciate the studied clutter of California's version of the Victorian era should stick to motels or the **Belle de Jour Inn $$** *16276 Healdsburg Ave; tel: (707) 431-9777; web: www.belledejourinn.com*, a luxurious collection of refreshingly simple cottages and carriage house. If money is no object, book into **Madrona Manor $$$** *1001 Westside Rd at Dry Creek Rd; tel: (707) 433-4231 or (800) 358-4003; web: www.madronamanor.com*, a rambling manor house surrounded by exotic gardens and a citrus orchard amid the vineyards. The best town centre choice is the **Healdsburg Inn on the Plaza $$$** *110 Matheson St; tel: (707) 433-6991 or (800) 431-8663; web: www.healdsburginn.com.*

Most of Healdsburg's best restaurants are on or near the plaza:

Bistro Ralph $$ *109 Plaza St E; tel: (707) 433-1380, open Mon–Fri 1130–1430, daily 1700–late*, is an intimate bistro and long-term survivor in a turbulent restaurant scene. The **Downtown Bakery & Creamery $** *308A Center St; tel: (707) 431-2719, open Mon–Fri 0600–1730, Sat 0700–1730, Sun 0700–1600*, and **Flying Goat Coffee Roastery and Cafe $** *324 Center St; tel: (707) 433-9081, open Mon-Fri 0700-1800, Sat-Sun 0800-1800*, are favourite local breakfast stops. The **Madrona Manor Restaurant $$$** is one of the most sought-after tables in Healdsburg, known for its ambience, presentation and fresh garden ingredients.

Grapes ripening in the Californian autumn sun

ROHNERT PARK❖

Rohnert Park began as a seed farm, but is sprouting more shopping malls than plants in recent years. The sole reason to stop is the **California Welcome Center** (*5000 Roberts Lake Rd, Rohnert Park, CA 94928; tel: (707) 586-3795; web: www.sonomawine.com; open daily*), the wine country's best visitor facility, with helpful staff, an extensive wine-tasting selection and wine shop, and computerised trip planning and itinerary help.

SANTA ROSA❖❖

ℹ Greater Santa Rosa Conference & Visitors Bureau
9 Fourth St, Santa Rosa, CA 95401; tel: (707) 577-8674; fax: (707) 571-5949; web: www.visitsantarosa.com. Open Mon–Fri 0830–1700, Sat–Sun 1000–1500.

Santa Rosa is ringed with shopping malls and plagued by traffic jams. It also has splendid residential neighbourhoods and more than its fair share of quirky museums, gardens and other attractions.

In the running for quirkiest are **Snoopy's Gallery & Gift Shop❖**, the world's largest collection of 'Peanuts' cartoon strip memorabilia, compliments of creator Charles Schultz, a local resident, and the **Church of One Tree** (*492 Sonoma Ave*), built of wood milled from a single redwood tree.

① Sonoma County Tourism Program
401 College Ave, Suite D, Santa Rosa, CA 95401; tel: (707) 524-7589; fax: (707) 524-7231; web: www.visitsonoma.com. Open Mon–Fri 0830–1700.

① Luther Burbank Home & Gardens $
Santa Rosa & Sonoma Aves; tel: (707) 524-5445. Gardens open daily 0800–1700, building tours 1000–1600 Apr–Oct.

Sonoma County Museum $ *425 7th St; tel: (707) 579-1500. Open Wed-Sun 1100–1600.*

Jesse Peter Native American Art Museum
Santa Rosa Junior College, 1501 Mendocino Ave; tel: (707) 527-4479. Open Mon–Fri 1200–1600.

California Museum of Art $ *Luther Burbank Center for the Arts, 50 Mark West Springs Rd; tel: (707) 527-0297; web: www.lbc.net. Open Wed, Fri 1300–1600, Thur 1300–2000, Sat–Sun 1100–1600.*

① Snoopy's Gallery & Gift Shop $ *1665 W. Steele Ln; tel: (707) 546-3385. Open Wed–Sun 1000–1600.*

A more down-to-earth attraction is the **Luther Burbank Home & Gardens**✦✦✦, the long-time home and gardens planted by the horticulturist who created more than 800 new varieties of commercial fruits, flowers, vegetables and other plants around the turn of the century.

There are several other traditional museums worth visiting. The **Sonoma County Museum**✦✦, in a restored 1909 post office and federal building, spans the eras from Native American habitation through the Victorian era. **Jesse Peter Native American Art Museum** displays Native American arts and crafts from across the continent, while the **California Museum of Art** features rotating exhibits by local artists.

Grapes are only one of many products that have made Sonoma County famous; the area is at least as well known for apples, escargot, berries, salad greens, lamb, goat's milk cheese, duck and other comestibles. The best guide to local farms, seasonal produce and agricultural tours is **Sonoma County Farm Trails**✦✦✦ *(tel: (707) 571-8288)*, a free self-guiding tour map available at most wineries and visitor centres.

Accommodation and food in Santa Rosa

Hotel La Rose $ *308 Wilson St; tel: (707) 579-3200 or (800) 527-6738; web: www.hotellarose.com*, occupies a historic landmark building. **John Ashe & Co $$$** *4330 Barnes Rd; tel: (707) 527-7687. open Tue-Sun, 1130-1400, daily 1400-2100*, blends Asian, French, Italian and Southwestern American flavours. **Kenwood Restaurant and Bar $$$** *9900 Hwy 12, Kenwood; tel: (707) 833-6326, open daily 1130–2100*, is a wine country favourite just south of Santa Rosa.

California poppies blaze through the gardens of the Preston Vineyard

SONOMA***

Sonoma Valley Visitors Bureau
453 First St E., Sonoma, CA 95476; tel: (707) 996-1090; fax: (707) 996-9212; web: sonomavalley.com. Open daily 0900–1700, to 1900 June–Oct.

Sonoma State Historic Park $
20 E. Spain St; tel: (707) 938-1519. Open daily 1000–1700.

Buena Vista Winery
1800 Old Winery Rd; tel: (707) 938-1266. Open daily 1030–1700.

Gundlach-Bundschu Winery *2000 Denmark St; tel: (707) 938-5277; web: www.gundbun.com. Open daily 1100–1630.*

Sebastiani Sonoma Cask Cellars
389 Fourth St E.; tel: (707) 933-3206; web: www.sebastiani.com. Open daily 1000–1700.

Viansa Winery & Italian Marketplace
25200 Arnold Dr. (Hwy 121); tel: (707) 935-4700. Open daily 1000–1700.

Sonoma town retains much of its original Mexican flavour despite years of wine country gentrification, thanks in large part to the 8-acre **plaza***** designed by General Mariano Vallejo in 1835. The Bear Flag Revolt of 1846 that catapulted California into America began in Sonoma. The revolt, which looms large in California history books, involved about three dozen American settlers who seized control of the unused and unguarded *presidio* at Sonoma. Their chief prisoner was General Vallejo, a long-time supporter of American annexation for California. Both the revolt and the California Republic dissolved a month later when the US Navy sailed into Monterey Bay.

A monument to the revolt sits in the middle of the shady plaza, across from **Sonoma State Historic Park**, which includes **Mission San Francisco Solano de Sonoma**, **Vallejo's home** and the **Sonoma Barracks** once occupied by a handful of Mexican soldiers. A dozen or so Mission-era buildings surround the plaza, most of them now used as restaurants, shops or boutiques. One of the more interesting is the 1850 **Swiss Hotel**** (*18 W. Spain St*), a stunningly good restaurant and small hotel.

California's modern wine industry was born at **Buena Vista Winery****, a large estate with a stone winery, hillside tunnels, an art gallery and picnic area. **Gundlach-Bundschu Winery*** is nearly as scenic with rich, up-to-date vintages. **Sebastiani Sonoma Cask Cellars*** has the area's most informative tour. Look for the hand-carved casks. **Viansa Winery & Italian Marketplace**** has Sonoma's best winery shop and picnic area overlooking a wildlife refuge.

Accommodation and food in Sonoma

The pink stucco **Sonoma Mission Inn & Spa $$$** *18140 Sonoma Hwy (at Boyes Blvd); tel: (707) 938-9000 or (800) 862-4945; web: www.sonomamissioninn.com*, is the most elegant and most expensive spa in Sonoma County. The luxurious spa is the main draw, but the inn is a traditional favourite for visiting Hollywood types. Two inn restaurants serve basic California cuisine: **The Grille $$$** is overpriced; **The Café $$** is more reasonable.

Not far from French-inspired **Babette's Restaurant & Wine Bar $$** *464 First St E.; tel: (707) 939-8921, open daily 1200-2200*, is a fine American-style choice, **Cafe La Haye $$** *140 E. Napa St; tel: (707) 935-5994.* **Della Santina's $$$** *133 E. Napa St; tel: (707) 935-0576, open daily 1100-1500 and 1700-2130*, does Italian. **The Swiss Hotel $$$** *18 W. Spain St; tel: (707) 938-2884, open daily 1130-1430 and 1700-2100*, concentrates on current California cuisine with period photographs and artefacts on the walls.

VALLEY OF THE MOON✧✧✧

🏛 Jack London State Historic Park $
2400 Jack London Ranch Rd, Glen Ellen; tel: (707) 938-5216. Museum open daily 0930–1700; park open 0930–1700 in winter, to 1900 in summer.

🐴 Sonoma Cattle Company $$
tel: (707) 996-8566. Trail rides Apr-Nov.

This is the capital of the Jack London cult. The author of *Call of the Wild* and numerous other stories that celebrate nature, manhood and the nobility of suffering in the Great Outdoors named the valley for the way the moon seems to appear and disappear behind the surrounding mountain peaks. London and his wife settled at the well-named **Beauty Ranch✧✧✧**, 800 acres that have become **Jack London State Historic Park✧✧✧**. London was the highest-paid writer of his era, which makes more intriguing the collection of rejection letters displayed in his house, now the park museum. A series of trails lead to the ruins of **Wolf House**, built for the couple in 1913 and destroyed by arson just before they moved in. Both are buried on a hilltop above Wolf House. **Sonoma Cattle Company✧** *(tel: (707) 996-8566)* offers horseback tours of London's lands.

Accommodation and food in Valley of the Moon

Beltane Ranch $$$ *11775 Sonoma Hwy; tel: (707) 996-6501*, is a buttercup yellow ranch bunkhouse become bed and breakfast. **Gaige House Inn $$$** *13540 Arnold Dr.; tel: (707) 935-0237; web: www.gaige.com*, a seemingly staid Victorian house, actually contains an eclectic collection of modern art.

Acclaimed food writer M F K Fisher lived in Glen Ellen for years. Her presence seems to have inspired the **Glen Ellen Inn $$** *13670 Arnold Dr; tel: (707) 996-6409, open 1730–late*, which specialises in dishes prepared with local ingredients.

Mes Trois Filles $$ *13648 Arnold Dr; tel: (707) 938-4844, open 1730–late*, offers French country cuisine with a touch of Japanese.

Driving guide

Follow Hwy 101 north from San Francisco across the **Golden Gate Bridge ❶** through Marin County to **Rohnert Park ❷**, **Santa Rosa ❸** and **Healdsburg ❹**. Take Healdsburg Ave and Alexander Valley Rd north, then east to **Jimtown ❺** and Hwy 128. Turn south to **Kellog ❻** and Franz Valley Rd to Porter Creek Rd and follow Calistoga Rd to Hwy 12 and **Kenwood ❼**. Take Warm Springs Rd south to **Glen Ellen ❽**. Continue south to **El Verano ❾** and turn east to **Sonoma ❿**. Return to San Francisco via the Carneros Hwy and the Napa Valley or take Hwy 121 to Hwy 37 and back to Hwy 101.

Detour

From **Healdsburg ❹**, take Dry Creek Rd through the **Dry Creek Valley ⓫** to Canyon Rd, then turn east on Canyon Rd to Hwy 101. Either follow Hwy 101 south to Alexander Valley Rd or take Hwy 128 to **Geyserville ⓬** and **Jimtown ⓭**.

Marin Coast

Ratings

Nature	●●●●●
Scenery	●●●●○
Children	●●●○○
Coastal villages	●●●○○
Wildlife	●●●○○
Museums	●●○○○
Beaches	●●○○○
Food	●●○○○

The western edge of Marin County (pronounced 'mah-rinn') offers the most civilised, most accessible and most crowded stretch of Northern California coast. The possibilities run from fine beaches with frigid water to shady, almost dank redwood groves, open pastures, sheer cliffs, windy picnic sites and elegant hideaways.

Marin's scenic bounty is natural, albeit highly modified by early loggers and farmers who stripped the forests from miles of coastal hills. But the style in which the coast is enjoyed, the roads, the parks, the restaurants and country inns, are imports from East Marin, the San Francisco Bay side of the county.

The Bay side of Marin is a striving, style-conscious enclave whose tone has largely been set by 1960s Flower Power survivors. Most have long since traded psychedelic trips for more prosaic journeys by BMW, Mercedes and top-of-the-line mountain bikes, but personal gratification remains central to life in Marin – thousands swarm across the open hillsides, beaches and trails of West Marin each weekend to keep bodies and auras well exercised.

BODEGA BAY*

ⓘ Bodega Bay Chamber of Commerce *575 Hwy 1; tel: (707) 875-3422 or (800) 905-9050. Open Mon–Fri 0900–1700.*

ⓣ University of California Bodega Bay Marine Station *Westside Rd, Bodega Head; tel: (707) 875-2211. Open Fri 1400–1600.*

Pomo and Miwok bands lived along the sheltered curve of Bodega Bay when Juan Francisco de la Bodega y Quadra Mollineda stopped by on his way north to British Columbia in 1775. The Native Americans were long gone by the time Alfred Hitchcock portrayed the fishing village as a town under siege from the air in *The Birds* (1963). Squawking hordes of sea gulls and other birds still haunt the harbour, but they're far more interested in stealing scraps from fishermen than in dive bombing tourists and school children.

Bodega was failing fast as commercial fishing declined in the 1970s, but holiday-makers discovered the pleasant seaside setting and turned the economic tide. The best walks are over **Bodega Head**, across the Bay, one of the first California sites where local opposition successfully derailed utility schemes to build nuclear power stations along the coast. The **University of California Bodega Bay Marine Station***
offers public tours.

Bolinas is an anti-social, but not unfriendly, beach town west of Bolinas Lagoon. It's worth the short drive off Hwy 1 (look for the unmarked paved road beyond the Lagoon) to get picnic supplies from the **People's Store $** (*end of the gravel drive, next to Bolinas Bakery; tel: (415) 868-1433*), famous for locally grown produce and sublime service.

Duxbury Reef Nature Reserve✳✳✳ (*end of Elm Rd*) is a rocky shelf with wonderful tide-pooling. Keep an eye on the water, especially on a rising tide. Bird-watchers usually opt for the **Point Reyes Bird Observatory** (*Mesa Rd; tel: (415) 868-1221*), which has a self-guided visitor centre and nature trail at one of America's few full-time ornithological research stations.

Accommodation and food in Bodega Bay

The Sonoma Coast Visitor Center has information on availability throughout the region. Bookings are essential in summer; at weekends all year.

Bodega Bay Lodge $$$ *103 Hwy 1 (Doran Beach Rd); tel: (707) 875-3525* or *(800) 368-2468; web: www.woodsidehotels.com*, is a condominium-like resort.

Bodega Coast Inn $$$ *521 Hwy 1; tel: (707) 875-2217 or (800) 346-6999; fax: (707) 875-2964; web: www.bodegacoastinn.com*, has large view rooms.

Breakers Café $$ *1400 Hwy 1; tel: (707) 875-2513*, serves *nouvelle* California seafood.

Lucas Wharf Restaurant $$ *595 Hwy 1; tel: (707) 875-3522; web: www.lucaswharf.com*, concentrates on more traditional seafood. **Lucas Wharf Deli and Fishmarket**, next door, is the best source for picnic supplies.

JENNER *

The tiny village marks both the mouth of the Russian River and the end of Hwy 116, which follows the river inland to dozens of wineries. The 'logs' on the sand at the mouth of the river are most likely seals warming themselves. Beaches north of Jenner are wild, windy and fabulously popular for hiking, beachcombing and enjoying the scenery.

Accommodation in Jenner

Below
Arcadian countryside around Jenner

Jenner Inn & Cottages $$$ *Hwy 1; tel: (707) 865-2377; fax: (707) 865-0829; web: www.jennerinn.com*, is a collection of several houses and bed-and-breakfast establishments.

MARIN HEADLANDS✥✥✥

❶ Golden Gate National Recreation Area
Headquarters on MacArthur St, upper Fort Mason; tel: (415)556-0560; web: www.nps.gov/goga/.

❶ Nike Missile Site *tel: (415) 331-1540. Open Mon–Fri 1230–1530 and the first Sun of every month.*

❶ Marin Headlands Visitor Information Center *tel: (415) 331-1540. Open daily 0930–1630.*

❶ Marine Mammal Center *tel: (415) 289-7325. Open daily 1000–1600.*

❶ Fort Barry Youth Hostel *Bldg 941; tel: (415) 331-2777.*

The windswept, nearly naked headlands directly north of the Golden Gate Bridge are the least-changed hillsides in Marin. They have been a military preserve since the US Civil War, when artillery batteries were installed to repel an invasion that never happened. Slopes facing the Pacific Ocean and the Golden Gate were honeycombed with batteries, observation posts and supply bunkers during World War II; anti-aircraft and Nike missile batteries were added during the Cold War years. The demilitarised Headlands is now part of the **Golden Gate National Recreation Area** (*see page 138*).

Most of the old batteries survive as scenic vantage points. Among the best is **Battery Wallace**✥✥✥ (*above the southwestern tip*), with nicely framed views of the Pacific and the Golden Gate Bridge. The last surviving **Nike Missile Site** is complete with decommissioned missiles. **Point Bonita Lighthouse**✥✥✥ (*western tip of the Headlands*) is open for tours at weekends.

Most Headlands activities begin around the Point from the lighthouse turn-off at the **Marin Headlands Visitor**. A wide, sandy beach separates the cold Pacific surf from the warmer waters of **Rodeo Lagoon** (no swimming, to protect nesting birds). Near by is the **Marine Mammal Center**, a rescue and rehabilitation centre for injured and sick marine mammals. The centre is open daily for tours, volunteer staff and workload permitting. Officers' quarters at the former **Fort Barry**, just inland, have been converted into a spacious youth hostel.

MARSHALL✥

❶ Tomales Bay Oyster Company
(15479 Hwy 1, just south of Marshall; tel: (415) 663-1242. Open daily 0900–1700.

Marshall was once a major oyster and fishing port for San Francisco. The fishing is long gone, but the oysters are back, courtesy of the **Tomales Bay Oyster Company**✥✥✥, which sells oysters fresh from the water. The other reason to stop is **Tony's Seafood Restaurant $** *18863 Hwy 1; tel: (415) 663-1107*, which has specialised in oysters for half a century. Barbecue is the preferred preparation.

MONTE RIO✥

This Russian River resort town 3 miles west of Guerneville (*see page 169*) is filled with gracefully crumbling Victorian houses and a few more modern resorts. The town is best known as the entrance to the **Bohemian Grove**, a private camp that lets out San Francisco's Bohemian Club for an annual camp-out for the world's biggest boys – former heads of state, bank presidents, media moguls, military leaders, politicos and the like, with neither women nor cameras allowed.

Accommodation in Monte Rio

Huckleberry Springs Country Inn $$$ *8105 Beedle Rd; tel: (707) 865-2683* or *(800) 822-2683*, is a collection of very private cottages surrounded by towering redwoods. The restaurant (guests only) is among the Russian River's best.

Rio Villa Beach Resort $$$ *20292 Hwy 116; tel: (707) 865-1143*, has pleasant views of the Russian River.

MOUNT TAMALPAIS STATE PARK✦✦✦

Mount Tamalpais State Park $
801 Panoramic Hwy; tel: (415) 388-2070; fax: (415) 388-2968; web: www.cal-parks.ca.gov/DISTRICTS/marin/mtsp239. Open daily 0700–1700.

Mount Tamalpais (Mount Tam to locals) dominates the Marin skyline. Ridges leading up to the 2571ft peak neatly divide the county into wild western slopes leading to the Pacific Ocean and surburanified slopes leading to San Francisco Bay. More than 50 miles of trails wind through the park to connect with another 200 miles in surrounding recreation areas. If fog and smog permit, panoramic views stretch from the Farallon Islands (26 miles west) to the Sierra Nevada (150 miles east). The Panoramic Hwy is the most direct route from Hwy 1 to Muir Woods, but traffic on the winding road can be extremely slow at weekends and in summer.

MUIR BEACH✦✦✦

Just down the road from **Muir Woods National Monument** (*see below*), Muir Beach (*tel: (415) 388-2596*) is one of Marin's prettiest beaches, a deep crescent of sand behind a semicircular cove. It is seldom crowded during the week, but can turn into a zoo (with almost no parking) at weekends and holidays during fine weather. Swimming is not recommended on account of ferocious rip-tides.

Accommodation and food in Muir Beach

The **Pelican Inn $$$** (*10 Pacific Way, tel: (415) 383-6000*) is the creation of a homesick British expatriate, who conjured up a dark and inviting 16th-century Tudor inn. Book as early as possible – the Inn is even more popular for its food, drink and boarding than its romantic atmosphere.

MUIR WOODS NATIONAL MONUMENT✦✦✦

This 560-acre virgin grove of Coastal redwoods is all that remains of the vast redwood forests that once cloaked Mount Tam and most of

Muir Woods National Monument $ Mill Valley, CA 94941; tel: (415) 388-2595; fax: (415) 389-6957; web: www.nps.gov/muwo/. Open daily 0800-1700.

the rest of coastal Marin, Sonoma and Mendocino counties – Mill Valley, just over the flank of Mount Tam, was named for the many lumber mills the town once supported. The next significant stand of easily accessible redwoods in **Redwood National and State Parks** (see page 203), is towards the Oregon border.

Muir Woods sits in a steep canyon that was uneconomic for early lumbermen to log. Today, it's a calm and majestic place, with tatters of fog and beams of sunlight filtering through 250ft-tall redwoods to the valley floor carpeted with ferns and laurel.

Paved, self-guided trails circle the flat canyon floor. Unpaved trails climb the canyon walls to connect with Mount Tam and

A hundred shades of green: Muir Woods National Monument

Pacific Ocean routes. The monument was named for pioneer conservationist John Muir in 1908.

Easy access also makes Muir Woods impossibly popular. The small car-park fills up early at weekends and holidays and sightseeing coaches from San Francisco clog the road every day. Crowds are smallest mid-week and in winter, which is also when salmon and steelhead trout migrate up **Redwood Creek**✷ to spawn. For salmon viewing updates during the Nov–Mar season; tel: (415) 388-2595.

POINT REYES NATIONAL SEASHORE✦✦✦

Bear Valley Visitor Center off Hwy from Olema; tel: (415) 663-1092. Open Mon–Fri 0900-1700, Sat–Sun 0800-1700.

Ken Patrick Visitor Center Drakes Beach; tel: (415) 669-1250. Open Fri–Tue 1000-1700 May–Sept, Sat–Sun 1000–1700 rest of year.

Point Reyes is a patch of semi-wilderness surrounded by the Pacific Ocean and Tomales Bay. This wing-shaped peninsula of rolling hills, sheer cliffs and drifting fog is a mecca for hikers, cyclists, bird-watchers, backpackers, mountain bikers, sea kayakers, wildflower enthusiasts and just about anyone else who enjoys outdoor activities.

It is also the most itinerant piece of California. Five million years ago, Point Reyes was south of San Francisco Bay, about where Monterey now stands. A hundred million or so years earlier, it was part of the Tehachapi Mountains in Southern California. Presuming it hasn't been swamped by erosion and global warming, the whole peninsula will eventually end up in the Gulf of Alaska.

Lighthouse Visitor Center *above the lighthouse; tel: (415) 669-1534.* **Visitor Center** *open Thur–Mon 1000–1700; lighthouse stairs and exhibits open to 1630, lens room open as staffing permits.*

Johnson's Oyster Farm *tel: (415) 669-1149; fax: (415) 669-1262. Open Tue–Sun 0800–1600.*

Point Reyes National Seashore *Point Reyes Station, CA 94956; tel: (415) 663-1092; fax: (415) 663-8132; web:www.nps.gov/pore/*

Point Reyes is drifting northwestwards along the San Andreas fault, which produced California's most famous earthquake. The 1906 quake that destroyed San Francisco was centred beneath Point Reyes; the entire peninsula jumped 16ft to the north in the blink of an eye. The only damage was to a few fences, which can be seen along the easy **Earthquake Trail** from the Bear Valley Visitor Center.

The park, which is adjacent to, but not part of, the Golden Gate National Recreation Area, has several distinct areas.

Bear Valley Visitor Center is the main visitor centre. The huge, barn-shaped building houses exhibits covering local history and ecosystems.

The easy one-mile **Earthquake Trail**✦✦✦ displays some of the more notable effects of the 1906 San Francisco earthquake, which was far stronger at largely uninhabited Point Reyes than it was in San Francisco. Behind the visitor centre stands the **Morgan Horse Ranch**✦, a working ranch for the Morgan horses used to patrol seashore wilderness areas. **Kule Loklo**✦ is a re-created Miwok village that offers a glimpse of local life before European contact. An easy ½-mile walk with self-guiding exhibits leads from the visitor centre to the village.

Several popular hikes leave from the Bear Valley centre, including an 8-mile return walk to **Arch Rock** on the coast. Check with rangers before setting out; the coast can be dramatically wetter, colder and windier than this protected valley.

Drakes Beach✦✦✦ (*off Sir Francis Drake Blvd*) is a calm strand backed by white sandstone cliffs behind the crook of Point Reyes. The beach and **Drakes Estero**, a shallow, sheltered estuary, are generally accepted as the place Sir France Drake careened the *Golden Hinde* in 1579 during his round-the-world pursuit of Spanish booty. Exhibits in the **Ken Patrick Visitor Center** focus on 16th-century maritime explorations as well as the local marine environment. Contemporary accounts have Drake remarking upon the white cliffs behind his makeshift shipyard and their resemblance to the white cliffs of Dover. A weathered copper plaque claiming *New Albion* for Queen Elizabeth I was discovered in the 1930s, but it is widely regarded as a forgery. Harder to dismiss are English coins of the era found in Native American encampments as far inland as **Olompali State Historic Park**, off Hwy 101 between **Novato** and Petaluma. As Drake's logbook was burnt in an Admiralty fire, the truth may never be known.

Also on the estero is **Johnson's Oyster Farm**, one of several oyster producers in the area selling the bivalves for about half the price in area restaurants.

Great Beach✦✦✦ (*off Sir Francis Drake Blvd*), sometimes called 'Point Reyes Beach', is more than 10 miles of undeveloped beach, backed by untrammelled dunes and beach grasses. The beach is open to the full force of the Pacific, which makes swimming dangerous (and cold), but the wave action inspires awe, particularly during the winter storm season. Snowy plovers nest north of the north entrance May–Oct.

Sir Francis Drake

Francis Drake was the first English tourist to California, a sometime-pirate, sometime-privateer who found fame, fortune and Point Reyes in the course of 'annoying' King Phillip of Spain. Drake was so successful that his tiny *Golden Hinde* was splitting at the seams from the Spanish treasure his crew had captured during 18 months in the Caribbean and the Pacific. In 1579, he put ashore in a place whose physical description matches Drakes Bay for five weeks of rest and repair, then posted a brass plate claiming *Nova Albion* for Queen Elizabeth I before sailing west for Plymouth.

In 1937, University of California archaeologists announced that they had found Drake's plate; x-ray diffraction tests in the 1970s revealed that the plate was made in the 20th century, not the 16th. Silver sixpenny coins found in local Native American encampments support Drake's Bay as Drake's landing place, but this has never been confirmed. Drake's three-year round-the-world voyage earned him a knighthood, but England never tried to capitalise on his claim to *Nova Albion*.

Limantur Beach✧✧✧ (*end of Limantur Rd*) is one of the best swimming beaches in the area, protected from the full force of the Pacific by the Point Reyes headland. The nearby estuary is a good spot for bird-watching.

Mount Vision Overlook✧✧✧ (*Mt Vision Rd, off Sir Francis Drake Blvd*), at 1282ft, provides the best panoramic view of the entire Point Reyes Peninsula, especially for colourful sunsets.

One of the oldest and most successful of the many dairy ranches established on the Point Reyes in the 19th century is **Pierce Point Ranch**✧✧ (*Pierce Point Rd, Tomales; tel: (415) 669-1534*). A short self-guided trail guides visitors through the historic complex.

Point Reyes Light Station✧✧✧ (*end of Sir Francis Drake Blvd; tel: (415) 669-1534*) stands 300 weather-whipped steps below the visitor centre at the tip of Point Reyes. Panoramas are stunning on clear days, but the winter whale migration is visible even on many foggy days. The visitor centre is ¼-mile from the car-park. Dress warmly, even on sunny days, as temperatures can drop as precipitously as the cliffs surrounding the lighthouse.

Tomales Point✧✧✧ (*off Pierce Point Rd*), the northern end of Point Reyes, protects Tomales Bay, immediately to the east. Herds of dairy cattle and tule elk wander the windy moors.

Tule Elk Reserve✧✧✧ (*end of Pierce Point Rd*) protects re-introduced tule elk which once ranged over coastal grasslands throughout Northern and Central California.

Right
The Point Reyes Light Station

POINT REYES STATION✢

❶ West Marin Chamber of Commerce *Box 1054, Point Reyes Station, CA 94956; tel: (415) 663-9232; fax: (415) 663-8818 or (800) 887-2880.*

This former ranching town is turning from milking dairy cows to milking tourists, an easier, less odorous and more lucrative task.

Accommodation and food in Point Reyes Station

West Marin accommodation is booked out early, especially at weekends and in summer. For help, try **Inns of Marin**; *tel: (415) 663-2000 or (800) 887-2880*, **Inns of Point Reyes**; *tel: (415) 663-1420; fax: (415) 663-9292*, or **Point Reyes Lodging**; *tel: (415) 663-1872 or (800) 539-1872; fax: (415) 663-8431.*

Bovine Bakery \$ *tel: (415) 663-9420*, has heavenly muffins and pastries.

Point Reyes Roadhouse & Oyster Bar \$\$ *10905 Hwy 1; tel: (415) 663-1277*, is popular for lunch as well as its excellent selection of microbrews and local wines.

STINSON BEACH✢

❶ Marin County Convention & Visitors Bureau, *Avenue of the Flags, San Rafael, CA 94903; tel: (415) 472-7470; fax: (415) 499-3700; web: http://marin.org. Open Mon–Fri 0900–1700.*

⊞ Audubon Canyon Ranch Bolinas Lagoon Preserve, *3 miles north of Stinson Beach; tel: (415) 868-9244; fax: (415) 868-1699; web: www.egret.org. Open Sat–Sun 1000–1600 mid Mar–mid July.*

Stinson is where Marin teenagers (adults, too) head when they need a taste of sand, Southern California beer-and-bikini-style. Swimming is allowed (there are life-guards on duty in summer), but the bone-numbing water tends to discourage more than perfunctory dips. For recorded weather and surf conditions *tel: (415) 868-1922.*

Just north along Hwy 1 is **Bolinas Lagoon✢✢✢**, a usually sunny resting spot for seabirds and harbour seals which haul out on sandbars. Off the eastern side of the Lagoon is **Audubon Canyon Ranch Bolinas Lagoon Preserve✢✢✢**, the premier place on the entire West Coast to observe majestic great blue herons, as well as dozens of other species.

Accommodation and food in Stinson Beach

Casa del Mar \$\$\$ *37 Belvedere Ave; tel: (415) 868-2124 or (800) 552-2124; fax: (415) 868-2305*, offers splendid views of the Pacific and Mount Tam, its backyard.

The Parkside Café \$\$ *43 Arenal Ave; tel: (415) 868-1272*, is a popular neighbourhood café for breakfast and lunch with more complex offerings at dinner. Weather permitting, go for an outdoor table.

Stinson Beach Grill \$\$ *3465 Hwy 1; tel: (415) 868-2002*, is an informal grill serving everything from osso bucco to hamburgers.

Suggested tour

Total distance: 60 miles.

Time: Half to full day.

Links: San Francisco south, Mendocino Coast north, Sonoma Wine Country east.

Route: From San Francisco, follow Hwy 101 north over the Golden Gate Bridge ❶ to the Hwy 1 exit at the south end of Sausalito ❷. Take Hwy 1 to the Panoramic Hwy; follow Panoramic Hwy through **Mount Tamalpais State Park** ❸ to **Muir Woods National Monument** ❹ and back to Hwy 1 at Muir Beach ❺. Turn north past Stinson Beach ❻ and Bolinas Lagoon ❼ along the **Point Reyes National Seashore** ❽ to Olema ❾ and Point Reyes Station ❿. If time allows, follow Sir Francis Drake Blvd west through Point Reyes National Seashore ❽ to the Point Reyes Light Station ⓫. Otherwise, continue north on Hwy 1 along Tomales Bay ⓬, then inland to Valley Ford ⓭ and back to Bodega Bay ⓮ and on to Jenner ⓯.

Detour: Tired of ocean? From Valley Ford ⓭, take Valley Ford Rd north to the Bodega Hwy. Turn east to the Bohemian Highway, then go north through Camp Meeker ⓰ to the Russian River ⓱ at Monte Rio ⓲ and Hwy 116. Take Hwy 116 west along the Russian River ⓱ to Hwy 1 and rejoin the main route at Jenner ⓳.

Mendocino Coast

Ratings

Birding	●●●●●
Nature	●●●●●
Scenery	●●●●●
Food	●●●●○
Beaches	●●●○○
History	●●●○○
Outdoor activities	●●●○○
Art and craft	●●●○○

The Mendocino Coast, once a fishing and redwood lumbering centre, has become one of the most sought-after and pleasantest tourist destinations in the United States. This 100-mile stretch of Pacific Coast is legendary for its dramatic cliffs and coves, quaint but artistic towns and varied flora.

It also has a hidden secret which confounds visitors expecting Southern California's sunny strands: thick fog which rolls in year-round, treacherous for fishing boats entering the narrow coves and adding a drippy nip to a climate where forests, rhododendrons, roses and heathers thrive. The fog can be invigorating, inviting exploration of the half-hidden scenery just around the next bend of Hwy 1.

FORT BRAGG✢✢

ⓘ Fort Bragg-Mendocino Coast Chamber of Commerce *332 N. Main St, Fort Bragg, CA 95437; tel: (800) 726-2780 or (707) 961-6300; fax: (707) 964-2056; web: www.mendocinocoast.com. Open Mon–Fri 0900–1700, Sat to 1500. Covers Point Arena–Westport.*

Fort Bragg is the pragmatic commercial centre between San Francisco and Eureka. Eight miles north of Mendocino, Fort Bragg has an historic railway excursion, a tidy downtown, a commercial fishing harbour and economical accommodation and dining.

Pomo and Coast Yuki Native Americans, permanent residents when Russians settled Fort Ross in 1812, became otter pelt suppliers. By 1855, with the Russians and fur trade gone, the tribes were confined to a reservation, pushed out by Western US settlement. An army base on reservation land marked Fort Bragg's founding in 1857.

Local coast redwoods provided strong, fire-resistant lumber for San Francisco's Gold Rush era construction; by 1869, mills on headlands above every cove were rendering lumber for shipment south. Noyo Harbor, south of the main section of Fort Bragg, was the largest port for over 100 miles, and Fort Bragg's mills were among the largest.

A railway east to Willits was begun to enable shipment of lumber

Mendocino Coast Botanical Gardens $
18220 N. Hwy 1; tel: (707) 964-4352; fax: (707) 964-3114. Open Mar–Oct 0900–1700, Nov–Feb 0900–1600.

Skunk Train $$$
foot of Laurel St; tel: (707) 964-6371 or (800) 777-5865) (Willits Depot; tel: (707) 459-5248); web: www.skunktrain.com. Check in advance for schedule.

south. Most of Fort Bragg was rebuilt after the 1906 San Francisco earthquake levelled it and 1950s redevelopment removed most, but not all, architectural distinctiveness. A Georgia Pacific Mill still fills a major section of town, a reminder of the industry that made the region prosperous for over a century.

Mendocino Coast Botanical Gardens*** is 47 acres of plants, flowers, landscaping and eroded ocean bluffs where coastal fog and surprisingly mild winter temperatures permit an astounding variety of flora in formal plantings, fern canyons, wetlands and a pioneer cemetery. A nursery sells the gardens' signature rhododendrons and heathers. Bloom schedules include rhododendrons (Feb–May), camellias, flowering plums and Pacific Coast irises (Feb–Mar), wildflowers, heritage roses and cacti (May–July), dahlias, fuschias and heathers (Aug–Oct) and winter heathers and mushrooms (Nov–Jan).

Grey whales migrate Dec–Apr, and butterflies swarm in summer. The gardens and Mendocino Coast Audubon Society bird list covers 100 resident species, including humming-birds, ospreys, pelagic cormorants and black oystercatchers.

California Western Railroad's wonderfully-named **Skunk Train***** hauls 65,000 holiday-makers a year on a 40-mile route through the redwoods from Fort Bragg to Willits. The all-day return excursion, named Skunk for 1920s cars which had an unbearable stench, crosses 31 bridges and manoeuvres 381 curves and two tunnels in a 1740ft

Getting ready to ride the Skunk Train through the redwood forests

rising journey east. The railway offers fair-weather open cars and closed passenger carriages pulled by diesel locomotive engines, or by No 45, a classic 1924 Baldwin Steam Engine. The loud steaming up whenever No 45 is rolled out is an attraction in its own right, worth arriving 45 minutes before scheduled departure to see the spectacle.

Accommodation and food in Fort Bragg

Chain and independent motels abound and Fort Bragg has its share of bed-and-breakfast inns. Book summer and holiday weekends in advance as reasonable prices make accommodation so close to Mendocino very popular.

Lodge at Noyo River $$$ *500 Casa del Noyo Dr.; tel: (800) 628-1126 or (707) 964-8045; web: www.mcn.org/a/noyoriver/,* has walking paths and fine views of the harbour.

Restaurants use fresh, locally grown ingredients and freshly caught fish.

Gardens Grill $$ *Mendocino Coast Botanical Gardens, 18220 N. Hwy 1, 1 mile south of Fort Bragg; tel: (707) 964-7474, open Sun 1000–1430, Mon–Sat 1100–1430, Thur–Sat 1700–2100,* takes advantage of the gardens' landscaping.

Harvest Market $ *Hwys 1 and 20, Boatyard Shopping Center; tel: (707) 964-7000; web: www.harvestmarket.com, open daily 0500–2300,* is stocked with a huge assortment of picnic provisions, preserves, fresh produce and local fare.

North Coast Brewing Co $$ *444 N. Main St; tel: (707) 964-3400; web: www.ncoast-brewing.com, open Tue–Sun 1200–2100* is relaxed, with tasty salads, appetisers and entrées, seafood, fine beer and cheerful service.

FORT ROSS STATE HISTORIC PARK✧✧✧

Fort Ross State Historic Park $ *Hwy 1, 12 miles north of Jenner; tel: (707) 847-3286; web: www.mcn.org/1/rrparks/parks/fortr. Open 1000–1630.*

Fort Ross's reconstructed wooden stockade beneath rugged hills encompasses two blockhouses, officials' quarters, two houses, a well and a chapel. Re-enactment of Russian-era daily life, the formal contact between the Russians and the Mexicans who had succeeded the Spanish in California, the arrival of a cutter, and soldiers and colonists in early 19th-century costume re-create Russian Fort Ross on Living History Day (last Sat in July). Russian Orthodox services are conducted on Memorial Day and Fourth of July weekends. Schoolchildren and volunteers re-enact the daily life and dances of California's Russian settlement throughout the year.

GUALALA*

ℹ **Redwood Coast Chamber of Commerce** *tel: (800) 778-5252, takes phone enquiries for Hwy 1 communities between Fort Ross and Gualala.*

'Water-coming-down place' residents can spot visitors to their town, 100 miles north of San Francisco, by how they say the name. *Wah-la-la*, once a lumber centre, now has posh inns, fine restaurants, a pleasant rock-sheltered coast, artists, film stars, musicians and a few metaphysical devotees left from the 1960s.

Accommodation and food in Gualala

Gualala is blessed with accommodation and dining venues good enough to be destinations in their own right.

St Orres $$$ *36601 Hwy 1; tel: (707) 884-3303; fax: (707) 884-1840; web: www.saintorres.com,* stops traffic with the inn's weathered old redwood and Douglas-fir dome turrets *à la Russe*. Succulent game specialities include wild boar, venison, quail and pheasant. The chef gathers wild mushrooms for the vegetarian tart selection herself.

Whale Watch Inn $$$ *35100 Hwy 1, 5 miles north of Gualala; tel: (800) 942-5342* or *(707) 884-3667; web: www.whale-watch.com,* has large rooms and a golden strand of private beach below.

JUG HANDLE STATE RESERVE**

🔟 **Jug Handle State Reserve** *Hwy 1, 5 miles north of Mendocino; tel: (707) 937-5804; web: www.mcn.org/1/mendoparks/ jug and www.mcn.org/1/ mendoparks/jugtrail (virtual tour).*

Looking at wave action against rocks and cliffs along the Mendocino Coast gives little hint of geological formation at **Jug Handle State Reserve**. The **Ecological Staircase** (preview on web virtual tour) takes a path upwards through five successive and distinctive land/vegetation areas, each one 100ft and 100,000 years older than the one before.

A combination of earth crust uplift, repeated cycles of rising seas when retreating glaciers melted and thawed, and layering of gravel and sand upon the terraces that formed have created a natural west-to-east staircase. The 2½-mile path within a one-mile-wide strip crosses Hwy 1. The forests become more dwarfed with each higher terrace, gnarled pygmy forests of Mendocino cypresses, rare Bolander pines and dwarf Fort Bragg manzanita growing in rock-hard soil which has been leeched of nutrients by wind and rain over the ages.

MENDOCINO***

Views of the sea in three directions, artists and galleries galore, Victorian buildings, inns, restaurants, saloons, occasional solitude and the ever-mysterious fog make the town of Mendocino (and its almost

Fort Bragg-Mendocino Coast Chamber of Commerce, *332 N. Main St, Fort Bragg, CA 95437; tel: (800) 726-2780 or (707) 961-6300; fax: (707) 964-2056; web: www.mendocinocoast.com. Open Mon–Fri 0900–1700, Sat to 1500. Covers Point Arena-Westport.*

Ford House Museum *735 Main St; tel: (707) 937-5397. Open daily 1100–1600. Incorporates Mendocino State Park Visitor Centre.*

Kelley House Museum *45007 Albion St; tel: (707) 937-5791. Open daily 1300–1600 in summer, Fri–Mon in winter.*

indistinguishable southern neighbour, Little River) a mecca for all who can take the time to drive there and can afford it. It's a free-spirited place, where the neat grid of blocks disappears close to the ocean, dogs abound, hikers are determined to get somewhere, seals mimic surfers waiting for waves in the bay, canoeists paddle rivers and honeymooners walk hand-in-hand. Mendocino is also a ready-made film set, often used to represent quaint New England seaside towns, as it did for Angela Lansbury's television series *Murder, She Wrote.*

Ford House Museum✳✳ is the **Mendocino Headlands State Park Visitors Center,** with a fine museum explaining lumbering, 'doghole port' (*see Point Cabrillo Light Station, below*) and schooner history. The restored 1854 home originally had a basement kitchen and dining-room, requiring 23-year-old newlywed Martha Hayes Ford to illuminate her house with candles even on sunny days. Rangers maintain a fine herb garden outside, resembling the one cultivated around Mendocino's second house in the 1880s.

Owner Jerome Ford stopped in Mendocino while searching for the valuable Asian cargo carried in the hold of the *Frolic*. What he found were redwoods, a discovery followed by his establishing lumbering operations to supply the heavy demand of newly rich San Franciscans.

Kelley House Museum✳ shows a family home constructed from local redwood which was built by a couple from Prince Edward Island, Canada, in 1861. Restored period rooms display photographs of early coastal shipping and artefacts from the family whose patriarch, William Henry Kelly, once owned most of the Mendocino Headlands, sawmills and lumbering operations for miles around.

The scenic coast of Mendocino

Mendocino Headlands State Park *north, west and south of Mendocino town; tel: (707) 937-5804; web: www.mcn.org/11mendopark/mndhdld.*

Point Cabrillo Light Station *at the north side of Russian Gulch State Park; ¾ mile west on foot; tel/fax: (707) 937-0816.*

Van Damme State Park *Hwy 1 at Little River, 3 miles south of Mendocino; tel: (707) 937-4016 or (707) 937-5804. Visitors Center open daily in summer, Sat–Sun 1000 in winter.*

Mendocino Headlands State Park✦✦✦ combines the beach and surf at the mouth of the Big River, favoured by surfers and aquatic mammals, grassy headlands, eroded cliffs, nestled coves, bluffs, carpets of wildflowers and prime grey whale-spotting Nov–Apr. The fog rolls over the western headland as a blanket, with nothing to define the horizon; just as suddenly, it retreats.

Point Cabrillo Light Station✦ is a small, well-proportioned 1908 lighthouse – under restoration, with several keeper houses nearby. The walk from the car-park to the shore traverses the Point Cabrillo Reserve meadows with grasses and wild blackberries lining the route. Guides conduct exterior tours with winter whale-watch weekends.

Craggy coast broken by narrow, rocky coves offered little protection from shipwreck and weather. These 'dogholes' (inlets only large enough, it was said, to permit a dog to go in, turn around and depart) became ports for lumber schooners plying to San Francisco. Specially designed wharves, chutes and cables from the tops of cliffs transported goods and people back and forth over the water. The invention of a steam engine attached to windjammer-style doghole schooners made for swifter shipping of milled redwood lumber south.

Van Damme State Park✦✦ is popular for camping. The 1864 lumber mill site on the Little River is now the park recreation hall. The park and **Fern Canyon Trail**✦✦ extend 5 miles east of the ocean to the **Pygmy Forest. Lost Coast Kayaking**✦✦ *(tel: (707) 937-2434)*, departs from the beach for summer season sea cave tours.

It's easier to drive than hike to the **Pygmy Forest**, *(3½ miles east of Hwy 101 on Little River Airport Rd)*, a segment of the dwarf species forest formed by the terracing of the ecological staircase along the Mendocino Coast *(see Jug Handle State Reserve, page 190)*. Periodic signs for the 10-minute circuit around a boardwalk indicate California huckleberries, Bolander pines, Mendocino cypresses, bordering Bishop pines and red-pink California Rose Bay rhododendrons, five times smaller than relatives in the redwood forest.

Shopping in Mendocino

Mendocino could be the only tourist town in California that boasts more art galleries than T-shirt emporia. The **Mendocino Art Center**✦✦ *45200 Little Lake St; tel: (707) 937-5818 or (800) 653-3328, open daily 1000-1600,* offers arts and fine crafts classes with resident artists, exhibitions, and a retail shop with reasonably priced visual art and sculpture by Mendocino artists. Ask at the Chamber of Commerce, galleries or museums for the *Mendocino Gallery Guide,* which lists 20 venues for openings and artists' receptions, *1700-2000 on the second Sat of the month.*

William Zimmer Gallery *Kasten and Ukiah Sts; tel: (707) 937-5121; fax: (707) 937-2405,* has an upper-crust attitude with one-of-a-kind *objets d'art,* including glass, wooden furniture and jewellery. **Highlight Gallery** *45052 Main St; tel: (707) 937-3132; fax: (707) 937-5300,* joins clothing shops, wine tasting and real estate brokers on Main Street. **Lark in the Morning** *10460 Kasten St; tel: (707) 937-5275,* sells unique musical instruments.

Accommodation and food in Mendocino

Mendocino's attractions and ambience drive prices high and accommodation availability low, especially in summer, at weekends and during holidays. Camping in state parks *(tel: (800) 444-7275)* can be an alternative, but pitches fill quickly. Enough restaurants are deliberately vegetarian to make a full meat, fowl and fish menu a surprise – and most post menus outside. Call ahead to reserve dining and arrive early to ensure a seat.

Cafe Beaujolais $$ *961 Ukiah St; tel: (707) 937-5614,* known for its fresh ingredients, is open for dinner 1745–2100. Gardens offer picnic-sized brick-oven-baked breads from 1100.

MacCallum House Inn & Restaurant $$$ *45020 Albion St; tel: (800) 609-0492* or *(707) 937-0289.* The restaurant *(tel: (707) 937-5763)* is an 1882 mansion surrounded by flower gardens.

Stanford Inn By the Sea $$$ *Hwy 1 and Comptche-Ukiah Rd, south of Big River; tel: (707) 937-5615 or tel: (800) 331-8884.* The owners have created a luxury inn on the south side of Big River, and with their resident cats, dogs, llamas and other animals welcome pets, from dogs and cats to iguanas. An extensive organic produce and herb garden supplies the innovative vegetarian restaurant; ferns decorate an indoor pool and spa area. The inn offers **Catch a Canoe & Bicycles, Too!** for recreation around the area.

POINT ARENA❖

Point Arena Cove❖ *(½ mile west of Point Arena),* is a lovely cove with a fish-packing plant, several restaurants and an inn. It was once a late 19th-century whaling station and lumber boom town.

   Point Arena Light Station❖ *(Lighthouse Rd, 2 miles north of Point Arena (town); tel: (707) 882-2777,* a 115ft white beacon, is visible for miles south. The light station property is fenced to discourage after-hour visitors and the 145-step circular climb to the first-level fresnel lens is

Russians in California

Europe was at war over Napoleon when the Russians built Fort Ross in 1812. Distant turmoil mandated extension of Russian imperialism, a direct challenge to the Spanish whose northernmost California outpost was at San Francisco. The lucrative fur trade with China was the impetus to send factors, soldiers and colonists south from the Russian settlement at Sitka, Alaska, to hunt and grow crops in a longer growing season. With the Russians came Aleuts from Alaska, adept with kayak-type ocean craft.

Russian officials had not counted on the coastal fog which limited farming productivity, nor on the colonists' general lack of interest in farming, or the almost total extinction of the fur seals, harbor seals and river otters within three decades. In 1841, the Russians sold the fort to John Sutter (of subsequent Gold Rush fame), and left forever. Fort Ross became a ranch. The 1906 San Francisco earthquake destroyed most traces of the Russian era.

frustrated by canvas covers over most of the already filthy windows. The lighthouse museum and tower are open for tours 1100–1430 most days – phone ahead. Three **vacation rental cottages $$** (*Point Arena Lighthouse Keepers, Inc; tel: (707) 882-2777*) are on site.

Russian Gulch State Park★★★ (*Hwy 1, 2 miles north of Mendocino; tel: (707) 937-5804*) offers beautiful views from every angle: the Hwy 1 arch bridge over the gulch near a blowhole, the gulch beach popular with abalone and urchin divers and sea kayakers, the canyon trail with redwoods and Douglas fir, and inland to a waterfall and pygmy forest.

Salt Point State Park★★ (*Hwy 1, 20 miles north of Jenner; tel: (707) 847-3221*) is supplemented by **Kruse Rhododendron State Reserve**, and **Gerstle Cove Marine Reserve**. Damage from a 1993 campfire is obvious, but attractions include the **Gerstle Cove Visitors Center**, spring wildflowers, abalone diving, ocean fishing and the only state park permitting mushroom hunting for king boletes and chanterelles.

The Sea Ranch★ (*29 miles north of Jenner*). Unique, skylit, weathered wooden homes, developed in the 1960s to harmonise with landscape and vegetation. Widely copied, these homes along 10 miles of Hwy 1 are exclusive and gated or landscaped away from public areas. An 18-hole golf course provides fine views to the Pacific. Real estate companies handle rentals (*tel: (888) 732-7262*), or stay at **Sea Ranch Lodge $$$** (*60 Shore Walk Dr.; tel: (707) 785-2371*).

Suggested tour

Total distance: 100 miles.

Time: 3 hours driving; speed limits are slow, traffic congested, lanes narrow. There are few restaurants or services between Jenner and Albion except in Gualala. Picnicking overlooking the Pacific Ocean is a local tradition. The 8-mile stretch north from Albion to Mendocino (town) has some of the most popular inns and bed and breakfasts in California, with dining, art galleries and ambience to match.

Links: From Jenner at the beginning of this route, join the Marin Coast Route (*see page 176*). To continue north, for redwoods, Victorian homes and more coastline, join the Coast Redwoods Route (*see page 204*) from Point Bragg. For a Wine Country experience, follow the Anderson Valley Detour from Hwy 1 (via Hwy 128) to Hwy 101, one mile north of Cloverdale. Take Hwy 101 south 10 miles, then turn left at Canyon Rd on to the continuation of Hwy 128 to Jimtown and Calistoga (*see Sonoma Wine Country (page 166)* and *Napa Valley Wine Country, page 154*).

Route: From Jenner ❶, at the mouth of the Russian River ❷, follow Hwy 1 north to Mendocino ❸ and Fort Bragg ❹.

Anderson Valley Chamber of Commerce *Boonville; tel: (707) 895-2379.*

Anderson Valley Winegrowers Association *Box 63, Philo, CA 95466; tel/fax: (707) 895-9463; web: www.avwines.com*

Navarro River Redwoods State Park *11 miles west from Hwy 1 on Hwy 128; tel: (707) 937-5804; web:www. mcn.org/1/mendoparks/nrrsp*

Boonville Hotel $$$ *Hwy 128 and Lambert Lane; tel: (707) 895-2210. Ten bright, simply furnished rooms and a renowned wood grill restaurant for lunch and dinner.*

Anderson Valley Brewing Company $ *Buckhorn Saloon, 14081 Hwy 128; tel: (707) 895-3369. A wide range of tasty beer and food to match.*

Also worth exploring

The **Anderson Valley ❺** along Hwy 128 between Hwy 1 and Hwy 101 at Cloverdale offers magnificent coast redwoods at **Navarro River Redwoods State Park ❻**, fine wines and sparkling wines around **Navarro ❼**, apples at **Philo ❽**, and **Boonville ❾**, one of the state's quaintest towns. *Boontling*, a locally invented dialect, has faded a little with the influx of tourists, but three Buckey Walters remain (telephone booths named after the cost of early calls).

Ratings

Birding	●●●●●
Nature	●●●●●
Scenery	●●●●○
History	●●●○○
Children	●●●○○
Outdoor activities	●●●○○
Walking	●●●○○
Architecture	●●●○○

Coast Redwoods

Towering forests of coast redwoods, pastoral dairies, an historic Victorian town, lighthouses, sea stacks and rocky bluffs isolate this northwesternmost section of California, while preserving its regional personality. Timber and fishing were Redwood Empire economic mainstays, and much of the region has not recovered financially or emotionally from the diminishment of both.

Coast redwoods are preserved in the Redwood National and State Parks, a series of mixed-use parks and groves along Hwy 101 appearing a few miles south of Garberville. Despite former President Ronald Reagan's comment that, having seen one redwood, you've seen them all, the clumps and groves differ in character. Second growth allows much more light to penetrate the canopy, but the size and magnitude of one or more old-growth giants is simply astounding.

Fog clings to this coast much of the year with a mild coolness which stimulates vibrant green ferns, redwood sorrel and surprising numbers of wildflowers twined with mint underneath the redwoods. Roosevelt elk and birds – even foot-long yellow banana slugs – thrive.

ARCATA✛✛

ⓘ Arcata Chamber of Commerce/California Welcome Center
Arcata, CA 95521; tel: (707) 822-3619 or (800) 908-9464; fax: (707) 822-3515; web: www.arcata.com/chamber/ Call for address and hours and ask for the excellent Victorian Building walking tour brochure.

Youth, counterculture, environmentalism, organic produce and vegetarianism are bywords in this youthful enclave by Humboldt State University. Sand dunes and marshy wetlands are within a mile of an urban forest sheltering magnificent redwoods along trails. Bicycles are common, especially by the marshes and estuaries of the Mad River between Arcata Bay and McKinleyville.

Arcata Community Forest/Redwood Park✛✛ (*east on 14th to Redwood Park Dr.*) is this town's answer to timber clear-cutting: the preservation of 575 acres on a slope east of Hwy 101 near Humboldt State University, with 10 miles of trails.

Arcata Marsh and Wildlife Sanctuary✛✛✛ (*G-I Sts*), is a birdwatchers paradise year-round, but especially mid July to mid May. River otters and 200 species of birds are visible from trails and blinds on a flat track by grassy uplands. There is also a freshwater marsh, a tidal slough, a brackish lake and mudflats, and a system designed to purify waste water naturally and return it to nature.

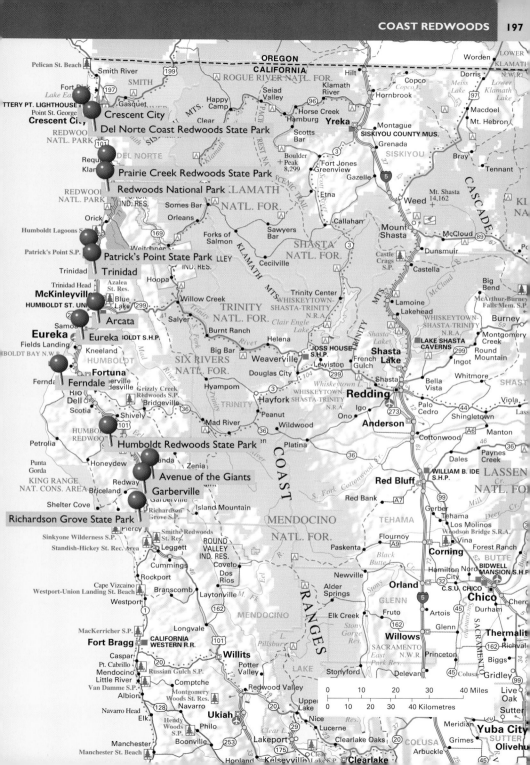

OREGON
CALIFORNIA

Pelican St. Beach

Smith River

SMITH
199
ROGUE RIVER NATL. FOR.

Lake Ea
Fort Dick

Gasquet

Point St. George
TTERY PT. LIGHTHOUSE
197

Crescent City

Del Norte Coast Redwoods State Park

REDWOOD
NATL. PARK

DEL NORTE

101

Requa
Klan

Prairie Creek Redwoods State Park

REDWOOD
NATL. PARK
IND. RES.

Redwoods National Park

Orick

169

Humboldt Lagoons S.

Patrick's Point S.P.

Patrick's Point State Park

Trinidad

Trinidad

Trinidad Head
Azalea
St. Res.

McKinleyville
HUMBOLDT ST. UNI

Blue
Lake

Arcata

Samoa

Eureka
Fields Landing

BOLDT S.H.P.
Eureka

BOLDT BAY N.W.R.

Kneeland

HUMBOLDT

Fortuna

Ferndale
Ferndale

Rio
Dell

Scotia

Petrolia

HUMBOL
REDWOO

101

Shively

Humboldt Redwoods State Park

Punta
Gorda

KING RANGE
NAT. CONS. AREA

Honeydew

Redway

Avenue of the Giants

Garberville

Briceland
Garberville

Shelter Cove

Richardson Grove State Park

Richardson
Grove S.P.

0   10   20   30   40 Miles

0   10   20   30   40 Kilometres

Arcata Plaza *(8th-9th, G-H Sts)* is the town square set aside by original lumber company owners as a park and meeting place. Among well-restored buildings near the plaza are the 1857 **Jacoby's Storehouse** *(8th and H Sts)* with 2ft-thick stone walls sheltering two restaurants; the 1914 **Minor Theatre** *(10th and H Sts; tel: (707) 822-3456),* the oldest operating cinema in the US, enhanced by isinglass door panels; and the 1915 **Hotel Arcata** *(9th and G Sts).*

The **World Champion Kinetic Sculpture Race**, Memorial Day weekend in May, begins at Arcata Plaza, and takes three days for contestants to navigate the 38 miles to Ferndale. Whimsical people-powered contraptions, the essence of clever design, ornamentation and wackiness are in keeping with Arcata's nickname, Ecotopia, and race founder Hobart Brown's belief in a 'New Race, conceived in insanity, and dedicated to the proposition that all mechanical nightmares definitely are not created equal.' The mechanical sculptures are displayed in **Ferndale's Kinetic Sculpture Race Museum** *(see page 201).*

Accommodation and food in Arcata

Chain motels cluster around E. Guintoli Lane, downwind of fumes from the Louisiana Pacific processing plant. Closer to downtown, a smattering of bed and breakfasts offer Victoriana. Book in advance for **Kinetic Sculpture Race weekend** in May.

Hotel Arcata $$ *708 9th St; tel: (800) 344-1221* or *(707) 826-0217,* on Arcata Plaza, is a central and cheerful 1915 hunting lodge.

Vegetarian and vegan is easy to find in this organic-produce conscious town, but freshness of ingredients is what counts.

Abruzzi $$ *780 7th St in Jacoby's Storehouse; tel: (707) 826-2345,* offers Italian dinners nightly in an historic building on Arcata Plaza.

Golden Harvest Cafe $$ *1062 G St; tel: (707) 822-8962,* has a wide range of dishes with a salad bar two blocks north of Arcata Plaza.

North Coast Co-Op $ *811 I St; tel: (707) 822-5947, open 0700–2100.* This is forthright socialism applied to food, selling groceries to all.

AVENUE OF THE GIANTS❖❖❖

ⓘ Avenue of the Giants Association
PO Box 219, Miranda, CA 95553; tel: (707) 923-2555; fax: (707) 923-3947.

Just north of Garberville, coast redwood groves extend for a narrow 31-mile strip along both sides of Hwy 101 from Phillipsville to Pepperwood, cutting left and right over the south fork of the Eel River. Most of the groves are named in tribute to the group of people who, in the early 20th century, worked to save a small number of redwoods before they disappeared. **Humboldt Redwoods State Park**❖❖ *(see page 202)* surrounds and helps interpret the long life span and predator-resistant coastal species. Most of the groves have a lay-by to park in so that you can explore the forest.

CRESCENT CITY❖

Crescent City/Del Norte County Chamber of Commerce *1001 Front St, Crescent City, CA 95531; tel: (707) 464-3174 or (800) 343-8300; web: www.delnorte.org. Open Mon–Fri 0900–1800, Sat–Sun 0900–1700 Memorial Day–Labor Day.*

Battery Point Lighthouse *west end of Front St; tel: (707) 464-3089. Open for guided tours Apr–Sept.*

As elsewhere on the north coast, Crescent City, 18 miles south of the Oregon border, was dependent upon fishing and timber. It is also a crossroads for over-the-border traffic and eastward routes to more redwood parks and the Hwy 199 Smith River Wild and Scenic River drive to the Rogue River Region in Oregon.

The city is named for the shape of its bay. A tsunami tidal wave caused by a major Alaska earthquake in 1964 wiped out the harbour and downtown; the rebuilt version gives it a modern but bland character.

Favourite local activities include fishing, bicycling, scuba diving and surfing in frigid waters.

Battery Point Lighthouse❖❖, perched since 1856 on well-eroded golden rock, has lovely proportions from any angle and at any time of day or night when it is illuminated around the outside. Check in advance about walking from the beach to a causeway at low tide.

North from Battery Point Lighthouse, scenic **Pebble Beach Drive**❖❖❖ looks west to sea stacks and **Castle Rock National Wildlife Refuge**❖❖, home to screeching birds and noisy sea lions. Go left on Washington Blvd to **Point St George** where there are vistas, beaches and trails, with its namesake lighthouse 6 miles offshore.

Battery Point Lighthouse

Accommodation and food in Crescent City

Proximity to Oregon (where prices are lower and there's no state sales tax) keep prices at Crescent City motels to bargain levels. Hwy 101 divides into north *(M St)* and south *(L St)* throughways between Front and 9th Sts; most motels are found here. Others are near the harbour at Anchor Rd.

Dining is basic, but seafood is an excellent choice. Ask for the fresh-caught special of the day.

Jefferson State Brewery *400 Front St; tel: (707) 464-1139; open 1100–2300*, has a flavourful selection of beers in the 'state of mind' style of this region which, with southwestern Oregon, periodically declares its independence from the US.

DEL NORTE COAST REDWOODS STATE PARK*

One of the Redwood National and State Parks (*7 miles south of Crescent City, tel: (707) 464-6101 ex 5120*), Del Norte Coast Redwood State Park has old-growth forest which includes redwoods with spectacular rocky coast and uncrowded trails.

EUREKA*

Eureka/Humboldt County Convention & Visitors Bureau *1034 2nd St, Eureka, CA 95501; tel: (707) 443-5097 or (800) 346-3482; fax: (707) 443-5115; web: www.redwoodvisitor.org. Open Mon–Fri 0900–1200, 1300–1700.*

No building in far Northern California is more recognisable than the green Victorian **Carson Mansion**, built in 1885 by a lumber baron's employees to fill time. Now a private club, this centre-piece of Eureka's Historic Old Town (*B-I Sts, Waterfront-7th St*), shows the 19th-century value of a good fishing harbour with access to lumber. Attractions from horse-drawn carriage rides to galleries, stores, restaurants and bed and breakfasts, can be found in this area. Salmon and Dungeness crab are still menu staples, though fisheries are restricted.

Carson Mansion, centrepiece of Eureka's Old Town

Food in Eureka

Samoa Cookhouse $ *Samoa Peninsula in Humboldt Bay; tel: (707) 442-1659, open daily 0700–1530, 1700-2100*, serves large, family-style portions of stick-to-the-ribs lumberjack fare in keeping with its status as the last surviving lumber camp cookhouse in the west. Prices are low, and the draw of a free museum to one side with artefacts and old-time pose-with-your-log lumber camp photographs is irresistible.

Café Waterfront $$ *102 F St; tel: (707) 443-9190*, has fine seafood, salads, a long wooden bar, a stained-glass window with a heron, and, most remarkable in the landmark Old Town Eureka building, wall paintings of flowers and natural scenes, even in the loo!

FERNDALE***

Ferndale has trademarked its moniker, 'The Victorian Village', but for once, the preciousness is justified. Settled in 1852, the town's low-lying, lush pastures were perfect for dairy cattle. Prosperity arrived, and by the 1890s dairymen in Cream City were building heavily-embellished Victorian mansions called 'Butterfat Palaces'. Two subsequent earthquakes wreaked havoc, but the homes, mansions,

Ferndale Chamber of Commerce *PO Box 325, Ferndale, CA 95536; tel/fax: (707) 786-4477; web: www.victorianferndale. org/chamber*

churches and Main Street shop-fronts were repaired, repainted and ooze charm whatever the weather.

Ferndale is a walker's paradise. **Main Street** is the place for shops, galleries, restaurants, bakeries, a meat market, a pioneer museum and the **Kinetic Sculpture Race Museum** *(580 Main St; see also Arcata, page 198)*. The **Ferndale Carriage Co** *(from Main and Washington Sts)* offers horse-drawn carriage tours of Main Street and mansions.

Ferndale's *de facto* image is the **Gingerbread Mansion Inn** *(400 Berding St),* an 1899 turreted and gabled froth of Victorian style, with magnificent English formal garden landscaping and a perfect and perfectly incongruous palm tree.

Accommodation in Ferndale

Ferndale is about 5 miles southwest of Hwy 101 from the Fernbridge/ Ferndale exit. Five bed-and-breakfast inns, one hotel, three motels and a county fairground camping area should be booked in advance, as Ferndale is popular with local tourists from San Francisco and Los Angeles.

Gingerbread Mansion Inn $$$ *400 Berding St; tel: (800) 952-4136 or (707) 786-4000.*

GARBERVILLE✢

Garberville Redway Chamber of Commerce *773 Redwood Dr.; Garberville, CA 95542; tel: (800) 923-2613 or (707) 923-2613; fax: (707) 923-4789. Open Mon–Fri 0900–1700, shorter hours in winter.*

Garberville serves as a hub for forestry, for holidaymakers seeking the redwoods, a base for exploring the **Avenue of the Giants** *(see page 198)* and a convenient stopping point for travellers taking Hwy 101 between San Francisco and Eureka/Crescent City. The friction between environment protection and lumbering is notable, while musicians and young counterculture types hang out for the atmosphere.

Accommodation and food in Garberville

As a services hub, Garberville is well supplied with motels.

Benbow Inn $$$ *445 Lake Benbow Dr., 1 mile south of Garberville; tel: (707) 923-2124 or (800) 355-3301; fax: (707) 923-2122; web: www.benbowinn.com,* is a stunning redwoods version of Tudor style, with lovely flower gardens outside and a high-ceilinged lobby and dining room. *Open Apr–New Year's Day.*

Sicilitos $ *445 Conger St; tel: (707) 923-2814,* with old advertising and sports memorabilia around the walls, serves tasty Mexican food and traditional American fare.

HUMBOLDT REDWOODS STATE PARK❖❖

① Humboldt Redwoods State Park tel: (707) 946-2409; web: www.northcoast.com/~hrspl/. **Visitor Center** 2 Miles north of Weott on Avenue of the Giants. Open Mar–Oct 0900–1700, Nov-Feb 1000–1600.

Most visitors encounter **Humboldt Redwoods State Park** as the **Avenue of the Giants** (see page 198), but its 52,000 acres include the awesome trees of **Rockefeller Forest**❖❖❖, estimated to constitute 10 per cent of remaining old-growth redwoods. Stop at the convenient and informative **Visitor Center** (2 miles north of Weott on Avenue of the Giants); a short path outside gives a rare opportunity to see all three redwood species side-by-side: dawn (Metasequoia glyptostroboides), coast (Sequoia sempervirens) and giant (Sequoiadendron giganteum).

PATRICK'S POINT STATE PARK❖❖

① Patrick's Point State Park $ west of Hwy 101, 4150 Patrick's Point Dr., 5 miles north of Trinidad; tel: (707) 677-3570 or (707) 488-2041; web: www.north coast.com/~hrsp/patricks

Patrick's Point State Park has superb views offshore to whale migrations, northward to Agate Beach and Big Lagoon and south to Trinidad Head, a blufftop **Rim Trail** and a **Yurok (Native American) Village**, with wooden houses, a sweat house and dance pit still reserved for use by tribal members.

PRAIRIE CREEK REDWOODS STATE PARK❖❖❖

① Prairie Creek Redwoods State Park $ west of Hwy 101, 50–58 miles north of Eureka, tel: (707) 464-6101, ex. 5301; web: www.nps.gov/redw /prcreek

Prairie Creek is best known for the Roosevelt elk which roam around three areas from Aug–Oct: **Davidson Rd, Elk Prairie** and **Gold Bluffs** (remote). These huge animals can ause traffic jams on Hwy 101.

Prairie Creek is rich in redwoods, with connecting trails circling through the major groves. Try **Newton B Drury Scenic Parkway exit** from Hwy 101. The most dramatic redwoods, however, are near the south exit where **Elk Prairie** and the **Elk Prairie Visitor Center** offer previews of what's ahead. Stop and hike to **Big Tree**, a fenced specimen 304ft high and 216in in diameter, and to the twined multiple trunks of the **Corkscrew Tree.**

REDWOOD NATIONAL AND STATE PARKS❖❖❖

① Redwood Information Center Hwy 101, 2 miles west of Orick. Open daily 0900-1700 with excellent whale-watching.

① Redwood National and State Parks ❙❙❙❙ 2nd St, Crescent City, CA 95531; tel: (707) 464-6101; web: www.nps.gov/redw

The jointly-managed park, with three state parks: **Prairie Creek Redwoods** (visitor centre 8 miles north of Orick on Hwy 101, open daily), **Del Norte Coast Redwoods** and **Jedediah Smith Redwoods** (east of Crescent City) protect old growth (250 years or more) coast redwoods, among the tallest, biggest and oldest natural objects on the planet. The parks are a **World Heritage Site** and an **International Biosphere Reserve,** accessible by vehicle, but much better enjoyed on foot, by bicycle, or on a horse (trails are well marked). Dress for frequent fog and rain. While coast redwoods and elk are the focus, the parks conserve coastline, tide-pools, waterfalls, oak woodlands and prairies.

As tame as the stately trees look, it's a wild world out there full of ticks, banana slugs, cougars (mountain lions), bears and elks.

RICHARDSON GROVE STATE PARK*

Richardson Grove provides services and an early glimpse of major stands of coast redwoods on the Hwy 101 route north. Families can swim in the Eel River south fork in summer, while anglers fish for steelhead later in the year.

TRINIDAD*

Greater Trinidad Chamber of Commerce *PO Box 356; tel: (707) 677-1610.*

Trinidad qualifies as a hamlet, just south of Patrick's Point State Park (*see page 202*), with more than its share of bed-and-breakfast inns and a fishing fleet. Its symbol is the red-roofed, white replica of an 1871 **Memorial Lighthouse. Trinidad State Beach*** (*off Trinity St, north of Main St; tel: (707) 677-3570*) is a good spot to watch a dramatic sunset behind jewel-sharp rocks rising from the sea, with diving and swooping black oystercatchers. Trinidad Scenic Drive (*south from Trinity St; parallel to Hwy 101*) provides access to **Luffenholtz Beach County Park** and **Houda Point.**

Suggested tour

Total distance: 221 miles.

Time: 6 hours driving. Allow a day for the main route, two days with **Detour 2**. Add a minimum of three extra days to drive into and hike the Lost Coast (*see Also worth exploring*).

Below
Some of the world's oldest and largest trees

Links: From Fort Bragg, the beginning of this route, connect with the Mendocino Coast (*see page 195*). For direct access from San Francisco, take Hwy 101 180 miles north to Leggett and on to Crescent City.

Route: Take Hwy 1 north from Fort Bragg ❶, turning inland north of Rockport ❷ for a winding, 16-mile drive over the mountains to Leggett ❸. Continue north on 101 to Eureka ❹, Arcata ❺ and Crescent City ❻.

Detour 1: Weaving in and out of the Avenue of the Giants ❼ parallel to Hwy 101 for 31 miles between Phillipsville ❽ and Pepperwood ❾ will take 45 minutes longer than going straight through on Hwy 101.

Detour 2: Two miles north of Weott ❿ at Dyerville ⓫, take the Rockefeller Forest exit west from Hwy 101. Follow the slow, winding Mattole Rd ⓬ from the redwood groves, over rolling, forested hills, to Honeydew ⓭, a small apple-growing hamlet. Continue northwest on the same road through more forests and mountain passes to Petrolia ⓮ and the coast south of the conical mass of Cape Mendocino ⓯. As Mattole Rd ⓬ turns to rise steeply inland, the narrow road narrows further, with 10mph speed limits all the way to Ferndale ⓰. Add half a day to the driving time for this slow and scenic 75-mile route.

Also worth exploring

The **Lost Coast** ⓱ is an isolated stretch of coast legendary amongst Californians, but little known because of its remoteness from roads and settlements. North of Rockport ❷ off Hwy 1 on Usal Rd, south from Honeydew ⓭ from Wilder Ridge/Kings Peak Rd, or west 24 miles from Redway ⓲ to Shelter Cove ⓳, is a barely touched section of coast, with sheer mountain peaks, slate black sand and teal blue water echoing with barking sea lions.

The coast, park and conservation areas are not signposted from any highway. Ask rangers or locally for directions, as some north and south roads are unpaved, and can be treacherous or even washed out from October to March from heavy rainfall when even four-wheel-drive vehicles can get stuck. RVs can't manoeuvre the steep, narrow, rugged roads.

Shelter Cove ⓳, with its working fishing fleet, has recently seen an influx of the rich and celebrated who are building homes on the hills, *à la Malibu*.

South of Shelter Cove, the 7367-acre **Sinkyone Wilderness State Park** ⓴, *PO Box 245, Whitethorn, CA 95589; tel: (707) 986-7711*, has a 17-mile trail through the wilderness.

King Range National Conservation Area ㉑, *Arcata Resource Area, US Bureau of Land Management, 1695 Heindon Rd; Arcata, CA 95521; tel: (707) 825-2300, office open Mon-Fri 0800-1630*, has 60,000 acres of rugged hiking and camping.

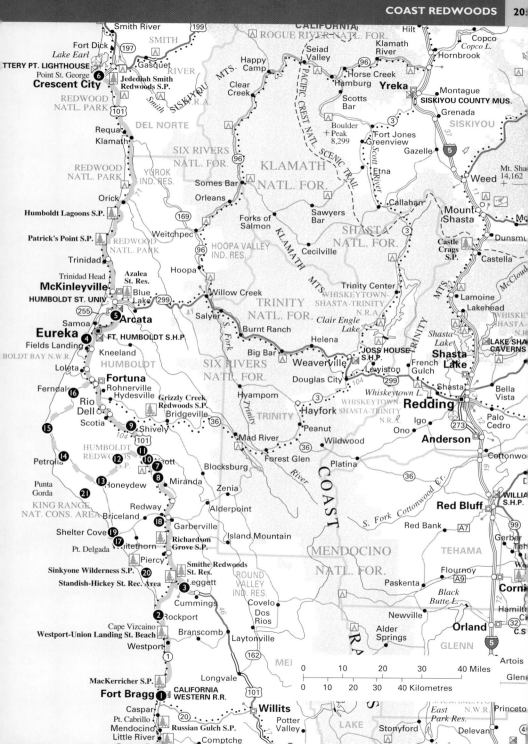

Monterey Peninsula

Ratings

Scenery	●●●●●
History	●●●●●
Food and wine	●●●●○
Children	●●●○○
Wildlife	●●●○○
Coastal villages	●●●○○
Beaches	●●○○○
Art and craft	●●○○○

Highway 1 from San Francisco to the Monterey Peninsula is surrounded by flower fields and vast vegetable farms, fringed by an ever-changing panorama of lighthouses, beaches and crumbling cliffs. Coastal attractions run the gamut from the ponderous mating of elephant seals on the sands of Año Nuevo to the theme park atmosphere of the Santa Cruz Beach Boardwalk, historic buildings in Monterey and the contrived artistic atmosphere of Carmel.

The whale-watching season runs from November to April, depending on location. Some areas, notably Point Reyes, Gualala and the north Mendocino coast, offer good views of whales passing just offshore. Ports from San Diego to Crescent City offer closer views from whale-watching cruises. Whale-watching boats aren't allowed to pursue whales, but if a canny captain manages to place his vessel ahead of the pod and a curious whale just happens to surface a few yards away, expect the view of a lifetime.

AÑO NUEVO STATE RESERVE✦✦✦

Año Nuevo State Reserve $ *Hwy 1, 22 miles north of Santa Cruz; tel: (650) 879-0227 or (800) 444-4445; web: www.anonuevo.org. Open daily. Advance reservations required Dec–Mar.*

This state reserve is a 4000-acre promontory of bluffs and beaches with the only northern elephant seal rookery on the California mainland. There are always a few of these huge aquatic mammals in residence, but the main show is between winter and spring, when immense bulls (up to 2.5 tonnes) battle for harems and females give birth. Access is by guided tour only, Dec–Mar, self-guided Apr–Nov.

CARMEL✦✦✦

This one-time artists' colony has tried to legislate its rustic past. Local ordinances prohibit parking meters, street addresses, postal delivery, high-heeled shoes and digging on the beach unless building a sand castle. Instead of the usual franchise stores and T-shirt shops, the town centre, **Ocean Avenue**, has mock Tudor art galleries, overpriced

Sonoma
Fairfield
Walnut Grove
TRAVIS A.F.B.
Galt
ma
116
Thornton
121
12
160
Napa
Rio Vista
Isleton
0   10   20 Miles
ato
29
680
Brannan I. S.R.A.
160
0   10   20 Kilometres
37
Termin
Frank
VALLEJO
SOLANO
Tract
Linden
fax
Benicia
Pittsburg
Antioch
S.R.A.
afael
Martinez
19
4
STOCKTON
Valley
14
CONCORD
Brentwood
4
Farmington
Richmond
Walnut Creek
32
French Camp
24
CONTRA
4
Lathrop
Manteca
BERKELEY
OAKLAND
COSTA
J6
Escalon
SCO
San Francisco
Danville
580
Ripon
108
NCISCO
880
San Ramon
Tracy
205
Empire
ly City
101
San Leandro
580
15
Salida
acifica
HAYWARD
21
Livermore
580
Vernalis
MODESTO
San Br o
30
Pleasanton
16
Ceres
San
ALAMEDA
13
Hug
Redw od City
84
FREMONT
Westley
C.S.U. STANISLAUS
Key
Moon Bay
Montara
880
Milpitas
Patterson
Hilmar
AN MATEO
Half Moon Bay
SUNNYVALE
33
Livingsto
Venice Beach
Newman
28
84
280
SAN JOSE
5
Pescadero
Cupertino
Campbell
STANISLAUS
165
Bu a
Pescadero
oga
85
Anderson
Gustine
Los Gatos
101
L.
Henry W.
Big Basin Redwo
SANTA
Coe S.P.
Volta
Lo
Pt. Año Nuevo
Año Nuevo State Reserve
LARA
Morgan Hill
Ba
Boulder Cre
Forest of
San Martin
e Lake
48
Ben Lomond
20
17
N
Santa Cruz Mountains
San Luis
Scotts Valley
Marks S.P.
152
Res. S.R.A.
Dos
Davenport
Aptos
Corralitos
Gilroy
San Luis
S
U.C. SANTA CRU
Santa Cruz
San Felipe
Res.
Santa Cruz Beach Boardwalk
m
Los Banos
Santa Cruz
San Juan
Res.
SANTA CRUZ
Watsonville
Bautista
Hollister
MERCED
Monterey Bay
Elkhorn Slough
ale
Tres Pinos
Moss Landing
Paicines
Castroville
Seventeen Mile Drive
remont
ister
DIABLO
Marina
Peak S.P.
Hills S.V.R.A
J1
Pacific Grov
FORT
Pacific Grove
SALINAS
Monterey
aside
Chualar
Pebble Beac
Monterey
55
San Benito
Carmel-by-the-Sea
Carmel
Gonzales
San B
MISSION SAN CARLOS BORROMEO
101
146
DEL RIO CARMELO
Garrapata S.
Point Lobos State Reserve
Valley
Soledad
PINNACLES
Bitterwater
1
NATL. MON.
POINT SUR S.H.P.
MISSION NUESTRA
Greenfield
Point Sur
Big Sur Pfeiffer
SENORA DE LA
Lonoak
Andrew Molera S.P.
Big Sur S.P.
SOLEDAD
King
25
Tassajara
City
San
Posts
Hot Springs
MONTEREY

ℹ **Carmel Business Association** *above Hog's Breath Inn, San Carlos, between 5th and 6th Sts; tel: (831) 624-2522 or (800) 550-4333; fax: (831) 624-1329. Open Mon–Fri 0900–1700.* **Info Kiosk** *Carmel Plaza, Ocean and Junipero. Open Fri–Sun 1100–1600.*

🏛 **Mission San Carlos Borromeo del Rio Carmelo** $ *2080 Rio Rd, Carmel; tel: (831) 624-3600. Open Mon–Sat 0930–1630, Sun 1030–1630.*

Point Lobos State Reserve $ *Hwy 1, 3 miles south of Carmel; tel: (831) 624-4909. Open daily.*

Tor House $ *26304 Ocean View Ave; tel: (831) 624-1813; fax: (831) 624-3696; web: www.torhouse. org. Open for hourly guided tours Fri–Sat 1000–1500.*

antique shoppes, traffic congestion and an unending stream of weekend events to keep the tourists coming. Parking is scarce, pavements uneven and prices high. The area from Junipero to the beach, between 5th and 8th Sts, is filled with unique homes, from ersatz adobe to shingled cottages and 'dolls houses' trimmed with Victorian finery.

The emerald-blue cove of **Carmel City Beach**✦✦✦ (*foot of Ocean Ave*) is bordered by soft white sand and green cypress trees. Enjoy the sand, but beware, a fierce undertow makes swimming dangerous.

Mission San Carlos Borromeo del Rio Carmelo✦✦✦ (*3080 Rio Rd; tel: (831) 624-3600*) is the very stereotype of a California Mission (*see page 259*), with golden sandstone walls, Moorish towers and contemplative gardens splashed with scarlet bougainvillaea. Mission founder Fra Junípero Serra is buried beneath the sanctuary of the rebuilt complex. Carmel is also one of the most-visited of the California missions; try to go early in the day before the crowds arrive. The church is closed during services, but the courtyard and grounds remain open.

Point Lobos State Reserve✦✦✦ has 6 miles of jagged shoreline above hidden aquamarine coves favoured by scuba divers, known as much for rolling meadows filled with spring wildflowers as the sea lions, whales, sea otters, seals and flocks of sea birds in permanent residence. Rangers lead nature walks daily, but parking is limited. Arrive early, especially between May and October.

Tor House✦✦ is Carmel's most imposing residence, a medieval-looking structure built of golden boulders hauled from the beach below by poet Robinson Jeffers. The family still live in the house.

Accommodation and food in Carmel

Nothing in Carmel is inexpensive. **Carmel Valley Ranch $$$** *One Old Ranch Rd, Carmel, CA 93923; tel: (831) 625-9500 or (800) 422-7635; fax: (831) 624-2858*, escapes the crowds (and coastal fog) in Carmel Valley, a few miles inland.

The **Highlands Inn $$$** *Box 1700, Carmel, CA 93921; tel: (831) 624-3801 or (800) 682-4811; fax: (831) 626-1574*, sits above the coast just south of Point Lobos.

Golfers gravitate to **Pebble Beach** and **The Inn at Spanish Bay $$$** or **The Lodge at Pebble Beach $$$** *Box 567, Pebble Beach, CA 93953; tel: (831) 647-7500 or (800) 654-9300; fax: (831) 644-7955; web: www.pebble-beach.com*, on the famed 17-Mile Drive.

Hog's Breath Inn $$ *San Carlos and 5th Sts; tel: (831) 625-1044, open daily*, is owned by film star Clint Eastwood.

Mediterranean Market $$ *Ocean Ave at Mission St; tel: (831) 624-2022, open daily*, has a good selection of picnic ingredients.

The **Tuck Box English Tea Room $$** *Dolores and Ocean Aves; tel: (831) 624-6365, open daily*, is kitschy, entertaining and anything but English.

ELKHORN SLOUGH NATIONAL ESTURINE SANCTUARY✣✣✣

ℹ Elkhorn Slough National Esturine Sanctuary $ *3 miles north of Castroville; tel: (831) 728-2822; fax: (831) 728-1056; web: www.elkhornslough.org. Open Wed–Sun 0900–1700.*

This is California's largest surviving coastal wetland, teeming with birds, seals, sea otters and fish. Trails provide shoreline access. **Elkhorn Slough Safari Nature Tours** *(tel: (831) 633-5555)* offer boat tours; **Monterey Bay Kayaks** *(tel: (831) 373-5357 or (800) 649-5357)* offer guided or self-guided kayak tours. Advance bookings are required for tours.

HALF MOON BAY✣

ℹ Half Moon Bay Coastside Chamber of Commerce *520 Kelly Ave, Half Moon Bay, CA 94019; tel: (650) 726-8380; fax: (650) 726-8389. Open Mon–Fri 0800–1600.*

Half Moon Bay is part dormitory community for San Francisco Bayside and Silicon Valley cities, part old-fashioned farming town, part artistic community and part surfing destination. The Chamber of Commerce has free self-guided walking maps to several of its charming Victorian buildings, including one built in 1849.

Bay and town are named for the half-moon shaped beach stretching south from **Pillar Point Harbor✣** and **Princeton-by-the-Sea✣**. **St Francis Beach✣✣✣** may be the most beautiful local beach; surfers head for **Surfer's Beach** (*El Granada*) and **Mavericks** (off Pillar Point), renowned for enormous and occasionally lethal waves. **Venice Beach✣✣** and **Dune Beach✣✣** are the least crowded.

Coastside Harvest Trails✣✣ *(765 Main St; tel: (650) 726-4485)* publish a free map to vegetable, fruit and flower farms in the area, many of which invite visitors to pick for themselves.

Accommodation and food in Half Moon Bay

Pillar Point Inn $$$ *380 Capistrano Rd, Princeton-by-the-Sea; tel: (650) 728-7377 or (800) 400-8281; web: www.pillarpointinn.com*, is more bed and breakfast than motel.

Barbara's Fishtrap $$ *281 Capistrano Rd at Hwy 1; tel: (650) 728-7049, open daily for lunch and dinner*. This rustic bayside diner is a long-time favourite with San Franciscans.

MONTARA✣

ℹ Fitzgerald Marine Reserve✣✣✣ *off Hwy 1, just north of Pillar Point; tel: (650) 728-3584; fax: (650) 728-3621. Open dawn–dusk.*

The coastal hamlet of **Montara** is known primarily for the **Point Montara Lighthouse Hostel✣** (*16th St at Hwy 1; tel: (650) 728-7177*), a former lighthouse converted to a youth hostel, and **Fitzgerald Marine Reserve✣✣✣**. At high tide, the reserve could be any stretch of rocky coastline, but low tide uncovers broad rocky terraces and innumerable tide-pools inviting exploration.

Food in Montara

Moss Beach Distillery $$ *Beach Way at Ocean Blvd; tel: (650) 728-5595; fax: (650) 728-8135. Open daily 1200–2100.* The 'distillery' was an illicit spirits storehouse and bar/restaurant/brothel during Prohibition. The bar and restaurant remain, one of the better eating spots along the coast and a popular protected vantage point for sunsets.

MONTEREY***

Monterey Peninsula Visitors and Convention Bureau
380 Alvarado St, Monterey CA 93940; tel: (831) 649-1770; fax: (831) 648-5373; web: www.monterey.com. Open Mon-Fri 0830-1700. **Visitor Center** *201 El Estero (Historic Monterey). Open daily 0900-1700.*

Monterey Bay Aquarium $$ *886 Cannery Row; tel: (831) 648-4888 or (800) 756-3737; fax: (831) 644-7580; web: www.myayaq.org. Open daily 0930-1800 mid-June-Labor Day, 1000-1800 rest of year.*

Monterey State Historic Park $ *20 Custom House Plaza; tel: (831) 649-7118; fax: (831) 647-6236; web: www.mbay.net/~mshp/. Open daily 1000–1700 Memorial Day weekend–Labor Day, 1000–1600 rest of year.*

Monterey was the capital of California under Spanish, Mexican and American flags. Overfishing in the 1940s killed the gritty sardine canneries immortalised in John Steinbeck's *Cannery Row*, but the town has been successfully trolling for tourists ever since.

Cannery Row** (*west of Fisherman's Wharf*) lost its last cannery decades ago, but the area has been resurrected as Monterey's main tourist district. The mile-long bayfront street is lined with restaurants, art galleries, shops and similar attractions. Don't miss construction site **murals**** of Monterey history just east of the Aquarium.

Fisherman's Wharf* has traded its commercial fishing fleet for a bevy of restaurants, galleries, handicraft shops, sport fishing boats and whale-watching operations.

Built around Monterey's last cannery, **Monterey Bay Aquarium**** has a wide range of exciting attractions. **Open Ocean**** displays creatures native to the open seas off Monterey Bay, including sharks, tuna, barracuda and 3000-lb ocean sunfish. **Live video**** transmissions from research submarines in Monterey Canyon show rare sea life from 6000ft deep. An open-air **kelp forest**** tank is so realistic that wild sea birds use it as an extension of the real Monterey Bay a few yards away. The **Great Tide Pool**** includes sea otters and harbour seals.

The best way to see the real bay is by kayak; **Monterey Bay Kayaks** (*tel: (831) 373-5357*) is the biggest operator.

Monterey State Historic Park** operates 37 historic buildings, sites and museums detailing Monterey from the 17th to 20th centuries. Daily guided tours begin from the visitor centre at **Pacific House**** on **Custom House Plaza****, next to Fisherman's Wharf. A 1½-mile **Path of History**** self-guiding walk connects the sites, most of which are closed except to guided tours.

Accommodation and food in Monterey

Casa Munras Garden Hotel $$$ *700 Munras Ave; tel: (831) 375-2411 or (800) 222-2558; fax: (831) 375-1365,* incorporates one of the first homes built outside the walls of the original Presidio in 1824. If you absolutely *must* have a harbour view, the **Monterey Bay Inn $$$** *242*

Cannery Row; tel: (831) 373-6242 or *(800) 424-6242; fax: (831) 373-7603*, has private balconies and stunning bay views.

Rappa's $$ *end of Fisherman's Wharf; tel: (831) 372-7562*, combines good seafood with great views. **The Poppy $** (*444 Alvarado St; tel: (831) 646-1021*) café served as the model for Steinbeck's Golden Poppy Cafe in *Sweet Thursday* (breakfast and lunch). **Alvarado St** is Monterey's trendy dining and shopping area.

PACIFIC GROVE❖❖

ⓘ Pacific Grove Chamber of Commerce *584 Central Ave, Pacific Grove, CA 93950; tel: (831) 373-3304; web: www.pacificgrove.org. Open Mon–Fri 0930–1700.*

The most scenic way out of Monterey is Pacific Grove (via the **Seventeen Mile Drive❖❖❖**), but the town has its own attractions. **Monarch Grove Sanctuary❖❖❖** (*Lighthouse Ave and Ridge Rd*) is winter home to millions of monarch butterflies, which congregate on trees between October and March before migrating north in summer. **Point Piños Lighthouse❖❖**, in operation since 1855, shows how lighthouse keepers lived and worked in the 19th and early 20th centuries (*Asilomar Blvd and Lighthouse Ave; tel: (831) 648-3116. Tours by costumed guides Thur, Sat–Sun 1300–1600*).

PESCADERO❖

🍴 Duarte's $–$$ *202 Stage Rd; tel: (650) 879-0464, open daily,* is one of the most talked-about fish restaurants on the coast.

This former Portuguese fishing and farming town presents a tidy face, but is best known for **Pigeon Point Lighthouse❖❖** (*Pigeon Point Rd; tel: (650) 879-0633*), now a scenic and popular youth hostel, and **Año Nuevo State Reserve❖❖❖** (*see page 206*). The coast north and south is lined with popular beaches.

SANTA CRUZ❖❖

ⓘ Santa Cruz County Conference and Visitor Council *701 Front St, Santa Cruz, CA 95060; tel: (831) 425-1234 or (800) 833-3494; fax: (831) 425-1260; web: www.scccvc.org*

🏛 Joseph M Long Marine Laboratory *$ end of Delaware Ave above Natural Bridges State Park; tel: (831) 459-4308. Open Tue–Sun 1300–1600.*

Perched on the north end of Monterey Bay, Santa Cruz began as a Mission town in 1791 and boomed as a beach resort with the coming of the railway. A University of California campus adds one more layer to this hard-working, relaxed, blue-collar, intellectual and artistic surfer city. The city **beach❖❖❖** is one of the widest, warmest, sunniest and busiest strands north of Santa Barbara.

Art galleries and studios❖❖ are concentrated in the city centre along **Pacific Ave** (*between Water and Cathcart Sts*), rebuilt following the 1989 earthquake.

Joseph M Long Marine Laboratory❖ is a University of California marine research lab. A small museum and guided tours explain current research projects, and there are aquaria, touch tank creatures and marine mammal pools. The lab overlooks **Natural Bridges State**

Santa Cruz Beach Boardwalk 400 Beach St; tel: (831) 423-5590; fax: (831) 460-3335. Boardwalk free, rides $. Open daily 1100 Memorial Day-Labor Day (closing times vary), Sat–Sun 1100–1900 Jan 1–Memorial Day and Labor Day–Nov 30.

Santa Cruz Surfing Museum ground floor of the lighthouse, West Cliff Dr.; tel: (831) 429-3429. Open daily 1200–1600.

Wilder Ranch State Historic Park $ Hwy 1, 2 miles north of Santa Cruz; tel: (831) 426-0505. Open daily.

Beach***, named for mudstone arches (only one is still standing).

Roaring Camp & Big Trees Narrow Gauge Railroad** (*Box G-1, Felton; tel: (831) 335-4484*) is America's last steam-powered railway with a daily, year-round passenger service. The line runs through redwood forests in the Santa Cruz Mountains.

Santa Cruz Beach Boardwalk*** was California's first beach boardwalk amusement park (1904) and the only one to survive. Top rides are the **Hurricane**** roller-coaster and the 1924 **Giant Dipper***** wooden roller-coaster, one of America's Top Ten Coasters. The 1911 Charles Looff **merry-go-round***** has its original organ and ring toss. There's also an assortment of lose-your-lunch rides for adrenaline addicts and free rock 'n' roll concerts Friday nights in summer.

Exhibits hearkening back to 100lb redwood surfboards of the 1930s are on display at the **Santa Cruz Surfing Museum***, which overlooks prime surfing beaches.

Wilder Ranch State Historic Park** has 34 miles of coastal hiking, cycling and equestrian trails as well as preserved ranch buildings. Guides in period costume explain the life of early Central Coast ranchers.

Accommodation and food in Santa Cruz

Casa Blanca Inn $$$ *101 Main St; tel: (831) 423-1570 or (800) 644-1570; fax: (831) 423-0235*, is a converted mansion across the street from the Beach Boardwalk. The **Dream Inn $$$** *175 Cliff Dr; tel: (831) 426-4330 or (800) 662-3838; fax: (831) 427-2025*, has ocean balconies or patios in every room. **Gabriella Cafe $$** *910 Cedar St; tel: (831) 457-1667, open daily*, is one of the area's best Northern Italian restaurants. **Santa Cruz Brewing Co & Front Street Pub $–$$** *516 Front St; tel: (831) 429-8838, open daily*, is Santa Cruzs' original brewery-restaurant.

SEVENTEEN MILE DRIVE***

This is the scenic coastal route (*tel: (831) 625-8426*) from Monterey (Pacific Grove) to Carmel by way of the coast, Pebble Beach and 21 marked points of interest. Don't miss **The Lone Cypress*****, one of California's most-photographed trees clinging to a bare rock (with significant help from guy wires). The Drive exits on to Ocean Ave in Carmel.

Suggested tour

Total distance: 90 miles.

Time: 2½ hours driving. Allow a full day or overnight in Santa Cruz, plus a day exploring the Monterey Peninsula.

Links: San Francisco and the Marin Coast to the north, Big Sur and Southern California to the south.

Route: From **San Francisco** ❶, follow Hwy 1 south over the spine of the San Mateo Peninsula to **Pacifica** ❷, the self-proclaimed Fog Capital of California. The road south follows golden cliffs set with small beaches and fronted by rocky reefs and lighthouses at **Montara** ❸ and Pigeon Point. Beach parks at **Pomponio** and **Pescadero** ❹ are local favourites.

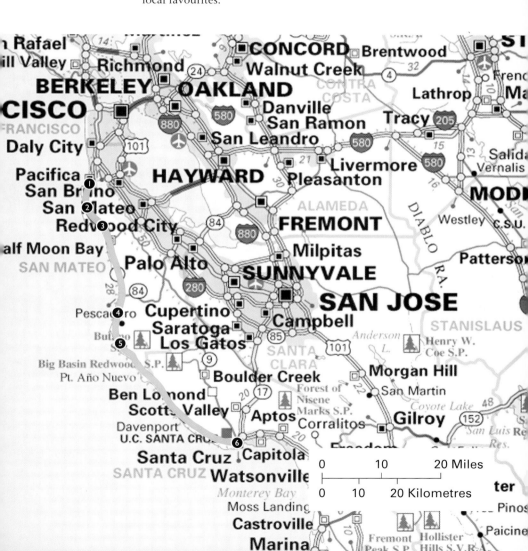

Big Sur and the Central Coast

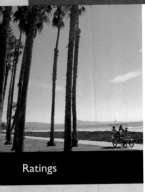

Ratings

Scenery	●●●●●
Nature	●●●●○
Children	●●●○○
Beaches	●●●○○
Sport	●●●○○
Food	●●○○○
History	●●○○○
Architecture	●○○○○

Big Sur is elemental California, undeveloped and seemingly untouched. Hwy 1 is the sole access, a route routinely blocked by winter rains and mudslides and just as routinely clogged with summer weekend traffic. South of Big Sur, the road becomes wider, straighter and less crowded, but no less scenic for the easier access. The Central Coast, Hearst Castle to Santa Barbara, offers an alluring combination of good weather, easy driving and rolling countryside that invites leisurely exploration.

Big Sur and its series of state parks is one of the most visited parts of California, yet manages to retain an air of isolation, mystery and mysticism. The 90 rugged, craggy miles of Hwy 1 were carved into trackless cliffs by convict labour in the 1930s. Enjoy the ethereal magic of the cobalt and turquoise Pacific Ocean battering soaring mountains cloaked in swirling mists and dense forests.

BIG SUR✦✦✦

ⓘ **Big Sur Chamber of Commerce** Box 87, Big Sur, CA 93920; tel: (831) 667-2100. Open Mon, Wed, Fri 0900–1300.

Big Sur Multi-Agency Station ½-mile south of Pfeiffer-Big Sur State Park; tel: (831) 667-2315. Open daily 0800–1800 in summer, to 1700 in winter.

The best views are south-bound, driving on the ocean side of Hwy 1. The scenery is unendingly stunning, but the winding road demands full driving attention – drivers should wait for the frequent lay-bys before taking in the views. The most complete local guide is the *El Sur Grande* newspaper, free at ranger stations and shops. The best information stop is the **Multi-Agency Station** (*just south of Pfeiffer-Big Sur State Park*). Big Sur ends at **Piedras Blancas Lighthouse✦✦**, just north of **Hearst Castle✦✦✦** (*see page 218*).

Andrew Molera State Park✦✦ (*south of Point Sur Lighthouse; tel: (831) 667-2315*) is the largest and least-developed of the Big Sur parks. Miles of trails wander its open beaches, meadows and hilltops.

Big Sur Valley (*25 miles south of Carmel*), the centre for tourist services, stretches for 6 miles along Hwy 1.

Bixby Creek Bridge✦✦ (*3½ miles south of Garrapata State Park*), a solitary and much-photographed arch, soars high above Bixby Creek. Best **views✦✦✦** are from an overlook at the north end. **Esalen Institute✦**

ond
Valley
Forest of
Nisene
Marks S.P.
San Martin
Coyote Lake
Volta Los
Banos
MERCED
N.W.R.
Santa
Rita
Park
El Nido
Red Top
Chowchilla
Fairmead
Berenda
Deulton
O'N
L.
Mille
41
Aptos
Corralitos
Gilroy
152
San Luis
Res. S.R.A.
48
Dos Palos
S. Dos
Palos
152
Madera
Fresno
145
Madera
Friant
S.R.
Clo
FRE

TA CRUZ
A Cruz Capitola
Watsonville
Monterey Bay
Moss Landing
Castroville
Marina
acific Grove
Monterey
by-the-Sea
ebble Beach
RIO CARMELO
Garrapata S.P.
Freedom
San Felipe
Res.
Hollister
San Juan
Bautista
Prunedale
Tres Pinos
Hollister
Peak N.H.S.V.R.
SALINAS
FORT
ORD
Chualar
Seaside
Gonzales
Soledad
Carmel
Valley
Paicines
MISSION NUESTRA
SENORA DE LA
SOLEDAD
183
16
101
SANTA LUCIA
146

Dos Palos
S. Dos
Palos
33
Oro Loma
Firebaugh
Mendota
5
180
Highway City
Rolinda
Biola
C.S.U.
FRESNO
Ripperdan
Kerman
Easton
Raisin
City
Fowler
Malaga
Conejo

COAST
DIABLO

Panoche
San Benito
Bitterwater
Idria
San Benito
Three Rocks
San Benito
Mtn.
5,241
Tranquillity
San Joaquin
Cantua
Creek
33
Helm
Caruthers
Monmouth
Burrel
Riverdale
Kingsbur
Laton

MONTEREY
25
RANGE
San Benito
PINNACLES
NATL. MON.
Greenfield
King
City
Lonoak
25
San
Lucas
Priest
Valley
198
Five
Points
Lanare
269
FRESNO
145
LEMOORE
NAVAL
AIR STA.
Lemoore
Armo
22
Hanf

Lonoak
Priest
Valley
198
Coalinga
Avenal
33
41
Westhaven
Huron
Stratford
Corcoran
Kettleman City
TULARE
LAKE BED
An

DINT SUR S.H.P.
Point Sur
ndrew Molera S.P.
Posts
108
Tassajara
Hot Springs
Julia Pfeiffer Burns S.P.
LOS PADRES
NATL. FOR.
Lopez Pt.
Lucia
JADE COVE
Cape
San Martin
Nacimiento Res.
San Antonio Res.
Junipero
Serra Pk.
5,862
MISSION SAN
ANTONIO DE
PADUA
Lockwood
HUNTER
LIGGETT
MIL. RES.
G18
Bradley
Parkfield

Big Sur
Sur S.P.
MISSION SAN
ANTONIO DE
PADUA
San Ardo
Cottonwood
Pass
2,000
KETTLEMAN HILL
KINGS
COL. ALLEN
41
Lost
Hills

HEARST SAN SIMEON S.H.M.
Pt. Pie
Hearst Castle
Pine Mtn.
3,594
San Simeon
San Simeon Pt.
San Simeon St. Beach
CAMP ROBERTS
MIL. RES.
San Miguel
Cholame
MISSION SAN
MIGUEL ARCANGEL
Shandon
Devils
Den
Blackwells
Corner
KERN
N.W.R.
5
46
38
46

Cambria
Harmony
Pt. Estero
Atascadero
Paso
Robles
Templeton
Creston
101
24
46
229
SAN LUIS OBISPO
Simmler
TEMBLOR
RANGE

Morro Bay
Morro Bay S.P.
Los Osos
Montana de Oro S.P.
MISSION SAN LUIS OBISPO DE TOLOSA
Cayucos
41
101
San Luis
Margarita
Obispo
San Luis Obispo
58
Machesna
Mtn. 4,061
California Valley
58
Buttonw
McCl

PACIFIC
OCEAN
Avila Beach
Pismo Beach
Grover Beach
Oceano
Pismo Dunes S.V.R.
Guadalupe
Point Sal
Arroyo Grande
Nipomo
1
Santa
Maria
Orcutt
Sisquoc
LA PANZA RANGE
Twitchell Res.
Cuyama
R.
Soda
Lake
CARRIZO PLAIN
166
Fellows
Cuyar
Ma

Casmalia
Purisima Pt.
VANDENBERG A.F.B.
Vandenberg Village
Lompoc
Pt. Arguello
Santa Barbara Wineries
Pt. Conception
Purisima Pt.
Los Alamos
135
LA PURISMA MISSION S.H.P.
246
Los Olivos
Santa Ynez
154
SIERRA
MADRE
MTS.
McPherson Pk.
5,749
New
Cuyama
Ventuco
SANTA BARBARA
Big Pi
6,828
SAN RAFAEL
RANGE

Las Cruces
NC
FA
Santa Barbara
Gaviota
101
30
Vista
Santa Barbara Beaches
Carpinteria
a
U.C. SANTA
BARBARA
Mont
leta

0	10	20	30	40 Miles
0	10	20	30	40 Kilometres

Below
Big Sur's scenic coastline

(*8 miles south of Julia Pfeiffer Burns State Park; tel: (831) 667-3000*) is America's original New Age retreat. The public are allowed as far as the famed outdoor hot tubs, *daily 0100–0300.*

    Garrapata State Park✦ (*10 miles south of Carmel; tel: (831) 624-4909*) contains 4 miles of undeveloped coast, but has no car-parks or other facilities. Park paths from lay-bys around **Soberanes Point** run to beaches, through stands of cacti and into dense redwood groves. **Henry Miller Memorial Library**✦ is a shrine to the infamous writer who lived in Big Sur for 18 years. The library is filled with Miller memorabilia, much of it for sale. The toilet has erotic tiles by local artist Ephraim Doner, and oversized sculptures grace the lawn.

    Julia Pfeiffer Burns State Park✦✦✦ includes some of Big Sur's best coastline. Don't miss the easy ½-mile return trail to **McWay Waterfall**✦✦✦, which drops from a bluff into the ocean. Another easy ½-mile return trail leads from Hwy 1 to **Partington Point**✦✦✦, overlooking the surging, kelp-filled waters of Partington Cove. **Nepenthe**✦✦ is a restaurant best known for its **views**✦✦✦. The multi-storey structure, 800ft above the crashing surf, was built by Hollywood director Orson Welles for his bride, Rita Hayworth, in the 1940s. **Café Kevah** has the best views.

    Pfeiffer Beach✦✦✦ (*no sign; off Sycamore Canyon Rd, the only paved road west off Hwy 1 between the Big Sur Post Office and Pfeiffer-Big Sur State Park*) is Big Sur's best and hardest-to-find beach. The white strand is dominated by a rock hump that changes from brown to fiery orange as the sun sets. Richard Burton and Elizabeth Taylor produced some of their steamier cinematic love scenes here for *The Sandpiper* in 1965. Their beach scenes notwithstanding, a fierce undertow makes swimming extremely hazardous.

    Pfeiffer-Big Sur State Park✦✦ (*tel: (831) 667-2315*) sits in the midst

of the Big Sur Valley, groves of redwoods, conifers and oaks interspersed with open meadows along the Big Sur River. There are miles of hiking trails and deep, clear river swimming-holes amongst the boulders in summer. Pfeiffer-Big Sur is headquarters for all of the Big Sur State Parks, with the best visitor and information centre.

Point Sur State Historic Park*** (*19 miles south of Carmel; tel: (831) 625-4419*) contains the **Point Sur Lightstation*****, in operation since 1889. The light is automated, but the building's interiors are being restored to their turn-of-the-century appearance. The station is open for guided tours as part of a 2½-mile return hike, with moonlight tours in summer.

Accommodation and food in Big Sur

High demand and low supply tends to keep prices high. Advance bookings are essential. **Big Sur Lodge $$–$$$** *Pfeiffer-Big Sur State Park; tel: (831) 667-2171; fax: (831) 667-3110*, is the only non-camping accommodation in the Big Sur state parks, with modern cabins around a swimming-pool. **Deetjen's Big Sur Inn $$** *tel: (831) 667-2377; fax: (831) 667-0466*, is a rambling, old fashioned inn popular with long-time visitors. **Post Ranch Inn $$$** *tel:(831) 667-2200* or *(800) 527-2200; fax: (831) 667-2824*, a post-modernist retreat below Hwy 1, has stunning views and rooms. **Ventana Inn $$$** *tel: (831) 667-2331* or *(800) 628-6500; fax: (831) 667-2419*, is a rougher-hewn equivalent above Hwy 1.

Deetjen's Big Sur Inn Restaurant $$ serves good Euro-Californian cuisine with larger than average portions. **Sierra Mar $$$** (*Post Ranch Inn – see above*) keeps to cutting-edge California dishes. **Ventana Restaurant** (*Ventana Inn – see above*) tends to traditional California offerings.

GUADALUPE*

Guadalupe is a California time capsule, a town that never lost its past. The traditional **Italian Cemetery*** at the intersection of Hwys 1 and 166 is filled with ornate funerary monuments; the brick shop-fronts lining Main St still display the names of the Italian, Mexican, Chinese and Basque merchants who erected them.

Food in Guadalupe

Santa Maria Barbecue $$$ a holdover from Californio days, is the best reason to stop in Guadalupe. The **Far Western Tavern $–$$** *899 Guadalupe St; tel: (805) 343-2211*, specialises in thick steaks, grilled with salt, pepper, garlic and olive oil and sliced paper-thin.

HEARST CASTLE✧✧✧

ⓘ Hearst San Simeon State Historic Monument $$ *750 Hearst Castle Rd, San Simeon, CA 93452; tel: (805) 927-2020 or (800) 444-4445; web: www.hearstcastle.org. Advance bookings essential in summer and recommended all year. Walk-in space may be available mid-week mid Nov–mid May.*

The rolling hills of the Central Coast have long been a magnet for dreamers with money to bring their fantasies to life – none with more extravagance than William Randolph Hearst. Hearst called his 165-room Renaissance-Moorish-Medieval holiday house 'The Ranch'. The official name was *La Cuesta Encantada*, The Enchanted Hill, but the world knew it as **Hearst Castle**.

More estate than castle, *Casa Grande*, the Big House, is surrounded by guesthouses and an outdoor swimming-pool complex, the whole set within lush gardens and a private zoo with free-roaming zebras and other exotic creatures.

Hearst, an only child, inherited a failing *San Francisco Examiner* and turned it into a hugely profitable chain of papers. In the euphoria following World War I, America's most famous media personality decided to build America's most famous house. With the help of architect Julia Morgan, Hearst got an eclectic pastiche of European treasures. The grand façade to *Casa Grande* once graced a Spanish cathedral; the ceilings were pulled from European monasteries. No museum of the day could outbid Hearst's buyers, who filled the Castle with priceless treasures.

Never one to underplay his own success, Hearst invited the social and political elite of the world to visit The Ranch for as long as they wished. Charlie Chaplin, Winston Churchill, Greta Garbo, Clark Gable, Charles Lindbergh, George Bernard Shaw and hundreds more accepted. Hearst's 'home movies', seen as part of the tour, show just how carefree life could be at The Ranch; Orson Welles's 1941 film *Citizen Kane* gives an equally accurate – if fictionalised – rendition of Hearst, castle and company.

Below
Sybaritic luxury – the Neptune Pool at Hearst Castle

The property eventually passed to the State of California and became **Hearst San Simeon State Historic Monument** (*tel: (805) 927-2020*), open by guided tour. **Tour One** is an overview of the property. **Tour Two** concentrates on the unfinished upper floors of *Casa Grande*, including Hearst's library and bedroom suite. **Tour Three** looks at one of the guesthouses in detail. **Tour Four** (summer only) inspects the grounds and gardens. **Tour Five** (Fri–Sat evenings, spring and autumn) is a living history tour with guides dressed as famous guests and servants from the 1930s. It's possible – but ill-advised – to cram all five tours into a single day. After the first few hours, one baroque tapestry starts looking much like any other.

The **Visitor Center** is worth a visit even if tours are fully booked. One wall opens on conservation laboratories and the free museum provides a good overview of the Castle and architect Julia Morgan's other and far more original work.

LOMPOC*

ℹ Lompoc Valley Chamber of Commerce *III S. I St, Lompoc, CA 93436; tel: (805) 736-4567 or (800) 240-0999; fax: (805) 737-0453; web: www.lompoc .com. Open Mon–Fri 0900–1700.*

🏛 La Purisima Mission State Historic Park *$ 2295 Purisima Rd; tel: (805) 733-3713. Open daily 0900–1700.*

Lompoc Museum *$ 200 S. H St; tel: (805) 736-3888; fax: (805) 736-2840. Open Tue–Fri 1300–1700, Sat–Sun 1300–1600.*

Many of the flower seeds sold in America are grown on more than 600 acres of fields in Lompoc, which blaze with colour between May and September. The Chamber of Commerce publishes a free self-guided flower field map.

La Purisima Mission State Historic Park*** (*see page 256*) is the most authentically restored of the 21 California Missions. The park includes ten buildings restored to their 1820s glory, the historic water system, replanted gardens and period barnyard animals. **Lompoc Museum*** has a large collection of artefacts from local Native American bands.

Right
Commercial flower farms blaze with colour in the Californian summer

MORRO BAY**

ℹ Morro Bay Chamber of Commerce *880 Main St, Morro Bay, CA 93442; tel: (805) 772-4467 or (800) 231-0592; fax: (805) 772-6038; web: www.morrobay .com. Open Mon–Fri 0830–1700, Sun 1000–1500.*

Once a lively port for the area's ranchers, Morro Bay has become a busy fishing port and holiday destination. The town and bay are named for **Morro Rock*****, first in a line of volcanic cores stretching south to San Luis Obispo. The sand spit which protects the harbour is accessible only by boat. Kayaking around the protected estuary at the south end of the Bay is popular in all seasons.

The Embarcadero* is the town's main tourist and commercial fishing area. Many fishing boats unload directly into restaurant kitchens or sell straight to consumers. **Harbour Cruises*** (*tel: (805) 772-2257*) aboard the stern wheeler *Tigers Folly II* pass Morro Rock, the Embarcadero and the harbour entrance.

Harbour Cruises $
1205 Embarcadero; tel:
(805) 772-2257; fax: (805)
772-1034. One-hour trips
daily June–Sept, Sat–Sun
Oct–May.

**Montaña de Oro
State Park $** end of
Los Osos Valley Rd, south of
Morro Bay; tel: (805) 528-
0513.

**Morro Bay State Park
and Museum of Natural
History $** south end of
Morro Bay; tel: (805) 772-
7434. Museum open daily
1000–1700.

Montaña de Oro State Park✢✢, 'Mountain of Gold' in Spanish, was named for the mounds of golden California poppies, wild mustard and other wildflowers that bloom each spring. There are more than 50 miles of walking paths in the park; among the most popular is **Hazard Canyon**✢✢, ½-mile from gum forests to tide pools.

Morro Bay State Park✢✢ takes in most of the south end of Morro Bay, including a public 18-hole golf course. The **Museum of Natural History**✢ covers the Bay's complex ecosystem, including a network of walking paths.

Morro Rock✢✢ (578ft) has been mined for building materials for nearly four centuries, but still dominates the bay and town. The Rock itself is closed to protect peregrine falcons nesting on the upper slopes.

Food in Morro Bay

Fish is the obvious best choice in town at the **Great American Fish Company $–$$** 1185 Embarcadero; tel: (805) 772-4407.

PISMO BEACH✢

**Pismo Beach
Chamber of
Commerce** 581 Doliver
St, Pismo Beach, CA 93449;
tel: (805) 773-4382 or
(800) 443-7778. Open
Mon–Sat 0900–1700, Sun
1000–1600.

**Pismo State Beach
$** 2 miles south; tel:
(805) 489-2684; fax: (805)
473-7229.

The town took its name from the Pismo clam, a local mollusc once so plentiful that newspapers talked of 45,000 clams being dug in a single day. Few legal-sized clams survived decades of depredation, though hardware stores hire digging gear and sell the requisite fishing licences. The fishing pier offers excellent views of surfers riding the waves toward shore.

At the **Monarch Butterfly Grove**✢✢✢ (tel: (805) 489-1869) just south of the **Pismo State Beach North Beach Campground** between Pismo Beach and Grover City, the orange and black butterflies hang in great clusters from the gum and Monterey cypress trees from November to February.

Pismo Beach, Grover City and Oceano are often lumped together as the **Beach Cities**. The **Nipomo Dunes**✢✢✢ begin south of the Beach Cities, a sand sea stretching 18 miles to **Point Sal**✢. Cecil B De Mille filmed the original *Ten Commandments* in the dunes beyond West Main St (Hwy 166) in Guadalupe. Bits of his faux-Egypt set occasionally reappear as the dunes shift.

Food in Pismo Beach

Splash Café $ 197 Pomeroy Ave; tel: (805) 773-4653, is famous for clam chowder, its surfing murals inside and out and a surfboard above the entrance.

SAN LUIS OBISPO✧✧

ⓘ San Luis Obispo Chamber of Commerce *1039 Chorro St, San Luis Obispo, CA 93401; tel: (805) 781-2777; fax: (805) 541-8416; web: www.VisitSLO.com. Open Tue–Wed 0800–1700, Thur–Fri 0800–2000, Sat 1000–2000, Sun–Mon 1000–1700.*

ⓘ California Polytechnic University *tel: (805) 756-5734. Tours Mon, Wed and Fri.*

Mission San Luis Obispo de Tolosa, *Chorro and Monterey Sts; tel: (805) 543-6850. Open daily 0900–1700 Jun–Dec, 0900–1600 Jan–May.*

San Luis Obispo County Park

San Luis grew up as a Mission farming community that blossomed when the railway arrived in 1894. The Mission heritage remains, both in the pronunciation (Lou-iss, Spanish-style) and the town's common appellation, SLO, as in 'slow', the relaxed pace of life.

The town centre, **Higuera and Monterey Sts**✧, contains some of the finest small-town commercial architecture in the state, from adobes to art deco and Frank Lloyd Wright. The Chamber of Commerce has free self-guided walking and driving maps, or ride the free **SLO Trolley** around a circular route covering the main tourist sites.

California Polytechnic University✧, usually called Cal Poly, offers free campus tours. Don't miss the **Botanic Garden**✧ or **Poly Canyon**✧, an outdoor laboratory for experimental architecture and construction.

Generations of teenagers have festooned **Chewing Gum Alley**✧✧ (*Higuera-Marsh Sts, between Garden and Broad Sts*) with graffiti, names and freeform designs, all carefully executed in well-used chewing gum. The oral appliqué changes slightly almost every night.

Mission San Luis Obispo de Tolosa✧✧ (*Chorro and Monterey Sts; tel: (805) 543-6850*) pioneered the red-tile roof that became the Mission hallmark – the 1772 Mission needed something more substantial than thatching to withstand fiery attacks by local Native American tribes (*see page 261*). **Mission Plaza**✧✧, fronting the Mission, is a shady park sloping down to **San Luis Creek** and the business district. Music wafts through the trees from several restaurant patios that open on to the plaza.

San Luis Obispo County Historical Museum $ *696 Monterey St; tel: (805) 543-0638. Open Wed–Sun 1000–1600.*

San Luis Obispo County Historical Museum✦ has a collection of local artefacts in the historic Carnegie Library building.

Accommodation and food in San Luis Obispo

Madonna Inn $$ *100 Madonna Rd; tel; (805) 543-3000 or (800) 543-9666*, is a shocking pink temple of kitsch, from the 200-tonne boulders in the Jungle Rock Room to the crimson silk Love Nest and equally whimsical décor for the Fabulous 50s, Cave Man and other theme rooms.

The **SLO Brewing Company $** *1119 Garden St; tel: (805) 543-1843*, is popular with students for its enormous servings as well as the beer brewed on the main floor.

SLO Perk $ *1028 Chorro St; tel: (805) 541-4616*, is a pleasant breakfast, lunch and coffee stop overlooking the Mission.

SANTA BARBARA✦✦✦

Santa Barbara Visitor Information Center, *1 Santa Barbara St, Santa Barbara, CA 93101; tel: (805) 965-3021 or (800) 927-4688; web: www.santabarbara.com. Open 0900–1800 in summer, 0900–1600 in winter.*

Santa Barbara began as a Mission town, but the Mission-look of downtown, red-tile roofs, whitewashed plaster walls and colourful wall tiles, dates from a 1925 earthquake. Faced with rebuilding nearly the entire city centre, authorities opted to create their own historic look with a strict architectural code. The result is one of the most gracious, visually pleasing cities in Southern California. Built on a series of rolling hills between broad beaches and the rugged Santa Ynez Mountains, Santa Barbara happily lives up to the name Lotusland bestowed by an early opera diva who retired here.

El Presidio de Santa Barbara State Historic Park *100-200 E. Canon Perdido St; tel: (805) 965-0093; fax: (805) 568-1990. Open daily 1030–1630.*

El Paseo and State St✦✦ are centre-pieces of the 1920s reconstruction. **El Paseo** is an early shopping arcade, filled with delightfully sunny niches and fountains. **El Paseo Nuevo** is an updated version with the same Mission motif, while **State St** is Santa Barbara's high street.

Mission Santa Barbara *E. Los Olivos and Laguna Sts; tel: (805) 682-4149. Open daily 0900–1700.*

El Presidio de Santa Barbara State Historic Park✦✦✦ is the site of the 1782 Spanish fort that first lured settlers to Santa Barbara. The restored **El Cuartel** is among the oldest structures in California. The padres' quarters, chapel, commandant's office and other buildings are reconstructions.

Santa Barbara Botanic Garden $ *1212 Mission Canyon Rd; tel: (805) 682-4726. Open Mon–Fri 0900–1700, to 1800 Sat–Sun Mar–Oct, 0900–1600 and 0900–1700 Nov–Feb.*

Mission Santa Barbara✦✦✦ *(see page 262)*, the 'Queen of the Missions', starred in numerous early cinematic epics. Buildings, gardens and the church interior are beautifully preserved.

Santa Barbara Botanic Garden✦ is devoted to native trees, cacti, shrubs and flowers.

Santa Barbara County Courthouse✦✦✦, in an extravagant take-off on the Mission style, has echoing tiled corridors, heroic furnishings,

ⓘ Santa Barbara County Courthouse
1100 Anacapa St; tel: (805) 962-6464. Open Mon–Fri 0800–1700, Sat 1000–1700.

Santa Barbara Historical Museum $
136 E. De La Guerra St; tel: (805) 966-1601; fax: (805) 966-1603. Open Tue–Sat 1000–1700, Sun 1200–1700.

Santa Barbara Museum of Natural History $
2559 Puesta del Sol Rd; tel: (805) 682-4711. Open Mon–Sat 0900–1700, Sun 1000–1700.

and a red-tiled roof. To top it all, the courthouse also has a Moorish tower from which there are fine views of city and sea.

Santa Barbara Historical Museum✦ offers local historical exhibits, while the **Santa Barbara Museum of Natural History✦✦** specialises in Native American tribal artefacts, as well as local flora and fauna.

Stearns Wharf✦✦ (*foot of State St; tel: (805) 564-5518*), built in 1872, now houses small speciality shops, restaurants and the **Sea Center✦**, a small museum devoted to marine and bird life of the Channel Islands National Marine Sanctuary.

Accommodation and food in Santa Barbara

Santa Barbara's popularity as a quick getaway for Los Angelinos keeps accommodation demand and prices high.

El Encanto Hotel $$$ *1900 Lasuen Rd; tel: (805) 687-5000 or (800) 346-7039*, has sweeping views and a mix of Craftsman and Spanish-style cottages.

The **Hotel Santa Barbara $$$** *(805) 957-9300 or (888) 259-7700*, is a posh stop in the city centre.

Citronelle $$$ *901 E. Cabrillo Blvd; tel: (805) 963-0111*, is famed for its French-California dishes and the view.

The **Enterprise Fish Co $$** *225 State St; tel: (805) 962-3313*, is the best fish house in town.

Wine Cask $$ *813 Anacapa St; tel: (805) 966-9463*, has one of Santa Barbara's best Central Coast wine lists. Don't miss the five-course tasting menu Sun-Mon.

SANTA BARBARA BEACHES✦✦

El Capitan✦✦, **Gaviota✦✦** and **Refugio State Beaches✦✦** (*Hwy 101, N. of Santa Barbara; tel: (805) 968-1033*) are three of Santa Barbara's most popular beach parks. **El Capitan** has rocky tidepools, a sandy beach and stands of sycamore and oak trees. **Gaviota** boasts a wooden fishing pier. **Refugio** offers stands of palm trees along the mouth of a small creek. All three have picnicking and camping.

Also worth exploring

San Luis Obispo to Port San Luis✦✦✦

Take San Luis Bay Rd west from Hwy 101 just south of San Luis Obispo through stands of spreading valley oak trees to Avila Beach Dr.

Avila Hot Springs* (*250 Avila Beach Dr; tel: (805) 595-2359; fax: (805) 595-7914*) was a favourite party stop for Hollywood stars on their way to Hearst Castle (*see page 218*). Today the resort is a family stop.

Sycamore Mineral Springs** (*1215 Avila Beach Dr.; tel: (805) 595-7302; fax: (805) 781-2598*) is a more expensive, full-service spa with an excellent California cuisine restaurant, **The Gardens of Avila $$** *tel: (805) 595-7365.*

The fishing village of **Avila Beach** is being dug up to remove decades of petroleum pollution. **Point San Luis Lighthouse*****, at the tip of Point San Luis, can be visited on easy 3½-mile walks guided by the **Nature Conservancy** (*tel: (805) 541-8735*, advance booking required). It is also possible to visit the nearby **Diablo Canyon Nuclear Power Plant** (*tel: (805) 595-7647*) by advance booking. The visitor centre is open Mon–Fri 0900–1200.

SANTA BARBARA WINERIES***

Santa Barbara County has three dozen wineries, most of them in the Santa Ynez Valley, off Hwys 154 and 246 near Solvang, or near Foxen Canyon Rd in the Santa Maria Valley. The Santa Maria Mountains funnel ocean breezes far inland, producing a long, cool growing season and some of California's most flavourful grapes.

For information on visits and tasting facilities, contact the **Santa Barbara County Vintner's Assn**, *Box 1538, Santa Ynez, CA 93460; tel: (800) 218-0881* or *(805) 686-5881; fax: (805) 688-0881*, and the **Edna Valley Vintners Assn**; *tel: (805) 541-5868.*

Suggested tour

Total Distance: 245 miles.

Time: 6 hours driving. Big Sur deserves at least a day to itself. Allow half a day to tour **Hearst Castle**, with an overnight stop in **Morro Bay** or **San Luis Obispo**.

Links: Monterey Peninsula to the north, Southern California to the south.

Route: Follow Hwy 1 south from **Monterey ❶**/**Carmel ❷** past **Point Lobos ❸** into **Big Sur ❹**. **Hearst Castle ❺** marks the start of the rolling **San Luis Obispo ❻** coast. From **Morro Bay ❼**, Hwy 1 runs inland to join Hwy 101 at **San Luis Obispo ❻**. Hwy 1 returns to the coast at **Pismo Beach ❽** and runs south towards **Guadalupe ❾** and **Lompoc ❿** before rejoining Hwy 101 28 miles north of **Santa Barbara ⓫**.

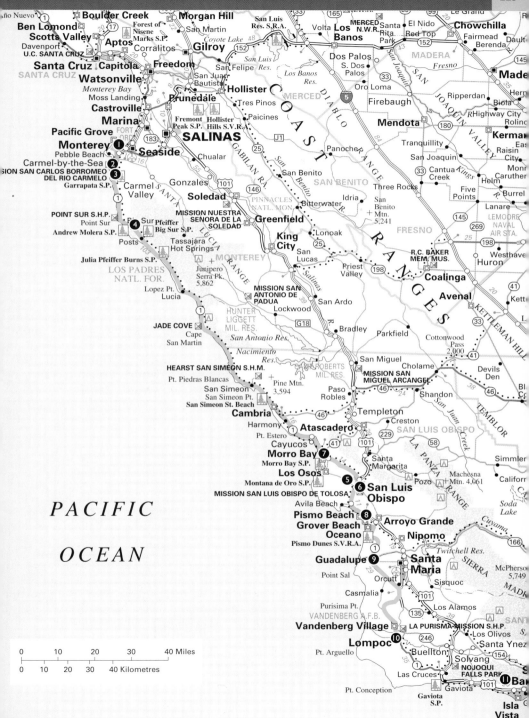

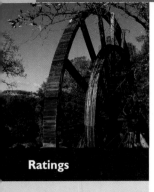

Gold Country to Yosemite

Ratings

Scenery	●●●●●
History	●●●●○
Children	●●●○○
Mountains	●●●●○
Food	●●●○○
Museums	●●●○○
Wine	●●○○○
Architecture	●○○○○

The discovery of gold in 1848 catapulted California from backwater to powerhouse and created Sacramento as its capital. Gold Country, the Sierra Nevada foothills from Sierra City south to Mariposa, shaped the California psyche far more dramatically than today's placid landscape would suggest. The rough-and-tumble promise of riches just over the next hill was fulfilled often enough that Californians still embrace calculated risks that many Americans might consider foolhardy. Try to visit in spring or early autumn; winding roads are congested in summer and most attractions are closed Mon-Wed in winter. Yosemite Valley is a summertime city, complete with crowds, traffic, noise and pollution, but the rest of the park is delightfully calm.

ANGELS CAMP✣

ⓘ Calaveras Lodging and Visitors Bureau
1211 S. Main St, Angels Camp, CA 95222; tel: (209) 736-0049 or (800) 225-3764; fax: (209) 736-9124; web: www.calaveras.org/visit

Jensen's Pick & Shovel Ranch $$ *4977 Parrotts Ferry Rd; tel: (209) 736-0287, call in advance.*

⚲ Calaveras County Fair $ *Calaveras County Fairgrounds, 2 miles south; tel: (209) 736-2561, third weekend in May.*

A young prospector with literary ambitions heard the story of a jumping frog contest here, and *The Celebrated Jumping Frog of Calaveras County* brought fame and the beginnings of fortune to Mark Twain. Twain may have written the short story in a rebuilt cabin just outside of town. Fans flock to the **Jumping Frog Jubilee** at the **Calaveras County Fair** *(tel: (209) 736-2561)*. Bring your own frog or hire a jumper on the spot.

Angels Camp Museum✣ has photographs and relics of gold mining equipment from the old days. **Jensen's Pick & Shovel Ranch✣✣** offers a taste of the romance – and the backbreaking labour – of panning gold by swirling gravel, sand, mud and water in an oversized pie tin to wash away the dross and recover a few flecks of precious metal.

OARS✣ *(tel: (209) 736-4677)* offer river trips from local half-day floats to whitewater expeditions. Calavaras winery tours make pleasant terrestrial expeditions; ask at the visitors bureau for local maps and suggestions.

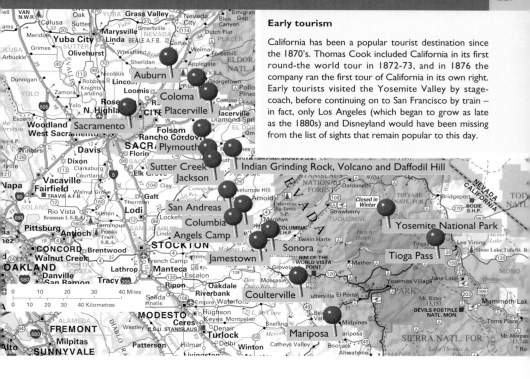

Accommodation and food in Angels Camp

ℹ️ **Angels Camp Museum** $ 753 Main St; tel: (209) 736-2963 Open daily 1000–1500 Mar–mid Nov, weekends Jan–Feb.

Cooper House Bed and Breakfast Inn $$ 1184 Church St; tel: (209) 736-2145, was the town physician's home and office. The **B of A Café** $$ 1262 Main St; tel: (209) 736-0765, a former Bank of America, is the liveliest local café.

AUBURN✦✦✦

ℹ️ **Placer County Visitor Information Center** 13464 Lincoln Way, Auburn, CA 95603; tel: (530) 887-2111 or (800) 427-6463; fax: (530) 887-2134; web: www.placer.ca. gov. Open Mon–Fri 0900–1700, Sat 0900–1500.

ℹ️ **Placer County Museum** 101 Maple St; tel: (530) 889-6500. Open Tue–Sun 1000–1600

Like most Gold Country towns, Auburn was an accident. Prospectors headed somewhere else hit pay dirt here first, but unlike hundreds of ragtag tent camps that disappeared as quickly as they sprouted, Auburn endured. Placer gold, panned from stream beds, gave way to hard rock gold, mined underground, which in turn gave way to more enduring riches from the Transcontinental Railroad in the 1860s.

Placer County Museum✦✦ has excellent regional gold displays and Native American tribal artefacts. The real Gold Rush was in **Old Town**✦✦, a warren of narrow streets and 19th-century buildings surrounding the red-and-white striped **Firehouse No 1** and an 1849 **Post Office**✦, California's oldest. The **Gold Country Museum**✦ has a demonstration mine shaft as well as period equipment.

Gold Country Museum $ *Country Fairgrounds, 1273 High St; tel: (530) 889-6500. Open Tue–Fri 1000–1530, Sat–Sun 1100–1600.*

Accommodation and food in Auburn

Power's Mansion Inn $$$ *164 Cleveland Ave; tel: (530) 885-1166*, is a bright pink mansion built by a powerful state politician.

Best stop for traditional burgers and milkshakes is **Ikeda's $** *13500 Lincoln Way; tel: (530) 885-4243*. **Bootlegger's Old Town Tavern & Grill $$** *210 Washington St; tel: (530) 889-2229*, serves an eclectic mix of French, Creole and steaks.

COLOMA*

Marshall Gold Discovery State Historic Park $ *310 Back St; Coloma, CA 95613; tel: (530) 622-3470; web: www.isgnet.com/coloma. Park open daily 0800–sunset; museum open 1000–1700 Memorial Day–Labor Day, call rest of the year. Try to avoid visiting in summer or at warm weather weekends, when Coloma is awash with school groups, family picnickers and river rafters.*

The California Dream started in Coloma, when a sawmill contractor named James Marshall spotted a few shiny flecks in January, 1848. **Marshall Gold Discovery State Historic Park**** (*surrounding Hwy 49*) contains about 70 per cent of the once-booming town. Historic buildings are concentrated along Main, Back and Brewery Sts; Marshall's restored cabin is below his hilltop grave and monument.

Start with the visitor centre and an excellent video detailing the geology of California gold, Gold Rush history and the often ruinous impact of miners digging, blasting and washing everything in sight – 150 years have barely begun to heal the environmental havoc that set California on the path to riches.

A working replica of Marshall's sawmill sits on the banks of the American River, which has changed course since 1848. Trails lead to the site of the original mill. Visitors still find traces of gold by panning the riverbank using pans from the visitor centre.

COLUMBIA***

Columbia State Historic Park *Columbia, CA 95310; tel: (209) 532-4301 or (209) 532-0150; web: www.sierra. parks.state.ca.us/coconten.htm*

Museum and visitor centre *Main & Spring Sts. Open daily 0900–1700.*

California's most appealing Gold Rush relic is an almost-ghost town, complete with brick storefronts, iron shutters, wooden sidewalks, spreading trees, stage-coaches and men (plus a few women) in real frontier garb. The park museum and ranger office have free self-guiding tours to the dozens of restored Gold Rush structures and businesses.

Accommodation and food in Columbia

The **Fallon Hotel $$** offers an opulent 1890s look. **City Hotel $$** *Main St; tel: (209) 532-1479 or (800) 532-1479; web: www.cityhotel.com*, more resembles the 'Gem of the Southern Mines' that 1856 visitors knew. The **City Hotel Restaurant $$$** is a French-California culinary delight, advance bookings required.

COULTERVILLE*

**Coulterville
Visitors Center**
*5009 Main St; tel and fax:
(209) 878-3074. Closed
Tue.*

**Northern Mariposa
County History Center**
*Hwy 49 and 132; tel: (209)
878-3015. Open Wed–Sun
1000–1600.*

Coulterville remains a mining, ranching and tourist supply town. The **Northern Mariposa County History Center*** is a pair of 1865 brick and stone buildings with period guns, Paris gowns and local Chinese furnishings. The 1851 **Sun Sun Wo Company Store** (*Main and Kew Sts*) is the sole survivor of a once-thriving Chinatown. The 1920s goods on the shelves here disguise an opium den behind. The **Whistling Billy*** locomotive engine, under the **Hanging Tree** in front of the History Center, once hauled ore from a nearby mine.

Accommodation and food in Coulterville

The **Hotel Jeffrey $$** *1 Main St; tel: (209) 878-3471* or *(800) 464-3471*, began as a Yosemite stage stop. Walls are still covered in the original stamped tin. **Yosemite Sam's Grill $$** *5006 Main St; tel: (209) 878-9911*, is the busiest local gathering place.

Right
Brewing up around the
camp fire

JACKSON*

ⓘ Amador County Chamber of Commerce *125-B Peek St, Jackson, CA 95642; tel: (209) 223-0350 or (800) 649-4988; fax: (209) 223-4425; web: www.cdepot.net/chamber. Open Mon–Fri 0900–1700.*

🏛 Amador County Museum *$ 225 Church St; tel: (209) 223-6386. Open Wed–Sun 1000–1600.*

Kennedy Mine Tailing Wheels *N. Main St, in a park one mile north of downtown. Open daily dawn–dusk.*

Kennedy Mine Tours *$ tel: (209) 223-9542, run mid Mar–Oct. Advance bookings required.*

Jackson grew and prospered with the Kennedy and Argonaut Mines, which survived until World II. The **Amador County Museum*** offers a good overview of daily life through the 1920s. The most striking remnant of the past is the **Kennedy Mine Tailing Wheels****, ruins of wooden wheels used to move mine debris (tailings) over several ridges to a holding pond. A well-marked **viewpoint*** 1½ miles north of town overlooks what remains of the mine headframe at the top of an abandoned 6000-ft shaft, once the deepest in North America. **Kennedy Mine Tours*** explores the surface structures. **St Sava Serbian Orthodox Church*** (*724 N. Main St; tel: (209) 223-2700*) is the Serbian Orthodox mother church in America.

Accommodation and food in Jackson

Linda Vista Motel $$ *Hwy 49, Martell, CA, one mile north of Jackson; tel: (209) 223-1096*, is outstanding value accommodation. The **National Hotel $$** *2 Water St; tel: (209) 223-0500*, claims to be the oldest operating hotel in California (since 1862), but without air-conditioning, rooms are insufferable in summer. The **Louisiana House** restaurant **$$** is in the cellar.

JAMESTOWN**

🏛 Railtown 1897 State Historic Park *$ Two blocks east of Historic Downtown Jamestown on 5th Ave; tel: (209) 984-3953; web: www.csrmf.org. Grounds open daily 0930–1630 for self-guided tours. Call in advance to book periodic steam train excursions Apr–Dec.*

Gold Prospecting Expeditions *$$ 18170 Main St; tel: (209) 984-4653 or (800) 596-0009 Advance booking required.*

'Jimtown' still uses original false-front buildings and wooden sidewalks, many of which have featured prominently in films such as *Butch Cassidy and the Sundance Kid*. Jamestown's working gold mine, an open pit operation outside town, is off limits, but **Gold Prospecting Expeditions** sells prospecting and panning trips for individuals and families. These can be great fun, but expect to get dirty and wet, and dress accordingly.

Locomotive engines and carriages from **Railtown 1897 State Historic Park***** have appeared in more than 200 films. The museum contains the original roundhouse and workshops of the Sierra Railroad, organised in 1897 to serve the Mother Lode.

Accommodation and food in Jamestown

The National Hotel $$ *77 Main St; tel: (209) 984-3446 or (800) 894-3446; fax: (209) 984-5620*, is an 1859 antique; many of the furnishings are original to the building. The **Jamestown Hotel $$** *18153 Main St; tel: (209) 984-3902 or (800) 205-4901; fax: (209) 984-4149*, is a bed and breakfast of similar vintage.

MARIPOSA*

Mariposa County Chamber of Commerce Visitors Center *5158 Hwy 140, Mariposa, CA 95338; tel: (209) 966-2456 or (800) 208-2434; fax: (209) 966-6168. Open daily 0800–1700.*

This southern gateway to Gold Country is the home of the **California State Mining and Mineral Museum***** (*Fairgrounds Rd, tel: (209) 742-7625*), one of the world's finest mineral and gem museums.

Government has been holding court in the white **Mariposa County Courthouse**** (*Bullion St, open Mon–Fri*) since 1854, the state's oldest official building still in use. Most courtroom furnishings are original, including the potbellied stove. **St Joseph's Catholic Church**** (*top of Bullion St*) is a striking example of traditional Gold Country church architecture. The **Mariposa County Museum and History Center*** (*5119 Jesse St, tel: (209) 966-2924*) has an exhaustive collection, from a working stamp mill to ancient bottles of Guinness Stout.

PLACERVILLE*

El Dorado County Chamber of Commerce *542 Main St, Placerville, CA 95667; tel: (530) 621-5885 fax: (530) 642-1624. Open Mon–Fri 0900–1700.*

El Dorado County Historical Museum $ *Fairgrounds, 100 Placerville Dr; tel: (530) 621-5865. Open Wed–Sat 1000–1600, Sun 1200–1600.*

Once known as 'Hangtown' for its favoured method of law enforcement, Placerville was more supply centre than mining town, a breeding ground for early entrepreneurs. The town's most famous product is the 'Hangtown Fry', eggs scrambled with bacon and oysters. The **El Dorado County Historical Museum*** focuses on local manufacturing and other mining support services. The **Gold Bug Mine*** (*1 mile north via Bedford Avenue and Hwy 50, tel: (530) 642 5232; open daily mid Apr–Oct*) has 352 feet of lighted tunnel with wooden floors, a stamp mill, museum and hiking trails. Nearby **El Dorado wine***** valleys are best known for Zinfandel, Syrah and Merlot. The **El Dorado Winery Association** (*tel: (800) 306-3956*) has free winery maps and touring suggestions.

PLYMOUTH*

Plymouth is a convenient starting point for tours of the **Amador wine country*****. **Amador Vintners** (*Box 667, Plymouth, CA 95669; tel: (209) 245-4309; fax: (209) 245-5636; web: www.amadorwine.com*) have free tasting and touring information.

SACRAMENTO**

California's capitol city began as **Sutter's Fort**** (*27th and L Sts; tel: (916) 445-4422*), built by Swiss immigrant John Sutter, whose Coloma sawmill sparked the Gold Rush. Sutter's adobe administration building is largely original, but the rest of the fort is reconstructed. The self-guided audio tour is a lively introduction to daily life of the era, aided by interpreters in period dress during summer and holiday periods.

ℹ Sacramento Convention and Visitors Bureau *1303 J St, Ste 600, Sacramento CA 95814; tel: (916) 264-7777; fax: (916) 264-7788, open Mon–Fri 0800–1700;* **Old Sacramento Visitor Center** *1102 2nd St; tel: (916) 442-7644, open daily 0900–1700.*

🏛 Sutter's Fort State Historical Park $ *27th & L Sts; tel: (916) 445-4422, open daily 1000–1700.*

California State Indian Museum $ *2618 K St; tel: (916) 324-0971, open daily 1000–1700.*

Golden State Museum $ *1020 O St; tel: (916) 653-4255, open Tue–Sun 1000–1700.*

California State Capitol *10th St between L & N Sts; tel: (916) 324-0333, open daily 0830–1700, free guided tours hourly 0900–1600.*

Old Sacramento *I-L Sts along the Sacramento River; tel: (916) 442-7644, open daily.*

California State Railroad Museum $$ *2nd & I Sts in Old Sac; tel: 916-445-7387; web: www.csrmf.org, open daily 1000–1700.*

Crocker Art Museum $ *2nd & O Sts; tel: (916) 264-5423, open Tue–Sun 1000–1700, to 2100 Thur.*

The adjoining **California State Indian Museum**✻ has a rich collection of photographs and artefacts. The **Golden State Museum**✻ is California's official museum, drawing upon the 120 million items in state archives.

The domed **California State Capitol**✻✻ is one of the West's most elegant public buildings. It is also an outstanding museum, thanks to extensive 1980s renovations that returned ground-floor gubernatorial and administrative offices to turn-of-the-century splendour. Visitors can watch Senate and Assembly sessions, but the magnificent **Capitol Park**✻✻✻ surrounding the building can be more revealing than many legislative debates.

Old Sacramento✻✻✻, or 'Old Sac' is Sacramento's original city centre. Brick buildings date to the 1850s, skilfully mixed with modern construction, wooden sidewalks and shade trees. The **California State Railroad Museum**✻✻✻ is America's largest railway museum, filled with splendidly restored locomotive engines, luxurious private carriages, sleepers and extensive displays on America's first transcontinental railway. A new **Waterfront Promenade**✻ links Old Sacramento and the **Crocker Art Museum**✻, the oldest art gallery west of the Mississippi River.

Sacramento's State Capitol building

Accommodation and food in Sacramento

The **Delta King Hotel $$** *1000 Front St; tel: (916) 444-5464* or *(800) 825-5464*, is an original paddlewheel steamboat permanently moored at Old Sacramento. **Amber House $$$** *1315 22nd St; tel: (916) 444-8085* or *(800) 755-6526*, a trio of historic homes, has the latest hotel amenities. The sleek **Sterling Hotel $$$** *1300 H St; tel: (916) 448-1300* or *(800) 365-7660*, is even better known for its stunning **Chanterelle** restaurant $$$.

Biba $$$ *2801 Capitol Ave; tel: (916) 455-2422*, is one of Northern California's better Italian restaurants as well as the star of a television cooking programme. **Buffalo Bob's Ice Cream Saloon $** *110 K St; tel: (916) 442-1105*, is Old Sacramento's best old fashioned ice-cream parlour.

SAN ANDREAS*

This tiny mining camp was known largely for the capture, trial and conviction of notorious highwayman Black Bart, actually a San Francisco dandy, famous among victims for his courtesy and poetry. The courthouse where the trial was held is now the **Calavaras County Historical Museum** *(30 N. Main St; tel: (209) 754-1058, open daily 1000–1600)*.

SONORA*

Tuolumne County Visitors Bureau *55 W. Stockton Rd, Sonora, CA 95370; tel: (209) 533-4420 or (800) 446-1333; fax: (209) 533-0956; web: www.thegreatunfenced.com. Open Apr–Oct Mon–Thur 0900–1900, Fri 0900–2000, Sat 1000–1800, Sun 1000–1700; Nov–Mar Mon–Fri 0900–1800, Sat 1000–1700.*

Tuolumne County Museum $ *158 W. Bradford Ave; tel: (209) 532-1317. Open daily 0930–1600.*

Once the wildest town on the Southern Mother Lode, Sonora has remained a busy crossroads with skiers, snowboarders, hikers and loggers mixing with Gold Country tourists.

The **Tuolumne County Museum**, in the 1857 county jail, has an interesting mix of old photos and curios. **Old Sonora*** stretches along **Washington St** from the dark red **St James Episcopal Church** into the town centre. The County Museum and visitors centre both have self-guiding walking maps.

Accommodation and food in Sonora

Ryan House $$ *153 S. Shepherd St; tel: (209) 533-3445* or *(800) 831-4897; web: www.ryanhouse.com*, is an 1855 house with all the details, from square nails to the original glass. **Banny's Café $$** *83 S. Stewart St, Ste 100; tel: (209) 533-4709*, has San Francisco quality for half the price. **Good Heavens: A Food Concern $$** *49 N. Washington St; tel: (209) 532-3663*, serves Sonora's best lunches in a former bordello.

SUTTER CREEK❖❖

ℹ **Amador County Chamber of Commerce** *Box 596, Jackson, CA 95642; tel: (209)223-0350 or (800) 649-4988, has Sutter Creek information.*

Sutter Creek does not have a very Gold Rush-like appearance. Main St is filled with galleries and antique shops in 19th century storefronts; side streets are lined with still more original buildings. **Knight's Foundry**❖❖ (*81 Eureka St*) was the last water-powered foundry in America.

Accommodation and food in Sutter Creek

Sutter Creek has the largest collection of accommodation in Gold Country. **The Foxes in Sutter Creek $$** *77 Main St; tel: (209) 267-5882* or *(800) 987-3344; web: www.foxesinn.com*, is one of Gold Country's most popular bed and breakfasts. Victorian **Grey Gables Inn $$** *161 Hanford St; tel: (209) 267-1039* or *(800) 473-9422*, is run by a pair of British expatriates.

Chatterbox Café $ *39 Main St; tel: (209) 267-5935*, is a classic diner with home-made burgers, pies and chips. **Zinfandels $$$** *51 Hanford St; tel: (209) 267-5008*, serves California specialities.

YOSEMITE NATIONAL PARK❖❖❖❖

ℹ **Yosemite Valley Visitor Center** *Yosemite Village; tel: (209) 372-0265. Open daily 0900–1700;*

Tuolumne Meadows Visitor Center *Tuolumne Meadows; tel: (209) 372-0263. Open early summer–Sept.*

Yosemite has been the target of adoring adjectives since the 1850s – all of them with waterfalls cascading down sheer, half-mile high granite walls, meadows laced with oak, cedar and maple trees, stupendous stands of sequoia redwoods and mountain vistas punctuated by rocky domes and spires.

The only problem is that the most famous sights, **Half Dome, El Capitan, Yosemite Falls, Bridalveil Fall** and more, are in Yosemite Valley. Nearly all of the four million-plus people who come to Yosemite each year come to Yosemite Valley. The rest of the park is practically deserted, including hiking trails barely beyond shouting distance of the gridlocked valley floor.

If possible, *don't* visit the valley in summer, but if you absolutely must come during high season, park your car, hire a bicycle (about $20 per day) and bypass the traffic jams. Free shuttles make non-stop loops around the valley from early dawn until midnight, an even easier alternative to driving. The main visitor centre, as well as most accommodation, restaurants and services are in **Yosemite Village.**

Instead of crawling through the valley, visit **Glacier Point**❖❖❖. The view is better than anything in the valley, spanning **Vernal Falls, Nevada Falls, Little Yosemite Valley, Yosemite Falls** and more. The vista is even better in winter, when the only access is by ski or snowshoe. The 60 miles across Yosemite National Park from **Crane Flat** over **Tioga Pass**❖❖❖ and down to **Lee Vining** is one of California's

Nevada City Chamber of Commerce *132 Main St, Nevada City, CA 95959; tel: (530) 265-2692 or (800) 655-6569; web: www.ncgold.com. Open Mon–Fri 0900–1700, Sat 1100–1600.*

Grass Valley Nevada County Chamber of Commerce *248 Mill St, Grass Valley, CA 95945; tel: (530) 273-4667 or (800) 655-4667; web: www.gvncchamber.org. Open Mon–Fri 0930–1700, Sat 1000–1500.*

Miners Foundry Cultural Center *325 Spring St; tel: (530) 265-5040). Open Mon–Fri 0930–1600.*

best short drives, threading through lush alpine meadows along the spine of the Sierra Nevada. The road is usually closed by snow in Oct and seldom reopens before the end of May.

Accommodation and food in Yosemite

All accommodation in Yosemite National Park is run by Yosemite Concession Services. Advance bookings are essential Apr-Sept and at weekends and holidays all year through **Yosemite Reservations** *5410 East Home, Fresno, CA 93727; tel: (209) 252-4848*. Valley choices include the grand **Ahwahnee Hotel $$$** motel-like **Yosemite Lodge, $$** and several clusters of **tents, cabins** and **camping grounds $$**. Choices at the south end of the park include the **Wawona Hotel $$$** and **camping $$**. Towns surrounding the park also offer accommodation.

Eating choices within Yosemite are limited to the same concessionaire-operated facilities, ranging from the **Ahwahnee Hotel $$$** to fast food and supermarket fare **$–$$**.

Right
Yosemite National Park's Bridalveil Fall

Suggested tour

Northstar Powerhouse Mining and Pelton Wheel Exhibits *across Hwy 49; tel: (530) 273-4255, open May–mid Oct 1000–1700.*

Firehouse No 1 *214 Main St; tel: (530) 265-5468), open 1100–1600 in summer.*

Total Distance: 175 miles

Time: Two days, plus at least one night in Yosemite

Links: Lake Tahoe to the north; Spine of the Sierras to the east

Route: From Sacramento ❶, take I-80 east across the flat Sacramento Valley ❷ to **Auburn** ❸ and the foothills of the Sierra Nevada Mountains ❹. Follow Hwy 49 south through Gold Country to **Coloma** ❺, where gold was discovered in 1848, **Placerville** ❻, **Plymouth** ❼, **Jackson** ❽, **San Andreas** ❾, **Angels Camp** ❿, **Columbia** ⓫, **Sonora** ⓬, **Jamestown** ⓭ and **Mariposa** ⓮. Turn east on Hwy 140 to the canyon of the Merced River and follow the river into **Yosemite National Park** ⓯, or take Hwy 120 from south of Jamestown to **Groveland** ⓰ and **Yosemite** ⓱.

Detour 1: Grass Valley and Nevada City prospered on deep mines drilled by immigrants from Cornwall and other European mining centres; Cornish pasties remain a local speciality. Follow Hwy 49 north from Auburn to Nevada City; either return to Auburn on Hwy 49 or take scenic Hwy 20 to I-80 and loop back to Auburn.

Grass Valley grubbed more than $400 million in bullion from tunnels beneath the town. **Empire Mine State Historic Park** $ (*10791 E. Empire St; tel: (530) 273-8522*) provides tours of the famous mine entrance, the 1850 owner's home, formal gardens and other buildings. The **Northstar Powerhouse Mining and Pelton Wheel Exhibits** is one of the most comprehensive mining museums in the Mother Lode.

Nevada City, 4 miles north, is quieter and more scenic. Don't miss the filagree-balconied **National Hotel** (*211 Broad St; tel: (530) 265-4551*). The white wedding-cake **Firehouse No 1** has pioneer relics, including Donner Party artefacts (*see page 36*). The **Miners Foundry Cultural Center** is an arts centre and winery tasting room. **Malakoff Diggins State Historic Park** $ (*54-mile return trip; Hwy 49 11 miles to Tyler Foot Crossing Rd, turn right for 17 miles and follow the signs; tel: (530) 265-2740*), is a rust-red badlands created by hydraulic mining that washed away entire mountains.

Detour 2: Follow Hwy 88 east from Jackson to **Indian Grinding Rock State Historic Park** $ (*14881 Pine Grove-Volcano Rd; tel: (209) 296-7488, open Mon–Fri 1100–1500, Sat–Sun 1000–1600*). The park protects an immense limestone slab with nearly 1200 holes worn by generations of Miwok women grinding acorns and other seeds into meal. A reconstructed Miwok village and the **Chaw'Se Regional Indian Museum** are near by.

Less than 2 miles away, **Volcano Daffodil Hill** turns golden with more than 300,000 daffodils in March and April.

Also worth exploring

This backroads route to Columbia passes two of California's finest public caves. **Mercer Caverns $** (*tel: (209) 728-2101; web: www.mercercaverns.com, open Sun–Thur 1000–1630 (0900–1800 in summer), Fri–Sat 1000–1800 (0900–2000 in summer)* is an intimate hole filled with dripping stalactites, towering stalagmites, congealed waterfalls and delicate strands of limestone pasta. **Moaning Cavern, $**, (*tel: (209) 736-2708; web: www.caverntours.com, open 1000–1700 weekdays (0900–1800 in summer), 0900–1700 winter weekends)* has a free-standing spiral staircase; the more adventurous explorers can abseil 120ft to the bottom. The moaning emanates from bottle-shaped holes at the bottom of the cave, not abseilers.

Murphys✦✦ is centred around the 1865 **Murphys Hotel✦✦** (*457 Main St; tel: (209) 728-3444*), temporary home to Mark Twain, Brett Harte, J P Morgan, Horatio Alger and other Gold Rush luminaries who left bullets in the woodwork.

The 60 miles across Yosemite National Park from **Crane Flat** over **Tioga Pass** and down to **Lee Vining** is one of California's best short drives, threading through lush alpine meadows along the spine of the Sierra Nevada. The road is usually closed by snow in Oct and seldom reopens before the end of May.

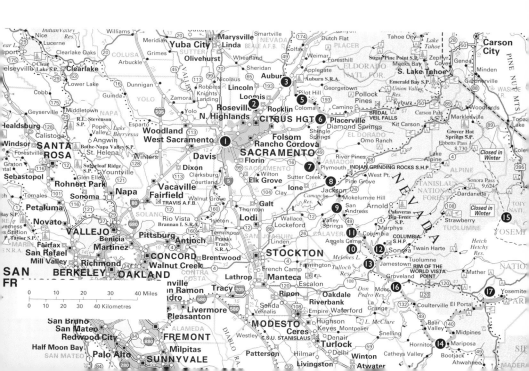

Sequoia and Kings Canyon National Parks

Ratings

Scenery	●●●●●
Outdoor activities	●●●●●
Children	●●●●●
History	●●●●○
Geology	●●●●○
Wildlife	●●●○○
Architecture	●○○○○
Food	●○○○○

These two contiguous parks contain some of California's most spectacular mountain scenery, from the biggest living things on earth to vast tracts of Sierra Nevada wilderness. The human-made attractions of Sequoia and Kings Canyon are warnings: valleys filled with rotting stumps larger than houses, fallen logs big enough to support a car, awe-inspiring views very nearly turned into theme park ski-runs. Tortuous trails lead eastward over the spine of the Sierra to Mount Whitney and the Owens Valley, but innumerable easier paths wandering a few miles into the wilderness are an indelible introduction to the glories of outdoor California.

BOYDEN CAVERN❖

Festooned with marble draperies, stalactites and stalagmites, the interior of **Boyden Cavern** (*Hwy 180, 22 miles northeast of Grant Grove (Kings Canyon NP); tel: (559) 736-2708; open daily June–Sept 1000–1700, May and Oct 1100–1600*) is a constant 55°F (13°C), which sends birds, small animals and under-dressed tourists into quick hibernation.

CRYSTAL CAVE❖❖

Crystal Cave is more difficult to reach. Vehicles over 20ft are prohibited on the access road and a steep ½-mile trail leads from the car-park to the cave entrance. Marble stalactites, stalagmites and flowstone adorn the chilly 48°F (9°C) caverns. (*off General's Hwy, 8 miles south of Giant Forest (Sequoia National Park); tel: (559) 565-3341; open daily 1100–1600 mid Jun–Labor Day, Fri–Mon 1100–1699 mid*

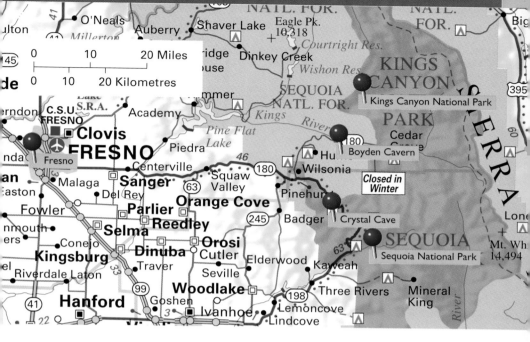

May–mid Jun and Labor Day–end Sept. Advance tickets required from Lodgepole Visitor Center or Foothills Visitor Center, see page 243).

FRESNO

Fresno Convention & Visitors Bureau, *808 M St, Fresno, CA 93721; tel: (209) 233-0836 or (800) 788-0836; fax: (209) 445-0122. Open Mon-Fri 0800-1700.*

Forestiere Underground Gardens $ *5021 W. Shaw Ave; tel: (209) 271-0734; open June-Sept Wed-Sun 1000-1600, Oct-Nov Sat-Sun 1200-1500*

The agricultural heart of California is blazingly hot in summer and blanketed by thick fogs in winter. Local farms produce one-third of all grapes grown in the US and over half the figs, cotton, nectarines and turkeys.

The **Fresno Art Museum**✦ *(2233 N. First St (Radio Park); tel: (209) 441-4220; open Tue–Fri 1000–1700, Sat–Sun 1200–1700)* has modest collections of French postimpressionist prints as well as American, Asian and Mexican art and sculpture. Asian art and alternating exhibits featuring regional history and European and American still-life paintings are on offer at the **Fresno Metropolitan Museum of Art, History and Science**✦ *(1555 Van Ness Ave; tel: (209) 441-1444; open Tue–Sun 1100–1700)*.

Forestiere Underground Gardens✦✦ *(5021 W. Shaw Ave; tel: (209) 271 0734; open June–Sept Wed–Sun 1000–1600, Oct–Nov Sat–Sun 1200–1500)* is an underground labyrinth of 50-odd rooms created between 1905 and 1946 to protect fruit orchards and other crops from the blistering summer sun. Descendants of builder Baldasare Forestiere conduct the tours.

ⓘ **Meux Home Museum** $ *1007 R St; tel: (209) 233-8007. Open daily 0900–1700 Mar–Oct, 1000–1600 Nov– Feb.*

The **Kearney Mansion Museum**✦ *(7160 W. Kearney Blvd; tel: (209) 441-0862; open Fri–Sun 1300–1600)* began as an opulent French Renaissance-style mansion for turn-of-the-century raisin mogul M Theo Kearney. Kearney's extensive canal system introduced industrial-scale vineyards and orchards to Fresno.

Meux Home Museum✦✦ brought Fresno the latest in urban elegance, 1889-style. The town's first two-storey home and the first embellished with Victorian finery, it remains Fresno's most stylish building.

The self-guided **William Saroyan Walking Tour**✦✦ *(920 E. Yale Ave; tel: (209) 221-1441)* explores many of the sites used by native son and novelist William Saroyan in his tales of Armenian immigrant life in America. Saroyan is best known for *The Human Comedy* and the stage play *The Time of Your Life*.

KINGS CANYON NATIONAL PARK✦✦✦

ⓘ **Grant Grove Visitor Center** *Grant Grove Village; tel: (559) 335-2856. Open daily 0800–1700.*

Cedar Grove Visitor Center *1/4-mile west of Cedar Grove Village; tel: (559) 565-3793; open daily 0800–1800 late Jun–Labor Day, Thur–Mon May and Sept.*

ⓘ **Kings Canyon National Park** $ *Sequoia and Kings Canyon National Parks, Three Rivers, CA 93271; tel: (559) 565-3341; web: www.nps/gov/ seki/.*

The park is named for a gaping canyon ripped into the salt-and-pepper granite of the High Sierra by the raging torrent of the Kings River, then gouged into a broad valley by ponderous glaciers. Just downstream from the confluence of the middle and south forks of the Kings River, the canyon plunges 8200ft from the peak of Spanish Mountain, the deepest gorge in North America.

King's Canyon Highway

Kings Canyon's most popular attractions are concentrated around Grant Grove. Just one road penetrates the park proper, the Kings Canyon Highway (*Hwy 180*), open only in summer. From the flat river meadow at Roads End, canyon cliffs soar nearly another mile straight up.

Cedar Grove✢✢ is as close as Kings Canyon comes to civilisation. The seasonal village and visitor centre are named for surrounding groves of incense cedars. The flat valley floor is ideal for leisurely cycling 5 miles to Roads End.

The 'U' shape of Kings Canyon, the unmistakable sign of past glacial activity, is most obvious from **Canyon Viewpoint**✢✢ (*1 mile east of Cedar Grove*). The 'V' shape of the lower canyon, beyond the reach of glaciers, is typical of canyons carved by rivers.

Knapp's Cabin✢ (*1 mile east of the viewpoint*) stored equipment for opulent fishing expeditions staged by Santa Barbara businessman George Knapp during the 1920s. One mile east of the cabin is the car-park for **Roaring River Falls**✢✢. An easy 5-minute paved path leads to the falls, roaring (and sometimes trickling) through a narrow granite chute.

The 1-mile loop trail through **Zumwalt Meadow**✢✢✢ is one of the most scenic walks in either park. The trail crosses a suspension bridge to a view over the grassy meadow and **North Dome**✢✢✢ (8717ft), then descends through the meadow. Expect to see a variety of birds, as well as a profusion of wildflowers – leopard lilies, shooting stars, violets, Indian paintbrush, lupines and others, depending on the season. Pick up a self-guiding map at the visitor centre.

Just beyond is **Grand Sentinel Viewpoint**✢✢✢, with clear views of one of the most striking rock formations in the area, the Grand Sentinel (8504ft).

Roads End✢✢✢ is the literal end of the road and the start of a vast network of trails. Gruelling tracks cross the Sierras over passes above 11,000ft and into the Owens Valley (*see page 116*). The 8-mile return hike to **Mist Falls**✢✢✢ is an easier glimpse of the backcountry. The sandy trail is relatively flat, but gains 600ft in the final mile to the largest waterfall in the twin parks. Allow between 4 and 6 hours.

Return to Cedar Grove on the road, or, more interestingly, via the **Motor Nature Trail**✢✢✢ on the north side of the river. The rough corrugated road is passable by passenger vehicles but is *not* recommended for RVs.

Grant Grove✢✢ is administratively part of Kings Canyon National Park, but the dense stand of sequoia, sugar pine, incense cedar, black oak and mountain dogwood looks more like Sequoia National Park. The grove is named for the **General Grant Tree**✢✢, officially the world's third largest tree at 267ft tall and 107ft in circumference. A ⅓-mile paved path wanders through the grove. Most of the major trees have been fenced off to protect their shallow root systems from trampling by enthusiatic crowds.

The trail also passes the **Fallen Monarch**✢✢, which has been a house and a stable, and the **Gamlin Cabin**, a rebuilt 1872 loggers cabin. A quieter alternative is the seldom-visited **North Grove Loop✦✦✦**, a 1½-mile trail from the Grant Grove car–park. The 2.2-mile **Dead Giant Loop✦✦✦** (*lower end of Grant Grove car-park*) passes a historic lumber mill pond on the way to a giant sequoia that was killed by girdling, or cutting through the living cambium layer (just beneath the bark), which cut the flow of nutrients to the tree. The walk offers an instructive comparison between the ways National Park and National Forest lands are managed.

Big Stump Basin✦ (*Hwy 180, 2½ miles southwest of the visitor centre*) is just what the name suggests, a valley filled with gigantic stumps – how the Grant Grove would appear today had early loggers been allowed to continue. A self-guiding 1-mile **loop trail✦✦✦** highlights regenerating sequoias and other natural features.

The **Mark Twain Stump** is what remains of a giant sequoia felled in 1891 so sections could be displayed in the American Museum of Natural History in New York and the British Museum in London. A similar tree-cutting exercise was conducted for the 1876 Centennial Exhibition in Philadelphia.

The **Kings Canyon Highway✦✦✦** runs from Grant Grove to Cedar Grove. Much of the road follows the canyon of the Kings River, here a sharp 'V' filled with the rushing boom of the river. The sheer granite walls are laced with blue marble, pocked with yellow yucca plants and splattered with green and orange lichen, more easily visible beyond **Junction View**. Numerous lay-bys offer excellent views of the canyon and High Sierra peaks rising in the distance.

Panoramic Point✦✦✦ is one of the most accessible vistas across the spine of the high Sierra, with **Lake Hume** to the north below. The 4.7-mile return **Park Ridge Trail✦✦✦** offers views from the high peaks to the east down the descending western ranges into the Central Valley (on clear days).

Accommodation and food in Kings Canyon National Park

All accommodation in the park is booked through **Kings Canyon Park Services**, *Box 909, Kings Canyon NP, CA 93633; tel: (559) 335-5500.*

Grant Grove Lodge $$ is open all year; **Cedar Grove Lodge $$** is open in summer. Accommodation is also available outside the park, including **Kings Canyon Lodge $$$** *Hwy 180; tel: (559) 335-2405.* Advance booking is necessary all year.

In summer, picnic supplies and restaurant meals are available in **Grant Grove Village $$**, **Cedar Grove Village $$** and **Kings Canyon Lodge $$–$$$**. Grant Grove remains open in winter. There are no petrol stations in the park, but Kings Canyon lodge has a supply at premium prices.

SEQUOIA NATIONAL PARK❖❖❖

ⓘ Ash Mountain /Foothills Visitor Center *tel: (559) 565-3341. Open daily 0800–1700.*

ⓘ Sequoia National Park $ *Sequoia and Kings Canyon National Parks, Three Rivers, CA 93271; tel: (559) 565-3341; web: www.nps/gov/seki/.*

Sequoia has a variety of natural attractions, from caves and Mount Whitney to alpine meadows and crashing rivers – all of which pale next to the dense stands of giant sequoia redwood trees (*Sequoiadendron giganteum*), the largest living things on earth.

Sequoia was created in 1890 to protect these massive trees, then in danger of extinction by logging. **Big Stump Basin❖**, near the entrance to Kings Canyon National Park and the **Generals Highway❖❖❖**, which leads to Sequoia National Park, is the result of still-current logging techniques.

Three-mile **Crescent Meadow Road❖❖❖** leaves the main road from the former Giant Forest Village. The scenic detour passes several famous sites, but is not recommended for RVs. **Auto Log❖**, a sequoia felled and flattened for drive-on passenger cars, gives visitors a sense of just how huge sequoias can grow. A set of nearly 400 concrete steps leads 300ft up the side of **Moro Rock❖❖❖** (6725ft) and a splendid 360-degree view stretching 150 miles from the spine of the Sierras to the Central Valley – save the staircase climb for clear days when valley vistas are visible rather than swathed in haze.

Tunnel Log❖ fell across the road in 1937; crews cut an 8ft-high tunnel through the log the next summer. A bypass accommodates taller vehicles. **Crescent Meadow❖❖❖**, like most naturally grassy areas in the park, is actually a marsh, too wet to support sequoias and other trees. A flat 1½-mile trail circles the meadow to **Tharp's Log❖**, a

A few centuries of growth – section through a giant sequoia tree

ⓘ **Lodgepole Visitor Center** tel: (559) 565-3782. Open May–Oct daily 0800–1800, Nov–Apr Fri–Sun 1000–1600.

Mineral King Visitor Center Open May–Sept daily 0700–1500.

Mineral King Pack Station $$ Box 61, Three Rivers, CA 93271; tel: (559) 561-3404 (summer) or (559) 561-4142 (winter). Advance booking required.

Giant Forest Village

Giant Forest Village was Sequoia's original centre for visitor services. Recognising that the year-round pounding of traffic and visitors was harming Giant Forest trees, the US Park Services removed accommodation and other services to **Wuksachi**, near the **Lodgepole Visitor Center**, in 1998 and 1999. Car-parks and a visitor centre remain, but most of the Village site is being re-seeded and returned to the Giant Forest.

sequoia hollowed into a cabin for Hale Tharp, who grazed sheep in the meadow in the 1850s. **Chimney Tree***⁺ is a still-living sequoia hollowed out by fire; look inside from the base to see blue sky through the crown. The **John Muir Trail** which follows the crest of the Sierras crosses 74 rugged miles to Mount Whitney.

Giant Forest*⁺⁺⁺ (*30 miles from Big Stump Entrance, 16 miles from Ash Mountain Entrance*) was named by John Muir. Four of the largest known sequoias grow in this grove. Most visitors spend their time staring in awe at named trees and dodging other visitors. Fortunately, the many hiking trails through Giant Forest provide a serene, almost deserted introduction to the 8000 or so mature sequoias in the area.

The biggest of them all is the **General Sherman tree***⁺, 275ft tall and 103ft in circumference. The trunk alone contains more than 52,000 cubic feet of wood, but with so many other slightly less monstrous trees nearby, it's hard to grasp General Sherman's extraordinary dimensions. One of the best easy walks is the 2-mile paved **Congress Trail***⁺⁺⁺ (*from the Sherman tree*); pick up a self-guiding trail guide at the Sherman tree or the **Lodgepole Visitor Center**, just north.

Hospital Rock*⁺⁺ (*5 miles beyond Ash Grove Entrance toward Giant Forest*) marks an ancient Native American village site. Look for **pictographs***⁺⁺⁺ on surrounding boulders and 71 mortar holes once used to grind acorns and seeds into flour.

Mineral King*⁺⁺⁺ (*turn off 5 miles north of Three Rivers, no RVs or trailers*) is a scalloped bowl at 7800ft, the only bit of the park's Sierra high country accessible by vehicle. Walt Disney tried to turn the scenic bowl into a ski resort in 1965. Thirteen litigious years later, it was added to Sequoia National Park instead.

Seven hundred-odd twists and turns in 25 miles of part-paved, part-gravel road discourage most visitors, but the summer-only route along the East Fork of the Kaweah River is worth the time, the driving effort and the occasional terror of meeting another vehicle on a blind corner with neither verge nor guard-rail.

Silver City has general supplies, petrol and food, but the only facilities in Mineral King itself are a seasonal ranger station and a basic campground. Hiking into the golden **Sawtooth Mountains***⁺⁺⁺ to the east is superb, as are wilderness horsepacking trips from **Mineral King Pack Station**. The ¼-mile **Cold Springs Nature Trail**✦✦✦ is a less strenuous alternative.

Accommodation and food in Sequoia National Park

All park hotels, including **Wuksachi Village $$** *open all year*, are operated by **Sequoia National Park Reservations**, *Sequoia and Kings Canyon National Parks, Three Rivers, CA 93271; tel: (559) 565-3134 or (888) 252-5757; fax: (559) 456-0542.*

Montecito-Sequoia Lodge $$ *Hwy 180 (Generals Hwy) between Sequoia and Kings Canyon; tel: (559) 565-3388 or (800) 843-8677; reservations, 2225 Grant Rd, Ste 1, Los Altos, CA 94024; tel: (650) 967-8612 or (800) 227-9900,* is open all year, as are motels in the town of **Three Rivers**, *Hwy 180, south of Ash Mountain Entrance.*

Silver City High Sierra Rustic Family Resort $$ *2420 E. Hillcrest Ave, Visalia, CA 93292; tel: (209) 734-4109 (late Sept–early May) or Box 56, Three Rivers, CA 93271; tel: (559) 561-3223 (late May–early Sept)* has lantern-lit cabins and chalets on the road to Mineral King in summer.

Meals and picnic supplies are available in Wuksachi Village, Lodgepole and Montecito-Sequoia all year. **Silver City Bakery and Restaurant $$** near Mineral King, and an adjoining general store are open in summer.

Giant sequoias

Sequoiadendron giganteum aren't the tallest living things – coastal redwoods top them by 100ft – nor the largest around – a Montezuma cypress in Oaxaca, Mexico, has a larger girth. But in sheer volume, giant sequoia redwoods are the largest living things on earth, and Sequoia National Park has more of them than anywhere else.

Sequoias that survive their first few centuries are practically invulnerable. High tannin levels discourage insects and rot; bark nearly 3ft thick is impervious to fire. Even if the heartwood burns away, the tree can survive – forest fires actually help propagate sequoias. The intense heat releases its tiny seeds and burns away brush that would compete with its seedlings.

The sequoia's weakness, however, is its roots, which penetrate just between 3 and 5ft into the soil. Without a firm anchor, high winds or heavy snows can topple the top-heavy giants. Foot or vehicle traffic atop the fragile roots can further weaken the trees, the reason so many sequoias are behind fences.

Cascade Volcanoes

California's Cascade peaks, Lassen and Shasta, begin a string of active volcanoes stretching north into British Columbia. This jumble of volcanic peaks, razor-edged river valleys and deep forests is one of California's most alluring – and forbidding – natural areas. Don't be deceived by mild Sacramento Valley weather. A few miles east – and a few thousand feet up – temperatures can drop to freezing in any month. The highway through Lassen Volcanic National Park is closed in winter, though snowploughs keep most other paved roads open.

The Sierra Nevada volcanoes are largely dormant, but the Cascades are very much alive. Mount Shasta last erupted around 1786, but steam vents near the peak are still hot. Mount Lassen erupted between 1915 and 1917, the most recent eruption in the continental US until Mount St Helens (in southern Washington State) blew up in 1980. Bookmakers aren't fixing odds, but geologists are betting on another major California eruption in the next few centuries.

Ratings

Scenery	●●●●●
Geology	●●●●●
Waterfalls	●●●●○
Lakes	●●●●○
Wildlife	●●●○○
Steam trains	●●●○○
Walking	●●●○○
Children	●●●○○

CASTLE CRAGS❖❖

ⓘ **Castle Crags State Park** *Castella Exit from I-5; tel: (530) 235-2684. Ranger station usually open summer and weekends.*

The granite ramparts of Castle Crags rise dramatically from the west side of I-5, resembling the remnants of some enormous castle wall towering more than 4000ft above. A narrow road twists 2 miles from the park entrance to a wooded **Vista Point**❖❖❖ and a cluster of picnic tables with unobstructed views of the Crags and Mount Shasta. The best views are late in the day (Mount Shasta) and early morning (Castle Crags), when the setting sun casts a rich, smouldering glow.

DUNSMUIR❖❖

The railway made Dunsmuir a popular mountain resort between the 1920s and 1940s, known as much for its wonderful fly-fishing and mineral water as the pristine mountain scenery and a cinema palace called the California Theater. Celebrities pulled into town by the carriage-load, from baseball home-run king Babe Ruth to Hollywood

Gazelle

CASCADE

KLAMATH NATL. FOR.

Etna

Mount Shasta
Mt. Shasta 14,162

Callahan

Mount Shasta City

Shasta

McCloud

Pondosa

Lookout

Ahjumawi Lava Springs S.P.

Dunsmuir

Dana

Big L.

Biel
Nubie

Castle Crags S.P.

Castle Craggs

Castella

McCloud R.

Big Bend

Glenburn

McArthur River

Little Valley

Center
TOWN-
ITY
.A.

Lamoine

Lakehead

WHISKEYTOWN-
SHASTA-TRINITY
N.R.A.

McArthur-Burney
Falls Me

McArthur-Burney Falls
Memorial State Park

Burney

SS HOUSE
H.P.

Shasta Lake

Montgomery
Creek

Hat Creek

LASS

NATL.

wiston

French Gulch

LAKE SHASTA
Shasta Lake FERNS

Round
Mountain

SUBWAY
CAVE

RANGE

Whiskeytown L.
EYTOWN-
TRINITY
N.R.A.

Sha

Ingot

Bella
Vista

Whitmore

SHASTA

Redding

Redding

Viola

LASSEN
VOLCANIC
NATL. PARK

Igo

Palo
Cedro

Mount Lassen
10,457

Closed in
Winter

Ono

Anderson

Shingletown

Manton

Chester

Cottonwood

A6

Mineral

Dales

Paynes
Creek

Almanor

Canyondam

Red Bluff

WILLIAM B. IDE
S.H.P.

Red Bluff

LASSEN

Butte Meadows

Indian Fa

Red Bank

NATL. FOR.

Belden

Twa

Gerber

Tehama

Stirling

Storrie

Flournoy

Los Molinos

Woodson Bridge S.R.A.

Vina

Paskenta

Black
Butte L.

Corning

Forest Ra

0   10   20 Miles

0   10   20 Kilometres

Newville

Hamilton Nord
City

BIDWELL
MANSIC

Paradise

Alder
Springs

Orland

C.S.U. CHICO

Chico

Cherokee

Oroville

FEATHER FALLS
SCENIC AREA

GLENN

Dunsmuir Chamber of Commerce *4118 Pine St, Dunsmuir, CA 96025; tel: (530) 235-2177 or (800) 386-7684; fax: (530) 235-0911; web: www. dunsmuir.com.*

The Railroad Park Resort $$ *100 Railroad Park Rd; tel: (530) 235-4440; fax: (530) 235-4470,* features accommodation in boxcars with bay windows or roof-top cupolas.

Café Maddelena $$ *5801 Sacramento Ave; tel: (530) 235-2725,* serves Sardinian dishes to rival anything San Francisco can offer.

luminary Clark Gable. As more powerful diesel-electric locomotives replaced steam in the 1950s, Dunsmuir sank into obscurity.

Once I-5 bypassed the town in 1961, most of California forgot it ever existed, until 1991, when the railroad put Dunsmuir back in the spotlight. A Southern Pacific train derailed, spilling tank cars loaded with a powerful herbicide into the Sacramento River. The poison killed everything in the river for 45 miles downstream into Shasta Lake, and nearly killed off the town.

The Sacramento River eventually recovered. So did Dunsmuir, with the help of a hefty financial settlement from the railway. Trophy-sized trout returned to the river while the town refurbished and rebuilt Dunsmuir and Sacramento Aves.

Don't miss **Hedge Creek Falls**✢ (*north edge of town, Frontage Rd*), a 30-ft waterfall cutting through basaltic lava that once flowed down the slopes of Mount Shasta. A gazebo next to the trailhead offers a pleasant view of the Sacramento River Canyon.

Right
The McArthur-Burney Falls

McArthur-Burney Falls Memorial State Park✢✢✢

The 129-ft double cataract of **McArthur-Burney Falls**✢✢✢ cuts through millions of years of moss-covered lava flows in a lush conifer forest.

McArthur-Burney Falls Memorial State Park 24898 Hwy 89, Burney, CA 96013; tel: (530) 335-2777. Open year-round for camping and day use.

Half-way between Shasta and Lassen, the Falls, like the rest of the region, owe their existence to volcanoes.

Shasta, Lassen and other Cascade peaks are noted for their explosive power, generated when thick, sticky lava builds up pressure in underground chambers until it blasts through to the surface. McArthur-Burney is shield volcano country.

Shield volcanoes begin life belching a mixture of magma, superheated steam and other gases. Bits of magma shoot into the air, cool quickly and fall back to earth to form steep-sided hills called cinder cones. In later stages, lava floods from vents in vast sheets, building up successive layers called shields. Hwy 89 between Lake Britton and the park entrance cuts through a shield, as do the Falls.

An easy 1-mile **Falls Trail Loop**✦ winds to the bottom of the Falls and back up. The slightly more difficult 1½-mile **Headwaters Loop**✦✦ passes the point where underground rivers emerge to feed the falls. **Lake Britton**, a reservoir popular for fishing, swimming and boating, is a 1-mile walk or 1½-miles by road (Hwy 89) from the park entrance.

McCloud✦✦✦

McCloud Chamber of Commerce 205 Quincy St, McCloud, CA 96057 tel & fax: (530) 964-3113 or tel: (877) 964-3113; fax: (530) 964-3113; web: www.mccloudca.com

McCloud Ranger District Hwy 89 east of McCloud; tel: (530) 964-2184. Open 0800–1630 Mon–Fri, Sat in summer.

McCloud Railway Company $–$$ across from the McCloud post office; tel: (530) 964-2142. Sightseeing May–Dec, lunch and dinner weekends.

McCloud looks much as it did in 1965, when the McCloud River Lumber Company abandoned the town it had built. Heavy winter snows can cut power and phone lines for days, but urban refugees have revitalised a town that most expected to die.

McCloud's attractions are largely natural – vast forests, modest ice caves, streams and waterfalls. Among the most popular are the Upper, Middle and Lower **Falls of the McCloud River**✦✦ (*near River Loop Rd and Fowlers Campground off Hwy 89, 5 miles east of McCloud*), torrents shooting from crevices in the rock. Lower Falls has carved a deep swimming hole. **Jot Dean Cave** (*9 miles south of Medicine Lake on County Rd 49*), a shallow, collapsed lava tube, is usually cool enough to hold ice in summer but shallow enough to explore without a torch.

The easiest way to enjoy McCloud's off-road sights is aboard open-air carriages on the **McCloud Railway Company**✦✦ sightseeing trips, or its weekend **Shasta Sunset Dinner Train**✦✦.

Accommodation and food in McCloud

The carefully-restored 1916 **McCloud Hotel $$** 408 Main St; tel: (530) 964-2822, a National Historic Landmark building, was originally company-owned housing for mill workers and town teachers. The hotel now offers bed with breakfast in the Garden Room. **Raymond's Ristorante $$** 424 Main St; tel: (530) 964-2099, offers dinner with home-made soups, lasagne, ravioli and gnocchi.

MOUNT LASSEN✦✦✦

Lassen Volcanic National Park $
38050 Hwy 36 East, Mineral, CA 96063; tel: (530) 595-4444; fax: (530) 595-3262; web: www.nps.gov/lavo.

Loomis Museum and Seismograph Station
tel: (530) 595-4444, ext 5180. Open June–Sept daily 0900–1700.

Drakesbad Guest Ranch California Guest Services, 2150 N. Main St, Ste 5, Red Bluff, CA 96080; tel: (530) 529-1512; fax: (530) 529-4511.

Mount Lassen is the southernmost link in the Cascade volcano chain that runs through **Mount Shasta✦✦✦** and **Lava Beds National Monument✦✦✦** in California, north to British Columbia. It is also one of California's least-visited national parks, an eerie, volcanic landscape that is virtually devoid of people, even at the height of summer.

Lassen, the mountain (10,457 ft), is a fraction of **Lassen Volcanic National Park**, 100,000 jumbled acres where Cascade volcanoes meet the Sierra Nevada. Prominent features include Lassen Peak and smaller volcanoes, as well as mud pots, fumaroles, hot springs, boiling lakes, emerald green meadows and stupendous wildflower displays – and that's just what's visible from the highway. Drive slowly (the speed limit is 35mph) and buy the *Road Guide to Lassen Volcanic National Park*, $, at park entrances.

Unfortunately, the road, Hwy 89, is covered by 50ft of snow in winter. From Nov to June, it's possible to explore both the north (from Redding) and south (from Red Bluff) edges of the park, but the only transport between are snowshoes, skis or snowmobiles, none of which are recommended.

From the north, the **Loomis Museum and Seismograph Station✦** (*tel: (530) 595-4444*) covers regional geology and history. Lassen erupted around 1700, creating the **Chaos Crags✦**, which were still steaming in 1850, and a vast rockfield called the **Chaos Jumbles**. The mountain went into violent action in 1914, with an earth shattering eruption in 1915 and small bursts that continued through 1921. The 1915 eruption blasted boulders to Reno, Nevada, shot a plume of dust 25,000ft into the air and cast a pall over Sacramento. Time and advancing vegetation have hidden most visible signs of that last eruption. The best views are from the half-mile **Devastation Trail** (*Road Marker 44*).

Park rangers lead free naturalist June–Aug programmes (guided walks and hikes), and Jan–Apr (snowshoe programmes). There are also many self-guiding walks. Remember, though, that nature has a thin skin in Lassen – literally. Most areas of visible thermal activity are vast pools of boiling mud covered by a solid-seeming, but fragile crust.

One of Lassen's other-worldly sights, **Bumpass Hell✦✦✦** (*3 miles return from Marker 17*) is named for an early Danish explorer who put a foot through the crust and saw his leg cook before he could pull away. *Stay on marked trails and boardwalks!*

One of the best high hikes is the 5-mile return **Lassen Peak Trail** (*5 hours from Marker 22*), a windy, sun-blasted trail that gains 2000ft. Bring water, sunblock, a hat and plenty of water. An easier 7½ mile return trail climbs **Brokeoff Mountain** near the south entrance. The peak is 1200ft lower than Lassen, but the trail is shaded until the summit.

Best stops for non-hikers are **Manzanita Lake✦✦** and **Reflection Lake✦✦** (*near the north entrance*) which provide serene reflections of

Marsh and mountain in Lassen Volcanic National Park

Lassen Peak in late afternoon. Thousands of 19th-century migrants walked **Nobles Emigrant Trail** (*Marker 60*) through the park. The trail can be seen through the chaparral to the northeast. Beyond the **Devastation Area**, look for trees with a curve at their base, the *snow bend*, caused by winter snows bending the trees as saplings.

Deep blue **Lake Helen****, between the Lassen Peak and Bumpass Hell car-parks, is frozen white at least eight months of the year. The lake was named for Helen Brodt, the first woman known to have climbed Mount Lassen. Lassen's most accessible thermal field is **The Sulphur Works***, a miniature Bumpass Hell near the south entrance. An easy boardwalk winds past small mudpots and fumaroles.

Accommodation and food near Mount Lassen

Sleeping in the park means camping. For a real roof, try secluded **Drakesbad Guest Ranch $$$** *Warner Valley Rd, Chester, CA 96020; tel: (530) 529-1512*, **Hat Creek Resort $$** *Hwy 44 & 89, Old Station; tel: (530) 335-7171;* year-round, **Lassen Mineral Lodge $$** *Hwy 36 E., Mineral; tel: (530) 595-4422;* or cabins at **Rim Rock Ranch $$** *13275 Hwy 89, Old Station; tel: (530) 335-7114.* All must be booked well in advance. Most visitors drive up from Redding or Red Bluff. The only food in the park is at **Manzanita Lake** (*north entrance*) and the **Chalet Café** (*south entrance*).

Mount Shasta✧ and Mount Shasta City

ⓘ Mount Shasta Convention & Visitors Bureau *300 Pine St, Mount Shasta, CA 96067; tel: (530) 926-4865; fax: (530) 926-0976; web: www.mtshasta.com/chamber/chamber.html.*

ⓦ Mount Shasta Ranger District *204 W. Alma St; tel: (530) 926-4511.*

Mount Shasta City is a former railway and lumber centre that has turned its attention to tourists and New Age believers. The latter revere 14,164ft **Mount Shasta✧✧✧** as an energy and spiritual centre inhabited by Limurians, ancient escapees from the lost continent of Mu. The rest of us see the tallest and most spectacular peak in Northern California, the source of the Sacramento River and a climbing challenge.

Mount Shasta Ski Park✧ (*off Hwy 89; tel: (530) 926-8610*) is a pleasant local ski area in winter, mountain bike park in summer and easy route up the mountain in any season. It's also possible to climb the peak in summer, a strenuous, occasionally fatal trek. Stop at the Ranger District station for advice on climbing, equipment rental or lessons. **Bunny Flat Scenic Trail✧✧** (*from Bunny Flat car-park*) is a gentle alternative that climbs to Horse Camp, the usual base for peak climbs. A still less strenuous outing is **Mount Shasta City Park✧** (*north end of town*), where the Sacramento River gushes from a lava tube.

Accommodation and food in Mount Shasta

Best bets are the **Mount Shasta Ranch Bed and Breakfast $$** *1008 W.A. Barr Rd; tel: (530) 926-3870*, a 70-year-old ranch, and **Mount Shasta Resort $$** *1000 Siskiyou Lake Blvd; tel: (530) 926-3030*, a golf resort on Lake Siskiyou. Classical French **Serge's Restaurant $$** *531 Chestnut St; tel: (530) 926-1276*, is Mount Shasta's best. **Lily's $$** *1015 S. Mt Shasta Blvd; tel: (530) 926-3372*, is Californian with Asian touches.

Below
Serene Mount Shasta

REDDING

A railway town that never stopped growing, Redding is the primary gateway to mountain escapes in three directions, a welcome compensation for the lack of attractions in town. The top historic sight is **Shasta State Historic Park**✷✷ (*Hwy 299, 6 miles west; tel: (530) 243-8194; open daily*). originally the town of Shaster, the area's Gold Rush settlement. Shasta was the richest, busiest town in the region until the railway route was built in Redding in 1872. The **Old Courthouse**✷ has been restored as an excellent museum.

The best stop in Redding itself is the **Turtle Bay Museums and Arboretum**✷ (*800 Auditorium Dr.; tel: (530) 243-8850*), a civic complex under development. The first unit, **Paul Bunyan's Forest Camp**, celebrates the logging industry. **Redding Museum of Art and History** (*Caldwell Park, tel: (530) 243-8801*) and the **Carter House Natural Science Museum** (*Caldwell Park, tel: (530) 243-5457*) will eventually move to Turtle Bay around 2001.

Accommodation and food in Redding

Jack's Grill $$ *1743 California St; tel: (530) 241-9705*, is a Redding institution for steaks.

SHASTA LAKE✷

Filled, Shasta Lake has more shoreline than San Francisco Bay. When it's partially empty, as it is most of the year, the lake is rimmed by red mud and slime. Either way, Shasta is used by more than two million people every year, which means a surfeit of whining jet skis and roaring motorboats near the lake's dozen or so marinas.

Shasta Dam, 3460ft long at its crest, 602ft high and 883ft thick at the base, contains enough concrete to build a 3-ft path around the equator. Behind the dam are five watery arms, stumps of the Sacramento, Pit and McCloud Rivers that were dammed for power and irrigation in 1945. The Visitor Center tells the story of this engineering feat, including a free tour that begins with an elevator plummeting into the bowels of the dam.

It's possible to plumb nature's bowels at **Lake Shasta Caverns**✷✷ (*tel: (530) 238-2341*), one of the state's more spectacular caves, complete with 'waterfalls' of solid calcium carbonate, masses of mineral straws that seem to defy gravity and delicate fluted columns. The two-hour tour begins with a 15-minute catamaran ride across the lake and an 800-ft climb by bus before descending into the chilly cave on foot.

Suggested tour

Total distance: 225 miles

Time: One day with no stops, but three days recommended

Links: The Gold Country (*see page 226*) and Lake Tahoe (*see page 122*), both lie to the south (follow I-5 to Sacramento, or Hwy 89 to Truckee). The Coast Redwoods (*see page 196*) are to be found by driving due west from Redding.

Route: Take I-5 north from Redding, climbing from soporific Sacramento Valley scenery toward **Lake Shasta** ❶, **Castle Crags** ❷ and the riverside town of **Dunsmuir** ❸ to **Mount Shasta City** ❹, at the base of **Mount Shasta** ❺. Follow scenic Hwy 89 east into the Cascades to the former logging town of **McCloud** ❻, then gradually turn south through lava flows and pine forests to **McArthur-Burney Falls Memorial State Park** ❼, **Hat Creek** ❽ and **Old Station** ❾ to **Lassen Volcanic National Park** ❿. In winter, take Hwy 44 west to Redding. In summer, continue south through the park to Hwy 36, then turn west to **Red Bluff** ⓫.

Also worth visiting

Mount Shasta Loop ⓬
A network of gravel roads loops around the north and east sides of Mount Shasta, making it possible to circumnavigate the mountain in a single day – but only in good summer weather and never in an RV. Check with the Mount Shasta Visitors Centre (*tel: (530) 275-1589*) for road conditions and maps before setting out. Local vehicles travel the back roads regularly, but most have high clearance and four-wheel drive. If rangers or the Visitors Bureau advise against the drive, heed their caution – blizzards can occur in summer.

Fortunately, paved roads offer a taste of Mount Shasta's more spectacular north face. Take I-5 north from Mount Shasta City past **Black Butte** ⓭ (6325ft), a volcanic plug cloaked with broken rock called talus. A 2½ mile trail leads to the peak, with sweeping views of Mount Shasta just east, the Sacramento Valley south, the Klamath Mountains west and **Weed** ⓮ just north. Continue 5½ miles north to the Central Weed exit, Hwy 97.

A lumber baron named Weed picked the windiest spot in the upper Sacramento Valley for a mill so the newly sawn lumber would dry quickly. Hwy 97 bypasses the late 19th-century town centre, which remains largely intact. The best Shasta views lie along the first 15 miles of Hwy 97 between I-5 and Military Pass Rd, just beyond the Hwy 99-Hwy 97 Cutoff.

Vulcanism in California

California was born of a 200-million-year collision between North America and the floor of the Pacific Ocean. As the Pacific Plate, one of the great tectonic plates that make up the earth's crust, was forced beneath the North American plate, islands and mountains scraped off against the edge of the continent. At the same time, a fraction of the titanic forces driving the Pacific Plate downward escaped to the surface as volcanic activity. The Sierra Nevada Mountains emerged about 170 million years ago, while the Cascade peaks are still emerging.

In Southern California, vulcanism is most obvious around Mammoth Lakes. Devil's Postpile National Monument is an ancient basalt flow that cooled into striking vertical columns. The hot springs dotting the Sierra are fuelled by geothermal activity, including mineral springs that created the striking tufa towers of Mono Lake. Mountains of black volcanic obsidian, once the source of arrowheads, are now used for fine surgical scalpels.

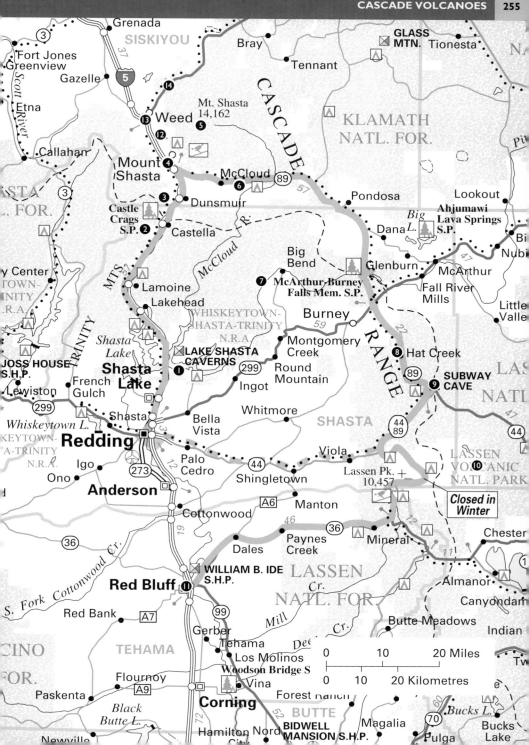

Ratings

Historical sights	●●●●●
Architecture	●●●●●
Scenery	●●●●●
Art	●●●●○
Churches	●●●●○
Gardens	●●●○○
Children	●●○○○

California Missions

A lways go forward and never look back' was the personal credo espoused by Fra Junípero Serra, the 18th-century Franciscan priest, university professor and missionary who created California.

Serra's missions are California's most visible link to the past, a chain of 21 whitewashed churches that define the state's most important highway as well as its very existence. For despite its secular excesses, modern California was born as a religious enterprise whose branches still flower in popular mythology and architecture.

In 1769, the Spanish crown sent Serra and military commander Gaspar de Portolá to head Spain's first attempt to settle Alta, or upper, California. It was called The Sacred Expedition, a gruelling desert march from Baja (lower) California to San Diego in mid-summer.

Serra's mission was simple and direct: Christianise the local tribes, teach them the Spanish language and European mores, put them to work and then start over again until California had been civilised under Spanish rule.

History

Visiting California's Missions All the missions described here lie off Hwy 101. If time is short All of the missions can be visited off Hwy 101. If time is short, Carmel, La Purisima, San Juan Capistrano, San Luis Rey and Santa Barbara are easily accessible and wonderfully evocative.

Serra founded a chain of 21 missions, stretching 600 miles north to Sonoma, just below Russia's southernmost settlement of Fort Ross (*see page 189*). Each outpost was a day's travel from the next, linked by *El Camino Real*, The King's Highway, a rough trail that became Hwy 101. Individual missions flourished and grew wealthy, but the system failed.

Supplies and equipment from Mexico often arrived late or disappeared. Earthquakes levelled adobe buildings. Imported diseases killed Native American converts, called *neophytes*, by the thousands.

The final blow came in 1834, when a then-independent Mexico secularised Church property. Mission holdings were sold or given as land grants. Most of the mission buildings dissolved back into the adobe mud from which they had sprung, surviving only as the names of the towns which had grown up around the long-vanished churches.

Nostalgic 19th-century artists pushed for the missions' restoration, aided by commercial interests, recognising profit in 'Old California'.

Santa Rosa

San Francisco de Solano

San Rafael Arcángel

San Francisco de Asis

Santa Clara

San José

Santa Cruz

San Juan Bautista

San Carlos Borromeo del Rio Carmelo

Nuestra Senora de la Soledad

San Antonio de Padua

San Miguel Arcangel

San Luis Obispo de Tolosa

La Purisima Concepcion (Lompoc)

Santa Inés

Santa Barbara

Santa Buenaventura

San Fernando Rey de Espana

San Gabriel Arcangel

San Juan Capistrano

PACIFIC OCEAN

La Purisima Concepción de Maria Santisima *La Purisima Mission State Historic Park, 2295 Purisima Rd (4 miles north of Lompoc); tel: (805) 733-3713. Open daily 1000–1700.*

Nuestra Señora Dolorosisima de la Soledad *36641 Ft Romie Rd, Soledad; tel: (831) 678-2586. Open Wed–Mon 1000–1600.*

San Juan Capistrano was converted back from a hay barn, San Luis Obispo from a gaol, while Carmel was rebuilt from a rubble heap.

The Mission Style, whitewashed walls, red-tile roofs, rounded arches and massive sprays of bougainvillaea, became the architectural rage from California to Florida. Generations of cinema-goers grew up with the imposing façade of Mission Santa Barbara as their image of Early California – modern pink paint apparently photographed better than the original whitewash.

Missions

La Purisima Concepción de Maria Santisima✦✦✦

La Purisima (1787) was rebuilt as a public works project in the 1930s, but it is the most authentic restoration amongst the missions. Workers used period tools and methods to bring an archaeological site back to life. The darkly ornate (but unconsecrated) church is furnished and painted as it would have been at its height in the 1820s. The kitchen garden is planted with typical food and medicinal plants, from garlic and chillies to elderberries and myrtle. Even the farm animals are period, down to the four-horned churro sheep that have come closer to extinction than the missions themselves.

Nuestra Señora Dolorosisima de la Soledad✦

Soledad (1791) is better known for its state prison than its mission, which is little more than a restored chapel, museum and adobe ruins in a pleasant, pastoral setting.

Father Serra's parlour in the San Carlos Borromeo del Rio Carmelo Mission

Why Missions?

Spain had little interest in California when Serra and Portolá were sent north to establish a chain of missions. Generations of Spanish monarchs had happily ignored Alta California since Sebastián Vizcaíno visited Monterey in 1602. But in the 1760s, Spain saw a new threat in the Pacific: Russia.

Russian fur-seal hunters were slowly making their way south from Alaska, posing a potential threat to undefended Alta California. A chain of missions and *presidios*, military forts, could block Russian advances.

The Russians got as far south as Fort Ross *(see page 189)* in 1812. What impact the missions had is unclear. After Mission Solano (Sonoma) was established a decade later, Fort Ross became a major buyer of California flour, beef and wine to provision Alaskan fur bases.

When the fur trade declined from overhunting along the entire Pacific Coast, the Russians unloaded Fort Ross on John Sutter, best known as the owner of Sutters Fort where the Gold Rush began in 1848. Sutter returned the favour by neglecting to pay most of the agreed selling price. The missions themselves went out of business in 1834.

San Antonio de Padua 23 miles southwest of King City, Mission Rd, Jolon; tel: (831) 385-4478. Open daily 1000-1630.

San Buenaventura 225 E. Main St, Ventura; tel: (805) 648-4496. Open Mon-Sat 1000-1700, Sun 1000-1600.

San Carlos Borromeo del Rio Carmelo 2080 Rio Rd, Carmel; tel: (408) 624-3600. Open Mon-Sat 0930-1630, Sun 1030-1630.

San Antonio de Padua◆◆◆

Sitting in a small valley surrounded by Fort Hunter Liggett, a quiet military reservation, San Antonio (1771) is more serene now than when it was a famed horse-breeding centre. The founding Franciscans are long gone, though the rough, rebuilt adobe arches and promenades match 19th-century photographs of the original building. Modern renovators have removed the candles, flowers and other devotional objects that once crowded the simple chapel, and stencilled designs along the walls and altar are based on original colours.

San Buenaventura◆◆◆

The stone church and surrounding gardens have been restored to a good approximation of their original appearance (1782). The tiered bell tower, topped by a striped dome, echoes Moorish motifs that distinguish California Mission styles from similar Mexican buildings. The museum has many of the mission's original furnishings, including the only wooden bells used in any of the 21 missions.

San Carlos Borromeo del Rio Carmelo◆◆◆

Carmel (1770) is a nearly perfect image of what a mission ought to be – golden sandstone, Moorish towers and contemplative gardens, all set off by splashes of brilliant bougainvillaea. Fra Serra is buried beneath the floor in front of the main altar; the rebuilt padre's quarters include Serra's spartan cell and a library with volumes dating to 1534. Carmel is also one of the most-visited of the missions. Try to go early in the day before the crowds arrive. The church is closed during services, though the large courtyard remains open and popular.

San Diego de Alcalá 10919 San Diego Mission Rd, San Diego; tel: (619) 281-8449. Open daily 0900–1700.

San Fernando Rey de España 15151 San Fernando Mission Blvd, Mission Hills; tel: (818) 361-0186. Open daily 0900–1615.

San Francisco de Asis 3321 16th St, San Francisco; tel: (415) 621-8203. Open daily 0900–1630.

San Francisco Solano Sonoma State Historic Park, Sonoma; tel: (707) 938-1519. Open daily 1000–1700.

San Gabriel Arcángel 537 W. Mission Dr., San Gabriel; tel: 626-282-5191. Open daily 0930–1630.

San José de Guadalupe 43300 Mission Blvd, Fremont; tel: (510) 657-1797. Open daily 1000–1700.

San Diego de Alcalá*

This was California's first mission (1769), and the first to be moved out of the reach of presidio soldiers. Not a wise move in San Diego's case, for the mission was sacked by neophytes (Native American converts) and unconverted tribes in 1775. Rebuilt with high adobe walls, the mission prospered until secularised in 1834, when it fell into ruin. The blindingly white walls were raised again in the early 20th century. San Diego buildings were particularly narrow because of the acute shortage of tall timber needed to span wider structures.

San Fernando Rey de España**

The graceful buildings and lush gardens of San Fernando (1797) seem to have survived the test of time, but the church is actually the youngest in the mission system. It is a copy of an 1806 church demolished by an earthquake in 1971. The mission once grazed more than 21,000 head of cattle in the San Fernando Valley, supplying candles, soap and leather goods to other missions. San Fernando's *convento*, or guest and missionary quarters, is the largest surviving mission building in the state.

San Francisco de Asis*

Usually called 'Mission Dolores' after a nearby lake that disappeared decades ago, the mission (1776) is San Francisco's oldest building. It is also among the most ornate, with a chapel restored to the 1791 period. The small mission museum holds artefacts from the colonial period, as does the cemetery, including California's first native-born Mexican governor (Luís Antonio Arguello), the city's first Mexican mayor (Francisco de Haro) and last Mexican mayor (José Noé).

San Francisco Solano*

This last of the missions to be established (1823) was also destroyed by Native American uprising and rebuilt in more durable adobe. All that remains of the rebuilt complex are the chapel and part of the priests' quarters, restored about 1913.

San Gabriel Arcángel**

San Gabriel (1771) has the oldest cemetery in Los Angeles County (1778) and has survived more earthquake damage than any major structure still in use locally. The original vaulted roof was damaged by a quake in 1804, as were the replacement in 1812 and its replacement in 1987. The choir loft, baptistery, sanctuary, sacristy and pulpit are all original. Landscaped grounds contain numerous ruins, including the original bell tower, which collapsed in an early earthquake.

San José de Guadalupe*

This copy was built on the site of the original mission church (1797). The interior shows the 1830-40s period, complete with ornate sculptures and gold-leaf replica furnishings.

San Juan Bautista, *San Juan Bautista Historic Park, centre of town; tel: 408-623-4881. Open daily 0930–1700.*

San Juan Capistrano, *31522 Camino Capistrano, San Juan Capistrano; tel: (714) 248-2049. Open daily 0830–1700.*

San Luis Obispo de Tolosa, *782 Monterey St, San Luis Obispo; tel: (805) 543-6850. Open daily 0900–1600.*

San Juan Bautista✦✦✦

If this largest of the California missions looks familiar, with its ponderous bells in the tower and an extended arcade fronting the monastery wing, it probably is. San Juan Bautista (1797) was used for the climactic stairway chase in Alfred Hitchcock's classic *Vertigo*. The bear and coyote tracks in the tiles along the church's central aisle were made while the tiles were drying in the sun nearly three centuries ago. The mission and surrounding square are one of the best surviving examples of an early 19th-century California town.

San Juan Capistrano✦✦✦

Forget the syrupy song and made-up legend about the swallows returning to Capistrano on 19 March. The mission (1775) is better remembered for its fountains, lush gardens, peaceful courtyards, the 1777 Serra Chapel, the oldest building still in regular use in California, and the ruins of the Great Stone Church which collapsed during morning mass in an 1812 earthquake. San Juan Capistrano is also one of the most popular missions. Get there at opening and flee when the tour buses start arriving.

San Luis Obispo de Tolosa✦✦

You'd never know by looking that Mission San Luis Obispo (1772) served time as the town gaol. Once among the richest of the missions (renowned for its wines), an 1830 earthquake sent San Luis' fortunes tumbling. It was eventually returned to the Roman Catholic Church, renovated into a vaguely New England-ish chapel, and finally returned to its adobe form from the 1930s. The imitation marble *reredos*, the decorated area behind the altar, is especially dramatic. So are the outstanding Chumash Native American exhibits that are displayed in the mission museum.

Mission organisation

Spain had more than a century of mission experience in New Mexico, Texas, Baja California and elsewhere before moving into California. The basic scheme combined religious, military and civilian authority.

Missionaries were to Christianise and Hispanicise the natives and turn them into a docile work force. Civilian settlers were responsible for creating a *pueblo*, or town, to instil civil authority, while soldiers built a *presidio*, or fort, to protect mission and town.

The scheme fared poorly in California. Early settlers and soldiers were largely conscripts who deserted at the earliest possible moment. The padres soon learned to establish missions as far from *pueblo* and *presidio* as possible to avoid abuse of their converts. Civilian and military authorities were just as distrustful of the missions, which seemed to concentrate on amassing wealth rather than building a new order.

None seemed to give more than a passing thought to the Native Americans they subdued, converted and unknowingly killed by way of imported diseases, poor sanitation and worse diet. Whether by design or by accident, the missions effectively destroyed every Native American group they encountered.

San Luis Rey de Francia *4050 Mission Ave, San Luis Rey (Oceanside); tel: (619) 757-3651. Open Mon–Sat 1000–1600, Sun 1300–1600.*

San Miguel Arcángel *801 Mission St, San Miguel; tel: (805) 467-3256. Open daily 0930–1630.*

Mission Santa Barbara

San Luis Rey de Francia**

The King of The Missions (1798) was the largest building in all of California for more than half of the 19th century. It is still the largest mission, its scalloped white façade almost a glaring mirage beneath the Southern California sun. The quadrangle once sprawled across six acres and mission fields stretched 15 miles. A unique wooden dome sits atop the cruciform church, an eight-sided lantern with 12 dozen panes of glass. The mission museum claims America's largest collection of old Spanish vestments and the sole surviving mission-era walking staff and padre's hat.

San Miguel Arcángel**

San Miguel (1797) is the best and the worst of missions. It has the best-preserved original artwork and interior of the 21, and its interior mineral pigments bound with cactus juice are as vibrant as any Pop Art creation from the 1960s. But the constant vibrations and wear-

San Rafael Arcángel 1104 Fifth Ave, San Rafael; tel: (415) 454-8141. Open daily 1100–1600.

Santa Barbara 2201 Laguna St, Santa Barbara; tel: (805) 682-4713. Open daily 0900–1700.

Santa Clara de Asis Santa Clara University, 500 El Camino Real, Santa Clara; tel: (408) 554-4023. Open daily 1300–1700.

Santa Cruz 126 High St, Santa Cruz; tel: (408) 426-5686. Open daily 1400–1700.

Santa Inés 1760 Mission Dr., Solvang; tel: (805) 688-4815. Open Mon-Sat 0930–1630, Sun 1200–1630.

and-tear of modern life have left the fragile paint, plaster and wood in the worst condition – the small parish church can't afford to restore its crumbling, but still stunning building. The multi-bell detached belfry, or *campanario*, has become the missions' symbol.

San Rafael Arcángel✦

Built as an *asistencia*, or branch, to Mission Dolores, San Rafael (1817) was primarily a sanatorium for its San Francisco parent house. The original mission was razed in 1870; the replica – on approximately the same site – was built in 1949.

Santa Barbara✦✦✦

Unique among the missions, Santa Barbara (1786) has remained a parish church from the day it was consecrated. Called 'Queen of The Missions' for its classic Roman façade (borrowed from a 27 BC architectural encyclopaedia), the mission starred in dozens of early films – it was convenient to Hollywood's favourite holiday destination, Montecito. The pink-hued, sandstone church is complimented by the lush courtyard gardens within and a spectacular city rose garden in front.

Santa Clara de Asís✦

The current church, built after fire destroyed the earlier building (1777) in 1926, mirrors an impressive original dedicated in 1784. The roof is covered in red tiles salvaged from the ruins of earlier mission structures. The wooden cross (inside a redwood frame) standing in front of the church dates to the founding of the original mission. Olive trees, roses and wisteria around the quadrangle beside the church have been growing since the mission days.

Santa Cruz✦

Santa Cruz (1791) was the smallest of the missions, but not this small – what you now see is a half-size replica built in 1931 to house a mission museum. The mission itself collapsed in 1857 from earthquake damage. The best reason to visit is **Santa Cruz Mission State Historic Park**, *144 School St; tel: (408) 425-5849*. A seven-room barracks is California's only remaining housing for mission *neophytes*. The building was later used by *Californio* and Irish residents.

Santa Inés✦

Santa Inés (1804) was admired for its cattle herds, fine leatherwork and delicate jewellery until 1824, when a guard chastised a convert with too much obvious enthusiasm. The neophyte community set fire to the church and mission affairs never recovered. Restoration began around the turn of the century, including a *trompe-l'oeil* painting behind the sanctuary. The marble panels separated by Ionic columns

Greater Las Vegas

Ratings

Gambling	●●●●●
Nightlife	●●●●●
Scenery	●●●●●
Architecture	●●●●○
Children	●●●●○
Shopping	●●●○○
Food and drink	●●○○○
History	●○○○○

The ads claim that Las Vegas never sleeps. It's true. The lure of easy money, clattering slot machines and flashing neon may slow in the hours just before dawn, but 'Vegas' has barely paused for breath since Nevada legalised gambling in the early 1930s.

'Show the suckers a good time and send 'em home broke' is how an early casino-owner might have put it. The public responded by turning what was once a dusty, sun-blasted oasis in the middle of nowhere into one of the most-visited, most talked-about cities on earth.

Vegas mirrors America's changing visions of itself, especially the 3-mile stretch of Las Vegas Blvd South lined with 40-plus casinos known simply as The Strip.

In recent years, circus acts and castles pushed half-naked showgirls and other more traditional attractions into the background. Extravagance, opulence and entertainment are today's watchwords, concepts that Las Vegas is more than happy to indulge with yet another round of bigger, grander and glitzier hotel-casinos.

Getting there and getting around

ⓘ **Las Vegas Convention & Visitors Authority**
3150 Paradise Rd, Las Vegas, NV 89109; tel: (702) 886-0770 or (800) 332-5333; fax: (702) 892-2824; web: www.lasvegas24hours. com (official) or www.las-vegas-real-estate.com (unofficial and practical). Open Mon–Sat 0700–1900, Sun 0830–1800, but the airport, car rental offices, hotels, restaurants, casinos, museums and souvenir shops are overflowing with brochures.

McCarran International Airport is just south of the Strip and 5 miles from the city centre. Taxi to Strip hotels averages $10. **Gray Line** *(tel: (702) 739-5700)* airport bus to strip hotels is slightly less for a return journey. **I-15** is the main highway access from California and the Grand Canyon.

Public transport
Citizens Area Transit (CAT) $ *tel: (702) 228-7433*, provide a bus service to most of Las Vegas. Strip buses run every 15–20 minutes 0700-0100, every 30 minutes 0100-0415 and hourly 0415-0700. **Strip Trolleys $** serve Strip casinos every 30 minutes until 0200. Traffic along the Strip, including buses, grinds to a crawl mid-afternoon-late evening.

Parking
Parking is plentiful, convenient and cheap. Casino car-parks are well-lit, patrolled 24 hours daily and almost always free. Free valet parking

Fremont Street
Experience
Downtown, 425 Fremont St;
tel: (702) 678-5600. Light
and sound shows nightly.

is available at the main entrance to all casinos; tip the attendant $2–$5 when the vehicle is returned. Car-parks which do charge, such as the **Fremont Street Experience** lot, normally waive the fee with validation (a stamp or paste-on sticker) from a nearby casino or merchant.

Sights

Fremont Street Experience❖❖
Four blocks of Fremont St have been transformed into the **Fremont Street Experience**, a walking street topped by a 90-ft canopy set with 2.1 million lights that explode into light and sound shows after dark. Downtown casinos are generally less flashy than their Strip counterparts, less expensive and less noisy.

Hoover Dam❖❖❖
About 726ft from base to dam-top highway, Hoover Dam is one of the highest concrete dams ever built. Finished in 1936, it backs the Colorado River into **Lake Mead**❖❖❖, a 140-mile strip of blue in the beige, grey and red landscape of the Mojave, Great Basin and Sonoran deserts that meet along its shores. The lake is a popular boating and outdoor recreation area from spring to autumn.

Imperial Palace Antique and Classic Auto Collection $
Imperial Palace, 3535 Las Vegas Blvd S.; tel: (702) 731-3311; web: www. imperialpalace.com. Open 0930–2330.

King Tutankhamun's Tomb & Museum
Luxor, 3900 Las Vegas Blvd S.; tel: (702) 262-4000. Open Sun–Thur 0900– 2300, to 2330 Fri–Sat.

Las Vegas pastiche – the skyline of the New York, New York Hotel

The **Dam Visitor Center**✤ has an excellent 40-minute multimedia presentation, with overlooks from both sides and the middle of the dam. The dam is also open daily for tours. Several river-rafting companies in Las Vegas offer easy whole- or half-day raft and canoe trips down the Colorado River from just below the dam.

Hoover Dam & Lake Mead *30 miles east of Las Vegas on Hwy 93; tel: (702) 294-3223. Dam visitor centre open daily 0830–1730. Tours $ tel: (702) 293-8321.* Lake Mead National Recreation Area is open 24 hours.

Imperial Palace Antique and Classic Auto Collection✤
One of the West's finer car collections includes an 1897 Haynes-Apperson. Rotating exhibits feature a 1928 Delage limousine owned by the late King of Siam, US President Dwight Eisenhower's parade limo and one of the world's largest collections of Model J Duesenbergs.

King Tutankhamun's Tomb & Museum✤
The tomb, an exact replica of King Tut's tomb as found by Howard Carter in 1922, is filled with reproductions of the furnishings recorded in Carter's expedition records.

Las Vegas Natural History Museum $
900 Las Vegas Blvd N.; tel: (702) 384-3466; web: www.vegaswebworld.com/lvn athistory/. Open daily 0900– 1600.

Liberace Museum $
1775 E. Tropicana Ave; tel: (702) 798-5595; web: www.liberace.com. Open Mon–Sat 1000–1700, Sun 1300–1500.

Old Las Vegas Mormon Fort State Historic Park $ *Washington Ave and Las Vegas Blvd; tel: (702) 486-3511 or (702) 486-5126. Open 0830–1530.*

Red Rock Canyon National Conservation Area $ *20 miles west, off Charleston Blvd; tel: (702) 363-1921. Scenic loop open daily 0700–2000. Visitor Center open daily 0830– 1630.*

Valley of Fire State Park $
52 miles northeast off I-15, near Overton; tel: (702) 397-2088. Park open dawn–dusk, visitor centre open 0830– 1630.

The Strip *Las Vegas Blvd S., Stratosphere to Mandalay Bay. Never closed.*

Las Vegas Natural History Museum✦

The museum is a good introduction to the plants and animals indigenous to Nevada as well as marine life from around the world.

Liberace Museum✦✦✦

Liberace was a classically trained pianist, technically astute and addicted to grand gestures of dazzling spectacle – audiences loved him. The museum displays many of his flashiest costumes, jewelled accessories, automobiles, pianos and other accoutrements.

Old Las Vegas Mormon Fort State Historic Park✦✦

This is where the entertainment began. In 1855, Mormon traders opened a fort in an isolated desert meadow ('Las Vegas' is 'meadows' in Spanish) to cater to pioneer wagon trains headed for California. The fort was eventually selected as a railway stop (steam locomotive engines needed regular infusions of water), which prompted an initial round of land speculation that resulted in today's Las Vegas. The Museum includes a late 19th-century Mormon living room.

Red Rock Canyon National Conservation Area✦✦✦

Best known for a 13-mile driving loop that winds through some of the most spectacular desert scenery within easy reach of Las Vegas, the conservation area is named for the 3000-ft high Red Rock Escarpment, as popular with rock climbers as with sightseers. Self-guided hiking trails lead to a spring, a waterfall, several small canyons and what remains of an old homestead. Wild *burros* frequent the loop road in search of handouts.

Man versus mountain in Red Rock Canyon

The Strip✦✦✦

The Strip *is* Las Vegas for most visitors, 3 miles of boulevard lined with more than 40 hotel-casinos and acres of neon. Traffic tends to move slowly, but the only way to see the full scope of creative casino architecture is to park and walk.

Valley of Fire State Park✦✦✦

This rugged valley is filled with eroded red sandstone formations that seem to catch fire in the sunlight – the effect is most spectacular at dawn and sunset. Some rocks and cliffs are covered with prehistoric petroglyphs. The most easily accessible set of petroglyphs lies along the ¼-mile trail to **Mouse's Tank**✦✦✦, a natural basin named for a Paiute Indian who successfully eluded capture in the natural maze.

Shopping in Las Vegas

As shopping evolved to become one of America's favourite forms of entertainment, casinos began to create their own themed shopping opportunities.

Glitziest of them all (for now, at least) is **The Forum Shops at Caesars Palace**◆◆◆ (*Caesars Palace, 3500 Las Vegas Blvd S.; tel: (702) 893-4800; open daily 1000–2300, to 2400 Fri–Sat; shows hourly from 1100*), a series of Italian streetscapes lined with 100-plus brand-name shops and restaurants. The hand-painted barrel-vaulted ceiling above cycles through the day from sunrise to sunset on a regular schedule. Highlights are fountains and imitation-marble statues that come to life on the hour with Vegas's own twist on Roman mythology.

Fashion Show Mall (*3200 Las Vegas Blvd S.; tel: (702) 369-8382; open Mon–Fri 1000–2100, Sat 1000–1900, Sun 1200–1800*) is the largest mall on The Strip, with more than 140 speciality and department stores to meet more mundane needs.

Accommodation and food in Las Vegas

Las Vegas is the hotel capital of the planet, with 110,000 rooms and still counting. Accommodation is concentrated along **The Strip** (*Las Vegas Blvd S.*) and **Downtown** (*Fremont St and nearby*). New Strip hotels are the most luxurious, the most touted and the most expensive; downtown hotels are less expensive. Prices drop even further at motels west of I-15.

Visit mid-week for the best value, but always book ahead to avoid major conventions or sporting events, which drive accommodation prices sky-high. The Sunday *Los Angeles Times* travel section is the single best source of current accommodation deals.

Casino food and drink prices have crept upward in recent years, but casino buffets are still good value for any meal. The **Fiesta**, **Rio** and **Station** (**Boulder**, **Palace**, **Sunset** and **Texas**) casinos get high marks for good food as well as good buffet prices.

Drinks are free to gamblers, though service is generally slow. Expect to pay standard prices at casino bars, where service is generally very good. The drinking age is 21 and alcohol may be served 24 hours a day.

Gambling

Gambling, or 'gaming' as the politically correct prefer, fuels the flash, the glitter and the hype that keeps Las Vegas moving. Take the rows of slot machines standing like sentries at the airport (locals warn the odds are terrible), petrol stations, supermarkets and wedding chapels as a hint: Vegas is a money machine oiled by the mathematical certainty that in the long run, the player *always* loses. The only question is how long it takes.

In general, the easier the game, the higher the house edge, or

ⓘ **The Word**
The best single source of practical Vegas information is the *Las Vegas Advisor* 3687 S. Procoyon Ave, Las Vegas, NV 89103; tel: (702) 252-0655; fax: (702) 252-0675. The monthly newsletter is filled with accommodation and show deals, gambling strategies, non-gaming activities and tips on local bargains – no adverts allowed.

Below
Antique slot-machines in Las Vegas

advantage. The house keeps around 45 per cent of the money bet on keno, less than 0.5 per cent of the cash bet on blackjack, Vegas' most popular card game. Most casinos offer free lessons for **blackjack** (also called '21' for the perfect hand) and **craps** (a high speed dice game). Try to graduate to low-stakes tables at slack periods, breakfast to mid-afternoon, before jumping into the heady night-time whirl.

Most gamblers opt for the ubiquitous **slot machines**, which require neither skill nor a rulebook. Pump in quarters, dollars or banknotes (occasional nickel slots are around) and pull the handle or push a button to set the reels spinning. If a winning combination appears, bells ring, lights flash and coins clatter reassuringly into a metal hopper. **Video poker** machines operate similarly, but require some knowledge of the rules of poker.

Other popular games include **baccarat**, a European card game similar to blackjack where the goal is nine rather than 21; **keno**, a lotto-like game; **roulette** and a number of different **poker** games. It is also possible to bet on sporting events at any casino sport book.

Casino themes

Most Vegas casinos have become gigantic theme parks in order to set themselves apart in a highly competitive market. The basic amenities are the same – accommodation, casino, restaurants, bars, cabarets and shows – but the packaging varies dramatically to lure different kinds of punters.

Bellagio *3400 Las Vegas Blvd S.; tel: (702) 791-7111 or (888) 987-6667; fax: (702) 693-8778; web: www.bellagiolasvegas.com.* An opulent village transplanted from Italy's Lake Como to Nevada. No one under 18 is admitted except registered guests, unless eating at a resort restaurant or attending a show or other event.

Caesars Palace *3570 Las Vegas Blvd S. tel: (702) 731-7110 or (800) 634-6661; www.caesarspalace.com.* Togas and other glories of Imperial Rome plus fabulous shopping.

Circus Circus *2880 Las Vegas Blvd S. tel: (702) 734-0410 or 800-444-2472; web: www.circuscircus-lasvegas.com.* Vegas's original family casino with circus acts, games and the **Grand Slam Canyon** theme park to keep the kids occupied.

The Luxor hotel, complete with Sphinx, in Las Vegas

Desert Inn *3145 Las Vegas Blvd S.; tel: (702) 733-4444 or (800) 634-6906.* Traditional luxury, and the only golf course on the Strip.

Excalibur *3850 Las Vegas Blvd S.; tel: (702) 597-7777 or (800) 937-7777; web: www.excalibur-casino.com.* Camelot on the Strip, complete with strolling dragons, King Arthur's Court and minstrels who deserve more attention than they usually receive.

Las Vegas Hilton *3000 Paradise Rd; tel: (702) 732-5111 or (800) 462-6535; web: www.lv-hilton.com. Star Trek* theme with Ferengis running the bar and Klingon warriors to keep the crowd in check.

Luxor *3900 Las Vegas Blvd S.; tel: (702) 262-4000 or (800) 288-1000; web: www.luxor.com.* Ancient Egypt within a black glass pyramid, a Sphinx crouching over the entrance and King Tut's tomb beneath.

Mandalay Bay *Las Vegas Blvd S.; tel: (702) 632-7900 or (877) 632-7900; web: www.mandalaybay.com.* The world's top tropical resorts distilled in the desert, with a separate **Four Seasons** hotel to punch the tone up-market.

MGM Grand *3799 Las Vegas Blvd S.; tel: (702) 891-7777 or (800) 929-1111; web: mgmgrand.com.* Cinema magic made real inside, a Disney-like theme park outside.

The Mirage *3400 Las Vegas Blvd S.; tel: (702) 791-7111 or (800) 627-6667; web: www.themirage.com.* Look for the erupting volcano outside, the tropical rain forest inside and white tigers in the showroom.

New York New York *3790 Las Vegas Blvd S.; tel: (702) 740-6969 or (888) 634-6969; web: nynyhotelcasino.com.* The New York City skyline compressed around a casino. The roller-coaster looping round the Statue of Liberty is real.

Treasure Island *3300 Las Vegas Blvd S.; tel: (702) 894-7111 or (800) 944-7444; web: www.treasureisland.com.* Caribbean Pirates on the Strip, with an epic sea battle in front – pirates sink the Royal Navy every 90 minutes from late afternoon.

The Venetian *3355 Las Vegas Blvd S.; tel: (702) 733-5000; web: www.venetian.com.* Renaissance Venice, complete with St Mark's Square, gondolas, the Doge's Palace and the Grand Canal but without the seaweed and winter floods.

That's entertainment!

Entertainment is the name of Las Vegas's game. The idea began with mobster Bugsy Segal, who imported musicians and comedians to give customers another reason to gamble in *his* casino rather than across the street. The ploy worked, then started feeding on itself.

Casinos began competing to create the flashiest shows and the most outlandish décor. Elegant drives were eclipsed by acres of neon, which gave way to erupting volcanoes, battling frigates and crooning gondoliers. Fantasy became a prelude to reality.

Big name stars, 'headliners' in Vegas-speak, come and go regularly. Traditional shows, **Enter the Night $$** (*Stardust; tel: (702) 732-6325*), **Folies Bergere** (*Tropicana; tel: (702) 739-2411*), **Jubilee $$** (*Bally's; tel: (702) 739-4567*) and **Splash $$** (*Rivera; tel: (702) 794-8301*) rely on lavish sets, singing, dancing and bare breasts. Most offer early-evening covered versions with topless shows later.

A few casinos have held on to child-orientated spectacles. The most lavish is **King Arthur's Tournament $$** (*Excalibur; tel: (702) 597-7777*), a dinner show with jousting knights. Vegas's finest magic show is **Lance Burton $$** (*Monte Carlo; tel: (702) 730-7000*), one of the world's top illusionists.

Supershows are the newest entry, lavish, expensive and heavily advertised. By far the best is **Cirque du Soleil $$$** (*Treasure Island; tel: (702) 894-7111*), with feats of balance, skill and timing by the eponymous Montreal-based circus. Cirque also produces **O $$$**

(*Bellagio; tel: (702) 791-7111*), which relies more on equipment than performers. **Siegfried and Roy $$$** (*The Mirage; tel: (702) 791-7111*) add white tigers and explosive lighting effects to a traditional magic show.

Vegas for kids

Vegas is the archetypal playground for adults, but children don't get left out entirely. Easy hikes at **Red Rock Canyon $**, **Valley of Fire $**, and **Lake Mead/Hoover Dam** are a good way to run off excess energy. Nearby Henderson (on the way to Hoover Dam) has three free attractions for kids of all ages. **Cranberry World West** (*1301 American Pacific Dr.; tel: (702) 566-7160*) has all you ever wanted to know about Ocean Spray cranberry and other juices. The unlimited free samples are especially welcome in summer. **Ethel M Chocolates Factory & Cactus Garden** (*1 Sunset Way; tel: (702) 458-8864*) has tours (and samples) of fine chocolate production with a well-labelled cactus garden outside. **Favorite Brands Marshmallow Factory** (*1180 Marshmallow Ln; tel: (702) 393-7308*) offers tours and samples.

Thrill rides are Vegas's latest attraction for grown-up kids. Both **Grand Slam Canyon $$** (*Circus Circus; tel: (702) (702) 734-3939*) and **MGM Grand Theme Park $$** (*MGM Grand; tel: (702) 731-7900*) have their share of screamers, but the top ride is the **Stratosphere Tower $** (*Stratosphere; tel: (702) 380-7777*), with a roller-coaster and free fall ride atop the 1149-ft tower. Best indoor-outdoor roller-coaster is **New York New York $** (*tel: (702) 740-6969*), which runs through the lobby and around the New York skyline. The best place for a hot afternoon is **Wet 'n Wild $$** (*2601 Las Vegas Blvd S.; tel: (702) 734-0088*) water park, with a choice of towering water slides or floating gently on quiet rivers.

At least three casinos provide artificial reality, kid-style. **Excalibur $** (*tel: (702) 597-7777*) has 'Magic Motion Machines' that offer the illusion of riding race cars, runaway trains and other high-speed vehicles. **Race for Atlantis $** (*Caesar's; tel: (702) 731-7110*) is a very real-feeling supernatural race to Atlantis, dodging thunderbolts and angry gods along the way. The space shuttle flight in **Star Trek: The Experience $** (*Las Vegas Hilton; tel: (702) 732-5111*) could have come straight from the latest *Star Trek* space battle sequence.

For free attractions, check out the **Buccaneer Bay Sea Battle** (*Treasure Island; tel: (702) 894-7111*) with cannons firing and ships sinking every 90 minutes from 1600-2330. Next door is the **Volcano** (*The Mirage; tel: (702) 791-7111*), which erupts every 15-30 minutes after dark. Downtown, the **Fremont Street Experience** (*Fremont St*) explodes into an overhead parade of moving images after dark.

The Mirage (*tel: (702) 791-7111*) offers a trio of animal attractions. The **White Tiger Habitat** has views of Siegfried & Roy's tigers at play, asleep and being themselves. **The Secret Garden of Siegfried & Roy $** is a small zoo with white tigers and other endangered species.

Dolphin Habitat $ is a large pool with trained dolphins.

Showcase (*3785 Las Vegas Blvd S.*) has three child-friendly attractions. **GameWorks $-$$** (*tel: (702) 432-4263*) is Vegas's largest video arcade, designed primarily for teenagers and young adults. **World of Coca-Cola $** (*tel: (702) 270-5965*) details the history and legend of Coke; a tasting station offers Coca-Cola brand drinks from around the world. **M&M's World** (*tel: (702) 458-8864*) is the ultimate M&M's candy shop, with colours available nowhere else.

Dragons and strolling minstrels entertain at the Excalibur Hotel, Las Vegas

Grand Canyon, Bryce and Zion

Ratings

Scenery	●●●●●
Geology	●●●●●
Sunsets	●●●●●
Children	●●●●○
History	●●●●○
Walking	●●●●○
Food and drink	●●○○○
Architecture	●○○○○

The Painted Desert vision of the American Southwest springs to life in these three National Parks. All were regarded as aberrations of nature and roadblocks to orderly development until recent decades. Today's visitors are more likely to stare with awe and vertigo into the mile-deep Grand Canyon, wonder at the fairy-like hoodoos of Bryce Canyon and gaze in silence at the mountain patriarchs of Zion – at least until the next tour bus or RV caravan pulls into the car-park.

The region ... is altogether valueless. It can be approached only from the south, and after entering it, there is nothing to do but leave. Ours has been the first, and will doubtless be the last, party ... to visit this profitless locality.

Thus wrote a member of the 1858 US government survey team, summing up the perceived economic value of the Grand Canyon. Today the Canyon receives more than five million visitors annually, all come to wonder at the red, white, buff, grey, yellow, orange, brown, pink and black rock.

BRYCE CANYON NATIONAL PARK❖❖❖

🏛 Bryce Canyon National Park $
Box 170001, Bryce Canyon, UT 84717;
tel: (435) 834-5322;
fax: (435) 834-4102;
web: www.nps.gov/brca/.

ℹ Visitor Center
1 mile south of Park Entrance. Open Oct–Apr daily 0800–1630 , late Apr and early Oct 0800–1800 , May–Sept 0800–2000 .

Bryce is a 17-mile canyon lined with hoodoos – ancient cliffs that have been eroded into parallel rows of sharp-edged pinnacles tinged with red, gold and chalk. Endless ranks of hoodoos form fanciful forests of stone that seem at times to resemble natural amphitheatres rimmed by fairy-tale cities of sheer-sided minarets, turrets, steeples and towers.

The drive south from the Park Entrance rises 1100ft to Rainbow Point. The road (Hwy 63) offers numerous lay-bys where you can pull in and enjoy the view, but longer-term parking is extremely limited. Arrive before 1000 if you are planning to park and explore from **Sunrise**, **Sunset**, **Inspiration**, **Bryce** or **Paria Viewpoints** during the spring to autumn. Trailers are not permitted beyond Sunset Campground, midway along the canyon drive. RVs longer than 25ft are prohibited from Paria View, at the end of the road, because of lack of turning space.

Minersville

UTAH

Modena

Newcastle

Paragonah

Parowan

Panguitch

Boulder

Escalante

Enterprise

Summit

Brian
Head

Cedar
City

Hatch

Bryce

Bryce Canyon National Park

Henrieville

Veyo

Kanarra

Kolob Canyons

Canyons

Rainbow Point

Bryce
Canyon
National
Park

Zion National Park

National

Alton   Junction

Orderville   Glendale

Mt Carmel

St George

Hurricane

Springdale

Washington

Mt Carmel
Junction

Kanab

Lake
Powe

Littlefield

Fredonia

Marble Canyon

Page

quite
lle

Jacob Lake

North Rim

Road closed
in winter

Colorado River

Colorado

Tuweep

Grand Canyon National Park

Grand
Canyon
National
Park

North

Phantom Reach

Tuba Cit

rce
ry

Grand Canyon Village

Grand
Canyon
Village

Tusayan

Desert View

Cameron

Colorado

Fraziers Well

Grand
Canyon
Railroad

Gray Mountain

ARIZONA

Peach Springs

Grand Canyon Caverns

Valentine

Seligman

Williams

Parks

Flagstaff

ngman

Ash Fork

SUNRISE

Walking the Navajo Trail in Bryce Canyon National Park

Arriving at dawn

Sunrise is one of the most striking times of day to see the hoodoos and the easiest time of day to park. Park at **Sunrise Point⁑** (*less than a mile beyond the Visitor Center*) to watch the low rays of light begin to pick out the spires, then follow the **Rim Trail⁑** down between the hoodoos to **Sunset Point⁑**, **Inspiration Point⁑** or **Bryce Point⁑**. Return via the main road.

During the day

Drive directly to **Rainbow Point⁑**, where visibility can exceed 90 miles and early visitors occasionally spot mountain lions. The 1-mile **Bristlecone Loop Trail⁑** threads through stands of rare bristlecone pines.

The return drive offers many lay-bys, most with hiking trails. **Agua Canyon⁑** has several named hoodoos, including **Hunter** and **Rabbit**. One of the park's biggest draws is **Natural Bridge⁑**, an 85-ft arch 6 miles north of Rainbow Point.

Bryce Point⁑ was named for Mormon settler Ebenezer Bryce, who farmed the Paria Valley for a short time in the 1870s and told the world of the mystical wonders that lay just to the south. **Inspiration Point⁑** is best known for **Silent City⁑**, a formation of 200-ft hoodoos packed in dense rows like some high-rise city emptied of people.

Arriving at sunset

Sunset Point⁑ is the obvious point from which to enjoy the

Garfield County Travel Council
Box 200, Panguitch, UT 84759; tel: (435) 444-6689, (800) 444-6689 or (800) 462-7923 (accommodation only).

sunset, though parking is a problem in summer. Vistas curve east toward **Queen's Garden**✦✦, **Wall Street**✦✦ and an illusory balanced rock called **Thor's Hammer**✦✦✦. Allow two hours to walk the 1.4-mile **Navajo Loop Trail**✦✦✦ that wanders past Thor's Hammer, through the narrow clefts separating the hoodoos and through forests of pygmy Douglas fir trees. The easiest canyon trail is a 1.8-mile stroll through Queen's Garden from Sunset Point.

If schedules are tight, the best one-hour park visit is **Fairyland Point**✦✦, just beyond the Visitor Center (also good for Nordic skiers). The stunning view is a preview of the magical scenery that lies beyond.

Accommodation and food in Bryce

The only non-camping accommodation in the park is **Bryce Canyon Lodge $$** *AmFac Parks & Resorts, 14001 E. Iliff Ave, Ste 600, Aurora, CO 80014; tel: (303) 297-2757; fax: (303) 237-3715, open mid-Apr-Oct.* Advance booking required. Nearby choices include **Best Western Ruby's Inn $$** *1 mile north of the Park Entrance on Hwy 63; tel: (435) 834-5341 or (800) 468-8660*, and **Bryce Canyon Pines** *12 miles west on Hwy 12; tel: (435) 834-5441 or (800) 892-7923*. Other accommodation is available in **Tropic**, east of the park on Hwy 12.

Best local restaurant, and well worth the 6-mile drive, is **Cowboy's Smokehouse Bar-B-Q $$** *95 N. Main St, Panguitch, Utah; tel: (435) 676-8030*, for authentic wood-smoked meats and enormous slabs of home-made pie. **Bryce Canyon Lodge Restaurant $$** is the only restaurant in the park open all year. **The General Store $$, Sunrise Point**, sells snacks and drinks mid–Apr–Oct.

GRAND CANYON NATIONAL PARK✦✦✦

Tour Information
tel: (520) 638-2631 for same-day bookings; tel: (303) 297-2757 for advance reservations.

The Grand Canyon is larger than it appears. The popular South Rim and the less-frequented North Rim are just 10 miles straight across the Canyon and 215 miles by highway. It is possible to see the Grand Canyon in a day, less if on a flightseeing package from Las Vegas, but the ever-changing colours and the utter vastness of the canyon beg to be absorbed at leisure, far from the vast crowds who stop at the South Rim and Grand Canyon Village. At the very least, skirt the crowds by walking or cycling the **South Rim Trail**✦✦✦ from **Hopi Point**✦✦ east to Grand Canyon Village and **Mather Point**✦✦ A free shuttle eases the return.

Bright Angel Trail✦✦✦ began as a Native American trail from the rim down to the springs at Indian Gardens. Private developers widened the trail in 1891 and began the mule rides that remain one of Grand Canyon's most popular organised activities.

ⓘ Main Visitor Center, *6 miles north from the South Entrance, open daily 0800-1700 in winter, 0800-1800 in summer.*

Desert View Information Center, **Yavapai Observation Station** *and* **Tusayan Museum** *keep similar hours.*

National Park Service Information Desk *Grand Canyon Lodge lobby, North Rim. Open mid-May-Oct daily 0800-1700 .*

Road Conditions; *tel: (520) 638-7888. Ask for Grand Canyon Magazine, free at visitor centres.*

ⓘ Grand Canyon National Park $$
Box 129, Grand Canyon, AZ 86023; tel: (520) 638-7888; www.nps.gov/grca/.

Grand Canyon Railway $$
123 N. San Francisco, Ste 210, Flagstaff, AZ 86001; tel: (520) 520-773-1976 or (800) 843-8724; fax: (520) 773-1610; web: www. thetrain.com. Open daily.

ⓘ The Park runs a **free shuttle bus** system mid-Mar-mid-Oct through the Village and the West Rim. From mid-Apr-mid-Oct, West Rim Drive, Yaki Point and the South Kaibab trailhead are accessible *only* by shuttle, tour bus, taxi or on foot.

The **Grand Canyon Railway**✳✳✳ (*tel: (800) 843-8724*) runs to the South Rim from Williams, 65 miles south of the Park. The 1901 line, originally run by the Santa Fe Railway, provided the easy access that turned the Grand Canyon from geographic curiosity into an American icon. A vintage steam locomotive engine pulls the restored 1920s Harriman carriages in summer; a 1950s diesel does the duty in winter.

Grand Canyon Village Historic District✳✳ is the central section of Grand Canyon Village from **Bright Angel Trailhead** east to **Verkamp's Curios** and the **First National Park Service Administration Building**. Many Village structures are historic landmarks, including the **Kolb Studio** and **Lookout Studio**, perched on the canyon rim, **Red Horse Station**, **Bright Angel Lodge**, the **El Tovar Hotel**, the **Santa Fe Railway Station**, **Verkamp's Curios** and the **First National Park Service Administration Building**. **Hopi House**'s Native American rugs, jewellery, pottery and tourist souvenirs are museum-class, as is the southwest-style adobe building.

Mule Trips✳✳ (*AmFac Parks and Resorts; tel: (303) 297-2757, open year-round for one-day rides and overnight to Phantom Ranch, mid Nov–mid Mar for three-day Phantom Ranch rides*) have been popular for generations. Riders must be at least 4ft 7ins tall and weigh less than 200lbs. Advance booking (*tel: (303) 297-2757*) is essential year round, but there *may* be last-minute cancellations the morning of the ride; contact the Bright Angel Transportation Desk.

One-day trips lead from the stone corral at the head of Bright Angel Trail to Tonto Platform and Plateau Point, 3200ft below. The blue-green Colorado River twinkles another 1300ft down. The ride takes about seven hours.

Phantom Ranch✳ rides stay overnight at Phantom Ranch cabins on Bright Angel Creek at the bottom of the Canyon. The trip can be made in two tiring days in the saddle or stretched to three days mid-Nov–mid-Mar.

The **North Rim**✳✳✳, 1000ft higher than the South Rim, is a different world. While the South Rim bakes in desert heat, the North Rim enjoys a cooler, mountain summer with spruce, fir and quaking aspen. And when the South Rim is dusted with snow, the North Rim is frozen beneath 25ft of white. The Grand Canyon Lodge and other North Rim facilities are open May–Oct; the park itself remains open to Dec, snow permitting.

A shorter season and more roundabout access mean that North Rim crowds are only about 10 per cent the size of South Rim mobs. The quickest way to enjoy the relative serenity is on foot. Easiest walks are the half-mile **Bright Angel Point Trail**✳✳✳ and the 1½-mile **Transcept Trail**✳✳✳. **Mule Rides** are another option; **Grand Canyon Trail Rides**✳✳ (*Grand Canyon Lodge Trail Rides Desk; tel: (520) 638-2292*) offer hour and half-day rides along the Canyon Rim or half- and full-day rides into the Canyon. Nordic skiing is available in winter, based in the **Kaibab Lodge** (*tel: (520) 638-2389*).

Rafting the Colorado River✧✧✧ *(tel: (520) 638-7888)* remains the most adventurous way to see the Grand Canyon. Allow a full day for a smooth-water float, including a picnic lunch. Water trips last from between three days and three weeks. Most outfitters depart from Lees Ferry, upstream from the park, but shorter trips start at Phantom Ranch. A few outfitters ride the river all year. Contact the Park *(tel: (520) 638-7888)* for a free *Trip Planner* that includes contact information for approved concessionaires, or check with local chambers of commerce. Summer trips book out early in the season. The waiting time for private river-running permits is 6–8 years.

Accommodation and food in Grand Canyon

Book as early as possible (6–12 months) to ensure a place to sleep at America's most popular National Park. South Rim is open year-round; North Rim is open May-Oct. All park accommodation and restaurants are operated by **AmFac Parks & Resorts**, *tel: (303) 297-2757; fax: (303) 297-3175.*

Grand Canyon National Park Lodges *tel: (520) 638-2631*, handles information and same-day bookings for the South Rim. Queen of the lot is the historic **El Tovar Hotel $$$** near the railway station. **Bright Angel Lodge $$$** is near the Rim; **Thunderbird Lodge $$$** and **Kachina Lodge $$$** offer a choice of canyon-side or park-side rooms. **Maswik Lodge $$** and **Yavapai Lodge $$** are removed from the

Village. Accommodation is also available in **Tusayan** (just outside the Park's south entrance), **Williams**, **Flagstaff** and **Sedona**.

All of the park hotels have restaurants, from the formal **El Tovar Dining Room $$$** to the ever-popular **Bright Angel Fountain $** with long midday queues for ice-cream. Best stop for picnic and other supplies is **Babbitt's General Store**, across the street from the Visitors Center.

The North Rim hotel is **Grand Canyon Lodge $$$** *tel: (435) 586-7686, open May–Oct*. Outside-the-park possibilities are **Kaibab Lodge $$** *HC 64, Box 30, Fredonia, AZ 86022; tel: (520) 638-2389* or *(800) 525-0924*, and **Jacob Lake Lodge $$** *30 miles north of the Park; tel: (520) 643-7232*. The only North Rim restaurant is the **Grand Canyon Lodge Dining Room $$$** but the lodge also has a tea-room and snack shop. The **General Store**, *North Rim Campground*, carries picnic supplies.

ZION NATIONAL PARK***

ⓘ Zion Canyon Visitor Center, *half-mile north of the South Entrance; tel: (435) 772-3256. Open daily.*

Kolob Canyons Visitor Center *Park Entrance near I-15. Open daily 0800-1900 in summer, shorter hours in winter.*

🏕 Zion National Park *$ Springdale, UT 84767; tel: (435) 772-3256; web: www.nps.gov/zion/*

Like Grand Canyon, Zion has two units: **Zion Canyon***** (south) and **Kolob Canyons***** (north). It is possible to combine the two in a single exhausting day, but more rewarding to allow at least a day for each.

Kolob Canyons is best known to backcountry hikers, but the easy 5-mile drive up Hurricane Fault to the picnic area at **Kolob Canyons Viewpoint***** is not to be missed. Look for stunning views of mesa formations dropping sheer to the Lower Kolob Plateau. The *Kolob Canyons Road Guide $* at the visitor centre, offers excellent explanations of Kolob geography and geology.

Zion Canyon is filled with names like Abraham, Isaac, Jacob and Moroni (the Mormon angel). The biblical names for the imposing formations were actually chosen by a Methodist minister, Frederick Vining Fisher, who explored the North Fork of the Virgin River.

The **Zion Canyon Scenic Drive***** follows Fisher's route up the canyon, starting from **The Watchman***** (6546ft), a mountain wedge standing sentinel near the South Entrance. A short path leads from the car-park to the **Court of the Patriarchs*****, the aforementioned Mounts **Abraham**, **Isaac**, **Jacob** and **Moroni** to the west.

Almost directly across from the Zion Lodge Complex lie the **Emerald Pools****, the lower pool at the base of a waterfall an easy half-mile from the road. A more strenuous one-mile trail leads to a larger pool at the base of the cliffs.

The natural hanging gardens of **Weeping Rock***** are a quarter-mile from the car-park. The gardens are watered by mists and rivulets seeping from the sandstone. Take a moment to duck beneath a well-watered overhang to see Zion's serrated peaks shimmer through the mist.

Climbers cling like ants to the cliffs beyond Weeping Rock that lead to the **Temple of Sinawava*****, end of the road and start of a one-mile **Riverside Walk***** along the Virgin River to another hanging garden.

ℹ **Cedar City Chamber of Commerce Visitor Center** 286 N. Main St, Cedar City, UT 84720; tel: (435) 586-4484.

Iron County Tourism and Convention Bureau Box 1007, Cedar City, UT 84720; tel: (435)586-5124.

Springdale Chamber of Commerce Box 111, Springdale, UT 84767; tel: (435) 772-3757.

Travel and Convention Bureau 425 S. 700 East, St George, UT 84770; tel: (435) 634-5747 or (800) 869-6635.

Grand Circle Association Box HH, Cortez, CO 81321; tel: (800) 554-2780.

Accommodation and food in Zion

Zion Lodge \$\$\$ *4 miles north of the South Entrance; tel: (800) 586-7686,* is the only indoor accommodation in the park. Reservations are essential, **AmFac Parks & Resorts** *140001 E. Iliff, Ste 600, Aurora CO 80014; tel: (303) 297-2757; fax: (303) 297-3175.*

Other accommodation is available in Springdale, just beyond the South Entrance, and the nearby towns of Hurricane and St George. Most convenient accommodation for Kolob Canyons visitors is in Cedar City.

The **Zion Lodge Restaurant \$\$\$** is the only restaurant in the park. Picnic supplies can be purchased in nearby towns, a better alternative than the Lodge snack bar.

Pitting human strength and agility against sheer rock in Zion National Park

Language

How To Talk Californian

Alternate: Means 'alternative', not 'every other' - - sometimes a source of confusion when reading timetables.

Bed & Breakfast (or 'B&B'): Overnight lodging in a private home, usually with private facilities and almost always more expensive than nearby hotels and motels.

Brewpub: A tavern that brews its own beer.

Buffalo wings: Chicken wings, usually fried and served with a spicy sauce as an appetiser or as bar food.

California cuisine: Anything the chef wants it to mean, as long as it's expensive, but usually based on fresh, organically grown foods.

Chili dog or chili burger: Hot dog or hamburger disguised with chili, onions, and cheese.

Chimichanga: A pseudo-Mexican concoction of a fried tortilla filled with meat, beans, cheese, tomatoes and lettuce.

Chips: Crisps, usually made from potatoes, but also from corn, taro, casava, rice or other starches.

Corn dog: Hot dog dipped in corn meal and fried. Usually served hot on a stick.

Dead head: Fans of the band the Grateful Dead; also a term for hippies.

Designer water: Pejorative term for bottled water.

Downtown: City or town centre

Holiday: A public holiday, such as Labor Day, not a private holiday, which is a vacation.

Lodging: The usual term for accommodation.

Natural ingredients: Food that has been grown, processed, and prepared without pesticides or other chemical additives.

Outlet shopping: Shopping at large stores specialising in factory overruns at reduced prices. Sometimes, factory outlets are simply low-priced retail stores selling direct from the factory.

Resort: A fancy hotel which specialises in leisure activities such as golf, tennis and swimming.

Road kill: Literally, animals killed by passing cars, but usually used to describe bad restaurant food.

Californian driving terms

Big rig: A large lorry, usually a tractor pulling one or more trailers.

Boulevard stop: Slowing at a stop sign, but not stopping.

CHP California: Highway Patrol, the state road police force.

CNG: Liquified petroleum gas used as fuel.

Crosswalk: Pedestrian crossing.

Connector: A minor road connecting two freeways.

Curve: Bend.

Divided highway: Dual carriageway.

DUI: Driving Under the Influence of alcohol or drugs, aka Drunk Driving. The blood alcohol limit in California is 0.08% and is very strictly enforced.

Fender: Bumper.

Freeway: Motorway.

Garage or parking: Garage car park.

Gas(oline): Petrol.

Grade: Gradient, hill.

Highway: Trunk road.

Hood: Bonnet.

Metering lights: Traffic signals controlling access to bridges, freeways, etc.

Motor home: Motor caravan.

Pavement: Road surface. A UK 'pavement' is a US sidewalk.

Ramp: Slip road.

Rent: Hire.

Rubbernecking: Slowing down to peer while driving past the scene of an accident or some unusual event.

RV (recreational vehicle): Motor caravan.

Shoulder: Verge.

Sidewalk: Pavement.

Sig-alert: An official warning of unusually heavy traffic, usually broadcast over local radio stations.

Shift (stick): Gear lever.

Switchback: Serpentine road.

Traffic cop: Traffic warden.

Trunk: Boot.

Yield: Give way.

Index

Acknowledgements

Project management: Dial House Publishing Services (tel: 01285 771044)
Series design: Fox Design (tel: 01373 834271)
Front cover design and artwork: Fox Design
Layout and map work: Concept 5D (tel: 0181 607 9858)
Repro and image setting: Z2 Repro, Thetford, Norfolk (tel: 01842 763003)
Print: Printed and bound in Italy by Rotolito Lombarda Spa

We would like to thank the following photographers and organisations for the photographs used in this book, to whom the copyright in the photograph belongs:

Front cover: Oakland Bay Bridge, San Francisco, Mannequin in Hollywood, Mission Santa Barbara (all courtesy of Maxine Cass).

Maxine Cass (pages 6 (=136), 8, 12, 13, 17, 22, 23, 24, 27, 28, 30, 32, 33, 34, 35, 36, 39, 42, 45, 47, 48, 51, 52, 59, 60, 62, 64, 66, 70, 73, 76, 78, 81, 85, 86, 88, 89, 90, 97, 98, 101, 102, 104, 109, 110, 121, 122, 127, 128, 134, 139, 140, 143, 146, 148, 151, 154, 157, 159, 164, 166, 168, 171, 172, 176, 178, 181, 183, 186, 188, 191, 193, 196, 199, 200, 203, 206, 214, 216, 218, 219, 221, 226, 229, 232, 235, 238, 240, 243, 246, 251, 252, 258, 262, 267, 270, 274, 276, 279 and 281).

Fred Gebhart (pages 18, 54, 56, 74, 94, 114, 118, 124, 131, 248, 256, 264, 266, 269 and 273).

Feedback form

If you enjoyed using this book, or even if you didn't, please help us improve future editions by taking part in our reader survey. Every returned form will be acknowledged, and to show our appreciation we will give you £1 off your next purchase of a Thomas Cook guidebook. Just take a few minutes to complete and return this form to us.

When did you buy this book? ....

....

Where did you buy it? (Please give town/city and, if possible, name of retailer)

....

....

When did you/do you intend to travel in California? ....

....

For how long (approx)? ....

How many people in your party? ....

Which cities, national parks and other locations did you/do you intend mainly to visit?

....

....

....

....

Did you/will you:
❏ Make all your travel arrangements independently?
❏ Travel on a fly-drive package?
Please give brief details: ....

....

Did you/do you intend to use this book:
❏ For planning your trip?   ❏ Both?
❏ During the trip itself?

Did you/do you intend also to purchase any of the following travel publications for your trip?
Thomas Cook Travellers: California ....
A road map/atlas (please specify) ....
Other guidebooks (please specify) ....

Have you used any other Thomas Cook guidebooks in the past? If so, which?

....

....

Please rate the following features of Signpost California for their value to you (Circle VU for 'very useful', U for 'useful', NU for 'little or no use'):

The Travel Facts section on pages 14–25	VU	U	NU
The Driver's Guide section on pages 26–31	VU	U	NU
The Highlights on pages 42–43	VU	U	NU
The recommended driving routes throughout the book	VU	U	NU
Information on towns and cities, National Parks, etc	VU	U	NU
The maps of towns and cities, parks, etc	VU	U	NU

Please use this space to tell us about any features that in your opinion could be changed, improved, or added in future editions of the book, or any other comments you would like to make concerning the book:

....
....
....
....
....
....
....
....
....
....

Your age category: ❏ 21-30   ❏ 31-40   ❏ 41-50   ❏ over 50

Your name: Mr/Mrs/Miss/Ms ....
(First name or initials) ....
(Last name) ....

Your full address: (Please include postal or zip code)

....
....
....
....
....

Your daytime telephone number: ....

Please detach this page and send it to: The Project Editor, Signpost Guides, Thomas Cook Publishing, PO Box 227, Peterborough PE3 6PU, United Kingdom.

We will be pleased to send you details of how to claim your discount upon receipt of this questionnaire.